FOREVER SHUNNED
AMISH REBEL

JONATHAN FISHER

A MEMOIR

Jonathan Fisher

This book is lovingly written in memory of my mother,
Rachel S. (Miller) Fisher,
who endured physical illnesses for many years
with amazing courage and quiet patience,
and who loved all of us
every day, equally and unfailingly.

Table of Contents

CHAPTER ONE

Humble Beginnings of My Early Years

EARLY IN THE MORNING, on August 23, 1951, at 2:14 A.M., there was born to Amos C. and Rachel S. Fisher, their sixth son who was also their eighth and final child. They were a very typical Old Order Amish couple with an average number of children. Devout, humble, and hard-working, they raised their family on a 56-acre dairy farm in the Lancaster County, Pennsylvania, Amish community between the sleepy little towns of Intercourse and Gap. When I arrived that morning, I was their only child who had been born in a hospital because I was bigger than any of the others, who were all born at home. No one could know then that I would later become more rebellious toward the ancient Ordnung than any of my siblings and that most Amish people would always consider me to be the "black sheep" of our family.

My mom told us that when their oldest child, Jacob, was born in 1937, Dr. Yunginger from Bird-in-Hand, only charged $16.00 to deliver him. My seven siblings and I all lived in a big white clapboard farmhouse that was built in 1879, the year that our Grandad Miller was born. That date was carved into the mortar of the chimney in the attic. Our house was two and one-half stories tall and had a full basement. It had a living room/kitchen combination that was heated by a big black Columbia stove which burned wood and coal. We also had a gas stove with four burners for cooking. There was a sitting/visiting room on the main floor, three bedrooms, a kettle "house," and a very primitive "bathroom" with no shower, no bathtub, no sink, and no running water. One might certainly ask, "Well, what *did* it have?" All it had was a large rectangular

1

wooden board with two oblong holes that we sat on, (sometimes in "double occupancy!") Still, it was better than the old "one-holer" outhouse, about thirty feet behind our house that we had used previously. And, of course, it was also equipped with an outdated Sears Roebuck catalog.

The kettle house was not really a house, it was simply a room with a concrete floor where the Briggs and Stratton engine-powered washing machine stood. It was located between the kitchen and bathroom and created a lot of noise and smoke and fumes every Monday morning during laundry time. Mom fed the wet laundry through the rotating rollers which squeezed the water out and was then hung out to dry on the eighty-foot long wash line strung between the house and barn.

Our house had five bedrooms upstairs but no bathroom. Two of those bedrooms were used for storage, leaving the other three for the eight siblings. My sisters, Suvilla and Lydia, shared one room while Brother John and I shared one and our four oldest brothers shared one. Since they only had one bed and a cot, one brother slept on the cot and the three others all slept together in the bed. There surely were many occasions of three-dimensional "spooning" then, especially in wintertime (as they nestled snugly together like spoons in a drawer). However, the "three in one bed" event was only on weekends as they all lived and worked at other Amish farms during the week.

Since our house didn't have any insulation at all, it was hard to heat in the winter and often sweltering hot in the summertime. Of course, our house had no electricity because the Amish bishops have always harshly condemned and prohibited that. So, we had no electric fans and most certainly no air-conditioning. On very warm nights, some of us occasionally slept outside on the open porch where there was absolutely no light except for the moon and stars.

Over the course of sixty years of marriage, my parents never told us to get off the phone or turn off the TV before bedtime because we never we had such things. Dad would turn off the kerosene lamp and lock the front door and the kettle-house door at about 8:30 P.M. Then they would dutifully and quietly retire to their dark, unheated, and sparsely furnished bedroom. With birds chirping and fireflies flitting outside their screened-in window, Dad would, with the help of a dim flashlight, wind up the old, metal alarm clock and set it for 4:00 A.M. in preparation for another long day of grueling farm work in the fields.

Dad and Mom were the quintessential, hard-working Amish husband and wife who labored daily, diligently and uncomplainingly, within the difficult and primitive reality of Amish farm life. One benefit for them was always being fit and trim with scarcely ever an ounce of fat between them, just like all us siblings. Dad, with his familiar long red beard, surely knew his role as "boss" of the barn and fields as he sternly commandeered his boys on a daily basis. Mom, a gentle and pretty lady whose dark hair was always neatly covered with the required white Amish "kapp," supervised her daughters at their duties in the house, gardens, and lawns. Life would just go by in a ceaseless, meandering ebb and flow as we worked six days a week, with Saturday being just another busy workday and Sunday being our only day of rest.

About twenty feet west of the house there was, and still is, a towering and majestic walnut tree, with great long gnarled branches reaching to the sky, and still producing walnuts and lots of shade where we played under as children. Its spacious branches were also the nighttime refuge for Uncle Benny's flock of guinea hens.

How excited I was, as an eight-year-old, when we first had running water in our house. It seemed like magic to me and was so much better than using the old-fashioned hand pumps. The water supply for the pumps was in the big metal cistern in the basement, which had always been periodically replenished by rainfall on the house's roof. In the past, someone always had to go to the pumphouse before our meals and pump a large pitcher full of well water. Now we had two new water faucets in the kitchen and the old hand-pumps and cistern were disposed of. We were elated that now there would be no more accidental drinking of that despised "rainwater." A well was dug and the big rust-colored steel tank up by the orchard now held our water supply. The forty-foot tall windmill next to it gallantly tried to keep the tank as full as possible.

At the north end of the house was another section that had been attached to the main house. It was called the "Dawdy" house and they're very common in Amish households. My grandparents, Benuel (also known as Benemel) and Suvilla Fisher had lived there with their daughter, Miriam, and mentally challenged son, Benny, who were both unmarried. Benuel had also been a farmer before he retired. Later, he had a little shop above their kettle house where he had a harness repair business. He also often helped Dad on the farm.

My grandmother, Suvilla, was born in 1871 and came from a large family. She proudly told people there had been thirteen of them and they all grew up. That rarely happened so long ago. Grandma lived to be eighty-nine years old. She had five siblings who lived to their nineties and her mother, Mary Kauffman, lived to be ninety-seven. Most of my grandmother's twelve siblings left the Amish and joined the Mennonite church at Maple Grove about 1915. Dad said Grandma would have wanted to do that too, but Granddad would never consider it at all. He died before I was born, but Dad said he had been a very humble and quiet man, fully dedicated to the often despised Ordnung. He was true-blue and "hard core" Amish, meaning he was extremely unlikely to ever leave the Amish church. And it seemed the die was cast early on for us to never leave the church either. If I had ever heard my parents discuss that, surely, my first thought would have been that I was either dreaming or hallucinating. For them, any other lifestyle would have been like fish being out of water.

My grandparents, Benuel and Suvilla, raised their family on the farm about a quarter mile east of our farmhouse. Previously, Menno Zook and his wife Mary, who was Granddad's older sister, had lived there. One night around 1900, there was a tremendous explosion in the barn because of a large steel-wheeled steam engine overheating. A few Amish farmers had steam engines, which were only used to provide belt power for certain farm machinery. The explosion ripped the steam engine completely apart. A big piece of red-hot steel, weighing about two hundred pounds, flew up through the barn roof and sailed over the house and landed several hundred feet away. The barn caught fire and was completely destroyed along with some cows and other livestock. The barn was rebuilt in about ten days, with the help of many friends and neighbors.

Eventually, my grandparents moved there and stayed until 1928 when Dad's oldest brother, Sammy, and his wife Mary moved there. They raised their nine children there, which included eight boys and one girl. They stayed until 1981 when Uncle Sammy died of a massive stroke at age seventy-five. He was a lot more lenient than Dad and eventually four of their eight boys left the Amish. When Sammy and Mary's oldest son, Jonas, first bought a car, he parked it behind their house which was something very few Amish parents would allow. Uncle Sammy threatened to hitch their huge Belgian workhorse, Bill, to the car and pull it away. But he never carried out that threat and Jonas continued to park there. Eventually some of his younger brothers bought cars and also parked there.

Uncle Sammy always put the family's trash under some trees in their meadow. One day while snooping around there, I found a non-working wristwatch which I eagerly snatched up. No doubt, it had belonged to one of Sammy's boys. I kept it well hidden and never told my parents since wrist watches are totally forbidden in the Amish church. I sometimes proudly wore it on the playground at school but didn't dare wear it inside for fear the Amish teacher would possibly confiscate it.

Uncle Sammy's house and barn was less than a quarter of a mile away, on the east side of Osceola Mill Road. Since my brothers and I grew up so close to Uncle Sammy and Aunt Mary's boys, we spent a lot of time with them, working and playing together during our childhood years.

The roof on the west side of Uncle Sammy's barn was almost flat and was about twenty feet high. Sometimes their boys rode their tricycles on top of it. Once, when my older brothers were doing that with them, Mom happened to see them. She ran over and sternly marched them back home and gave them all a good whipping. They never did that again!

My great, great, great, great grandfather, Jacob Kauffman, was born in 1737. He and his wife and their seven children lived in Chester Valley, Chester County, Pennsylvania during the Revolutionary War. One day the Continental and British armies came very close to their farm. General George Washington, who was later our first president, came to their house and notified them that a battle was likely to take place at their farm the next day. He strongly advised them to stay in their basement all day. The next morning a severe storm swept over the valley and the expected battle did not take place.

Grandma gave the nickname Barney Google to Dad when he was a young child, after a newspaper comic strip from that era. Nicknames are very common among the Amish and last a lifetime. Because there aren't many different names among them, it's very helpful to have so many nicknames. Dad's nickname, Barney, was passed down to us kids, and also to his grandchildren. But every day my siblings and I addressed our parents as Datt and Mamm, (Dad and Mom) just like most other Amish kids do.

My dad wore a dress from the time he was born until he was three years old because it was a lot easier to change a diaper than if he had been wearing pants. That was a strict Amish custom then. Dad sometimes begged Grandma to let him start wearing pants, but she didn't comply. One day when he was sitting on the floor cutting pictures out of a Sears Roebuck catalog with a pair of scissors, he "accidentally" cut a big hole in the front of his dress. Soon after that Grandma provided him with his first pair of pants!

I was told I was named after two different Amish men, Jonathan King and Jonathan B. Fisher. Mr. King was a close friend of Dad's; his farm was on Cattail Road, about one mile away. They had been childhood friends and had attended the same Amish church district. On my eighth birthday, Mr. King gave me a neat little wooden desk that he had made. I have always treasured it and would not consider ever parting with it.

Jonathan B. Fisher was a distant relative and was known as Traveling Yonie. He was said to be a world traveler which is very unusual for an Amish person. He was born about 1870 in a small house that had been at one end of our cow pasture. The only thing now left of it is a large, three-foot-tall vertical rock protruding from the ground, where cows and horses have rubbed themselves against for approximately the past one hundred years.

In 1934, Traveling Yonie spent nine months traveling around the world by ship, including a long stay in the Holy Lands. A familiar joke at our house (I *guess* it was a joke) was that one day he left the house and went out the *front* door as he started his world tour. When he finally arrived back home, he came across the backyard and in through the *back* door of the house, since he had just circled the globe. Unfortunately, he passed away a long time ago and I never did meet him.

My seven sibling's names were Jacob, Aaron, Benuel, Amos, Suvilla, John, and Lydia. The last three of us were all born in the "final spurt" of a twenty-eight-month time period. I went by the nickname Yonie, as do most Amish who have my name.

The big white rambling farmhouse was always a busy and noisy place, especially at mealtime. Of course, there was never any electricity or TV or radio or telephone, as those and many other modern things were totally forbidden in the Amish church Ordnung. That is their vast number of hundreds of unwritten "social order" rules and regulations.

The walls in our house were mostly drab and bare, with no pictures hanging there at all. But, throughout the house, there were always at least a dozen calendars which Lydia and I would eagerly hurry to on the first morning of each month and rip off the expired page. In the living room, the ugly old linoleum flooring was completely worn through in some spots but was still a happy place as we daily played on it with the few toys we had. They included some old building blocks, a small wooden barn, about six wooden horses and cows, and two old toy tractors. One was of orange metal and had both front wheels missing. The other one was a red plastic model with an attached driver whose head had been pulled or bitten off and had been like that since my earliest memory.

Outside in the pasture, of course, were the farm animals. The sixteen cows had to be milked twice a day, seven days a week, 365 days a year, on Sundays, holidays, and Christmas, no matter what. On frosty mornings when we chased them from the pasture into the barn, we often briefly stood with our bare feet on the spot where they had lain, to warm our cold feet.

We had six huge Belgian draft horses, known as the workhorses, or chunks, because they did all the slow, heavy, work pulling the farm implements in the fields. Their names were Charley, Bill, Prince, Frank, Jim, and Jerry. They were considered the blue-collar workers because they did all the "grunt" work. There were also at least two smaller driver horses, normally only used to pull a buggy or a carriage on the road. Sometimes, however, one might be used in an emergency to help the bigger horses in the fields.

We also had hogs, sheep, calves, heifers, and a big bad Holstein bull. During the winter months we kept seven steers in the south end of the barn to fatten and sell. We always kept one to butcher, which supplied us with meat all year. We also butchered a hog every winter. There were ducks, chickens, bantam roosters, hens, and little chicks which roamed around the barnyard. And, of course, Uncle Benny's small flock of beloved guinea hens. We always had plenty of cats and kittens, along with our two dogs, a brown and white fox terrier named Nellie, and an old reddish colored chow named Sporty.

My childhood and teenage years were very typical of most Amish boys, although it seemed more memorable things happened to me than to other boys. Since there were six boys in the family, and our farm was rather small, my older brothers worked full-time at other Amish farms. Each Monday morning, they'd drive their horses and buggies there. On Saturday eve when they came home Lydia and I would run out to greet them, as they drove in on the gravel driveway. I always loved it when all my brothers were home on Sundays, and we'd have a big noon-day dinner meal and they'd talk about their life at the other farms and, of course, about Rumspringa. There'd be lots of chatter and light-hearted banter while Dad might grin and sagely remind us, "Olly moll uss' Shipley blaht, faliehts unn mahl full," (Each time the sheep says "Baa," it loses a mouthful!)

When we went away with any of the driver horses, they always remembered where home was. Then, upon returning home, they would turn into our driveway without the driver even needing to pull the proper rein. Other Amish people's horses also did that. Interestingly, each of the cows knew their individual stall in the barn and went to it each time to be milked. Certain cows were always the eager beavers, so to speak, and would be first in line to come in. Of course, they knew that was also feeding time for them. There were also one or two "lingerers" that would dawdle around outside and had to be chased in. Of course, all our cows had been born and raised as calves on our farm, a consistently "generational" happening.

Mom often talked about her all-time favorite driver horse, Dewey. He was named after Tom Dewey, the Republican presidential candidate in 1948. Another horse that my parents had, died strangely and suddenly as they were coming home after visiting Aunt Miriam at the hospital. There was a lot of traffic along that big highway and they thought that might have stressed him out. Apparently, he had already died by the time the veterinarian arrived. It was presumed he had died of a heart attack.

Dad's favorite workhorse, Prince, died from eating too much green corn while in the binder team, as they were harvesting corn one day. He had gotten his wire mouth basket loose, without anyone noticing, and he ate so much corn that he got a severe case of colic. Dad called the vet to come and treat him but by the next morning he had died. We were all very sad about that.

Another sad incident involved a driver horse that I owned when I was in Rumspringa. He was a handsome, black thoroughbred named Fred and had one white ankle and a white spot on his forehead. I had been to a doctor's appointment in New Holland, about five miles away, on a rainy Saturday afternoon. As I was returning home, driving Fred in my enclosed buggy, it started raining very hard. I drove slowly, as we approached a steep hill which was called Dry Hill. It certainly was not dry then, it was very wet and slippery. Apparently, one of Fred's horseshoes had come off a little earlier, and while coming down the hill he slipped with the bare hoof and suffered a very bad fall. Being flat on the wet pavement on that steep hill, with the weight of the buggy pushing and making things worse, he slid on the road for some distance before he and the buggy got stopped.

I immediately jumped out and ran up to him, as he was still lying on the wet pavement. I saw that he had a horrifyingly bad front leg fracture, below the knee, at the leg which had lost the shoe. The main leg bone had fractured so badly that a section about eight inches long had broken off at both ends and was lying separately on the road. As soon as I saw that, I knew that I would have to put Fred out of his misery, or have someone else do it. Even the most valuable horses are usually euthanized when they have that kind of injury, so I knew I really didn't have a choice in the matter.

As I stood there in the pouring rain, wondering what to do next, Fred actually struggled to his feet. That is, the three feet that he could still stand on. I quickly unhitched him and took his harness off. Even though he must have been in great pain, he just calmly stood there and didn't try to run off. I talked to him, and petted him and stroked his neck, as the steam rose from his body in the pouring rain. Then I had to make a grim and sad decision. I decided to go to a nearby neighbor's farm, someone who was a friend of mine, and ask to borrow his shotgun. When I told Jake Zook what had happened, he listened sympathetically and willingly let me borrow his twelve-gauge shotgun. I went back to where Fred was still standing by the side of the road. I petted him and stroked his neck again. I talked to him and apologized for what I would have to do. I made sure the shotgun was properly loaded and raised it to my shoulder. I aimed directly between his eye and ear from about ten inches away and pulled the trigger. At the roar of the shotgun, it seemed as though Fred didn't move even one muscle, as he crashed down to the pavement. He died instantly, as I tried to convince myself that he surely didn't know I was going to do that. I returned the gun to Jake and called Messner's Rendering Company in Ephrata to come and get Fred. Then I walked more than two miles through the pouring rain to our house and told my folks what had happened. That certainly was a sad and distressing day.

CHAPTER TWO

Why Did My Grandmother Commit Suicide?

MY VERY EARLIEST CHILDHOOD memory is of my grandmother, Mary Miller, when I saw her in her coffin on August 20, 1954. That was just a few days before my third birthday. Probably, the reason I still remember it is because it was the first time I had seen a deceased person. It was in a little bedroom at my Uncle Sam and Aunt Bertha Miller's house, near Bird in Hand. My Uncle Eli and Aunt Lydia Miller and Uncle Jake and Aunt Mary Beiler and their families all lived at the two adjoining farms along Miller Lane, near Stumptown Road.

At my grandmothers viewing, as two tiny siblings and I stared down at her, I wondered why she just laid there and didn't move or say anything. Was she sleeping? And why were the people crying and looking so sad? Soon someone told us "Grussmommy iss schtarva," (Grandmother is dead). "Well, what does *that* mean?" I innocently wondered.

About ten years later, I was told there had been something very unusual and very tragic about her death. When I was thirteen years old, Dad told me that my grandmother had committed suicide on that fateful day, long ago. Apparently, she had suffered from depression for many years and finally decided to end it all by jumping into the water cistern in the basement. The cistern was the big holding tank used to collect rainwater from the roof.

Grandmother probably never had the opportunity to get counseling and it's very unlikely that she was advised to do so. Even though this had been her *third* suicide attempt. I suspect being married to Grandad Miller for fifty years had not been easy or pleasant for her since he was known to be hot-tempered and harsh at times. She was seventy-two years old at the time of her death and did not leave a suicide note. I'm sure it must have been a very hard thing for Mom, her siblings, and Grandad Miller to deal with. In fact, before the funeral he had gone out to the barn and, because of all the windows being open in that hot August weather, his grief-stricken sobbing and crying was heard, even from the house.

Despite many people's belief that the Amish lifestyle is peaceful and pleasant, suicides occur with about the same frequency as in the non-Amish community. When Amish people do that, there is usually a very small, hastily arranged, funeral held at the house, often just hours afterward. Sometimes, they are buried in an isolated location on the family farm, rather than at an Amish cemetery. I'm glad Grandmom was buried at Myers Amish cemetery, next to her husband, my granddad, Jacob B. Miller.

I've often wondered if living the bleak and austere lifestyle of the Amish may have been a factor in Grandmother's decision to commit suicide. I suppose her death may have almost devastated my mom and her siblings, but I really don't know because our family never talked about it. Our parents never said we shouldn't, but it seemed we had an implicit understanding not to. From the time Dad told me about it, until Mom died forty-three years later, I never heard her talk at all about her mother's suicide, and I don't remember any of us ever asking her anything about it. I think that, in addition to the sadness we felt, there was a continuing sub-conscious sense of shame that we felt. Many years later, I read an article which stated that, since the year 1880, there had been two Amish people who had committed suicide by drowning. My grandmother, Mary Miller, was one of those two people.

Granddad Miller was a hard-working Amish farmer and had somehow managed to buy those three farms along Miller Lane where all of them lived. Miller Lane, obviously named after him, was very narrow but was paved, which was considered a luxury. Mom said her dad was a stern man and he wouldn't hesitate to whip his children, both boys and girls. There were three boys and six girls, and their lives were much like slave workers on the farm. Mom had twin brothers, Eli and John, and Mom was the next one born after them. Oddly, Dad had twin sisters, Mary and Miriam, and he was the next one born after them.

Mom told us that one day, Eli and John, and their brother-in-law, Levi, loaded with hand forks, and spread one hundred loads of manure from the steer barn with the horse-drawn manure spreader. The average weight of the manure in each load was about thirteen hundred pounds. They didn't unload it by hand, as the spreader did that mechanically. They did, however, admit that they were extremely tired at the end of the day. Their older brother, Uncle Sam, may have been the hardest working farmer in Amish history. He would get up around 3:30 A.M. and literally work all day, till dark or later, only stopping for a short breakfast, lunch, and supper. He was a stern man like his father, Granddad Miller, had been.

One day one of Uncle Sam and Aunt Bertha's sons, who was seventeen years old, ran away and left no trace. That is an extremely rare event in Amish families. With relatives, friends, and neighbors, they searched diligently but could not find him. I strongly doubt that any police were notified. About one and a half days later, to their great relief, the runaway son returned home. I never heard why he did it, but I presume things were bad between him and his father. I never heard any details about it at all.

Mom said that Granddad Miller, at a fairly young age, bought a farm just a few miles east of Lancaster. He was excited and pleased that he had bought it at a bargain price. However, his father objected strenuously and said it was too close to Lancaster with all the wickedness in that city and demanded that he sell it again. Fortunately, he was able to sell it for a profit of one thousand dollars, which pleased him greatly, because that was considered a huge amount of money in 1915.

From the time of my first memories of Granddad Miller, he was already crippled from a major stroke and spent most of his time in a wheelchair. Fannie and Lydia, his two unmarried daughters, still lived at home and took care of him. I vividly remember whenever we visited him, we kids were always urged to shake his hand, which is a very important Amish custom. But we were very nervous and unwilling, as small children, because he always grabbed our wrist and held on tightly. He teased us this way as we struggled mightily to get loose. He only let go once we were in tears or very near so. What made it worse was that he couldn't really talk anymore and his attempts to do so resulted in incoherent groaning. He seemed to be laughing but at the same time was also drooling and slobbering, all of which was quite scary to us kids.

About 8:30 P.M., on Christmas Eve, 1964, as we sat around the living room, someone knocked on the front door. It was Uncle Sam, coming to tell us that eighty-five-year-old Granddad Miller was deathly ill. My parents immediately hitched up a horse and drove about five miles to be with him, expecting him to die at any time. He surprised everybody by living six more weeks and passed away in February, 1965. Grandmother Miller's tragic death had already occurred more than ten years earlier.

Their two single daughters, Aunt Fannie and Aunt Lydia, had a thriving business, making Amish straw hats. I believe they were the only source for homemade Amish straw hats in all of Lancaster County for a very long time, possibly thirty or forty years. Of course, store-bought straw hats made in other states were readily available at tourist attractions in Intercourse. But they were not as durable and were very much frowned upon and even prohibited in southern Lancaster County where the Amish bishops had the strictest rules and regulations.

My aunts grew the special rye straw which was somewhat like wheat, in their brother Eli's field. When the straw was ripe, they'd ride out to the field in their horse-drawn spring wagon and cut it by hand with a sickle and harvest it.

A few years after Granddad Miller died, Aunt Fannie, at the age of forty-seven, married a widowed man from the neighborhood, Christ King. He was twenty-two years older than her. Their "courtship" had started when he came to Fannie and Lydia's house one evening and told them he was looking for a wife and would take whichever one was most interested. That happened to be Aunt Fannie, so he married her. Christ, at that time, had a precocious young grandson, Lloyd Smucker, who would later become the first Amish-born U.S. Congressman, although Christ had passed away by then.

Uncle Christ and Aunt Fannie had a very unusual living arrangement after they got married. Even though Fannie and Lydia had been living in the same house, Christ moved in with them and they all shared the same living quarters. That seemed to work well for them until his death, fifteen years later. Uncle Christ was a very pleasant and friendly man and always helped with harvesting the straw and making the straw hats. Of course, we always bought our straw hats from them, although I did buy a worldly English one at Zimmerman's store in Intercourse when I was seventeen years old and already quite rebellious. Mom was very unhappy about that, but she did still allow me to wear it.

Each year my aunts had a special day planned for the summertime straw harvest and it was called a "frolic." All our uncles and aunts and cousins went there and helped with the straw that day. It was put on tables inside their little barn and the people would line up the dark knots on the straw stems. The knots were then chopped off and the straw was ready to be braided together and sewn into straw hats. Of course, my aunts were the only ones who did the sewing.

In the summertime, almost all the Amish men and boys in Lancaster County wore the homemade straw hats that my aunts made. Only those who were considered quite liberal wore the store-bought hats. In the wintertime, everybody wore the black felt hats, whether they were liberal or not. The ones who wanted to be the plainest and most conservative, wore the wider brimmed hats. The more liberal folks wore hats with more narrow brims, which were considered more worldly.

For a long, long time, there was only one place where the Lancaster County Amish got their black hats. That was at Haas Hat store in Lancaster, about twelve miles away. Harry Haas had been selling hats there for about fifty years and certainly was considered to be an honest merchant. However, he was often in a real dilemma, especially with the more liberal Amish customers who usually wanted narrower brimmed hats. Apparently, all the large hats came from the factory with brims of the same width, about four inches wide. The preachers and older men bought and wore their hats like that with a full width, untrimmed brim. Most of the younger married men would have Harry trim a small amount off the hats they bought. The unmarried boys who were in Rumspringa, would have even more trimmed off, and the most liberal and worldliest ones would have more trimmed off than anyone else.

Naturally, the preachers admonished and almost begged Harry not to trim the worldly and rebellious boy's hats brims down to as narrow a width as they wanted. So, Harry had to do somewhat of a diplomatic balancing act and was often, really, in a no-win situation. Probably, the narrowest brims that even the wildest boys ever got were two and one-half inches wide, which was considered almost unacceptable. However, a brim width of two and three quarters of an inch would be grudgingly accepted by the bishops. That slight difference might not seem like a big deal to most, but in the Lancaster County, Amish community it really was a big deal!

CHAPTER THREE

The School Life
of an Amish Child

THE MOST INTERESTING DAY in a young Amish child's life is their first day at school. Since Amish children don't go to nursery school or kindergarten, their first school attendance is when they enter first grade at age six. Their emotions on that first day range anywhere from eager anticipation to dread. Of course, most would be accompanied by older brothers and sisters. And, for the first time in their life, everyone will be speaking English instead of Pennsylvania Dutch.

I remember eagerly awaiting my first school day at Hatville School, along with my brother John and sister Lydia, who were in third and second grade. Like Amish kids everywhere, we walked to school every day and *never* rode a bus. The school was only about a quarter of a mile away, but we had to trudge up the Red Hill and the school was a short distance north of it. My siblings were teasingly calling me a beginner, or guinea, after Uncle Benny's guinea hens. As we approached the old wooden one-room schoolhouse I was nervous and excited, clinging to my sister's hand. Even though she was only one year older than me, that seemed like a lot to me. My brother and sister seemed like experienced old-timers compared to me.

Hatville School seemed very much like an Amish owned school. All the kids were Amish, except for two sisters who were English, (as the Amish call non-Amish people) Sharon and Carol King. In reality, though, it was a public school with a total of thirty-two students in grades one through five.

The kids converged toward the humble old one-room schoolhouse from all directions, swinging their lunch boxes and chattering away. They came down Hatville Road and from Osceola Mill Road. They came across the fields from as far away as Old Philadelphia Pike and Cattail Road, down across the Pequea valley, about a mile away.

My brother and sister and I, along with our cousin Omar, Moses and Verna Lapp, Ben and Mary Jane Smoker, and a red-haired boy named Joe Zook from down by Pequea Creek, were the only ones who had to walk up the Red Hill to school. The Red Hill got its name a long time ago, before it was paved, because of the ground being a deep reddish color.

Cousin Omar was a fifth grader, which seemed like an upper-class man to me, as I was just a lowly first grader, a beginner. He was a tall young lad and I literally looked up to him. Also, figuratively, and with near reverence, when I soon found out that he was quite the hard-hitting slugger in the softball games they always played behind the schoolhouse. Even at that early age I already had a rather intense interest in baseball because of my brothers often playing it out in our meadow. Omar was the youngest of Uncle Sammy and Aunt Mary's large family. They lived less than a quarter of a mile away, near the crossroad at Newport Road and Osceola Mill Road.

When we arrived at school that morning, I got my long anticipated, first look at our teacher, Mrs. Edith Shertz. Since Hatville was a public school, of course, she was an English lady. Her car, an old brown sedan from the early forty's era, was parked near the porch on the gravel driveway. Even then I was already fascinated by cars and sometimes admiringly gazed at it and wondered what it would be like to drive it. Mrs. Shertz was a large woman and had a rather unfriendly attitude and an intimidating manner. She also had a weird looking frizzy hairstyle which I thought was not very attractive. But what did I know about English women's hairstyles, anyway? Of course, nothing. Surely, I didn't expect her to have an Amish lady's hairstyle, did I?

A year earlier when Lydia was starting first grade, Mrs. Shertz frequently told her to pay attention. Since Amish kids are not taught any English at home, Lydia didn't know what that meant, so she asked Mom. So, I do think that Amish kids should be taught some English before they start school. But, like most other Amish traditions, that probably will never change.

During the recess periods at school we played Fox and Geese, Prisoners Base, and Kollyover, which involved about ten kids standing on each side of the schoolhouse. One kid threw a sponge ball over the schoolhouse and someone on the other side would catch it and they'd all run to the other side and try to hit somebody with it. Softball was also a favorite daily activity.

The lunchtime recess consisted of a full hour. Since we lived only about a quarter of a mile away, we'd run home for lunch and Mom would always have it ready. We'd gobble it down and hurry back to school so as to maximize our playing time. On the rare occasions when Mom was away for the day, she'd "pack" food into our lunchboxes and we'd eat at school. We always knew when the recess period was almost over when Mrs. Shertz strolled out to the girl's wooden outhouse at the east edge of the property. She always wore her old brown robe even in very warm weather. As soon as she was back inside, she'd ring the big bell on top of the schoolhouse, signaling that our recess period was now over.

There were six boys and two girls in my class, including Sharon King, one of the English girls. My studies were easy for me and I did very well, especially in reading and spelling. When we had homework in the evening, Dad often helped us with our math. We always called it arithmetic. I thought it funny that Dad always called the number zero, "aught." Of course, that's how he was taught when he went to school back in the twenties.

Dad had five older sisters and three brothers, including Michael, (Mikey) who died at age five of diphtheria. They had also attended Hatville School, along with an English boy, Willis Futer, who lived just west of us. Dad said when he attended school as a child, they had an English male teacher who threw erasers, pencils, and books at them when they misbehaved.

Hatville School was the only school my two oldest brothers ever attended, from first through eighth grade. Brother Aaron said that, other than an occasional substitute, he had only one teacher during his entire eight-year school "career" and her name was Mrs. Roberts. My brothers, Benuel and Amos, and sister Suvilla attended the modern brick schoolhouse at Intercourse during grades sixth through eighth after having "graduated" from Hatville School after fifth grade. Unfortunately, Amish student's formal education essentially ends after eighth grade, because the bishops think that going to high school is both unnecessary and sinful.

Unlike Hatville School, the school at Intercourse had far more English kids, which put the Amish kids in the minority. Since Hatville School was a one room schoolhouse, there was always only one teacher, Mrs. Shertz. She taught all the various subjects to all those kids, which kept her incredibly busy.

At Hatville School, each morning started with all the kids standing up alongside their desks while holding their right hand against their chest and reciting the pledge of allegiance, along with Mrs. Shertz. Of course, that was not done at any of the Amish schools because it has always been considered worldly and unnecessary. At Hatville and other public schools, the Amish grudgingly complied with that rule since they had no authority in the matter.

For the various classes, the kids went behind the teacher's desk and stood side by side on the platform. Near the far end of the platform stood a huge coal burning stove, which was the only source of heat in the wintertime. Each day the older boys had to bring buckets of coal up from the basement for the stove.

Mrs. Shertz was quite strict with us kids, but rarely resorted to whipping anybody. She did, however, sometimes have a strange way of doing things. One day, Joe, an eight-year-old, vomited on the classroom floor. She then demanded David, another eight-year-old, to clean it up. We would have expected her to make one of the two fifth-graders, Isaac or Stephen, clean it up instead. Or, perhaps she should have had the novel idea of cleaning it up herself! But, strangely, she did not.

When I was in second grade, my siblings told me I must be the teacher's pet because Mrs. Shertz gave me straight A's in every subject throughout the entire school year. Whether I was the teacher's pet or not, I was nevertheless quite proud of having had all A's that year. It was during second grade, also, that the kids in my class did a class project when we wrote a short essay of a historical American figure. We put a picture of him in a little folder, glued in place on a piece of green construction paper. Mine was of Daniel Boone and I read the whole story clearly and correctly as Mrs. Shertz had asked. She then praised me and said loudly enough that everyone could hear, that I had read it as well as any fifth grader could have. I was then so proud I think I almost burst!

There was another event which involved Mrs. Shertz, of which I was not proud of. Each afternoon just before school was over, she'd send two boys out to sweep the porch. One day she assigned me and my classmate, Ira Beiler, to do that. Ira was my best friend and lived at the farm on the hill, just a quarter of a mile north of us. After sweeping the porch we decided to play behind the schoolhouse for a while. Maybe we wanted to test Mrs. Shertz's authority. She soon sent another boy, Elias, out to summon us back in. Elias, however, also stayed out and played with us for quite some time. Eventually, Mrs. Shertz herself came out and sternly ordered us inside and up front. She then gave each of us a good paddling with a wooden paddle, right in front of all the other kids. Then she sent us back to our seats. We put our faces down on our desks and hid our faces with our hands and appeared to be deeply sorry. One of the other boys was crying, but I was brazenly peeking out between my fingers and evaluating the situation. I expected my siblings to tell my parents about it and, of course, they did so. Mom then also paddled me because of my paddling at school. I believe that was the first time I was a victim of Amish double jeopardy, having been punished twice for the same crime! By the way, that was the only time I was whipped by any of my teachers. That seems surprising, considering how much trouble I got into later at the three one-room schools I attended.

I vividly remember the day the two English sisters came to school with hula hoops. We had not even heard of hula hoops before, much less having seen any. We watched with great interest and amusement as they did their hula hoop performance and they did it very well. I'm sure the Amish girls wished their parents would get them one too, but I doubt if any ever did as that would have been frowned upon and considered very worldly and possibly even sinful.

CHAPTER FOUR

A Nineteen-Year-Old's Fatal Heart Attack

THE MOST VIVID AND painful event during my childhood years was the death of my older brother, Amos. He was my parent's fourth child and was born on August 21, 1943, which was also our Granddad Jacob Miller's birthday. Amos was nineteen years old and I was eleven at the time. Our birthdays were only two days apart.

Amos was a handsome dark-haired lad and he and Mom were the only family members with black hair. He was, of course, named after Dad and was known by everybody simply as Amy. It was then, and still is quite common for Amish who have that name to also be called Amy.

At a very young age, the family doctor did some tests on him because his physical progress was lagging. I think more tests were also done at the hospital and soon my parents were told the grim news. Sadly, Amy had a deformity in his heart which involved a growth that restricted the blood flow in his heart. And, shockingly, they thought he would only live to be about forty years old. The doctors did not advise any surgery, thinking that would be too risky. Heart surgery was rarely done at that time, especially on toddlers. Nevertheless, it was thought he still might be able to live a fairly normal life.

As a young child, Amy was quite small and weak, so Dad took him to a "braucher," or Pow-wow doctor, first in Lancaster and later in Intercourse. They went once or twice a week for about six months. They thought that helped him somewhat, although I never knew what the "braucher" treatments consisted of. Amy did not start walking until he was two years old, about the same time as Sister Suvilla, who was fifteen months younger. Still, he lived a fairly normal life and did most of the things our brothers did. He would be the shortest of us six brothers at five feet and five inches tall. We wondered if his heart condition had stunted his growth. When playing, running, or working at strenuous activities he became fatigued rather quickly. During his lifetime, his heart problem was rarely mentioned by any of us, because he himself rarely mentioned it. In fact, I can't remember ever having heard him talk about it at all.

Amy was a free spirited, happy-go-lucky lad who had a good sense of humor and liked to make people laugh. Soon after turning sixteen and starting Rumspringa he acquired the nickname "Funny" because of all his jokes. One day when he and John and I were playing baseball out in the meadow, one of us hit a foul ball into the weeds behind the henhouse. Since it was Amy's ball, and we were having trouble finding it, he promised John and me that he would give a "buck" to whoever found it. John eagerly explained to me that meant a dollar bill. So, we searched for it with renewed energy and determination. Suddenly, I found it and immediately showed it to him triumphantly, along with my other hand, palm up, waiting for the reward. He then laughingly lowered his head and butted me in my chest, which we always considered to be a "buck." So, I didn't get a dollar bill after all. Despite Amy's heart defect, he was very competitive in baseball and other activities and wanted to show that he could do as much as other boys.

In August of 1962, at the age of nineteen he, along with four Rumspringa buddies took a weeklong vacation to Virginia and Tennessee and toured Skyline Drive and various other places. Of course, they all had a great time. Two months later, we all were especially glad that he at least had the opportunity to do that.

He worked at Yonie Kauffman's farm that summer and at the home farm and always seemed to be in excellent health. In fact, Dad said Amy hung almost all of our large crop of nine acres of tobacco in the six weeks before his death. Dad hung very little of it because of his legs being crippled at that time. John and I were still in school and really weren't big enough to do it yet, anyway.

During apple picking season, Amy and Brother Benuel and our cousin, (Sammy's) Leroy sometimes spent the days at A.L. Kauffman's Fruit Farm, a few miles away, picking apples at their enormous orchard. They were paid a certain amount per basket, so the apple picking became quite competitive and they'd see who could pick the most in one day. This, despite the fact that they were not allowed to keep the money they earned. Of course, it all went straight to their fathers.

One day, Benuel picked one hundred bushelsful of apples, possibly a record for a single day. Amy, with his competitive nature, decided to see if he could also accomplish that amazing feat. It really is remarkable for anybody to pick that many apples in one day, with all the climbing up and down the trees and positioning the ladders that's required. We were all immensely proud of him a few days later when, with great effort and determination, he matched Benuel's recent feat. But he did admit that he was really tired at the end of the day.

The very next day was the unforgettable day of October 4, 1962, which started as a fairly normal day. John, Lydia, and I went to Newport School that morning as usual. Amy and Dad and several Amish farmers from the neighborhood were working at our farm, filling the fifty-foot tall silo, which was done every fall. Groups of farmers drive horse-drawn flatbed wagons into the cornfields to harvest the fully-grown corn crop. When the wagon is full, it is driven up alongside the big concrete silo. The corn bundles are thrown off onto a chopping machine which is powered by an "Amish" steel-wheeled tractor. The cutter also blows the chopped-up corn up a long steel pipe into the top of the silo and it is fed to the cows during the winter months.

On that fateful day, after they all ate lunch in the farmhouse, Amy said he felt a little tired and took a short nap while the other men lounged around briefly before returning to work. Dad climbed to the top of the silo to put the filler pipe in place while Amy, Leroy Esh, and Elam Zook went out to the cornfield in the horse drawn wagon. From the top of the silo, Dad watched them leave and never dreamed that would be the last time he'd see Amy alive.

At first, Amy and Elam loaded the corn stalks before Leroy took his turn at loading while Amy drove the horses. He had given no indication of not feeling well and was chatting and joking with the others when it, suddenly, all happened.

Meanwhile, at Newport school about three quarters of a mile away, it was raining lightly during our 2:00 P.M. recess period. Nevertheless, most of the kids were playing outside. One of my classmates, Twin Aaron and I were inside throwing a softball back and forth, playing catch. Suddenly the front door swung open. Aaron's twin brother, Amos, came running up to us and in a shocked tone of voice, blurted out, "Yonie, your brother died!"

As I stared at him in utter horror and anguish, I immediately thought he meant Brother John, who was outside playing with the other kids. Imagine being told in that way, without any warning, that my closest brother had suddenly died while playing right outside the schoolhouse.

During those first few awful moments, as my mind was reeling and I couldn't yet even speak, I knew without a shadow of doubt, what Amos had told me was absolutely true. I will never, ever forget the indescribable feeling of horror and grief coursing through my heart and I felt as though I'd just been punched in the stomach. Finally, while still thinking it was John who had died, I managed to ask in a shaky, quavering voice, "Wh-what happened"? He immediately replied, "It's your brother Amos, he died of a heart attack." Twin Amos then motioned toward the playground and said, "Leroy Esh (his cousin) is out there, he came and told us." Instinctively, I hurried to the window and looked outside. I saw Leroy out in the schoolyard and all the kids were gathered around him as he told them the sad news. I ran to the door but before I got there, Brother John came in. As we approached each other, I saw that he had tears in his eyes. He simply said to me, "Amy died, we're going home now." Sister Lydia then came in and she was also crying. I don't think any of us even told the teacher we were leaving but, of course, the other kids would tell her what had happened. We quickly got our lunch boxes out of the wooden cabinet and went outside and, along with Leroy, climbed into Manny Nafziger's old station wagon. Manny was a semi-retired man from Intercourse who often transported Amish people. Someone had flagged him down at the farmhouse and he'd brought Leroy to the schoolhouse to tell us.

Soon we arrived at our farmhouse and, as we pulled into the driveway, we saw Dr. Bauer's car there. Manny parked behind it and we all got out and started toward the house. As we went up the old faded blue wooden porch steps, we were still in stunned disbelief and filled with an unspeakable dread. We went in through the front door and into the living room. Dad and Mom and Suvilla were there, crying and sitting next to the old green sofa that Amy was lying on. Dr. Bauer was kneeling by the sofa and had put a long needle into Amy's chest and was trying to resuscitate him. A few moments later, Dr. Bauer slowly stood up and turned to us and sadly said, "There's nothing more I can do, Amy's gone."

As we sat there and the enormity of it all really hit us, Dad managed, but just barely, to tell us what had happened. Amy had been driving the horses while Leroy and Elam were loading the wagon. It was just west of the solitary cherry tree that stood near the middle of the field. Amy had been talking and joking with the others when suddenly he was quiet, and the horses had walked too far ahead. After calling and getting no answer, Leroy ran up front and saw Amy slumped down and lying motionless on the corn bundles. He anxiously called his name and shook him but there was no response. Shockingly and unbelievably, he apparently had died instantly of a massive heart attack. He had seemed perfectly fine moments before and had shown no signs of distress.

While Elam stayed with Amy, Leroy ran in to the silo and told Dad the shocking news. Then, Dad, overwhelmed with dread and anxiety, ran out to the field as fast as his crippled legs could carry him. When he saw Amy and it was obvious that life had fled, his most dreaded fear had become reality. He vainly tried to get him to respond but it was not to be. He could hardly believe that his young son had died this way after having seen him in a happy mood just a few moments earlier.

Leroy then desperately ran west on Newport Road to the nearest English neighbor's house, where Willis and Martha Futer lived and where the nearest telephone was located. Willis immediately called Dr. Bauer in the town of Intercourse, about one mile away. Dr. Bauer had already been our family doctor for a long time. Meanwhile, back at the farm, Elam drove the wagon to the barn with Dad sitting down and Amy lying beside him and Dad protecting him and holding his head in his lap.

As I write this today, more than fifty years later, these sad memories are still quite vivid in my mind. On that unforgettable day long ago, Leroy had the sad task of notifying Brother Benuel, who lived in Bareville, about Amy's death. Benuel and Amy were very close buddies and were born only a few years apart. Also, Benuel and Leroy were close friends, as Benuel had previously worked for him as a hired boy. Leroy found him at Harry's Furniture Auction and told him the sad news. Benuel was in such shock and anguish that Leroy had to tell him three times before he could fully comprehend and accept it. I remember, later at the viewing, seeing Benuel standing by the coffin with his hands on top of it and his head down low, while sobbing bitterly.

Elam Zook rode his horse more than a mile over the fields to Brother Jake's farm to tell him the sad news. Later, Manny took him in his car to Strasburg to the Amish farm where Brother Aaron worked. He was "A.C." Fisher's hired boy and had been helping with the corn harvest there. Then it started raining so they stopped working and went into the house. He was in his upstairs bedroom, putting on a dry shirt when someone unexpectedly knocked on the door. When he opened it and suddenly saw Elam standing there, he immediately feared there was bad news. He said it was like a dagger to his heart when Elam told him the shocking news of Amy's death.

Back home, Amy had been carried into the house and laid on the kitchen floor. Dr. Bauer asked Stevie Esh to push vigorously on Amy's chest in the faint hope of reviving him, but it was unsuccessful. Soon, he was taken into our parent's bedroom and laid on top of the bed. Preacher Stevie then read a lengthy prayer from Dad's old German prayer book as we all knelt down, utterly grief-stricken. Then Mom cut off Amy's white T-shirt and bathed and dried his upper body with a washcloth and towel, after the rainy weather earlier in the cornfield. Somehow, she was quite calm as she did that. Mom always was a strong woman in situations such as that.

Later, Mom combed Amy's hair the way she always wanted it to be, with bangs combed straight down rather than parted to each side as he always wore them. She said she was glad that he still had bangs and that she didn't have to cut any for him. It's always been a strict requirement for all Amish men and boys to have bangs and to always have them combed straight down.

After a while, the undertaker came and took Amy's body. There was no autopsy performed and I'm sure it was not even considered. Many friends, neighbors, and relatives, gathered at the house, grieving with us and offering support and help in any way they could. Much later, we eventually all went to bed and tried to sleep, with little success. The next morning at the breakfast table, Dad, grim and haggard, said he's certain he hadn't slept at all during the night. He said he's sure he heard the big old wind up Seth Thomas clock in the kitchen strike every hour and half-hour throughout that long, grief-filled night.

I'm sure my parents must have been haunted by the realization that Amy's strenuous and exhausting accomplishment of picking so many apples the previous day probably contributed to his fatal heart attack. Although they could not have anticipated it, they surely must have regretted not warning him. I'm sure they didn't know he was planning to pick so many that day.

Amy's funeral was two days after he died and was held at our house, as is Amish custom, with very many friends and relatives attending. As a young, impressionable eleven-year-old lad, I, along with my family, was hit especially hard with the stark and painful reality of Amy's passing, as that was the first-time death had claimed anyone in our immediate family.

Most Amish strongly believe when an adult Amish person dies and is not a member of the Amish church, they are far less likely to get to Heaven, even if that person professed to believe in Jesus Christ. They seem to think that specifically being a member of the church is more important than truly believing in Jesus and accepting Him as their Savior. Because Amy had not yet joined the church, his death was a particularly sad event for all of us. I'm sure the grief and sorrow my parents felt was almost beyond comprehension. I don't know if Amy had even planned to join the church. I don't think I ever heard him talk about it, other than possibly giving vague answers whenever Dad and Mom were urging him to join. I'm sure that Amy, and later myself, were the two most rebellious brothers in our family. Partly because of that, I had somewhat of a secret admiration for him and generally considered him to be my favorite brother.

A few days after his death, a classmate told me that Amy had owned an old black car of some sort. I doubt that Dad and Mom had known about that. I presume Amy kept it hidden behind Stauffer's Diesel Shop in Hatville where several other Amish boys parked their cars. I don't know if he even had a drivers' license. He had borrowed forty dollars from a friend, Aquilla's Dave, to help pay some of his car expenses. After Amy's death, Dave came to see Dad, hoping he would repay him the money. Dad flatly refused to pay him any of it and told him he shouldn't have loaned Amy any money for car expenses. I don't know what ever happened to Amy's car. I suppose Dad either gave it or sold it to Gap Auto Salvage.

I think Amy and I were the only of us six brothers who ever owned a car. If any of the others had owned one, I'm sure they would not have told me for fear that might tempt me to also get one. However, I'm sure that all those who never had one would readily tell me that if I asked them.

By a strange coincidence, the bi-weekly Sunday church service had been scheduled to be at our house the day after Amy's funeral. It also just happened to be the semi-annual Counsel service, which lasts about seven hours. So, in addition to the stress and sadness of Amy's funeral, we also had the responsibility of hosting Counsel service the next day. Several other families kindly offered to do it, but my parents said they might as well do it as planned since the benches were already in place because of the funeral. Dad said later it was hard to keep his mind on the preaching at the service, because of Amy's death and the funeral the previous day. But he said the Good Lord helped him and Mom to somehow get through it.

Amy was buried at Myer's Cemetery, near Leola, an Amish cemetery where many of our relatives have also been buried. His body was taken there in [Hen's] Christ Stoltzfus' horse-drawn hearse. [A few years later, Christ and his family suffered the immense grief and pain of their only son, Henry, being killed in an automobile accident.] Christ's hearse was at the front of the long procession of mourners, all riding in horse-drawn carriages and buggies.

The four pallbearers were Leroy Fisher, Christian Miller, Alvin Stoltzfus and Danny Beiler. They were all cousins and close friends of Amy and about the same age as him. Sadly, and solemnly, they lowered his plain wooden coffin down into the hand-dug grave with ropes. Then, as the minister read from the German prayer book, they slowly shoveled the dirt down on top of the coffin until the grave was completely full and mounded over at the top. Meanwhile, all of the men and boys had removed their hats or were holding them against the side of their head as a sign of sadness and respect and humility. It certainly was a sad, heart-breaking, and unforgettable event in my young life.

During the rest of the fall and throughout the long, dreary, winter months, Dad said he missed his beloved son terribly. Especially since the plan had been for Amy to work at home with him every day. So, since all of our older brothers were now married and not living at home anymore and John and I were still in school, it was a most sad and lonely winter for Dad. As a way to honor and remember Amy's much too brief life, Dad put a two-foot-high home-made wooden cross into the ground in the field where Amy had died, and it was there for many years.

CHAPTER FIVE

Aunt Lydia
and Childhood Hobos

I HAD A LOT OF uncles, aunts, and cousins while growing up, which is typical in Amish society. My favorite aunt was Aunt Lydia, who was one of Dad's older sisters. Aunt Lydia and Uncle Amos were semi-retired and lived on a small farm on the south edge of Intercourse, two miles away. Sadly, they had no children who grew up, having had one daughter, Suvilla, who only lived four days, and five other children who were all stillborn.

Once, while at their house during my summer vacation, Aunt Lydia and I walked to the little cemetery in Intercourse and she showed me where all her children had been buried. There were six little grave markers, all next to each other and they had been there for many years already. I thought it was very sad and I felt very sorry for her and Uncle Amos.

Among my earliest and fondest memories is of eagerly awaiting Aunt Lydia's arrival at our house every Tuesday morning. She'd walk all the way to our house to do Uncle Benny's cleaning and washing his clothes. We knew she'd always have some candy for us kids, which was something our parents almost never gave us. Aunt Lydia was also quite generous with birthday gifts for us. We never got any birthday gifts from our parents, so we really appreciated the gifts we got from Aunt Lydia and, occasionally, from some other aunts.

Aunt Lydia was a small woman, only about four feet and nine inches tall, but she was a very pleasant and generous lady and loved by all. My siblings and I always eagerly looked forward to the one week in the summer when we were allowed to stay at their house for our summer vacation. We did not go in the same week, but went one at a time, during separate weeks. Almost every day we'd take Uncle Amos's binoculars and look out the living room window at Brother Jake's farm down in the valley, about three quarters of a mile away. We hoped to see him or Arie, his wife, in the yard or garden or fields. Of course, we couldn't call them since we didn't have telephones. Down across the hayfield, about one hundred yards away, was Jake Eichelberger's house. Jake was the local blacksmith and he was an extremely busy man because he did all of the nearby Amish people's horseshoeing in his little shed behind Worst's Department Store in Intercourse.

During our summer vacation, we never had to work very hard at Uncle Amos's. Certainly, not nearly as hard as back home on our farm. Behind the barn in the small pasture were their two hen houses with a total of about five hundred hens. Aunt Lydia and I gathered all the eggs each afternoon and took them into the egg room and weighed each one on a quaint little weight scale device. Then we put them in the proper cardboard flats, small, medium, or large with an occasional jumbo. Finally, we carefully put all the flats into the large cardboard egg crates.

Uncle Amos was a thin, frail looking man with a wispy gray beard. He never helped us with the eggs, and we didn't expect him to because it really wasn't much work. After lunch, he'd walk out to the back pasture, then a quarter mile northward to his brother Aaron's farm and help him with his farm work. Uncle Amos always had a small flock of sheep in the back pasture. He'd solemnly remind us every day to make sure we shut the wooden gate so the sheep wouldn't get out while we were gathering eggs.

As a very curious young lad, I soon discovered where he kept his chewing tobacco. He did not make a secret of his chewing habit as he often boldly spit tobacco juice on the ground. I had never had any and wondered what it would taste like. One day when he was away, I took some from where he kept it hidden in his little tool shed. I was about eleven years old at the time. I eagerly put some in my mouth and quickly realized I didn't like the taste, but still gamely chewed it for a short time. Then I accidentally swallowed some tobacco juice. I soon started feeling sick and thought I might have to throw up. I spit it out somewhere where I felt sure Uncle wouldn't see it. My stomach felt rather queasy for a while but soon I was okay again. Even though the tobacco brand name was Good Bite, it was not a good bite for me, and I never tried it again!

Besides chewing tobacco, there apparently was another minor "vice" that Uncle Amos was guilty of. One day, to my surprise, I saw a bottle of Four Roses whiskey on their basement stairwell. Although I never saw him imbibing from it,

I suppose he secretly took an occasional nip or two sometimes. And, no, unlike with his chewing tobacco, I never sampled the contents of his whiskey bottle.

There were a few other interesting things about Uncle Amos. As is Amish custom, he would not say, but "think" the Lord's Prayer at mealtimes. Everybody knew how long it should take to think it, about the same length of time as saying it. The Amish do not actually recite it, not even in a whisper. They simply bow their heads together and then think the Lord's Prayer with their eyes closed. They do that at the beginning and end of each meal and everyone's hands must be down on their lap. Uncle Amos always thought the Lord's Prayer extremely fast at mealtime, faster than anybody could have spoken or thought it. We found that amusing, and privately accused him of cheating during the prayer because we knew that when he raised his head, he was done. Of course, we never actually mentioned it to him. Also, he had a strange habit of using his knife to eat off of, including even things like peas, and he was quite an expert at it. Maybe he should have been the first professional Amish juggler! After the lunch meal, he'd lay down on the old sofa for a nap and soon there would be thunderous snoring, so loud that he often woke himself up.

In Uncle Amos's orchard was a small wooden shed where little chicks used to be raised. It wasn't being used anymore, so it became the permanent home of Conrad. He was an older English man who'd had a lot of misfortune in his life and became a hobo in his old age. I never knew if Conrad was his first or last name. The Amish always pronounced his name "Con-erd."

His hair was even longer than any of the Amish men that I knew. His full gray beard did, of course, include a moustache, which seemed quite sinister to me. Since even Amish men don't wear mustaches, hoboes were virtually the only people who wore moustaches during that time, in the fifties.

Uncle Amos and Aunt Lydia let Conrad live in the little shed for quite a few years and, of course, never charged him any rent. The inside of the shed only measured about twelve feet by twelve feet square. Aunt Lydia would take Conrad a nice meal every day. She would also occasionally wash his clothes and cut his hair. One day when I was about nine years old, Conrad wasn't there anymore. Aunt Lydia told me that he had passed away. I suppose his body had been taken to the county morgue although I never heard any details of his death.

During and after the Great Depression of the 1930s, there were numerous hobos who traveled the countryside. They were also known, unkindly, as bums and tramps. They walked along the roads and creeks, and through the fields looking for food and possibly a hot meal at the Amish farmhouses. They often worked at certain farms for a few days before moving on. They'd carry a burlap bag on their back in which all of their earthly possessions were kept and they often slept in the farmer's barns at night. Most farmers would ask to keep their matches overnight if they had any. That's because there had been several instances when an angry hobo had burned down the barn at night where he was staying.

I remember as a young child, whenever one came to our house for food, Mom always gave him a nice meal. They'd eat it hungrily while sitting out on the porch steps as Lydia and I watched, shyly peeking around from behind Mom's dress. Then they'd say to Mom, "Thank you very much, Ma'am," and "God bless you, Ma'am." Mom told us that the Bible says, "Geib dem der bittet," which means, in German, to give to those who ask.

There were a few hobos who came to our house fairly regularly. Some of them we only had nicknames for. There was Mr. "Every Two Weeks," the Black Longhaired, and the Delahschleckah, which meant, "the plate licker," an amusing and self-explanatory title, indeed. Others we knew by their real names, such as Jack Donahue, Sam Cole, and Frank Collins.

Frank Collins liked to talk politics and seemed to know a lot about what goes on in Washington. He often complained about our elected "leaders" there, so his nickname around the neighborhood was President. His political rants did not interest the Amish farmers much, however, because they take pride in being as uninformed as possible about politics and world affairs. In fact, for many of them, it's considered honorable and praiseworthy to not have any interest or knowledge at all of such things.

One day some Amish boys hid Frank's worn old hat somewhere and he was *really* angry by the time they finally brought it back. I believe he died one night about 1959, in Uncle Sammy's barn. I don't know if he had been sick at that time or not, or if his death was completely unexpected. How sad and tragic for anybody to die completely alone and unattended in a barn at night like that, with only the various uncaring horses and cows nearby. Although no one will ever know, it's possible that Sammy's beagle dog, Pearly, provided some solace for poor old Frank during his final moments.

During the decade of the fifties, the number of hobos around the country declined greatly. By the early sixties there were virtually none left. This was largely due to the increasing availability of various welfare and other social safety net programs.

CHAPTER SIX

An Amish Child's Death by Shotgun

ONE OF THE SADDEST and most heartbreaking events that sometimes happen is when parents have to endure the heart-wrenching grief that accompanies the death and loss of a child. Especially when it happens because of a horrifying, tragic accident. My Uncle Stephen [Steffy] and Aunt Mary Stoltzfus experienced that on November 7, 1954 when their young son, Andrew, died in such a way. He was seven years old at the time.

It happened on a day which started with much happiness for Uncle Steffy and Aunt Mary, who went by horse and buggy that morning to a relative's wedding. Amish weddings are much anticipated, and eagerly attended, because they are all day events, filled with the solemn preaching during the wedding ceremony, and a lot of visiting, eating, and singing later in the day. So, this was supposed to be a day of celebration and happiness but ended with utmost horror and grief for them. Uncle Steffy and Aunt Mary were the parents of eight young boys, ranging in age from four to eighteen years old but they never had any daughters, which was a very unusual and odd phenomenon, and which almost never happens in that way.

For many years, Pennsylvania has always had the month of November designated as official hunting season for small game, including rabbits, squirrels, and pheasants. Any resident only needed to be at least twelve years old to be eligible to have a valid hunting license. Many of the Amish, especially teenagers, hunt frequently on their farms during that time. On that tragic day while the parents were at the wedding, some of the older brothers went hunting in the woods and fields that afternoon. Upon returning to the barn, they put their shotguns away, presumably in safe locations. However, one gun was left unsecured somewhere.

The older boys started milking the cows and feeding the horses and other animals and doing their barn chores. Meanwhile, two of the younger boys found the gun that had not been safely put away. Unfortunately, the gun had not even been unloaded. Seven-year-old Andrew and one of his brothers started playing with it, not knowing that it was loaded, and potentially extremely dangerous. While just playing around and certainly not meaning any harm, Andrew's brother pointed the gun at him and pulled the trigger. With a horrifying roar, the shotgun blast hit young Andrew directly in the stomach and he immediately fell to the ground, fatally wounded. The brother who had fired the gun, was horrified and in disbelief at what he had done. He immediately ran screaming and crying to tell his older brothers. They had heard the shotgun blast and came running quickly to where Andrew was lying on the ground. As indescribable dread and panic overwhelmed them, they soon came to the awful realization that the young boy would almost surely not survive.

One older brother ran as fast as he could out the long gravel driveway and up the road to the nearest non-Amish neighbors to tell them what had happened and to get their help. Since the Amish don't have cars or telephones, the neighbors took Andrew in their car to the nearest doctor but he had already passed away when they arrived. Then the brothers were faced with the unbearable task of going to the wedding where their parents were and telling them the sad news. When the parents saw the two older brothers hurrying up to them, they wondered why they had come. Never did they expect such dreadful news. They immediately all left together, and with deep sadness and broken hearts, went to where the young boy was.

As the family grieved through the long evening and night, one can only imagine their thoughts. Especially the thoughts of the young boy who had innocently and unintentionally, yet tragically, killed his little brother. Two days later, after a very sad and emotional funeral, the young boy was laid to rest in the Amish cemetery next to where other relatives had also been buried. Then the family faced the unending sadness and grief of the awful event that had cruelly snuffed out the life of their precious young child.

CHAPTER SEVEN

The Life of Uncle Benny

A MOST INTERESTING AND memorable person who was a legendary and long enduring figure in all our lives, was Uncle Benny. He was always known simply as Benny and he was Dad's older brother. He lived almost his entire life of eighty-five years in the smaller north section of the farmhouse where I grew up. Benny was slightly mentally challenged, which was thought to have been caused by a severe case of measles when he was three years old. He never married and he worked on Dad's farm and other farms in the neighborhood, helping to harvest crops of hay, wheat, corn, tobacco and potatoes. He had some very strange characteristics and lived a very humble life.

After his siblings were married, he continued to live with his parents and sister Miriam. Eventually, they all passed away. His father, Benuel Fisher, my grandfather, died of prostate cancer when he was seventy-five years old, in 1944. His mother, Suvilla, my grandmother, died at our house on a Sunday morning, January 1, 1961, at the age of eighty-nine. Uncle Benny and Aunt Miriam continued to live in the [Dawdy] grandfather end of the house until Miriam died in 1966. After that Benny lived there by himself until he was very old.

It seemed everything there, including the few items of furniture was old and decrepit. The ugly linoleum floor may not have been waxed in a decade or more. There was no running water in the house and only two small hand pumps, one at the kitchen sink and one at the wash bowl. To bathe, he used a bucket of water, a bar of soap, and a washcloth, although bathing was a relatively rare event for him. He simply used water to occasionally clean his teeth, using a funny looking antique toothbrush.

He dutifully joined the Amish church and participated in Rumspringa, but dated very little, if at all. One Sunday night, he and his twin sisters, Mary and

Miriam, were coming home from a singing with his horse and buggy. Suddenly, the horse became frightened and was soon out of control and running away at high speed. Benny jumped out and left his frightened sisters in the buggy. So, they both jumped out and suffered quite a few scrapes and bruises. The driverless horse made it home safely without being hit by a car. Of course, during that time in the twenties and thirties there were very few cars on the road at any time.

Benny always had several harmonicas which he loved to play. He also had a large black and white teddy bear that he bought after Granddad died. Grandma disapproved of it but did allow him to keep it. However, she cut the glass like eyes out of it because she said they looked too worldly. He also had a miniature piano that he liked to play. (We called it a PIE-ano because we thought that was correct!) Grandad probably would have confiscated it if he had still been living, but Grandma let him have it if he strictly kept it in his bedroom. Benny also had some old comic books that featured Bugs Bunny, Elmer Fudd, and Wiley Coyote which us kids liked to look at sometimes. At times when we misbehaved or teased Benny, he'd get agitated and run at us and pretend he was really going to hurt us but would only touch us lightly around our shoulders.

Granddad and Benny each used to have a horse of their own and their names were Maude and Pet. There was a ramshackle rat-infested old gray barn behind the big walnut tree where they were kept. After Granddad died, Maude was sold and eventually Pet was also sold. Later, Dad was often afraid Benny would someday get hit by a car because he did so much walking on the roads to various places. He often darted from one side of the road to the other, seemingly without looking to see if it was safe. But somehow the Good Lord seemed to always be watching over him and he never got hit.

He did, however, have a very narrow escape in the snow one day while sledding down the Red Hill. Cousin Omar was watching for him at the bottom of the hill, at the intersection of Newport Road. He signaled for Benny to wait as there was a big truck approaching. Benny must have missed the signal and, while face down on his sled, he crashed into the truck's rear tires and suffered some major bruises, and also had a front tooth knocked out. He could very easily have been run over and killed.

There had been one fatal accident at the Newport Road/Red Hill intersection many years ago, in 1950. One afternoon, my three oldest brothers were coming home from school, walking down the Red Hill. At the same time, two English classmates, Billy and Tommy Lefever, were riding their bikes home. They were the only children of Paul and Mrs. Lefever, our neighbors who lived by Pequea creek, between the farms of Mose Zook and Leroy Esh. While riding down the hill, Billy failed to see a truck in time and was hit by it in the intersection and was killed instantly. Of course, that was a most sad and heartbreaking event.

Uncle Benny loved to take his big Lightning Glider sled and go sledding on the Red Hill, whenever there was enough snow. Sometimes us kids would accompany him, but most times he went by himself. He also liked to go hunting for small game with his shotgun, but had some unsafe habits, such as often having the gun safety off. Once, while tinkering around with it in his upstairs bedroom, the gun discharged accidentally and the shot, reportedly, went through the floor, down into the kitchen and almost hit Grandma and Miriam. Sometimes he'd take the loaded gun into Zimmerman's grocery store in Intercourse. The Zimmerman brothers would ask him if it was loaded before he did any shopping there. He told them no, it wasn't LOADED, because it only had ONE shotgun shell in it! Since he probably was never able to shoot a live pheasant out in the fields, he eventually thought of a solution for that. He bought a pheasant from someone in Quarryville and put it in a burlap bag and rode the bus back home, with it in the bag. Unfortunately, it had suffocated by the time he got back.

Another large ring-necked pheasant that he had escaped in the living room. While flying wildly around and simultaneously ejecting excrement, it almost knocked down the big clock on the shelf near the ceiling. Then it flew into a windowpane and cracked it, which was accompanied to the sounds of Grandma's cries of distress. When Benny finally captured it, he tied it to the top of a fence post and shot it, strangely, during a driving rainstorm. He then proudly announced that he had finally shot a pheasant, even though the gun "kick" had given him a bloody nose. He kept the brightly colored neck and tail feathers for many years in his upstairs bedroom. Eventually, Dad confiscated and hid Benny's gun because of his unsafe habits with it.

Benny chopped almost all of the firewood that we used at the farmhouse. He would often be seen using his trusty axe and splitter at the woodpile up near the orchard. He had very little knowledge of technical skills of any sort. He did, however, once act the part of a dentist, in a very crude way. Once when Brother John had a loose tooth, Uncle Benny pulled it out with a pair of steel pliers. I guess that was better than having to go and visit Dr. Brett, the family dentist, because he would have charged two dollars to pull it!

Benny usually didn't eat much at the house after Grandma died, although Mom often took him a nice hot meal on a tray. He often had chocolate candy and saltine crackers with peanut butter for breakfast, washed down with copious amounts of orange soda or home-made root beer. He never bought any type of cereal or milk. We were certain, however, that he occasionally crept stealthily down to the barn at night and slyly ladled out a generous supply of milk for himself from the milk tank. At mealtimes, he'd eat a huge amount at all of the neighborhood farms where he worked. Sometimes he'd eat as many as ten ears of sweet corn, plus lots of other food. Whenever he had a tummy-ache, he would take some horrid-tasting, yellowish-green medicine called Greatfind from a little glass bottle. Once, he told my brothers that during the winter of his fifty-ninth birthday, he would plan on eating a huge amount of candy and not take any Greatfind, and then would expect to get so sick that he'd die and would "go down" with the March snow. So, before he reached that age, we sometimes reminded him about that statement, and he'd just grimace and have a wry grin on his face. Obviously, he never carried out that threat he had made.

After his sister, Miriam, died he lived at the Dawdy end of the house by himself for many years. He had a copy of {The Amish Year}, a hard-cover book from 1956 which was full of stories and photos of the Amish. He always kept it laying on top of his dresser, opened to his favorite page which had a picture of Miriam and his niece, (Josh's) Suvilla King standing outside of Uncle Ike's house in Intercourse. Of course, that was the only picture he ever had of her since the Amish are not allowed to have cameras.

Uncle Benny always had some white or speckled gray Guinea hens which he was very fond of. They roamed around our farmyard and usually slept in the big walnut tree behind the house. Sometimes, they'd sleep on the little wooden fence at the landing near the entrance to the kettle house. That was only about five feet away from the kitchen sink. In the morning, they'd get quite annoying to whoever was working at the sink when they did their unique two syllable squawk there. We were told when they did that, they were saying "Come back."

Benny was a very faithful worker at all the farms in the neighborhood. His misshapen, "squashed-down" straw hat and tangled, tortured, and "safety-pinned" suspenders were a familiar sight to all the neighbors. But he was a slow worker because he was considerably overweight. He might sometimes disdainfully disapprove when he thought others were working too fast. That was especially true the day that Brother Jake and his hired boy, Ezra, came to help us with the tobacco harvest. Ezra was like a whirling dervish and was spearing tobacco much faster than anyone we'd ever seen, probably at the incredible rate of one stalk per second, which was about fifteen times faster than Benny would do it. When we remarked in awe to Benny about Ezra's prowess, he grimaced and frowned and said disparagingly, "Dei Fishera sinn doch feal mae schteady," meaning that the Fishers are much steadier.

For many years, he only charged fifty-one cents per hour to the farmers he worked for, and we never knew why he insisted on that exact amount. He considered himself to be somewhat liberal by Amish standards, or "toney" as he called it. He'd have a certain neighbor cut his hair who he knew would cut it shorter than other people would. Even when he was quite old, he would sometimes give his beard a rough trimming, which is very much frowned upon, and is also blatantly disobedient to the Ordnung. Many Amish men trim their beards slightly but often it is so little that one can't be sure if it had been trimmed at all. A good analogy might be an old Clairol ad for women's hair coloring which claimed that "Only their hairdresser knows for sure!"

At the semi-annual Communion church service, Benny would take two gulps of wine from the cup that the deacon passed to him, rather than just one sip like everyone else. His birthday was on December 24 and he was genuinely concerned that, with it being one day before Christmas, people might forget his birthday. Whenever there was wrapping from a gift, even from someone else's gift, he'd take it and store it in his bedroom closet for years and never use it, and eventually it would be shredded by mice. He loved to watch Amish children playing and would laugh at them and play with them at church and family gatherings. Despite our best efforts at teaching him, he never quite understood how his stove would work most efficiently, so his house was often cold in the wintertime. The only light he ever had in the house was from a dim lamp that burned coal oil, although sometimes he'd momentarily use a flashlight in his upstairs bedroom.

Sometimes I wished I had offered him a small radio which could have provided him some entertainment during the many hours he spent alone. But the wrong person might have found it and gotten him in trouble with the church and I certainly wouldn't want that for the poor soul. So, maybe it's best that his music consisted only of his own humming and singing, in addition to his harmonicas, his Jews-harp, and the little old twelve key miniature piano.

Of course, there was no bathroom upstairs so at nighttime when he needed one, he improvised by opening the window and, inevitably, the green grass in the yard below became his "substitute" bathroom. Telltale evidence of what he had done included the grass strangely becoming brown and the paint on the windowsill eventually becoming faded and discolored.

He was a remarkably simple man and lived a very simple life, and never even had a checking account. Of course, he never received government benefits of any sort although he certainly would have qualified because of his extremely limited income. I thought the Amish church should allow him to at least receive Social Security benefits, but of course they didn't agree, and nobody ever helped him with that. In fact, I'm certain he didn't even have a Social Security number. He loved to play his harmonica and sing English songs from a hymn book in his unique halting style, especially when there was an audience. He had a very limited knowledge of the Bible, but sometimes quoted Scripture as best he could, which gave him a feeling of self-importance. He attended the Amish church services regularly and usually walked to them, sometimes as much as five miles away. He very much disliked when some rude and tactless boys from church called him Bachelor Benny. Nevertheless, he accepted it quite graciously and throughout his life was well liked by almost everyone. He always seemed to have a simple trusting faith that he would someday be reunited with his parents in heaven.

On June 1, 1993, Uncle Benny passed away at the age of eighty-five. Many people were surprised he lived to that age, considering his strange and unhealthy eating habits, as well as being as overweight as he was. And because of the dangerous way in which he'd often dart from one side of the road to the other. At his funeral, Preacher Stevie Esh, in his sermon, told the people to think about what Uncle Benny's life had really been like. Even a typical Amish person's lifestyle has much more to offer than what Uncle Benny's standard of living was. He certainly was very widely known in the Lancaster County Amish community and will always occupy a special place in our hearts and memories.

CHAPTER EIGHT

Our Long Walk to Harristown School

ALL AMISH KIDS ARE taught to work hard very early in life, often as young as four and five years old. When I was seven years old, I had to do several different chores every day after school. I would assemble the two Surge milker units which were used each morning and evening to milk our cows. It included the big stainless-steel bucket, with a tight-fitting top, and four rubber inflation's and teat cups. There was also a rubber hose which provided suction from the diesel engine which always had to be running during milking time, since we had no electricity.

Dad had first gotten two mechanical milking units around 1949. Before that he and Mom and my older brothers always had to milk the cows by hand. When they first used the milkers, however, the cows got extremely nervous and frightened and kicked wildly at them, so much that Dad threatened to discontinue using them, despite my brothers' earnest pleas. Fortunately, the cows soon adapted and didn't kick anymore.

My other evening chores were filling a five-gallon bucket with ears of corn from the corn crib and feeding them to the horses, along with grain and hay. One evening while doing that, I saw a mouse in the grain bin. Since the bin was small I decided to try to catch it, not knowing what I would do with it even then. As soon as I caught it, I ran into the house with it to show to my mom and sisters. But, by then it had already bitten my hand enough to make it bleed. I burst in through the door and yelled, "Look at this mouse," and threw that indignant squealing creature on the kitchen table. My sisters screamed and jumped on the nearest chairs and the mouse immediately ran off the table and hid somewhere, never to be found again. I was scolded, but that incident was good for a few laughs from our family.

During my childhood and teenage years, it seemed there were always lots of flies in our house in the summertime, especially in the kitchen and living room. This, even though the sticky brown strips hanging from the ceiling seemed to do a fairly good job of "capturing" them. Even so, Mom often recruited Lydia and I to wage war on the buzzing flies with our trusty plastic flyswatters. The pay scale was one "wheat back" penny for every thirty flies that we swatted and killed.

The most I ever earned in one day while doing that was three cents for my total of ninety flies killed. We envied our cousin Raymond, who was paid the princely sum of three cents per fly, when he did that at his grandparent's house. They were our Uncle Ike and Aunt Emma Smoker and they were wealthy so they could easily afford it. Of course, there were far fewer flies at Ike and Emma's house, as it always seemed in pristine condition in comparison to ours. Still, three cents per fly killed seemed almost like a "union scale" pay rate to us.

Since we didn't have a dishwasher, but *lots* of dishes to do after each meal, Lydia and I were almost always stuck with that chore. She washed them in the sink using Mom's big eighteen-inch-wide agate "tub." I did the drying, as I sat on the counter next to her while resting my feet on the seat of a chair. One form of entertainment during those boring times was throwing my drying towel up against the ceiling and catching it on the way down. I wonder now if the ceiling became cleaner or dirtier when I did that! Surely, I tossed the towel hundreds of times during my dish-drying career.

When Lydia and I were about eight and seven years old, Mom occasionally made good use of us on Saturday mornings in the summertime. She'd bake some fresh homemade bread and send us up to Hatville to sell them. With about eight loaves loaded onto our little green wooden wagon we'd trudge up the Red Hill, pulling the wagon past the schoolhouse where we attended. There were only about ten houses in Hatville for us to go to. About seven o'clock, we'd start ringing doorbells. Some of the women would still be in their nightgowns and we'd innocently ask them if they wanted some fresh bread. I guess we were too young to be afraid of being rejected and people possibly not wanting them. They usually sold pretty well. I believe they were priced at fifteen cents per loaf. When we were done, we were allowed to go to Stauffer's Diesel Shop nearby and each get a 5¢ Milky Way candy bar, which was a rare treat for us.

One morning, while coming home from a bread marketing excursion in Hatville, we met two boys from my class, Elias and Samuel, who lived nearby. They wanted me to come and play with them in Abram Beiler's wheat field. We really shouldn't have done that because the wheat would get trampled down. But, of course, we did it anyway. While playing in the wheat, which was almost as tall as we were, I discovered to my horror, that I had lost my candy bar out of my pants pocket. Even worse, I had not yet even eaten any of it. We searched for it unsuccessfully for a while, then had to give up and I was quite sad about that. Then, to my pleasant surprise, Elias gave me a nickel of his own and I happily went back to Stauffer's for a new candy bar. I guess Elias felt somewhat guilty because he had urged me to play in the wheat field with them.

When I finished second grade at Hatville School in the spring of 1959, Lydia and I both passed our exams and were promoted to the next grade in the fall. Unfortunately, Brother John did not pass, and would have been required to stay in fourth grade for another year. I think my parents were more bothered by that than about him having flunked. After all, one extra year in school would mean one less year of him working on the farm for them for free. So, they inquired at the nearest Amish school, Harristown School, to see if he would be allowed to go straight to fifth grade. He was allowed to do so, and we all were told to do our best to keep it a secret from Mrs. Shertz, back at Hatville School. I don't know what reason my parents gave her for not returning us to her school in the fall. As far as I know she never found out, or if she did, she made no controversy about it. Imagine anybody being able to do that nowadays! The three of us were never asked how we felt about changing schools. We really didn't have any choice in the matter. An indication of the truly congenial and forgiving spirit that Lydia and I had toward John, despite his flunking, was that we never resented at all that he *had* flunked, even though our required walking distance had now quintupled!

Of course, we were sad to leave all our friends at Hatville School. Harristown School was located along Osceola Mill Road, just north of the tiny hamlet of Harristown, which had about ten houses. At Harristown School, all the kids were Amish and the school was owned by the Amish. Of course, this school had an Amish teacher, a sinister looking man named Christ Esh. Christ had a bristling black beard and a piercing stare, which he often inflicted on misbehaving students. He was a strict teacher and wouldn't tolerate any nonsense. Unlike Hatville School, which only had grades first through fifth, at Harristown School it was grades first through eighth. So, Teacher Christ certainly had a full plate and was extremely busy teaching all those kids, a total of about forty students.

For John, Lydia, and me, we now had to walk *much* farther than before, a distance of about one and a half miles each way, which was an unwanted challenge, especially at first. There were about ten other kids who walked part of the way with us. Among them were Joe Beiler's three daughters, who always had to walk about two miles each way. Hatville School would also have been much, much, closer for them but Joe was far too strict to let them attend a sinful, secular English school like that.

One day we got a ride with an English neighbor lady, Mrs. Frankhouser, who lived in the house by Osceola Mill, the old mill by Pequea Creek. She stopped her old woody paneled station wagon and asked us if we wanted a ride and of, course, we said yes. I believe there were a total of thirteen of us, packed in like sardines. Of course, we loved it, as Amish kids always love riding in cars. She seemed quite amused by it all, but she never picked us up again.

There were some kids who never had to walk to school and we envied them. They were three families who lived over near Byerstown, about three miles away. Black Jake's, Sam Zook's, and the Yoder families had a total of about eleven kids. Black Jake's Levi or Henry Zook, both eighth graders, took turns driving a horse pulling an open spring wagon, and all those kids rode with him. No school bus but better than walking, like we had to.

Every morning before school started, two of the older boys took the big earthen stoneware five-gallon container and got drinking water for us because there was no water source of any kind at school. They'd take it to Bishop Henry Fisher's farm, about five hundred feet away and fill it with water. Then they'd walk back, carrying it between them with a sturdy wooden stick inserted under the handle. Of course, that water was strictly to be used for drinking only. Since there was no running water at the school and no way for anyone to wash their hands, everybody needed to be extra careful during any bathroom (outhouse) visits. Imagine any modern school today not having its own water supply!

One morning while walking to school, something happened that we would always remember. As we approached Deacon Davey's house on Osceola Mill Road, we saw him come out to meet us. Deacon Davey was the father of Christ, our teacher. We knew that Davey's aged father-in-law, Christ Glick, lived there with him and his wife, Katie. Davey then solemnly told us they were quite sure that Christ, who was a ninety-year old preacher, was dying during those very moments inside the house. Davey thought we should come inside and watch and be with them during those final moments. Some of our classmates, who were Christ's great-grandchildren, were also there as we watched old Christ draw his final breaths. It certainly was a solemn event for this innocent eight-year old Amish child.

The first event in school each morning was all the students standing on the platform behind the teacher's desk, boys on the right and girls on the left. Then two English gospel songs would be sung, chosen by the one boy and one girl who's turn happened to be that day. That is the typical format in Amish schools. One day, Rag's Sam, an absent-minded kid, forgot to mention the page number and started singing all by himself, which brought a few snickers from various kids.

We attended Harristown School for only one year and life there was pretty tranquil, almost idyllic. There were ten tall graceful white South Carolina birch trees standing in the schoolyard, often gently swaying in the breeze while providing welcome shade for us kids. All in all, it was a peaceful, picturesque, scene in a rural farmland setting.

During recess, we played Prisoners Base, Kollyover and softball. One day, Sammy Zook was standing on top of the wooden outfield fence when his sister Annie came up to bat. I guess she was a surprisingly good hitter, because she hit it all the way to the outfield, incredibly, right to Sammy on top of the fence and he caught it. We all thought that was hilarious and amazing, especially since Annie hadn't even been trying to hit it to him.

Teacher Christ ruled the school with an iron hand. I remember once poking a classmate during class, and simply pointing at a dog out in the field. Then I saw Christ staring angrily at me with that withering glare. I was glad he didn't punish me. Once a six-year-old girl misbehaved badly enough that Christ took her down to the basement and whipped her. We could hear her crying. I believe he accused her of lying to him.

None of the students ever uttered profanity at Harristown, not even the typical four-letter words. The "strongest" word spoken there was the word Holy and that was considered to almost be a "cuss" word. It was always spoken only as one word by itself and we didn't even realize that in itself was strange.

An eight-year-old boy who was in my class would pull the heads off of baby starlings when he found them in a nest. Starlings are plain looking spotted birds like sparrows. One day out on the playground, this boy exposed himself and deliberately walked and strutted past a group of young girls. The boy had told us earlier about one girl in the group that he really liked and he thinks he would cry if he didn't marry her someday. Well, I don't think what he did that day increased the chances of that happening! And, of course he never did marry that girl.

That boy's father, who was an Amish farmer, was said to have a terrible temper. One day while out in the field with his team of horses hitched to some farm machinery, one horse was lazy, or was misbehaving. The farmer, in a fit of rage, grabbed the three-foot-long steel jockey stick off the harness. He then hit the horse over the head a mighty blow with it and the horse fell dead on the ground. I'm sure it was never even reported to any authorities. Sadly, cruelty to animals was more common and was tolerated more than it is nowadays.

Harristown School was a very conservative school compared to Hatville School. Most of the students obeyed the school rules carefully. One rule was that the boys had to have their bangs combed straight down, as is Amish custom. They were not allowed to have the bangs parted to the side, which would have been an extreme violation of the Ordnung.

One day teacher Christ noticed during class that an eighth-grade boy, Elam, who was sitting at his desk, had his bangs parted to each side. Christ angrily demanded that he comb them straight down. Elam stared straight ahead and pretended not to hear. Christ told him again and was again ignored. Since Elam was a strong, sturdy teenager almost as big as Christ, we breathlessly wondered if there might be a physical confrontation, possibly even a fight. Christ then strode up to his teacher desk at the front of the classroom and yanked open a drawer and grabbed his whip. It was a menacing looking homemade contraption, with a custom-made handle securely attached to a section of thick gray belting, probably meant to be used on a gasoline-driven engine. He then started walking slowly toward Elam at the back of the room, while fondling the whip meaningfully in his hands and affixing him with that piercing glare. As we all watched with bated breath, the classroom became so quiet you could have heard a church mouse. Or, an Amish schoolhouse mouse. When Christ was about five feet away, Elam, still not looking at Christ, mumbled resentfully; "haub kenn comm," which meant he had no comb. Christ snapped angrily, "Well, I'll get you a comb." He went back to his desk and brought Elam a comb. Elam, then, obviously still unwillingly, combed his bangs straight down, a crisis was averted, and we all could breathe again. Interestingly, there was another eighth-grade boy, Benuel, who frequently parted his bangs, but teacher Christ never demanded that he comb his bangs down. We believed the reason Christ didn't dare confront him, was because Benuel's family was more worldly and liberal and they might have defended their son.

The long walk we had to school each day became more problematic whenever there was snow. One morning we woke up and saw a huge amount of snow on the ground. An amazing amount was clinging to the telephone wires and poles along the road and quite a few poles had snapped off from all the weight. It seemed there was a lot of snow each winter, and sometimes there were real blizzards, including one which left over four feet of snow during the winter of 1958.

During the year we went to Harristown School, there was a very heavy snow in March of 1960. That morning, Brother Aaron attempted to take us to school in the horse-drawn market wagon. Before we were even halfway there, we got stuck at Mose Zook's farm, down by Pequea Creek. The snow was about three feet deep and we had to turn back. I was very disappointed because I had not yet missed any school days in that term and had hoped to have perfect attendance that year for the first time.

Traveling by horse and buggy in deep snow can be extremely dangerous in frigid weather, with no heat in it as cars would have. One Sunday night, a young couple stopped at our house, and they appeared to be almost frozen. They had already gone about fifteen miles, by horse and open buggy, at a slow pace through deep snow, and in very cold weather. They had been at the young folk's Rumspringa singing in the Kirkwood area and still had about five more miles to go. The young girl, Susie, who we knew, was crying and was extremely cold, and might have been near death. They stayed at our house, huddled around the stove for a long time, till they were completely warmed up and eventually left and went home.

One afternoon, during a snowstorm that had virtually become a blizzard, we were very surprised to see Uncle Sam Miller pull into our driveway in his open horse-drawn buggy. He lived about five miles away, near Bird-in-Hand, and we wondered why he had come in such bad weather. He tied his horse to the fence post at the front yard and stumbled through the deep snow to our front door. Mom quickly invited him inside, and he immediately went to the big Columbia coal stove to warm up because he was very cold.

Of course, we had no phone so he could not have called us. Then he turned to us and said in a grim, sad tone, "Da Chek Beilah iss schtarva" (Jake Beiler died). We were very shocked and saddened to hear that. Jake was their brother in law, married to Sam and Mom's sister, Mary. Uncle Jake had a frozen water pump at his barn that morning and had driven by horse and carriage to Intercourse, about five miles away, when the weather was not yet really bad. While on his way back with a new pump, he encountered blizzard-like conditions. The strong winds whipped the snow and plastered it against his carriage windows and visibility became extremely poor. Suddenly, the fierce wind blew the carriage into a ditch and one of the wooden wheels was broken. He then unhitched the horse and walked all the way home, while leading the horse behind him. By the time he got home, he was very cold and probably in a state of hypothermia. He went into the house and sat down by the stove.

"I think I'm almost frozen," he just barely managed to say to Aunt Mary. A little while later, he suddenly just passed away, while sitting there on the chair. He was fifty-nine years old and he and Aunt Mary had seven sons. Uncle Jake was a genuinely nice man, very pleasant, and always seemed to be smiling and happy. His unexpected and untimely death saddened everyone greatly.

CHAPTER NINE

Willis,
Our English Neighbor

EVEN LONG BEFORE I WAS born, our closest neighbors were two English families who lived in an old wooden house, about two hundred yards west of us. They were Sam and Annie Futer and their only child, Willis, and his wife Martha. Annie's unmarried sister, Lizzie, also lived with them. They had a small farm of about fifteen acres which included a funny looking ramshackle old barn which Dad said had not been painted for about seventy years.

Sam Futer, a crusty, hard-bitten old German, (although not of Amish heritage) was a retired farmer and carpenter. On at least one occasion, he was known to have defiantly proclaimed, "I'll never die!" He grew a small amount of tobacco each year and kept the most prized stalks in a special place in his barn. One day, my buddy Ira found them and, as a mere toddler, innocently ripped a lot of the "valuable" leaves off. When Sam discovered that, his angry cursing shattered the calm, peaceful stillness of a quiet autumn morning, or "enheiliched" (desecrated) it, as Dad told me, years later.

Sam was proud of the fact that he had built the First National Bank of Intercourse, about one hundred years ago, at the intersection of Newport Road and Old Philadelphia Pike. He rented his farmland to an Amish neighbor, Abram Beiler. Sam was in his eighties and sat on his rocker on the front porch each day as we walked by on our way to school. It was said that his sister-in-law, Lizzie, was mentally deranged, and probably even insane. They kept her locked in the attic most of the time. We sometimes saw her forlornly looking out the attic window as we went by. We never got to meet her or talk to her and we all felt very sorry for her.

Willis Futer was self-employed, selling and repairing radios and television sets at his house, with Martha helping him on a daily basis. They never had any children. Willis and Dad were good friends and had attended Hatville School together in the twenties. Since we didn't have a telephone, Dad would go to Willis's house to make any rare necessary phone calls, such as to the veterinarian to come and treat a sick cow or horse. If it was a local call, Dad would give him a dime and they'd chat for a while, sometimes discussing politics, which Willis was passionate about. He was a staunch Republican, and often told Dad the Democrats spent way too much money.

It seemed to be an odd quirk of fate that this English neighbor who lived so close by, just happened to sell and repair TVs and radios which, of course, are anathema to the Amish bishops and parents. I'm sure my parents wished Willis had a different occupation. But, of course, my brothers and I felt fortunate that he was there and could provide us with such sinful entertainment. If Dad knew that my brothers and I bought various radios from Willis, or that he once repaired a battery-operated record player for me, I suppose that would have somewhat strained his friendship with him.

I bought my first radio from Willis when I was fifteen years old. It was early on a Monday morning, about 6:30 A.M., as I was walking by and making my usual trek over to Brother Aaron's farm where I worked as his hired boy. I boldly rapped on Willis's screen door and when he appeared, his swarthy crew-cut visage featured a five o'clock shadow and he seemed slightly annoyed at having a customer so early. His mood brightened considerably when I told him I was there to buy a radio.

The radio I bought from him was a battery-operated model, by necessity since we had no electricity. I paid him twelve dollars for it, which was a lot of money to me back then. Of course, I had to keep the radio well hidden from my parents. When I worked at Brother Aaron's farm over the next few years, I kept it hidden in my bedroom closet there and usually listened to the Baltimore Orioles baseball games at night after I went to bed. I'd turn it on very low, with it laying right on top of my ear, so no one else could hear it. To my great dismay, it was stolen out of my buggy, one Sunday night in Strasburg, about six years later.

I'm sure Willis never told Dad I had bought that radio from him. If Dad had ever found it, no doubt he would have destroyed it. He told us he had once found one of my brothers radios hidden in the buggy shed. Dad said he turned it on full blast and attacked it with a pitchfork. He said he stabbed it until that little devil inside shut up and, of course, by then it was ruined. He was laughing when he said it, but the point is, he ruined it!

Amish fathers who, unwittingly, find a son's hidden radio, have a real dilemma. Should he ruin it and say nothing, or should he ruin it and *admit* that to the angry son? Or, better yet, should he ignore it and pretend he had never found it? It often is quite a difficult decision!

One of my brothers had bought a large radio from Willis and was listening to it one evening when no one else was home. He was sitting back in the recliner chair and happened to fall asleep. Suddenly he heard loud knocking on the front door, about six feet away. He looked up and saw Bishop Moses glaring through the window at him. Brother had been caught red-handed with the radio blaring! That took some adroit diplomacy and explaining because he was already a member of the church. A week later he had to confess that sin at a special members' only meeting known as "Sits-Gma," which is for disciplinary matters at the end of the regular church service. However, that offence did not rise to the level of requiring ex-communication and shunning. But he *did* have to "bekkenn failah" (admit that he had failed) on his knees.

I don't think Dad ever found any of my well-hidden radios. However, an embarrassing situation occurred the day after President Nixon was elected in 1968. I had secretly heard the election results on my radio that morning, but Dad did not yet know. While working together forking horse manure that afternoon, I proudly told him that I "already" knew that Nixon had won. I said, "Husht du gvist uss da Nixon gwunna hutt," (Did you know that Nixon won?) I thought he would be glad because we had all hoped for that result. While he *was* glad that Nixon had won, he was upset because he correctly suspected I had a radio that had informed me, even though I refused to acknowledge that. I think I hid the radio even more carefully after that!

Brother Amy had a neat old portable wind up record player and some hillbilly records that he kept hidden up in the barn. A few months after his death, I saw it in our trash pile out behind the barn. I'm sure Dad had found it and thrown it out there. I checked and found that it didn't work anymore. I'm sure Dad was responsible for that, too. Mom always agreed with him, that my brothers and I should not have worldly things such as wrist watches, radios, record players, musical instruments, cars, etc. She called those things "dumm sach," which, in Pennsylvania Dutch, means dumb things.

There were several things in Willis and Martha's front yard that fascinated us kids. In addition to some worldly looking brightly colored yard ornaments, there was a little in-ground fishpond where we liked to watch the fish swimming around. They also had a water pump in the front yard that looked very much like our hand operated pump at home, and it also had a long wooden handle like ours did. It certainly looked as though the handle should be grabbed and moved up and down to pump water like we did with ours.

"No, that's not a hand pump, that's an electric pump," Willis proudly informed us. He'd push the switch and the handle would go up and down, as though an invisible ghost was pumping it, and soon the water would come out and us kids thought that was really neat. But, of course, we thought everything that operated with electric was neat!

There had been for many years, a huge flock of pigeons inside and on top of Willis's barn. They congregated there year around. During the spring, they'd fly down into Dad's fields and dig up and eat some of the newly planted corn, wheat and barley seeds. Dad sometimes complained about that, but I doubt if he ever said anything to Willis about it. However, one day when the Futer's weren't home, Dad encouraged me to go into their barn and catch some of those thieving birds which I could have sold later. So, I went into the barn's wheat granary where I knew some pigeons would be. But because of being in broad daylight, I couldn't catch them as they flapped and flew wildly around me. Soon, I heard Dad nervously calling me from outside, telling me to give it up. I'm sure he had second thoughts and realized how bad it would look if Willis caught us doing that! Another "bone of contention" Dad had was sometimes when Martha was high up on a ladder, painting the side of the house and only wearing what looked like an early rendition of a bikini bathing suit!

Despite all that, Willis and Martha were nice folks and good neighbors, and at Christmas time they'd invite all of us up to their house to look at and admire their Christmas lights and decorations. Of course, we had nothing like that since Amish are forbidden by the church to have electricity. Willis had a couple of antique Nash automobiles in the lower level of his barn, which we occasionally got to see. They were in storage and had not been driven for many years. We thought they were neat, even though they were mostly covered with cardboard and pigeon dung.

Willis and Martha had a fancy red sports car and a motorboat. The car was a 1965 Rambler Marlin fastback. On Saturday afternoons in the summertime, they'd drive past our house with the boat on the trailer and go down to the

Chesapeake Bay in Maryland, for a weekend of boating and swimming. I'd be working hard in the fields in the hot sun, watching enviously as they went by, resentfully feeling sure that I would never have a car or a boat.

One afternoon as two other boys and I were walking home from school, we noticed that Willis's old station wagon that he used to haul TVs was not in their driveway. We thought they were probably away somewhere, picking up or delivering a TV. We had always been curious to explore the upper floor of the old barn and thought this would be a good opportunity to do so. Especially, since Willis and Martha were the only ones still living there, as his parents and aunt had already all passed away.

We brazenly walked to the far end of the gravel driveway and up the barn hill. Then we went inside to the upper floor of the barn and eagerly looked around. There were some old farm implements, various types of antiques and, of course, a lot of the ever-present pigeons. Then we saw something in the granary that really excited us, an old bike. Of course, we had never had bikes of our own because the Amish Ordnung strictly forbids that. We eagerly took turns riding it on the wooden barn floor. Or, rather, took turns *trying* to ride it. Since we had no bikes of our own, we barely knew how to ride it, and fell down with it several times. Nevertheless, we were still having a lot of fun.

Suddenly we looked around and there was Willis, standing just a few feet away and glaring at us. He did not say a word to us. We were extremely embarrassed that we had gotten caught. I immediately put the bike back where we'd found it and we all quickly walked out of the barn without saying one word to Willis. He watched us go and never said anything to us about it.

Willis was born there, in his parent's house in 1912. Being an only child, he inherited the property after Sam and Annie passed away. After Martha passed away, Willis continued to live there by himself, as he was then in his eighties. After my mother died, Willis, who was then eighty-five years old, walked down to the viewing at our house to pay his last respects to Mother, and to visit his old childhood friend, my father. Dad and Willis had both lived their entire lives not more than a quarter of a mile away from each other, a period of eighty-four years. Six months after my mother's death, Willis also passed away and that was the end of a memorable era. Sometime later, Willis' property was bought by an Amish neighbor who then tore down the familiar old house and barn and built new ones. That brought an end to one of our most vivid and enduring childhood memories.

CHAPTER TEN

Ramblings of My Amish Youth

SINCE MY FIRST DAY at Hatville School, when I learned about Dick, Jane, and Sally, I have always loved to read and have had a very strong curiosity about many different things. Of course, during my childhood and teenage years, I did not get to read about nearly as wide a range of things as English kids did. Most of the time we did not even get a daily newspaper. Even when Dad did subscribe to the local Intelligencer Journal, he never read much of it. He would, however, always read his favorite comic strip, Bringing up Father, featuring Jiggs and Maggie. My siblings and I read most of the comic strips, or funnies, as we called them. Our favorites were Dagwood, Freckles, and Alley Oop. Family reading material consisted of Readers Digest and Words of Cheer. Dad normally had a subscription to Pennsylvania Farmer and Hoard's Dairyman. Two Amish related publications that we got were Family Life and Blackboard Bulletin, which were published by a well-known Amish writer from Canada, David Wagler. We also got the Budget, a weekly paper that dates back to 1890. It has a lot of Amish communication and gossip in it and is still immensely popular among the Amish. A more recent weekly Amish newspaper that's also very popular is Die Botschaft. However, the Amish scribes predictably and discreetly never report of any sins or disciplinary actions involving any church members, with the possible exception of the criminal trial of famous beard-cutter, Sam Mullett. Nevertheless, one could almost consider those publications to be the Amish versions of Facebook, although they're snail-paced in comparison.

We had very few storybooks or biographies at our house. Three books that I do remember were about Abraham Lincoln, Thomas Edison, and Buffalo Bill.

The "library" at school consisted of two shelves of books in the old wooden cupboard where we also kept our lunch boxes. It was pathetically understocked, with probably about fifty books, which included some ancient material like the Tom Swift series and the Rover Boys. It even had a few "modern" books like the Hardy Boys, Nancy Drew and the Bobbsey Twins. There certainly was nothing there that could be considered risqué, or "fahfeerish," that might lead the kids astray, or make them dissatisfied with the Amish lifestyle. Still, all the books were carefully examined by the hawk- eyed members of the Amish school board before they could reside in that quaint old cupboard.

In 1973, an English man named Dan Neidermyer from Lancaster County, wrote a book which was simply titled "Jonathan." It was about an Amish boy named Jonathan who became rebellious and disillusioned with the Amish lifestyle and stopped going to their church and eventually went English. Even though it was thought to be fictional, the Amish fathers thought it contained a lot of fahfeerish, deceptive, and dangerous information which might lead their teenagers astray. So, they begged the publishers and offered them four thousand dollars to stop printing it, to which they agreed. There are still some copies in circulation, although they are quite scarce.

My class at Newport school where I went to from fourth through eighth grade, was the largest of the eight classes. There were ten students in our class, with six of us having been born in the month of August. I guess the traditional "marriage" month of November had something to do with that! At the end of the school term evaluations I was always ranked second, behind the "brainiac" of the school, a girl named Mary B. At the spelling bee competitions that we frequently had, I think either Mary or I won every time. Sadly, other than the spelling bees, the *only* extra-curricular activities we ever had at the Amish schools were the over-hyped and underwhelming Christmas program and the annual end-of-the-year school picnic! How sad that there were *none* of the many social and cultural events that typical English schools normally provide.

We always went to the same dentist, Dr. George Brett, from Lancaster, who "took care" of all our family's dental needs. Most Amish at that time, including our family, only went to a dentist when they were already in pain. Which meant he would either install a filling or pull out the offending tooth. Because dental insurance was unheard of for them, Amish parents were very pleased that Dr. Brett only charged two dollars to pull a tooth or install a filling. We *never* had orthodontic work done, such as braces or anything like that, because that was considered an unnecessary and worldly luxury. We knew early on that such a vain and expensive procedure was never an option for us!

But far worse was the barbaric strategy that the Amish used regarding their kid's dental needs. Most teen-agers were not strongly urged to take proper care of their teeth because it was assumed, they would not only need, but would even want new upper teeth just before they entered Rumspringa at age sixteen. So, since everyone certainly wanted to have nice teeth *then*, the parents strategically arranged for the kid's upper teeth to all be pulled and a few weeks later they'd have a gleaming set of new "choppers," that is, a full upper denture. It was thought that in the long run, that was less expensive (and therefore *better*) than providing proper dental and orthodontic care like English kids had. So, about 90% of Amish kids back then, both boys and girls, were cruelly victimized in that way. Surely, Dr. Brett and other dentists must have been repulsed and horrified by it. But no Amish parents thought it to be cruel and it was considered normal and was fully expected, almost like a unique rite of passage!

Another way in which many Amish boys back then were routinely victimized was the shameful practice of *hardly ever* getting their hair washed. That was considered normal to both them and their parents. They could have washed it themselves but were taught to believe it wasn't necessary. An Amish friend told me he's certain his hair was never *washed* from age ten till age thirteen! He and his friends did, however, occasionally go swimming and diving in Pequea Creek, which may have provided a crude "washing!" Often, certain young boys' hair looked as though it had been dipped in oil! Back then, there also were lots of grown men who'd go for *years* without washing their hair. These were *not* isolated situations; they were very common! In their defense, however, it should be recognized that "bathing" from a small metal bucket on the floor does not really "inspire" one to wash their hair as much as standing under a shower head might! It does sadden and embarrass me, though, to tell these things, but I feel I need to, because it reveals just a few of the many little-known *odd quirks* of Amish society. And, also, because I'm certain no fawning "English" authors will ever reveal it.

One day when I was eight years old, Mom and I were at Dr. Brett's office. I saw a book in the waiting room that really fascinated me. It was a large hardback book with pictures and stories about all the u.s. presidents from George Washington to Dwight Eisenhower, who was then the current president. I found it extremely interesting and was totally enthralled by it.

When Mom was done with her dentist appointment, I still very much wanted to look at the book. So, Dr. Brett chuckled and said he would let me take it home, and we could return it the next time one of us came to see him. I was thrilled about that. I guess Dr. Brett was impressed that I would be so interested in our presidents. Maybe he thought I might become the first Amish politician. Or the first Amish president. Hardly!

The book stayed at our house for about four months. By the time it went back to Dr. Brett, I had easily memorized all the president's names and whether they served one or more terms. Also, how they all followed each other in order and even which ones died in office or were assassinated. With the innocent naivety of an Amish child, I assumed that they must all have been noble men. I also wrongly assumed that all future Presidents, Senators and Congressmen would be honorable and trustworthy because otherwise they surely would not receive enough votes to win an election. How wrong I was about that! In any case I did not become a politician as Dr. Brett may have hoped. In fact, I had virtually no interest in politics at all until much later in life. Suffice to say, I have never been as disgusted with our political "leaders," as I am now, as I'm writing this book, in the year 2015. But that might be a story for another day.

A book I remember very well was a 1957 volume titled Fisher Family History. It was compiled by my Uncle Levi Fisher and our neighbor, Joe Beiler. It was a large exhaustive hard back and listed almost all the Amish that had lived in Lancaster County since they first arrived from Europe, in the early 1700s. It listed all the families, in chronological order, and included birthdays, deaths, and marriages. Uncle Levi gave us a copy when I was about eight years old and I practically devoured it. Meaning, that I looked up so much information in it, that I systematically wore it out in a few years' time. Then we had to get a new one, but that one we had to pay for. I eagerly did a lot of reading and researching in that one as well. I soon noticed that there were 77 John Stoltzfus' listed, more than any other name. In the latest update version of Fisher Family book, there were 266 John Stoltzfus' listed. In both lists, there were all the John Stoltzfus' who had ever been a head of household in Lancaster County and nearby areas since the Amish arrived in the early 1700s.

Because virtually no non-Amish people ever join the Amish church, the list of last names remains quite small. Also, until recently, almost everybody had traditional Amish first names, usually Bible names. Now, there are many more non-traditional, modern first names than in the past. It's understandable that nicknames are very common and are very much needed because there are so many with similar names. My point is well made by the fact that three of the four preachers in one Amish church district were named Sam Stoltzfus!

Another Amish tradition is that the two oldest boys in any family are usually named after the two grandfathers. However, the oldest son is almost never named after the father, because that would be "ehr-geitzich," or conceited. One way in which that would almost be acceptable, however, would be if one of the grandfathers had the same name as the father. But what if both grandfathers had the same first name as the baby's father? That certainly happens sometimes, given that so many first names are similar. On the one hand, it would be considered "ehr-geitzich" to name the baby after his father. At the same time, it would be considered very rude if he was not named after one of the grandfathers. That sometimes created a real dilemma!

Also, many bishops preferred that only traditional names be used. An Amish man whose son was named Casper was scolded by his bishop and told that he should have given him a "decent" name instead!

As most people know, Amish families usually are quite large. When I attended the Amish schools, one of the families at Harristown School had eighteen children and all were single births. There was a family at Newport School that also had eighteen children. Eventually, all eighteen of them married and in due time, sixteen of them had a son named Daniel, which, of course, was a grandfather's name. Imagine having sixteen grandchildren with the same first name! Around 1860, there was an Amish family with twenty children, all born to the same father and mother. The mother was married when she was only seventeen years old. Some of the children died at a young age, however, so there were never twenty living children at any one time. Not to be outdone, an Amish family from a western state had twenty-three children!

A very unusual situation involved the Eli Smucker family which included seventeen children, of whom none were twins. Three had birthdays on OCT. 1 and two others were born on Jan. 1. And one of the New Year's babies later had a son born on JAN. 1!

My great-uncle, Danny Fisher, and his wife only had one child, Katie, who was married to "Black" Jake Stoltzfoos. They had eighteen children of their own, who later also procreated in an impressive way. When Katie died at age ninety, she had eight hundred and one direct descendants!

That, however, is not an Amish record. The record apparently is held by Mrs.

Bessie Hostetler of Buffalo, Mo. When she died in 1997 at the age of ninety-seven, she had nine hundred fifty-one direct descendants!

My parent's family was a very average family in many ways, including there being eight children, of whom I was the youngest. Over the past century, the Amish population has doubled approximately every twenty-two years. In 1900, the Amish population in America was about six thousand. Now, in 2020, it is approximately 340,000. While doing this research, I calculated that when I was born in 1951, there was about one chance in 4,500 that I would be born Amish. Those are very slim odds.

Something else that is very odd is how so many of my cousins are boys, and that so many were born consecutively in three different families. Uncle Stephen and Aunt Mary Stoltzfus had eight boys and no girls. Uncle Jake and Aunt Mary Beiler had seven boys and no girls. Uncle Sammy and Aunt Mary Fisher had eight boys and one girl, with seven of the boys having been born consecutively. It's also interesting that in each of these three families, the mother's name was Mary, which means I had three Aunt Mary's. I also had three Aunt Lydia's, two Aunt Katie's, two Aunt Annie's and two Uncle Sammy's. Dad had two older brothers and five older sisters. Sadly, three of his sisters, Katie, Mary, and Miriam all died of cancer within a twenty-one-month time period, from March, 1965 to December, 1966. Of course, that was a very sad and depressing time for all of us, with so many family deaths.

Mom had a diary that she wrote in regularly, even though her life, like most Amish women, was quite mundane and (in my opinion) very boring! When I was about eleven years old, I started a diary myself, but soon discontinued it, because I thought there weren't enough interesting things in my life to write about.

However, one day, when I was about seven years old, something very interesting happened to me at the noonday meal. I was eating some canned apricots which still had the pits in them. Suddenly I started choking on a pit that got stuck in my throat. I could not swallow it or cough it out. My parents and siblings saw my predicament and became very alarmed and tried to help me. They gave me lots of water to help me swallow it, but that didn't work. Then they held me upside down by my ankles, while pounding on my back, hoping I could cough it out. When that also didn't work, there was virtual pandemonium. I think my family was more scared than I was. I do remember wondering if I was going to choke to death, although I don't remember being absolutely terrified. Then, for some reason that I never understood, they rushed me over to Uncle Benny's end of the house to see if he could help. I don't think he had any great ideas, either. Then they again gave me copious amounts of water to drink. Finally, everybody was greatly relieved to hear me say "nawh iss's druna," which means, now it's down, and that I had swallowed it. Mom monitored me for the next day or two, until she knew that I had passed it successfully.

Each summer and fall, about six or eight men from the neighborhood came to our farm to help with the wheat threshing and corn harvesting. At the noon time meal, they all got to eat the scrumptious meal my mom and sisters had prepared. It would be homemade bread and jelly, mashed potatoes and gravy, peas, corn, beef or chicken, apple sauce, fruit and homemade pie. The men were all familiar to me, being members and regular attendees in our church district, and they were all friendly and congenial. Nevertheless, as I sat at the corner end of the table between Dad and Mom, I would never even utter a peep. If I wanted a certain dish or food, I'd poke Dad's arm to get his attention, and then I'd simply point at what I wanted. I still wouldn't say anything and would be hoping the men wouldn't even see me poking and pointing!

At Amish church services, there is always a big meal later. Young boys up to the age of eight years old usually eat with their dad. When I was about that age, I couldn't find Dad one day after church. I thought he might have already eaten. That meant I had to eat with all the older boys, and I was petrified at the thought. Or I could choose to go hungry. My buddy Ira told me I could eat with him and the older boys, but I was too shy to do that. He repeatedly encouraged me and practically begged me, but I refused. As I remember, I decided to go hungry instead.

When I first attended school, I was rather shy, but I eventually became quite bold and brash. By the time I was eight or nine years old, I sensed that Dad liked my brother John more than me. In any case, I'm sure he didn't normally show me as much attention as he could have or should have. He did, however, show me lots of attention when I misbehaved, by whipping me. He occasionally whipped Brother John too, and a few times he locked us into the corn crib after whipping us. Mom usually carried a leather strap in her dress pocket and would sometimes whip my siblings and me with it, whenever we deserved it. I will say that I never noticed any favoritism from her.

Like most other Amish at that time, we always lived an extremely frugal lifestyle. The biggest reason was that my parents were always struggling to make the mortgage payments on their other farm, where Brother Jake's lived. The financial status of that farm always bugged us kids greatly, because no matter how often we asked Dad how much was still owed, he'd never give us a clue. We hoped that when it was paid off our lifestyle would improve but, predictably, it never did.

In those days, almost all Amish farmers were making mortgage payment on their farms or already owned them outright. Many of the latter even owned an additional farm, which was thought to be an extremely impressive status symbol. Those farmers were considered to be the upper crust of Amish society and were admired, and even privately exalted, but also greatly envied by their less successful brethren.

My mom was a hard-working penny-pincher and made all of our clothes except for our Sunday pants, vest, and mutza. But it seemed that our work clothes were always too small. Maybe we grew so fast that Mom could hardly keep up. Because of all the hard work we did on the farm, our clothes would literally wear through, especially the pants. The solution for that was, Mom sewing patches on them, and later she would sometimes put patches on top of patches!

She would even, with her old foot operated treadle sewing machine, sew and repair the little plastic bags used for our sandwiches in our school lunch boxes. She had grown up in a very frugal family and spent hardly any money at all on herself. We told her she could squeeze a nickel so tightly that the buffalo would bellow. But, bless her soul, whenever there was not enough food on the table, she'd always be willing to share what she already had on her plate with my siblings and me. Sometimes when our yelling and quarreling got too loud, Mom would sing, "How beautiful Heaven must be" or "Blest be the tie that binds." In retrospect, it certainly is silly that we bickered and quarreled as much as we did. Now, many years later, I am truly sorry for Mom's sake, that there was so much of that.

CHAPTER ELEVEN

School Troubles and Selfies at Woolworth's

MY PARENT'S MAIN SOURCE of income was the biweekly milk check from the sale of milk from our herd of twenty Holstein cows. When we kids brought the mail in at lunchtime, Dad would eagerly watch for it when it was due, every other week. Everyone was always very concerned and interested to know how much it was. While we all sat at the table before eating, he'd open the envelope. Then he'd slowly pull out the check, intentionally prolonging everybody's anxiety, as he slowly peeked at the amount. If a grin came over his face, we'd all breathe a sigh of relief, because that indicated that it was at least an adequate amount. If it was three hundred dollars or more, that was cause for a celebration. After all, he usually only kept about five dollars or less in his worn old wallet at any given time. He kept no other items in it, such as a driver's license or social security card or credit card or ATM card because he never had any of those. The only time he carried the wallet with him was when he went away somewhere, such as to Zimmerman's Store. Otherwise, it was always kept in the third drawer of the combine along with the German prayer-book. On the rare occasion that they had any "big money" such as a twenty-dollar bill, it was kept "hidden" in the big Martyr's Mirror book in the desk in their bedroom.

Another major source of income my parents had was when the tobacco crop was sold in the winter. Raising tobacco requires a tremendous amount of hard work, which includes planting, hoeing weeds, topping, and suckering the tobacco. The next steps are cutting it, spearing each stalk on laths, loading it onto wagons, bringing it in from the fields and hanging it in the barn and tobacco shed. The five large stalks of tobacco on each lath weighed about thirty pounds. They'd be hung on long wooden rails about four feet apart from each other, side to side, and also up and down from each other, throughout the building. Whoever hung the laths in place always had to "straddle," which is standing with his feet on the rails about three or four feet apart. That is very tiresome physically and also dangerous, especially if it's nearly dark and if it's high up inside the building. There, the tobacco dries out for several months and is then taken down and all the leaves are stripped from the stalks and baled. That requires many hundreds of hours of manual labor and is a depressingly long and boring process. It would've been much less so if I'd have been allowed to listen to country and bluegrass music on my radio, but I knew better than to even try that with Dad working right next to us! So, we normally grew about eight acres of tobacco on the home farm and, in the 1960s, it was usually sold for about 20 to 27¢ per pound. The buyers always were various stingy, hard-bargaining, dealers from Lancaster, representing P. Lorillard, Bayuks, and Lancaster Leaf Tobacco Co.

The straw from threshing the wheat was always kept for bedding for the horses and cows. Most of the wheat was sold to Clem Hoober's feed mill in Intercourse for about a dollar and thirty cents per bushel. The rest we took to Mascot Roller Mills where old Frank Ressler ground it into flour that Mom used to make bread. Another source of income was selling the six or more fattened steers in the wintertime, except for one which we'd butcher for our meat supply. Last, but not least, was income from hiring out the sons to other Amish farmers for about one hundred dollars per month each, more or less.

My siblings and I rarely, if ever, got any birthday gifts from Dad and Mom. Also, at Christmas time, Santa's sleigh must have been nearly empty when he departed the North Pole. I remember Christmas in 1962, which was just a few months after Brother Amy died. We were, of course, still grieving his death, but things were also quite bleak financially. Brother John and I only got two shared gifts from Dad and Mom that year. The gifts were a 25-cent sponge ball and a $1.49 bow and arrow set, with three rubber tipped wooden arrows from Zimmerman's store in Intercourse. The bow was merely a flat piece of wood about three feet long with a nondescript blue and white string.

At least we got *something* for Christmas each year! But I don't remember my parents ever giving each other any Christmas OR birthday presents. They did not get anything from us either and did not expect anything and that was considered normal. Of course, most Amish people live very frugally and seemingly love to improvise and just "make do" with whatever they happen to have. In fact, many are so frugal that they don't even have lots of things that the bishops *do* allow!

When I was twelve years old, my parents gave me a beautiful 17 jewel railroad pocket watch for Christmas. That was a Cadillac compared to the plain-faced $1.99 Ingraham watch from Zimmerman's that I'd had for three years. And, when all my brothers and I reached our eighteenth birthday, we each got a genuinely nice gift from Dad and Mom that we treasured greatly. It was a beautiful hand-made hardwood desk meticulously hand-crafted and built by our great-uncle, Johnny B. Miller, Grandad's younger brother. He was an elderly furniture maker and very skilled at his trade. He was always very sociable, just a really warm and friendly guy who I liked very much.

Even though all my brothers and I had to work awfully hard on the Amish farms, we usually had very little spending money. That's because whenever we worked at another farm, that farmer would pay it all directly to Dad, leaving us with nothing. When we worked at home, we also were not paid anything. Mom thought that way we were less likely to buy "dumm sach," dumb things, such as radios or guitars or other things that were verboten.

When I was approximately twelve through fifteen years of age, I often didn't have more than one or two dollars to my name anywhere at home. We each had an appallingly small savings account at the Intercourse Bank, which we couldn't access even if we had wanted to. Practically our only source of income before Rumspringa was raising guinea pigs, cats, and bantam roosters and chicks and selling them at the weekly auction at the Green Dragon farmers market in Ephrata. We also sold the pigeons that we caught in barns around the neighborhood. We'd have old Manny Nafziger take us to the auction in his ancient station wagon. He had lost his right hand a long time ago in some accident at a feed mill but that didn't keep him from driving his car. He had a custom-made knob on the steering wheel which allowed him to steer with just one hand. He'd reach over the steering column with his left hand to move the gear shift handle, and, all in all, seemed to be quite adept at driving his car.

One day, a smooth-talking guy from Christiana named Joe Wright, who we didn't even know, pulled into our driveway. He asked Dad if there were any boys here that he could hire for a few days. He had a truckload of scrap metal that he wanted to take to the salvage yard in Ephrata, so Dad told John and me to go with him. On the second day, John didn't want to go, so my buddy Ira went along to help unload Joe's truck. It was hard work in the hot sun, and as it turned out, Joe cheated us out of most of our pay. Maybe he shouldn't have had the last name that he did!

That afternoon when we were almost done, we saw an old man walking down the sidewalk. He came up to us, carrying a brown paper bag and asked Ira and I if we were thirsty. Of course, we said we were. He then reached into the bag and gave both Ira and me an ice-cold can of beer. Joe was not there with us at the moment. I think Ira and I were both fourteen years old at the time. I don't think I had ever even tasted beer before, but I was more than willing to drink mine. I opened it up and drank quite a bit of it, trying to impress Ira, even though I didn't like it. Ira decided to not drink his beer, and he said I could have it. A little while later I drank his too, even though I didn't really want it. I believe I was slightly inebriated. But for fun, I pretended to Ira that I was very drunk. He just didn't know if I was pretending or not, and later we both had a good laugh about it.

Interestingly, none of my classmates or I ever had any alcoholic beverages at school. As far as I know, that has never been a problem at Amish schools. Or, at least, it wasn't where I attended. I do remember my brother trying to make some rhubarb or dandelion wine that he secretly tried to brew up in the orchard, but it didn't turn out very well. That was a few years later during Rumspringa.

There were other times when John wanted to be involved with dandelions, although for an entirely different reason. During his younger years, he was always "afflicted" with freckles, which he hated. Suvilla, had convinced him that there was an easy way he could get rid of them. She told him that May 1st each year was the only day that the unique freckle remedy would work. That morning, before he spoke even one word to anyone, he had to go out into the yard and rub some bright yellow dandelions over his face.

For about five or six consecutive years he meant to do that but Suvilla would spoil his plan each time by getting him to say something first. Then, when he'd get very annoyed, the rest of us would chuckle about it all. Our family was not known to be superstitious [except when Dad took Amy to the "braucher" as a baby] so I was always surprised that John seemed to really believe that the freckles remedy would actually work.

At school, some boys would occasionally pick up partially smoked cigarettes from along the roads and smoke them in the outhouse at school. When they burned down to the filter, it would then have an extremely bitter taste. Even so, we thought smoking them was cool. It probably sometimes *was* a Kool cigarette, as that was the name of an extremely popular brand at that time. As for illicit drugs, I'm sure there were never any at the schools I attended back then.

John and I also experimented with making homemade cigars from the tobacco crop that we raised at our farm. Of course, we didn't tell Dad about that. The cigars were very bitter tasting and didn't work very well. We had similar results from our home-made hollowed out corncob pipes. Also, one Sunday afternoon when I was about thirteen, I took one of Uncle Benny's cigars and was smoking it in our upstairs bedroom. I was right by the open window and thought Mom couldn't smell it from downstairs. She *did* smell it and came upstairs and gave me a severe scolding. In addition to that, the smoke made me sick, and I almost had to throw up.

I got into trouble again at Newport School when I kicked out the wooden boards from the back wall of the boy's outhouse. Maybe I thought it needed some "natural" air conditioning. Or, maybe just some fresh air to neutralize the bad smell that we were all so familiar with. As I might have expected, though, someone tattled and told the teacher what I had done. Dad and I went up to the school that Saturday to fix the damage and he really scolded me about it, as he should have.

There was another time that Dad and I had to fix damage that I had caused on Amish school property. One Sunday afternoon when several "church buddies" and I were walking home from church, we stopped for an unauthorized visit at Harristown School. While apparently feeling angry at Teacher Christ and thinking this would be a good time to do it, I threw a rock through one of the windowpanes. I didn't think any of the others would tattle on me, but I certainly was wrong about that!

One morning at Newport School, soon after the first bell had summoned all the kids inside, I hurried back out to get my lunchbox that I'd left on the porch. But there was still one boy out there and he was raiding my lunchbox. He was the resident school bully, a few years older than me, but not as tall as me. But he was tough and wiry, although I was not afraid of him. As I hastened over toward him, he saw me coming but kept hurriedly and greedily drinking from my jar of lemonade as long as he could. I had caught him red-handed!

"You bitch" I exclaimed angrily, which must have surprised him since that was an extreme epithet for any Amish kid to call another. He cocked his fist in my face and snarled belligerently at me "What did you call me?" I was extremely tempted to punch him, which could have resulted in quite a fight. Somehow,

I resisted that temptation and grabbed my lunchbox and lemonade and went back inside. For some reason, I didn't even tell the teacher. I guess I didn't want to be a tattletale. Later when I told Mom, she suggested I give the bully a chocolate bar and see what happens. Predictably, I wasn't at all interested in that "solution."

In today's English society, it's common for bullies to steal or demand lunch food or money from younger kids. But, to their credit, I've never heard of any other Amish kids doing that to each other, which is fortunate because there's no cafeteria or vending machines or other source of food whatsoever at Amish schools. The teachers also bring their own lunch and, (for what it's worth) I don't think any kids ever brought an apple along for any teacher!

I don't recall any boys ever fighting with each other at any of the school's I attended. There were instances of teasing and mocking which, of course, happens at every school. There were also some significant character and personal behavior problems involving two boys. One boy would occasionally grope one of the girls in his class, when no one was looking. Even though she was already an eighth grader, she was very naïve. Although I assume she was upset about it, I strongly doubt she ever reported it to the teacher. Another boy, who happened to be the lemonade stealing bully, would occasionally expose himself to girls in the classroom when the teacher had her back turned. There was a petite and innocent young girl that he often picked on and call horrible names so that she would sometimes be in tears.

I don't think any sexual activity ever occurred between the students at any of the Amish schools I attended. I don't even know of any sexual *talk* ever occurring between any of the boys and girls there. There were, however, two girls at Newport School, Sarah and Becca, who engaged in mild flirting occasionally. Another girl, Barbie, who's desk was directly in front of mine, would sometimes turn around and secretly chat with me briefly, while looking at me with "dreamy" eyes.

There have been girls as young as fifteen years old who taught at Amish schools. Sally, my sixth-grade teacher at Newport, started teaching when she was sixteen. Like other Amish teachers, she did not have proper accreditation, but only an eighth-grade education like us students! Her father, Andy, was the leader, or "chairman" of the school board. Our books included ancient material like McGuffey's Readers from the 1800s, the Strayer-Upton Arithmetic Series from the 1930s and the 1919 Essentials of English Spelling. I believe Sally had adequate knowledge of all the curricula *except* English, where her knowledge was so poor that all of our grades should have been a collective disaster! In fact, the only thing I remember having learned in that English class was that a noun was a place, person or thing! So, even though Sally gave all or most of us a passing grade, I'm sure we all should have gotten an F. And probably even a Z if that were possible!

Yes, I'm sure we all should have flunked English. And, I think we all hated that class, *including* Sally. Our hearts just weren't in it and we thought it was *so* unnecessary. All of us students (in addition to all our parents) had an appallingly poor knowledge of many, many commonly used English words which never entered our tightly confined little world. But I'm sure the bishops were happy that we knew so few worldly "big" words. They intuitively knew that the less such words we knew and the poorer our quality of education was, the less likely it was that we would ever leave the Amish!

One day during our reading class a seventh-grade student was reading about Mrs. Crabapple and she mispronounced it as Craybayple. Strangely, Sally did not even correct her. I wondered if perhaps Sally herself didn't know the correct pronunciation!

It's a well-known fact that some English words have strange pronunciations. In our history class at the Amish schools we were taught that the word colonel should be pronounced exactly as it appeared, with no "r" sound at all. Mom told us that when she went to school (there were no Amish-owned schools then) her English teacher taught them to pronounce the word colonel with an "r" sound in the middle, which actually *is* correct. There was no doubt in Mom's mind that her teacher had been completely wrong about that and there certainly was no doubt in our minds either!

Of course, there was a school dictionary that everyone was taught how to use. But what good is a dictionary if one doesn't know how the word is spelled? There was never a thesaurus at school and, surely, none of us would have known how to use one or even that such a thing existed!

Certainly, there were lots of words that were routinely mispronounced in our family because of our poor knowledge of English. Even though Dad and Willis sometimes talked about the second World War and the Vietnam War, Dad still mispronounced words such as Nazi's, (Nazzies) Allies, (Alliz) and Vietnam (VITEnam). Maybe he thought Willis was the one who was mis-pronouncing them instead of himself! And even in the present era, an Amish lady mispronounced President Obama's name so that it rhymed with the state Ala(bama). Obviously, she had never heard it spoken on radio or TV!

Something that we thought was neat about Teacher Sally was that she always pronounced each students' name in its entirety, such as Rebecca or Emanuel or Jonathan. Certainly, no one else there ever called me by my full first name!

I believe my first two teachers, Mrs. Shertz at Hatville School and Christ at Harristown School were the only teachers who ever paddled kids at any of the schools I attended. Apparently, Sally had a more modern style of punishment. She had a chart on the wall with each student's name on it, with two rows alongside, where she put check marks for good or bad behavior. To get a proper score, one's bad marks were deducted from the total of good marks. Whenever a student achieved twenty-five good marks, they were given a small prize such as a little booklet of picture stickers of flowers or animals.

My score frequently indicated that I was the "baddest" one in the whole school, as some students willingly reminded me. One day I decided to give myself a much-needed good mark when Teacher wasn't looking. But someone else saw me do it and told her about it. Teacher then angrily went to the chart, and gave me two bad marks, one as punishment for what I had done, and one to cancel out the good mark I had given myself!

My cousins, Henry and Sammy, who went to a different school, laughingly told me that their teacher had the same system and they would sometimes give themselves "good" marks during recess. Apparently, their teacher then got very frustrated and only used that chart system during one school year.

One day Teacher Sally had a private talk with me and offered me a reward of 25¢ if I truly tried to reform myself. I told her I would try hard to do so because I really was sorry about my frequent misbehavior. I can honestly say I did make a sincere effort at that. Every day I wondered with great trepidation if I would pass that test. After about six weeks, she rewarded me with the much longed for quarter. I certainly was elated and I'm sure Teacher and I both felt I had given my best effort. That nice big genuine silver quarter looked quite impressive with the meager group of other coins I had at home!

Each class would have at least one "stand-up" class at school every day. At that time, they'd stand on the platform in front of the blackboard. Occasionally, one of us boys would secretly reach behind his back with a piece of chalk and teasingly write Teacher Sally's boyfriend's name, Ike, on the blackboard. Later, when she noticed it, there'd probably be a slight grin on her face as she erased it.

One afternoon while walking home from school, a car with tourists from New York City stopped and asked if they could take pictures of us. That had happened occasionally before, but this time was different because they offered to send us some photographs later in the mail. We were very excited about that, because we'd never had or even seen photographs of ourselves before. We eagerly agreed, and one boy, Leroy, said they could send them to his parents' home in Hatville and he gave them the mailing address. Of course, at that time there was no such thing as "instant" photos so they could not immediately provide us with any. Leroy's parents were more liberal than most because the rest of us wouldn't have dared to have them sent to our homes, for fear our parents might destroy them. The tourists then took some photos and left, leaving us extremely excited about the prospect of soon having real photos of ourselves. Unfortunately, they never sent us any photos, which I guess could have been predicted. We were quite unhappy about that but, in retrospect, I guess we should have been thankful that the Ordnung *did* allow mirrors, as that was the only way we could see individual likenesses of ourselves!

About a year later, I finally was able to obtain some photos of myself, but through an entirely different process. One day when Suvilla and I were shopping at Woolworth's Department Store in Lancaster, I saw something that intrigued me greatly. There was a booth which one could sit in, and it had a built-in camera, which allowed four small black and white pictures to be taken. I immediately decided to do that, even though it cost fifty cents, which was a lot of money to me. After deciding how I would pose, I quickly put two quarters in the slot, and the camera flashed during each shot, about five seconds apart. I took two frontal pictures and two side shots of myself, all while I was wearing my big black Amish hat. I made sure that one frontal picture showed me with my bangs completely hidden, crammed up underneath my black hat. That was done to portray my rebellious nature and because I hated the bangs that I was forced to wear. Soon after the fourth camera flash, the strip of four pictures came out. I eagerly inspected them and was reasonably well satisfied, although in one frontal picture, I looked decidedly glum. I had not meant to look glum, I only meant for it to be a non-smiling pose to go along with the one in which I *was* smiling. It should be understood, of course, that I had absolutely no experience in posing for photos. Also, I was doing this initial event all by myself, (like taking a "selfie" today?) and had no one there to prompt me by telling me to say "cheese." I was fourteen years old and these were the first photos I had ever seen of myself, and I still have them to this day.

A few minutes later I told Suvilla about it and showed her the photos. She seemed amused and didn't seem to mind that I had done something so worldly. She did not tell my parents, and of course, I didn't either. About a year later, I was back at Woolworths again and took four more pictures of myself in the same way, all of which I also still have. And, I believe those were the *only* pictures I've seen or had of myself before I was nineteen years old, at which time I finally bought a camera!

The Amish Ordnung prohibits ownership of cameras, and even prohibits the Amish from taking photos at all, especially photos of themselves or other Amish people. However, they are allowed, somewhat grudgingly, to own photos of themselves, such as informal or random photos taken by a non-Amish person. For instance, it's fine for the Amish to buy the commercial photos of the Amish that were always available at Zimmerman's store in Intercourse, or at any of the many "tourist traps" in the area. This strange partial legality is somewhat like their rule which prohibits them from driving or owning a car, but it's perfectly fine to ride in one if an "English" person is driving. I'm sure the reason cameras are prohibited, along with taking pictures of themselves, is because of what the Bible says about graven images in Exodus, Chapter 20, verses four and five. It tells the Israelites not to make graven images to bow down to and worship. But it does not prohibit making images or pictures of themselves which would only be to look at. And besides, we're Amish, not Israelites, although I suppose we have a few things in common. So, it seems the Amish have taken those Bible verses completely out of context, along with many others that I became aware of, later in life. As far as family photos are concerned, I'm not aware of *any* of my siblings ever even having a camera! And I have often wished we had at least one photo of Brother Amy before he died, but we did not, and I think that is very sad.

CHAPTER TWELVE

Baseball and Mushball Follies

DESPITE DISAPPROVING FROWNS FROM the older folks, many Amish boys are very interested in sports. The sport that interests them most is softball, starting in elementary school. To the best of my knowledge, that has always been allowed while baseball, using the smaller, harder ball is frowned upon and usually prohibited, with those opposing it saying a baseball is more dangerous and definitely more worldly. But during Rumspringa, *only* baseballs are used, and using softballs would be considered sissy and silly!

When I attended the Amish schools, softball was almost always played during recess periods in the warmer months. Nowadays volleyball might be as popular as softball, whereas it was never played when I was in school. There were never any umpires because everyone wanted to play instead. A captain for each team would pick teams daily from the older boys and girls. Of course, it was coed, because there were barely enough older players to have two teams of nine each. The two teams usually consisted only of kids at least nine years old and above. Of course, there were no coaches, as there are at non-Amish schools, so one's level of skill was strictly achieved by their own amount of practice, watching others, personal ability and learning as you go, or on the fly.

With a motley assortment of fairly old and very old baseball gloves and cracked and taped wooden bats, we played very seriously and competitively. We even kept various statistics including batting averages and errors, of which there were many. One quaint and amusing example of our baseball phraseology was us calling a foul tip a tipper or a nipper. Since there was no umpire, the batters could take as many pitches as they wanted without swinging, which sometimes resulted in impatient yells of "Choicey!" from the players in the field. At the end of each season, in late fall, and just before the end of the school season in May, we'd have a mock World Series. Since even then we didn't have umpires, sometimes we had really serious arguments, although usually only among the boys.

The older boys followed their favorite major league teams by reading the box scores in the papers the next day, if you were lucky enough to have a newspaper sent to your house. A few boys had older brothers who had battery powered transistor radios at home and they could then provide early morning scores to the rest of us at school. We got daily updates from Rag's boys that way in 1961 when Mickey Mantle and Roger Maris, who both played for the Yankees, were chasing Babe Ruth's home run record of 60 homers in a season. Roger Maris broke that record by hitting 61 homers in 1961. But most of us hated the Yankees, because it seemed as though they won the pennant and World Series almost every year. I was a Baltimore Orioles fan, with Hall of Famer Brooks Robinson being my hero, and I wished I could someday play professional baseball like him. But, because I was Amish, I had absolutely no hope of that ever happening, even if I would have had exceptional talent.

My first baseball fiasco was in second grade at Hatville School. One day, I swung the bat and it flew out of my hands and hit a classmate, Levi, directly on his head. I was very sorry and scared when that happened. Levi cried briefly but soon appeared okay and didn't need any medical attention.

At Newport School where I went to in grades fourth through eighth, our permanent playing field was on the east side of the school yard in Benuel Stoltzfus's cow pasture. If someone really hammered the ball to left field, it might bounce or roll into their vegetable garden and would surely be a home run. No one ever hit a real home run on the fly into their garden because it was too far away. Even Rag's Davey never hit one that far despite consistently being the top slugger at Newport School.

The only "fans" we ever had at our games were Benuel's Holstein cows, sometimes watching disinterestedly from a safe distance. However, at times we weren't there, they might come up to the playing area and make some fertilizer deposits, that is, cow patties, which could be a problem for us later. In any case, whenever we slid into second or third base, we wanted to be sure it really was what we thought it was!

The oldest, ugliest and most worn-out baseball glove at Newport School was one that my brother John and I brought from home. I believe it belonged to our oldest brother Jake, quite a few years earlier. I estimate it may have dated back to the twenties or thirties during the Babe Ruth era. Everybody mocked, scorned, and ridiculed it because it had a huge thumb and a very small pocket. It was also so flat that sometimes we used it for a base!

We usually played with our big straw hats on to shield our eyes from the sun. However, there was one time I wished I had not been wearing my hat. That particular time, I was a base runner at second base. On the next pitch, the batter hit a line drive into left field. It was hit just a little in front of me and I saw it coming toward me as I put my head down and raced for third base. I scored easily and, as I hit home plate, I clapped my hands celebrating the run I had just scored. Or, thought I had just scored! At that moment, Ammon, a boy from the other team ran up, yelling, "No, no, you didn't score that run, you're out."

"You're crazy, there wasn't even a play at home plate," I yelled, angrily.

"I'm telling you, when Manny batted that ball, it hit the brim of your hat as it went by you, and you're *out*," Ammon shouted emphatically. We all knew that if a base runner is hit by a batted ball, he is automatically out. I thought about it a little, and sort of remembered, yeah, I think maybe I did feel something graze my hat. So, I relented and wound up not scoring the run after all and wishing I had not been wearing my big old Amish straw hat!

A few years later, I played with a more "professional" team, consisting of my Rumspringa buddies and me. We used real baseballs and professional style wooden bats. I had a modern baseball glove that I was quite proud of, but instead of wearing baseball shoes with cleats, I wore used golf shoes that I had fished out of the fifty-cent "bargain bin" at the Goodwill store in Lancaster.

One Sunday afternoon we were playing baseball in a cow pasture at an Amish farm. We weren't doing so well as fire balling Humpy Johnny was in the process of throwing a no-hitter against us. With two outs in the bottom of the ninth inning, I came up to bat as the last hope of our team not being no-hitted. Although desperate to get a hit, I swung and missed at strike three, and immediately thought the game was over. Then I realized that the catcher, Danny Lapp, had not caught the ball, and I knew if I could make it to first base before he threw down there, I would be safe, and the game would continue. The ball hit the big old barn door backstop and bounced far enough away that my mad dash enabled me to reach first base safely. But I had made a headlong dive and had cut my knee badly on a rock or a piece of glass, and it really hurt and even bled some. But I never considered coming out of such an exciting game.

My buddy and teammate, John Z. Esh, was the next batter, and to our great delight, he hammered the first pitch over the pasture fence in right field for a dramatic home run. My knee didn't seem to hurt as much as I eagerly raced home followed by the hero, John Z. Even though I certainly should have gone to a doctor to get my knee stitched up, I never did, and it took a long time before it healed properly. I still carry a scar there to this day.

During another Sunday afternoon game, I was batting with a runner on first base. As the pitch came in, he was running and trying to steal second base. The pitch was high and inside, and I ducked backwards to avoid being hit. As I immediately straightened up again, I felt an awful blow to the back of my head and fell to the ground as though I had been shot. Of course, I had not been wearing a batting helmet since no Amish wore those back then. I lay there in great pain, dazed and almost unconscious. I soon realized that the catcher, which happened to be my brother John, had hit me with the ball, while trying to throw to second base. Soon I managed to get up and I was not a happy camper. I became even more disgusted when the self- appointed umpire, Christ Binks, actually called me *out*. I had done nothing wrong, and I'm sure he really blew that call. But on the positive side, being called out gave me some time to rest my throbbing head. Of course, I stayed in and played the rest of the game. And John never even apologized for hitting me on the head with the ball!

In early springtime in the Amish community, there are always auctions held at various farms, where horses and cows and lots of esoteric Amish items are sold. When a newly married son and his wife take over his dad's farm, a lot of household goods, farm equipment, and various animals are sold. It's an excellent time and place for Amish to socialize and to watch the mush ball or corner ball games. There is always at least one being played at every farm auction. It involves two teams, with six men or boys on each team, and often it is an Amish team against a Mennonite team.

The Old Order Mennonite's are somewhat like the Amish, in that they also don't have cars, TVs, radios, telephones, or electric power. But they do have English clothes, English haircuts and bicycles. And they do take their mush-ball games every bit as seriously as the Amish do. The games are played in the barnyard, in an area about fifty by fifty feet square. At each of the four corners, a board is put down, and a thrower, or "chucker" stands behind it, with all four of them facing the middle. The baseball-sized mushball is made of leather and has horsehair inside. The whole playing area is covered with straw from the barn. Four players, known as "mushers" are grouped in the middle of that area. The chuckers at each corner throw the ball to each other. They throw it to any teammate, including across the middle, where the mushers are. After the ball is thrown at least three times without being dropped, it is now "hot." They can keep throwing to each other, or try to hit one of the mushers, as long as the ball is still hot. They may throw with either hand, if they're ambidextrous, (unlikely) or momentarily play the hidden ball trick, or pretend to be throwing it when they don't even have it. All four chuckers might pretend to be throwing at the same time, in order to confuse the mushers. They throw as hard and as fast as they can at all times. The mushers, of course, are trying their best to not get hit. There is no foul ground area, as there is in baseball, so the many spectators move as close as they can, while cheering boisterously. Of course, no one wears any protective equipment at all. So, the mushers *and* the spectators often get hit by hard throws, sometimes in very vulnerable places. As a spectator, I once got hit very hard in an extremely sensitive area. As I was in a lot of pain, I desperately wanted to rub the injured "part." But even Amish people would not rub there publicly, so I gamely tried to laugh it off and to grin and bear it until the pain subsided!

When a musher gets hit, he goes out and one of his remaining teammates goes in to replace him. The other team then gets one point. If all six mushers get hit, that gives the other team a maximum score of six points. If a chucker throws at and misses a musher, he goes out and a teammate replaces him. Eventually there may be less than four chuckers. They can then run to unoccupied bases, hoping to get a surprise advantage over the mushers. If there is only one chucker left, he is known as the "greaser." He can run with the ball to any other base at any time, including through the middle, right past the mushers. Eventually, when there is only one chucker or one musher left, that half inning ends, and the mushers becomes chuckers, and vice versa, as a new half inning begins, like the baseball format. A complete game lasts only three innings.

One day there was an auction at Danny Zook's farm at Dry Hill. A team of six Keffah boys, including myself, were playing mushball against a team of Happy Jack boys. I was the only chucker left, as all my teammates had each already thrown at a musher and missed. I faced the very daunting and virtually impossible task of hitting five mushers in a row, one at a time. Since I was the only chucker left, they were all at the opposite corner, about sixty feet away, rather than in the middle, so it would be much harder for me to hit them. I started off well as I hit one of them with my first throw. Then I decided that as long as I kept hitting them, I would just stay at that base, instead of running to any other base, which would have improved my chances slightly. Staying at the same base, though, was considered to be very cocky and arrogant. Somehow, unbelievably, and to everybody's utter amazement, I was able to hit all five guys, one at a time, from the same base, without having run to any other base. I was not known for superb mushball throwing skill, but somehow none of them was able to dodge away from my throws. Afterword, as the crowd roared deliriously, my teammates mobbed me and congratulated me. They would certainly have "high fived" me too, but there was no such thing as a high five back then. To put it into proper perspective, what I had done was probably as rare as a major-league pitcher pitching a perfect game. In fact, I haven't heard of anybody else ever having matched my feat. It definitely was the highlight of my Amish "sports" career.

CHAPTER THIRTEEN

Dad Was An Accident Waiting to Happen

OVER THE YEARS, DAD surely had more than his fair share of accidents, some of which caused him major physical injuries. They included two broken legs, a broken back, a broken wrist, a broken rib, the complete loss of one eye, and a concussion to his head. He came closest to losing his life on the day he was attacked by a vicious bull. Dad and Brother Amy had been cleaning out the bull's pen and Dad was alone in the barn while Amy was driving the horse-drawn manure spreader out to the field. A heavy chain was in place that kept the huge swinging oak gate secured to the wooden post by the bullpen. Dad loosened the chain and was planning to tighten it. For some reason the huge Holstein bull, which weighed almost a ton, started to push and bump against the gate with his head and body. Dad frantically tried to secure the gate with the chain, but by then the bull had worked himself into a rage. Soon he rammed the gate so hard that the post was broken, and the gate fell on Dad, pinning him underneath. As the raging bull was bellowing and stomping around, Dad knew he was in mortal danger of losing his life. The bull was butting the gate and trying to lift it up with his nose so he could attack Dad directly. Dad was trying to keep it on top of himself, so the bull couldn't get at him. He knew that if the bull got the gate off him, he probably would be gored to death. Suddenly, Dad noticed his big black Amish hat lying next to him. He grabbed it and threw it toward the far end of the stable. The bull immediately chased it and started butting it savagely. Dad quickly got out from under the gate and crawled as fast as he could toward the concrete feed trough. He had to crawl because he he'd suffered a very serious fracture of his knee and thigh from the falling gate. The upper edge of the feed trough was about three feet high, and had thick vertical pipes cemented securely into its concrete top. The pipes were about sixteen inches apart, wide enough for the bull to get his head through, but not his body. Dad knew that if he was able to climb up and get between and past the pipes, he would be safe. He had just gotten there when the bull ran up behind him and butted him savagely in his back, knocking him out into the feed alley. Thankfully, however, he was now safe. The bull was still bellowing and trying to get at him but could not. A few moments after Dad knew he was safe and the adrenaline slowed down, he started feeling tremendous pain in his leg. His knee and thigh were smashed so badly, that they later considered amputating his leg.

When Dad heard Amy returning from the field, he yelled at him to not come into the barn because the bull was still loose there. He told him to go into the house and tell Mom what had happened and that his leg was broken. Mom misunderstand Amy and thought he meant the bull's leg was broken, so she didn't come out right away. Eventually an ambulance was summoned and took Dad to Lancaster General Hospital.

Dad had told Amy to call the local livestock hauler, Jay Plank, to come and take the bull to the cattle auction at New Holland. Dad later said he really wished he had the twelve-gauge shotgun from the buggy shed, during those terror filled moments when he thought the bull would kill him. He was forty-four years old at the time. We were all thankful that God allowed his life to be spared that day. He lived forty-four more years and died in 2002 at the age of eighty-eight.

Meanwhile, at the hospital, after the decision was made to try to save his leg, they put a cast on it which extended from his heel to his hip. The cast had two wooden pins that went completely through his leg. He wore the cast for four months and later wore a large metal leg brace for a long time. It was bulky and uncomfortable and extended from his foot to his hip. He eventually recovered reasonably well but always walked with a limp after that.

Another serious injury that Dad suffered was when he was still a young man, just twenty-two years old. It was on a Sunday afternoon when my parents were dating each other. Dad was getting his horse and buggy ready to go see Mom at her house when he noticed one of his horse's shoes was loose. While trying to nail it properly back into place, a tiny piece of steel flew directly into his eye. It actually became imbedded in his eye and he couldn't get it out. The next day at the hospital he was in great pain because the tiny steel fragment had lodged in the pupil of his eye. This happened in 1936 when the knowledge of major eye surgery was primitive in comparison to today. Sadly, they were unable to save his eyesight and, in fact, decided to actually remove the eye. He was fitted with an artificial glass eye, which he wore after that. It was, of course, very inconvenient for him to only have one eye to see with for the rest of his life. He and Mom had been dating for some time but had not been planning to get married during the November marrying season, which was only two months away. However, with of all the angst and trauma from the injury and removal of his eye, they decided to get married at that time, rather than wait till the following November. Also, he knew that Rumspringa would not be nearly as much fun for him anymore, because of having lost the eye.

Another serious accident that he had was when he was about forty years old. One evening he was driving a team of horses pulling the big farm wagon on Newport Road, about a quarter of a mile from home and almost directly by Uncle Sammy's house. It was quite dark already when Abner Smoker's car slammed into the back of the wagon because Dad didn't have any lights. Dad was thrown off and landed on his tailbone on the road, breaking several vertebrae in his back. Uncle Sammy and Jonas ran out to help Dad and to get the horses up, which had been knocked down by the impact. Abner, a Mennonite man from Paradise, was not hurt and the horses only suffered minor injuries. Later at the hospital, Dad was put in a body cast from his neck to his pelvis. He wore it for three long agonizing months before it was finally taken off.

The accident in which he broke his other leg was two years after the attack by the bull. One evening Dad and I were on our way to Dad's other farm where Brother Jake's lived. We were traveling on the dirt road between the two farms. Dad was driving a team of two unruly young mules pulling a fertilizer drill, which he and I were sitting on. There was a fence along one side which had a lot of thick brush and vegetation growing around it.

Suddenly, the mules lunged forward and sideways toward the fence, apparently spooked by some animal running nearby, probably a rabbit or groundhog. The wheel hub caught in the fence, jerking violently, and both of us were thrown off onto the ground. Dad was thrown forward and down in front of the wheel, which went over his ankle and broke it. I fell forward and down on the ground behind the mule's legs. The fertilizer drill went over top of me but, fortunately, none of the wheels went over me, which could easily have killed me. The mules galloped wildly down the dirt road for about a quarter of a mile, till they got to Danny [Push] Esh's farm, where somebody ran out and managed to stop them.

In the meantime, Dad was lying on the ground in a lot of pain with a broken ankle. I was there with him, screaming for help. Soon one of Push's boys drove up with a horse and buggy and helped Dad and me into it. We went to their farm and an Amish taxi was called to take Dad to the hospital. They put a cast on his lower leg, and by the next day he was back home again. He spent a short time recuperating but was soon back out in the fields, hard at work as usual.

One day in 1964, Dad, John, and I were coming home from Intercourse in the spring wagon, with John and me sitting up front. Dad was sitting on the back holding the neck rope and "leading" a horse that had just been shod at Jake Eichelberger's blacksmith shop. Suddenly a big truck went barreling past us and scared the horse. He yanked sharply backwards and started to run away as Dad unsuccessfully tried to hang on to the neck rope. He was dragged off and hit his head on the pavement and suffered a concussion. He didn't even seek any medical attention for that, which seemed to prove he was a pretty tough guy back then.

When he was thirty-eight, Dad suffered from a serious bout of depression and spent almost three weeks at Philhaven Hospital. He said later that he didn't fully recover from that for several years.

In 1973 he suffered a ruptured appendix which was a very serious situation and could easily have been fatal, as he arrived at the hospital not a moment too soon. That was a most painful and traumatic event, but he recovered okay as he always seemed to do.

One day, at the age of eighty-two, he was attacked by a ram, a big male sheep. For some unknown reason, the ram charged at him and savagely butted him several times. He vigorously fought back, trying to hit it with a shovel, but it knocked him to the ground, and he suffered a broken rib and a broken wrist. He had a cast on his wrist for three months.

But there was more misfortune still to come. At the age of eighty-seven, he fell several feet from the wooden porch down to the ground and broke his left hip bone. Again, an ambulance ride to the hospital where a steel plate was attached with four screws. Amazingly, like always, he recovered and was still able to walk in his old age.

CHAPTER FOURTEEN

Of Runaway Horses
and Mules

SOMETHING THAT MOST AMISH families have experienced are various incidents with runaway horses. Certainly, our family was no exception to that. My first such experience was when I was ten years old. One day, Dad hitched up our family driver, Tony, a wild and unruly steed that he had recently bought from Bishop Moses. Dad, John, and I then went to New Holland to do some shopping at Rubinson's Department Store. The most longed-for item we got there was a metal washtub about three feet long. Since we didn't have a normal built-in bathtub at our house, we decided to buy the metal type. That turned out to be a big improvement over the small metal buckets we'd always used. Of course, with the new tub, we were far too frugal to use a lot of hot water while "bathing," but it was still much better than using a bucket.

At Rubinson's that day, we loaded the tub into the back of the market wagon and headed home. Soon the tub started rattling around in the wagon, which scared Tony. He started running wildly and was soon at top speed. Dad was desperately yanking on the reins and yelling "Whoa." I don't know if John and I were also yelling "Whoa," but we were yelling something because we were scared. The faster we went the more noise the tub made as it bounced around. That made Tony run even faster. Fortunately, we were on a quiet country road and there was very little traffic. Eventually, Tony got tired and slowed down and Dad got him under control, and we proceeded the rest of the way at a more leisurely pace.

An accident which happened to my Mom, Lydia, and I involved, not a runaway, but a misbehaving horse. I was eleven years old at the time. We were all in the covered carriage, the type Amish parents go visiting in. It had an open front, which is typical for that style of carriage. Mom was driving the horse, Bobby, through the town of Intercourse. Suddenly, Bobby got spooked or scared about something and reared high up on his hind legs. He reared so high that he lost his balance and tipped over backwards. To our horror, we thought he was going to sit right back in the open carriage with us. Fortunately, the wooden cross piece that connects the two shafts on each side of him prevented that from happening.

Nevertheless, he was tangled up in the shafts and the harness and couldn't get up. We happened to be right by Menno Glick's house, an Amish man whose children went to our school. Menno saw our predicament and ran out to help us. He got Bobby straightened out and fixed his harness and soon had him standing up and we started for home.

Unfortunately, Mom now had decided to not make a certain stop on the way home that she had planned. My siblings had often told me how delicious, and almost heavenly, the frozen custard tasted that was sold at the little stand at the corner of Old Philadelphia Pike and Pig Lane. I had never had any, either there or anywhere else, and today Mom had promised us we'd go there and get some on our way home. I guess she was afraid that Bobby might do his "rear up and tip over backward" stunt again, and she just wanted to get home. I was really mad at Bobby because his misbehavior was the reason we didn't go there after all.

One evening, as a teenager, I was riding home from Brother Jake's farm on our big strawberry roan, Bill. It was already completely dark, except for some moonlight and stars. Certainly, there was no artificial light anywhere nearby. I was riding through a hayfield on Bill, who was just calmly walking along. Suddenly we came to a single strand electrified fence, which Danny [Push] Esh had put up to keep his cows in the field. This is done frequently at Amish farms. A 12-volt battery connected to a shocking device sends an electric current through the wire and provides quite a jolt for possibly a mile or more.

As Bill was just ambling along in the dark, he walked right up against the fence without seeing it. Of course, I had not seen it either. I got two unpleasant surprises simultaneously. One was feeling that nasty shock going through my body. The other one was, old Bill rearing way up on his hind legs because of the shock he also had gotten. He reared so high, and jumped forward so fast, that I was thrown off on the ground. I believe Bill actually jumped over the fence, which was about three feet high. He then started galloping wildly toward home. I soon realized that I was just shaken up and not really hurt. I got up and ran after him, yelling "Whoa," but he had other ideas and was heading for home in high gear and in high dudgeon. Eventually he got tired and slowed down and I was able to catch him. I calmed him down and climbed back on and we made the rest of the trip home uneventfully.

Normally, old Bill was quite gentle as evidenced by the fact that I sometimes briefly slept on his back, early in the morning, when I was still feeling tired and lazy. I'd go to where he was in his stall and climb on his back. Then I'd turn around, and with my legs still straddling his back, I'd put my upper body and face down on his broad back. Then, with my hands under my face and Bill just patiently standing there, I'd take a short nap. His back would soon feel nice and warm, and he never seemed to mind at all when I did that.

Soon after I started Rumspringa, some of my friends and I occasionally went to the Guernsey Barn on Saturday nights to see various country and western and bluegrass music groups. The building was a converted cow barn, where livestock auctions had previously been held. Various entertainers that we saw were Jimmy Martin and the Sunny Mountain Boys, the Osborne Brothers and Mac Wiseman. One cold winter night, some of us went there to see Bill Monroe and his bluegrass band. I drove there alone in my buggy and it was very cold, with snow on the ground. When I arrived, I tied my horse to the hitching rail out back and put a blanket on his back. The horse was still hitched to the buggy, which is commonly done. I went inside and joined my friends and we enjoyed the show together.

Sometime later a friend hurried up to me and said that a runaway driverless horse and buggy had been seen racing up Hartman Bridge Road with no lights on. Realizing that it might be my horse, I hurried outside to check at the hitching rail. Sure enough, my horse and buggy were gone. Maybe the cold weather had made him restless and he pulled back hard enough to get loose. But I suspect some bad guy may have had untied him. I asked an Amish friend, Jake King, for a ride in his car. We jumped in and sped up the road hoping to overtake my horse. After about a mile and a half we got to the intersection of Old Philadelphia Pike in Smoketown. Then we saw an Amish man leading a horse along the side of the road. Of course, it was my horse. He was sweaty and steaming, which meant he had been running very fast for some time. He also had a large bloody gash in one shoulder. We were told that when he came to the T road intersection at Old Philadelphia Pike he turned left, but was going too fast and ran into a metal road sign on the far side of the road. The buggy got hung up on the sign and the horse couldn't go any further, and that's where the Amish man found him and freed him. He led the horse back to his barn and called a veterinarian. A lot of stitches were required for the shoulder cut but it healed up very nicely. He was fortunate he had not been hit by any vehicle in the intersection. I was nervous about how Dad would react when he found out I had been at that worldly entertainment event. Of course, since my horse had gotten hurt, I had to tell Dad all the details. I was very relieved that he took it calmly and even paid the veterinarian's bill rather than make me pay it.

The most serious accident that ever occurred to me involved a team of mules pulling a corn wagon when I was nineteen years old while working at Brother Aaron's farm. I was alone out in the cornfield husking corn by hand, which was an extremely slow and boring process. I doubt that anybody does it that way anymore. I suppose it's all done with a corn picker nowadays. Two of Aaron's mules were hitched to the big flatbed farm wagon. I had been husking and throwing ear corn into the wagon all day and by now it was heavily loaded. Since there was no driver, I controlled the mule's forward progress by yelling "giddyap" and "whoa" as we slowly moved over the length of the field. Each time we moved, I had a new length of cornrow to husk and would throw each ear of corn onto the wagon.

Eventually, the mules didn't want to obey me anymore. They were restless and wanted to move ahead faster. Probably they were hungry or bored as I also was. Several times they would move much too far ahead. Then I'd run to the front of the wagon and yell at them and yank very hard on the reins to make them back up and also to punish them. They didn't like that. The next time I did that they heard me coming and suddenly jumped ahead and started running at full speed. I had just stepped around the front corner of the wagon but had not yet grabbed the reins which were hung around the pole there. I was therefore in an extremely vulnerable position.

The front of the wagon knocked me to the ground as the mules leaped forward. As the big heavily loaded wagon started going over me, I knew that I could very easily be run over and killed under the six-inch-wide steel wheels. I didn't have time to yell at them to stop and they wouldn't have obeyed me anyway. I was lying on the ground on my stomach, completely helpless as one front wheel went over my ankle, but I wasn't concerned about that. During those frightening few moments, I was only concerned about whether one of the rear wheels would go over my head. I knew instinctively if that happened, it would surely kill me. I didn't have time to roll out of the way or to orient myself because the cornstalks were blocking my vision and also hindering any escape movements I might have made. Also, I had very little time, maybe a second or two. I could not see the rear wheels approaching me. One rear wheel rolled over my body, as I was lying face down on the ground. It went directly over my lower back and buttocks as I was laying at right angles with the path of the wagon.

Immediately, I was in a lot of pain but still very thankful that I had not been killed. I tried to lay very still in case I had a spinal cord injury. I soon felt certain that was not the case and rolled onto my side. Then I waited and desperately hoped someone would come and help me. Meanwhile, the mules were on a dead run heading toward the barn, about a quarter of a mile away. Fortunately, Aaron saw them coming and ran out and jumped on the wagon and turned them around and drove up to where I was lying on the ground. After telling him what had happened to me, we decided to try to get me on the wagon. We really should not have done that, not knowing what injuries I might have. He lifted me on the wagon by himself and as I lay there on top of the load of ear corn, he slowly drove the mule team back to the barn. An "Amish taxi driver" from Intercourse was called because it was much cheaper than an ambulance would have been. I was taken to Lancaster General Hospital and was soon in the emergency room. While flat on my back and waiting to be examined, I came extremely close to passing out. After all the x-rays were done it was determined that I had only suffered severe bruises where the two wheels had rolled over me. I was very sore for several days but was soon back to normal and very thankful to God for sparing my life.

During that time in my life I often wondered as I suppose anyone in my situation would, what would happen to me if I died suddenly. We were taught from early on that Heaven and hell were both very real. Also, that being a member of the Amish church was extremely important. To become a member, we were required to profess that we believed that Jesus Christ was the Son of God. But we were led to believe that membership in the church, specifically, was more important than that belief.

An incident involving runaway horses happened at the west end of our farm which bordered neighbor Henry Esh's farm. On that warm summer day, Dad and I were hoeing weeds in our cornfield. The corn was so tall that we were completely hidden. We were at the very end of the cornrows and were just stepping out into the open. Meanwhile, Henry and two of his sons were starting to bale hay at the edge of their field, just a few feet away. Henry was driving the three horses pulling the baler. The older son, Moses, was ready to load and stack the hay bales on the empty wagon. He was a muscular strapping young man about twenty-one years old. Nine-year-old Davey was sitting at the front of the wagon.

They were all going by, just a few feet away, as Dad and I suddenly stepped out of the cornfield, not thinking that we might startle the horses and cause a runaway. Dad told me later that horses are more likely to get spooked that way then mules would be. When the horses hitched to the wagon saw us suddenly and unexpectedly, they became frightened and immediately swiftly jumped forward. Within a few seconds, they were running at full speed, galloping wildly with reckless abandon toward Henry's barn, about two hundred yards away. Henry, Dad and I were left behind, helplessly watching in horror and dismay. Dad said later that, because horses don't have an instinctive sense of self-preservation like mules do, there's no way to know what they might do if they were not quickly stopped. They probably would have raced down the barn hill at full speed and might have crashed into the huge oak tree by the driveway. As the horses sprang forward so suddenly, Moses, who was standing at the back end of the wagon, came extremely close to losing his balance and being thrown off. I vividly remember seeing his one leg pointing straight backward horizontally as he desperately struggled to maintain his balance and stay on the wagon. If Moses had fallen off, little Davey surely could not have controlled the wildly galloping horses so he would have been in extreme danger. Meanwhile, Moses, instinctively knowing this, was fighting to stay on his feet while trying to get to the front of the wagon as it bounced crazily over the hard, bumpy field. He never even considered yelling whoa to the horses, knowing full well they wouldn't obey him. The pair of leather reins were hanging around the pole at the front of the wagon. When he got there, he grabbed them and quickly looped them around each hand. Then, with all the strength in his brawny arms he gave a mighty jerk, as Henry, Dad and I watched fearfully from behind, wondering if even he would be able to stop them. To our great relief, both horse's heads immediately jerked sharply upward, straight up in the air, which was a sure sign of capitulation and proof that Moses now had them under control. He turned them around and drove back to where we were standing. We were all thankful that a catastrophe had been averted that day.

Henry was a wonderful neighbor to us for many, many years. He and Becky arrived at their farm in 1938, as newlyweds, and lived there for the rest of their lives. Becky died in 2004 and Henry died in 2007 at the age of ninety. Because we admired him so much, his familiar slouching posture and long angular nose seemed to almost have endearing qualities to us. Henry was always very friendly and congenial with everyone. He was greatly respected as a father, husband, and Amish church member, always had a spirit of true gelassenheit (acceptance) toward the Ordnung and was certainly considered to be a pillar of the church.

He and Becky had a family of five boys and four girls. Their farm which bordered our farm to the west had a very long gravel driveway about one third of a mile long. Whenever Dad or any of my brothers or I went out to work in the western fields, we knew we should look and see if Henry was working in his fields, anywhere reasonably close by. We knew that if he was within a quarter of a mile of us when he first saw us, he would surely wave at us as a friendly greeting. It is a rare and heartwarming thing to have a neighbor who is that friendly.

Another unique thing about Henry, was that he could yell amazingly loudly. Not in anger, but as a means of communication. One warm and very calm summer evening, sister Lydia and I, along with Henry's daughter Lizzie, were picking cherries directly across from Willis Futers house. Lizzie had taken the scenic route there with their horse and buggy. She had gone out their long driveway, turned left on Osceola Mill Road then west on Newport Road past our house to where the cherry trees were. Henry was doing something near the end of their gravel driveway, probably repairing the pasture fence. He was way down across the hollow almost a half mile away. This was in the sixties, long before the era of the cell phone. As darkness approached, we heard his stentorian voice faintly wafting across the tobacco and hay fields from so far away. He was calling to tell Lizzie to come home, as her buggy did not have any lights. She waved to him to acknowledge that she had heard him, then gathered her baskets of cherries and climbed into the buggy and left. By the way, we survived quite well without cell phones back then!

Henry also experienced at least one life-threatening accident during his farming career. One day he was driving a pair of his huge draft horses, which were hitched to the big flatbed farm wagon. He was hauling a full load of corn fodder bales on the wagon. Henry was sitting high up on top of the bales while driving on the long gravel driveway toward their barn. The driveway was slightly down hill and the horses started running at a slow trot. He pulled back on the reins to try to slow them down. Then he realized he was in trouble because there were no vertical wooden poles at the front of the wagon for him to hold on to or to brace himself against.

As the horses ran faster, he pulled too hard on the reins and suddenly the bales he was sitting on tumbled out from underneath him. By now the horses were in full-fledged runaway mode, galloping wildly along at top speed. Henry fell forward over the front of the wagon and directly down between the two galloping horses. While in a horizontal falling position he somehow managed to grab and hold on to the three-inch-thick wooden wagon tongue between the horses. Of course, he had absolutely no control of the horses now as they raced on at full speed with their upper legs banging against his body. He desperately clung to the wagon tongue with both hands, knowing that otherwise he would get trampled by the horses or would get run over by the wagon, or both. The wagon tongue he was clinging to was only about two feet above the ground, directly between the horses wildly galloping legs. After running about a quarter of a mile they were near the barn and ran around behind it and into a corner somewhere and had to stop. Henry then slowly and carefully climbed out from between the horse's legs to safety. He could very easily have been killed and was extremely fortunate that he had only suffered a separated shoulder and some minor bruises.

CHAPTER FIFTEEN

Misbehavior
at the Amish Schools

IN THE SUMMER OF 1960, a new Amish schoolhouse was built about one half mile west of us, along Newport Road. Since it was much closer than Harristown School, our parents decided to have John, Lydia, and me attend there. So, after spending only one year at Harristown School we were now starting again at another school. Newport School was the third and final school that we would attend. It was a one-room schoolhouse, as Hatville School and Harristown School both had been. And, happily, Newport School had its very own water supply, a big hand-pump out in the schoolyard although I don't remember any drinking cups ever being provided!

Our teacher was a twenty-three-year-old Amish lady named Katie who we liked and respected. Certainly, more so than Christ at Harristown school. What also appealed to us was the fact that she was more liberal than stodgy, ultra-conservative Christ had been. During the very simple, quaint and amusing Christmas program "plays" that Katie arranged, she had daringly placed plain white curtains which were moved back and forth on a piece of wire at the beginning and end of the "show," which surely dismayed some of the watching parents. Also, unlike any other teacher that I've had, Katie played baseball with us during the lunchtime recess. I vividly recall seeing her running the bases with her untied Amish "kapp" streaming behind her head as a single pin on top valiantly tried to keep it from flying off completely. She also would kindly read a chapter from a storybook to us after lunch, often from the ancient series known as the Rover Boys or the Tom Swift series.

There were seven girls and three boys in my class which was the largest of all the classes, grades one through eight. The other two boys in my class were twin brothers, Amos and Aaron Stoltzfus. Their father, John, whose nickname had been Rags, had passed away when they were only five years old. Several years later, Ben [B.T.] Fisher, a widower, married their mother and then there was an exceptionally large "blended" family of nineteen children. I soon became close friends with the twin brothers, Amos and Aaron.

The class sizes at Newport School ranged from ten students to one student in each class. That's right, one class only had one student, and his name was John Petersheim. I always felt sorry for him about that, but I never heard him complain about it.

Softball was practically the only game we ever played at school where any kind of ball was used. One exception to that was when we played Kollyover, when we used a sponge ball. We also played Flying Dutchman, Fox and Geese and Prisoner's Base. One competition the boys sometimes had was walking on top of the school yard fence, which was about five feet high. It surrounded the school property on all four sides and measured a total of about five hundred feet in length. The boards measured one inch thick or less, and were very shaky and wobbly. The posts were about eight feet apart. Also, the tops of the posts were cut at a steep angle. So, no one could "relax" while standing on a post because that in itself was tricky and difficult. One memorable day, I somehow managed to walk all the way around on top of the fence without falling or jumping off at all. I'm not aware of anyone else ever having done that.

There never was a basketball hoop at any of the three schools I attended. Not even at Hatville, which was a public school. Also, football was never played at any of those schools. In fact, I don't recall ever even seeing a football there. The Amish parents probably considered basketball and football even worldlier than baseball. So, of course, they had no incentive to put up a basketball hoop.

Wilt Chamberlain, from the Philadelphia 76ers, scored one hundred points in a game at Hershey in 1962. It was then, and still is, the all-time single game NBA record. Hershey was only about thirty-five miles from our house. The Sixers only played one game each year at Hershey so it was extremely odd that Wilt set the record there that night. After that I became really interested in basketball. Since Dad would never have provided me with a "store-bought" hoop, I put up my own version of a basketball hoop on the back side of our wooden tobacco shed. I took an empty five-gallon metal bucket that previously had Milk Mizer in it.

Milk Mizer was powder mix that was mixed with water that we used to feed the calves. I used a pair of tin shears to cut the bottom out of the bucket, then nailed it to the outside of the shed. We didn't have a basketball, but we had a red rubber ball of similar size that I had found along the road. When I started shooting it at the metal bucket, I soon became perplexed that I wasn't making more of my shots. I thought that the professional players must have tremendous talent to shoot as well as they do. Eventually it dawned on me that nobody would make many shots shooting a nine-inch-wide ball at a twelve-inch-wide basket! Since I couldn't afford a real basketball hoop, I started throwing a softball at the Milk Mizer bucket from about thirty feet away and soon became quite proficient at doing that. All that could be considered improvising the Amish way!

One of my school friends, a mere ten-year-old who later went English, mysteriously seemed to always have money available to buy bubblegum, candy cigarettes, and similar luxuries. When I asked him about that, he slyly grinned and said he steals money from his mom's pocketbook. I was shocked to hear that and would not have considered or dared to do that myself.

One foolish and possibly dangerous thing that some boys, including myself, would occasionally do was hypnotize each other out on the playground during recess. Without going into much detail, it involved holding one's breath and extreme chest compression from another boy, and we really would be "out like a light" for a short time. We tried not to let the teacher know about it and apparently no girls ever tattled on us because the teacher never confronted us about it.

My first experience with bubblegum was when I was in fourth grade. Some boys who came from the Intercourse area sometimes stopped at Dorothy Brubaker's restaurant and bought bubble gum, or "fireballs," as we called them, which they then peddled to the other kids at school. We certainly didn't mind that they were somewhat contaminated from having been carried loosely and unprotected in the boy's pockets. Fireballs were hot tasting but I liked the taste and, of course, blowing bubbles was fun. We'd pay a penny for each one, but we weren't allowed to chew or blow bubbles during "books," or class.

Sometimes when we blew huge bubbles at home, Dad would look on with mild amusement, and would disparagingly call the bubbles "bull hide." Mom was afraid that our chewing the gum would pull the fillings out of our teeth. We kids earnestly tried to convince her that it would not, fearing she would prohibit our gum-chewing. Another source for bubble gum could have been from packs of baseball cards at Zimmerman's Store, but no boys from our school ever bought any there. However, some Amish boys who went to the English school in Intercourse did and later I wished I also had when I saw how valuable the baseball cards had become. We did cut baseball and football cards off the backs of Post Cereal boxes during the few years they appeared there, in the early sixties. Some cereal boxes had president's cards on the back which we would cut out. I traded some president cards for baseball cards with my buddy Ira, who went to the Intercourse school. One of the cards I got from him was a 1959 Topps Mickey Mantle and that certainly was a good trade for me. I still have that card to this day.

All the kids regularly walked to school although some of us would occasionally roller-skate back and forth. We used the clamp-on steel skates that were common then. One boy regularly rode a pony to school which he kept tied inside the schoolyard fence during the day. Often, the big yellow English school buses would pass us as we were walking to and from school. However, we were so indoctrinated to believe they were not for us that we hardly even envied those kids at all.

During the winter of 1960, my first year at Newport School, I went through an especially difficult period. I was nine years old and everything was going fine for me at school. Then, on New Year's Day on a Sunday morning, Dad's mother, my grandmother, Suvilla Fisher, died at our house. She had been a widow for a long time. She was eighty-nine years old and her death was not unexpected, because she had come down with pneumonia. I was sent around the neighborhood that morning to notify the neighbors of her death. During her last few years, she had lived month to month at her married children's homes, which is common in Amish culture since they don't put their old people in nursing homes.

A few days later at the graveside burial at Myers Cemetery, I saw Dad cry as he saw her for the last time in her coffin. Of course, that was understandable as some other people were also crying. However, seeing that, along with the sad atmosphere of the funeral and the loss of my grandmother, had a dramatic effect on me. Within a few days' time, I had sunk into a deep depression.

Because the Amish believe they have no assurance of salvation, death for them is often a much more frightening experience than it needs to be. It's frightening to them because they strongly believe that everybody will either go to Heaven or hell, but they just don't know which place. They believe that the more faithfully they keep the rules of the Amish church, and probably to a lesser degree, follow the teachings of the Bible, the better chance they'll have of getting to heaven. I was familiar enough with the Bible to know that it at least generally taught that sinners won't get to heaven. However, I also knew that sins could be forgiven if someone repented and prayed for forgiveness. I became very worried, though, about what would happen if I sinned at any given time but then died, possibly just a few moments later, before I had a chance to pray for forgiveness. Would I be eternally sentenced to hell because I was guilty of one unforgiven sin? I became very worried about that, and I didn't know where to turn to, or of whom to ask these questions. I assumed if I asked anyone in my family, or any Amish minister, they would consider me very strange. They would probably tell me to just live as good a life as I could and hope that I will eventually get to Heaven.

Usually, when an Amish person dies, others will say they have a good hope for that person, especially if he or she had lived an honest and obedient life. They don't think anyone should feel sure that they are saved and would think that to be arrogant and conceited. Because I was so troubled by all this, I was sad and depressed and didn't talk much. My family thought I might be close to having a nervous breakdown. They tried to talk cheerfully and optimistically to me, but it didn't help. Much later I realized that what I needed at that time, was Christian counseling from someone who could tell me how I could be saved, specifically to repent of my sins and believe and trust in Jesus Christ. However, I had no idea who I could or should go to, who might explain that to me. If I had wanted to go to an English person, even an English pastor, that would have been very much frowned upon and discouraged.

My parents thought I needed physical therapy provided by a chiropractor, even though I told them I felt fine physically. They decided to send me to a lady chiropractor in Lancaster named Paula Seitz, so Dad took me to see her each Saturday.

Dad and I would walk up to Hatville or Intercourse to catch the bus to Lancaster and then walk about six blocks to Paula's office. The usual highlight was when we stopped at the little confectionary on East King Street for a quarter pound of spearmint gumdrops in a little white paper bag. Then we'd each eat one, but only one, before we arrived there.

Paula was a friendly woman but, of course, I was still very bashful in her presence, as all Amish boys would be. She squeezed and poked and pulled me around vigorously, and I'm sure it all did help me physically to some extent. Meantime, Dad would be in the waiting room reading a newspaper or magazine.

Once, when Paula was treating me, she left the room before she was done. It seemed I had to wait a long time till she came back. I remember my bladder being very full, to the point where I was extremely uncomfortable. I looked around in vain for a door going into a bathroom. I wondered why Paula was gone for so long. I could have gone into the waiting room and told Dad of my dilemma. But I didn't, because I was too shy to even tell Dad that I had to use this English woman's bathroom. I would never have considered asking Paula herself because that would have seemed extremely personal and inappropriate. I looked around desperately, then saw a small metal wastebasket under a kneehole desk. So, I hurried over and picked it up and in a very short time my bladder was not full anymore! Soon, Paula came back and finished treating me. I was really glad she didn't check the wastebasket at that time. I felt bad and very embarrassed for having done that, but I really felt as though that was my only logical choice. I hoped that when she emptied it, she would not suspect that I had done it.

This somewhat illustrates the extreme degree to which Amish children and teenagers are taught, in a very subtle but earnest way, to never talk to anyone of the opposite sex about anything pertaining to pregnancy, sexuality, or anyone's genitalia. They are taught that any such talk is rude, crude, embarrassing and inappropriate. So, it's understandable that whenever any of my sisters-in law became pregnant, my parents never told me about it, even when I was already in my twenties. Neither would my brothers, who were the new fathers-to-be. And, most certainly my pregnant sisters-in-law would not tell me either. So, the only way I found out was when it became visually noticeable about halfway through the pregnancy.

Speaking of pregnancy, one way in which Amish women do *not* hide that, not even in the slightest degree, is how they dress at that time. Unlike non-Amish women who wear "bump-hiding" maternity dresses, Amish women always wear the same style dress with an apron tightly tied directly above the "baby bump," which greatly accentuates its visibility!

Brother John worked at Jake and Arie's farm as a teenager, in 1966. They had a new baby, Aaron, who was just a few weeks old. Their oldest son, Eli, who was four years old, had never been told or given even the slightest clue where the baby had come from. One day at lunchtime, as Arie was feeding the baby, Eli was watching with great interest and became curious about the baby's origin.

"Voo hen mah Bapy Aaron grickt?" he piped up, which means "Where did we get baby Aaron?" For a four-year-old Amish boy to ask his parents that question was thought to be totally taboo and shameful and disgusting and they would never consider telling him the truth about that. But of course, they could not punish him or even scold him because he had asked it in such complete innocence. John and Jake both immediately started grinning and had trouble hiding their amusement when Eli asked that question. Sister-in-law Arie was not amused, or if she was, she hid it very well. She kept a matter of fact appearance and both her and Jake ignored Eli's question. They urged him to eat and pretended that he was eating much too slowly. Eli was not to be deterred, however, on such an important question. He persisted and asked several more times where they had gotten baby Aaron. After again being told by his parents to hurry up and eat, Eli thought he had it all figured out.

"Shtoah, net"? he asked, which means, "At the store, not?" With my brothers still trying to hide their amusement, Jake sheepishly mumbled "I guess." Eli probably wondered why they were so unwilling to tell him because to him it really *was* important.

Dad took me to see Paula about six or seven times, then as spring approached, my depression lifted considerably. Soon I was back to my former self, although those important questions about Heaven and hell still had not been answered.

One day as Dad and I were returning from a visit to Paula, we stopped at Brubaker's Restaurant in Intercourse for a rare snack. A little black and white TV was playing on the counter, and I watched with great interest. It showed a boyfriend and girlfriend talking with each other. Suddenly, as they were standing there, they hugged and kissed each other in a very innocent way. I was very embarrassed that I had seen that in Dad's presence. He probably really wished I hadn't seen it, although he didn't say anything. We left the restaurant almost immediately afterwards. I'm sure he didn't want me to keep watching that TV program.

None of my siblings, as youngsters, were obsessed with watching TV like I was. Even many years later, one brother told me watching TV would be boring! He obviously didn't know of the huge number of *vastly* entertaining things that modern-day TV provides.

During all of my growing up years I never saw any of our family members hugging each other. Also, I don't recall my parents ever telling any of us that they loved us. In Amish families back then, that just wasn't done. At least, not that I know of. Even so, I'm sure Mom loved us, and I would hope Dad did, too. And, in our family, kissing was almost non-existent, other than when Lydia and

I, as young children, kissed Mom goodnight at bedtime. Once in a great while we would then also kiss Dad. However, it was with some reluctance because he would grin and try to "bristle" our faces with his beard which would bring childish giggles from Lydia and me. However, I never saw Dad and Mom kiss OR hug each other, and I suppose none of my siblings ever did either. So, it's understandable that I grew up thinking that would almost be immoral and sinful. In our family, it was thought to be silly and unnecessary. Sadly, I also did not ever even see my parents touch each other in an affectionate way. I suppose that was normal for many other Amish families as well. While Dad was never abusive to Mom, it didn't appear that they actually enjoyed being together. It seemed like a business relationship rather than a happy marriage.

CHAPTER SIXTEEN

Snowplow Attack
on a Schoolyard Fence

UPON ENTERING FIFTH GRADE at Newport School in 1961, I became more rebellious and got into minor trouble occasionally. Of course, my parents were concerned about that. I believe now my attitude was largely because I was angry at Dad and jealous of John. That's because my perception was that Dad favored and liked him more than me. However, I never accused Dad of favoritism or asked him about that at all.

One night in August, a few weeks before the 1961 school term started, there was a major thunderstorm late at night. When Dad went to the barn that morning it was still quite dark. But he saw a reddish glow on the eastern horizon, and immediately thought it was from a barn fire. He was afraid it was at Uncle Steffy and Aunt Mary's barn, about three miles away at Spring Garden. Later that morning our fears were confirmed. Uncle Steffy's very large barn had indeed been hit by lightning and had burned to the ground. It had been an extremely traumatizing event for all of them. One son, Ike, had desperately ran as fast as he could through a tremendous rainstorm and lightning and thunder, for more than a mile to call the nearest fire company. Back home, they had major difficulty freeing the huge, wildly bellowing bull from the burning barn. Then he ran off into the darkness, only to be found dead the next morning in the nearby Pequea creek. It wasn't known if he had drowned or had died from the serious burns he'd suffered. Later that morning, Dad hitched Tony to the hack buggy and drove over to Steffy's to help out and I desperately wanted to go along and be with my cousins, Willie and Sylvan, but I had to stay home and hoe weeds in the tobacco field instead.

About a week later, the new barn was ready to be built so we all went there to help that day. It was a typical Amish barn raising, which Lancaster County is well known for, and which tourists are always greatly interested in. I don't think any tourists came that day, though, probably only because the farm was in a secluded rural area. I was not quite ten years old, so I didn't actually help to build or "raise" the barn.

After a scrumptious Amish lunch meal, a bunch of us went down to Pequea Creek, which ran through their meadow a short distance away. How eager we all were to wade and swim in the creek! As I remember, it was Willie and Sylvan, also cousins Omar, Raymond, Toby Ben, my brother John and me and my buddy, Ira. Raymond was Uncle Ike and Aunt Emma's grandson. His parents were Mennonite, and he was the same age as I was. He could swim very well, while I couldn't swim at all, although I foolishly thought I could if I just tried to. After all, it looked fairly easy.

"Let's go swimming and race each other to the other side of the creek," I said to Raymond when that silly idea entered my mind. He agreed and we started out, while the others watched. Very soon I realized that I was not swimming, I was just paddling around in the water, and was now in deeper water than I could wade. As the water came above my mouth and nose, I panicked and thrashed around wildly. When my feet touched bottom, I jumped up and was able to see them briefly and yell for help, before going down again. A moment or two later when I jumped up again, I saw Raymond swimming toward me with one arm outstretched. No doubt, that was the happiest moment of my young life. I grabbed his hand and he swam back to shallow water, towing me with one arm. I had, of course, been very scared and was extremely grateful that he had rescued me. Some of the others seemed to think it was somewhat funny, but it was never funny to me. The lesson I learned very well that day was that, in order to swim, it's really helpful if you actually know how to do it!

A few weeks later I started fifth grade at Newport School. We had a new teacher, a pretty young lady named Fannie. She had five or six siblings who were students there. Fannie also only taught there for one year, like Katie the previous year. She had two particularly good reasons for teaching only one year. One reason was she got married in the fall after the school term was over. Also, she was only being paid five dollars per day, with no benefits, of course. Obviously, the Amish schools are run on a very tight budget. Most Amish teachers are teen-age girls who only teach for one or two years. And, of course, they have no official State certification at all to even be teachers!

There were about a dozen students who lived way over on the other side of Old Philadelphia Pike, commonly known as the Old Road. They all had quite a long hike each day. Some had to walk about two miles each way, including a long stretch on a dirt road by Benuel Stoltzfus's fields. Several times, probably out of boredom, some of the boys made a big bonfire on the dirt road from cornstalks and dried hay from the nearby fields. But I don't believe they ever got into any trouble for doing that.

One day, boredom also affected two of the older Stoltzfus brothers who were already out of school. They were stripping tobacco in their shed, very close to Newport Road. As we walked by on our way home from school, they came out and lured several of us inside. They were in a rowdy and jovial mood and, while entertaining us with several risqué Rumspringa tales, they noticed that I had a small hole in my upper pant leg, near my waist. So, one of them reached in with two fingers and really yanked and tore it completely down to the bottom. They seemed to think that was quite funny. I knew then that it was time to head home. Since I wasn't wearing underwear [I started that at about age fifteen] I had to hold the torn sections together so as not to be "indecent." In my naïve innocence, I even thought it was a little funny. When I told Mom about it, however, she definitely was not amused. Even though she was a very easy-going lady, that was a rare occasion when she really became quite perturbed at someone. But I'm sure the boy's parents were never told about it or held accountable.

The twin brothers, Amos and Aaron, told me about a "hot rod" that their older brothers had made, and I was desperately eager to visit them at their house and drive it with them. It was a flatbed type contraption powered by a Briggs and Stratton gasoline engine and had two steel wheels and two hard rubber wheels. It had a hand clutch, but no brakes. Dragging one's shoes on the ground was the normal braking procedure. If there was a rider in addition to the driver, the braking capability would double when he also dragged his shoes!

One Sunday afternoon, I got Dad's permission to go visit them. Of course, I didn't tell him about the hot rod because he probably would have said no. It was a long walk for me, a total of about four miles, but I was so excited about driving the hot rod that I didn't mind that at all. When I got there, I quickly asked them about the hotrod, but to my great dismay, they told me that it was "out of commission." Of course, I couldn't call ahead of time to ask about the hotrod's status, because we didn't have a telephone. As it turned out, we settled for a much less exciting thing to do, climbing up to the top of their fifty-foot-high windmill which, admittedly, was somewhat scary.

There was another intriguing thing that we occasionally did on our daily afternoon trek home from school. We'd step into Push's Reuben's little telephone shanty along the side of the road and call the local operator. We'd simply dial zero and when she answered, we'd innocently ask her what time it was. When she courteously told us, we would marvel at the wonders of "English" technology and unanimously agreed with each other that telephones certainly were a wonderful invention!

One day, after a heavy snowfall, some of us schoolboys got into trouble at Newport School. During the afternoon recess we saw a man out on the road, plowing snow with a big yellow snowplow. About eight or ten of us climbed onto the schoolyard fence to watch. Since the snowplow only had a flat steel roof, and no windows, we saw that an Amish man was driving it. We were surprised at that because Amish men didn't usually drive snowplows. Then we noticed that he had a trimmed beard and a zip up style jacket. So, we assumed he was a renegade Amish man who had left the Amish church and joined the newer, more liberal Amish. Since we had almost been "taught," in a subtle way to scorn and shun those people, we decided to pelt him with snowballs. We were only about forty feet away and did hit him a few times, but he pretended to ignore us. Suddenly he veered the big snowplow toward us and came at us really fast. We thought he was just trying to scare us, but we weren't going to stick around to find out. We jumped off the fence and ran backward like scared rabbits. To our amazement and consternation, he crashed right through the fence, breaking all three rows of boards like matchsticks. Then, as he was backing away, he yelled at us, "Ich tzill cel net patzallah, de Amishe kenna cel patzallah," meaning that he's not going to pay for that, and the Amish can pay for it!

Needless to say, we didn't throw any more snowballs at him. When Teacher Sally found out what we'd done, she made each of us write on pieces of tablet paper, about three hundred times, a certain sentence pertaining to the incident. I tried to mitigate that punishment by simultaneously holding two pencils in my hand instead of one but that didn't work out so well. Several days later some of the snowball-throwing boys' fathers came to the school and repaired the fence. I doubt if the snowplow driver was ever even billed for it.

One summer evening when Uncle Steffy and Aunt Mary and their boys came to visit we had a memorable baseball game. It was out in our front yard, between the house and barn where we often played. The teams consisted of our cousins Stevie, Willie, and Sylvan, against my brothers Amy and John and me. First base was the middle post of the garden fence, by the grape arbor. Second base was the maple tree nearest the barn, and third base was the tree on the far side of the gravel driveway. It was an extremely competitive game, and by the last inning it was very dark, so dark you could just see the faintest glimpse of the ball when it was thrown. The Fisher team, meaning my brothers and me, were batting in the bottom of the last inning, and we were behind by one run. Brother Amy represented the tying run at third base for us, and I was batting with two outs. I desperately wanted to get him home, because I knew if I made out, the game would be over, and we'd have lost. Willie was pitching, and I did manage to hit a foul ball. But then with two strikes on me, to my great dismay, I swung and missed and we lost the game, right then and there. Certainly, no one blamed me at all because it was so dark it was virtually impossible to see the ball. And, of course, there was no artificial light anywhere. I think the reason I remember it so well is because it was just a few weeks before Amy passed away. After his death, I remember thinking that, whereas I had failed to bring him home in the baseball game, I trust and believe that God did bring him home to Heaven soon afterward when he died at such a young age at that time.

Dad never played baseball with us, which was understandable, because of his two bad legs. I do remember him throwing the ball back to us a few times when he was working near the barn. Understandably, he got upset when I hit a foul ball that broke Aunt Miriam's bedroom window. But, as for batting, I never, ever saw him swing a bat and sometimes wondered what that would look like.

Whenever any of us went to Lancaster we always took the bus, either from Hatville or Intercourse. Of course, I always loved to go there because of all the worldly things that could be seen in that "evil" city. And, of course, riding on a bus or any type of motor vehicle was so much more fun than riding in a slow old horse-drawn buggy.

Practically the only time I ever got to go to Lancaster before Rumspringa, was to get a new hat from old Harry Haas, about once every three years. Or if I had a toothache, I would go to see Dr. Brett, our faithful old dentist. By the age of fourteen, I was allowed to take the bus to Lancaster by myself, if I had a good reason to. However, there were not many good reasons for me to go there, according to my parents.

Years ago, Amish people were prohibited from working in factories and were sometimes excommunicated for doing that. Even now, they are not allowed to live in Lancaster or other cities, as decreed by the Ordnung. Cities are thought to be hotbeds of iniquity and the bishops definitely would prefer their people live in rural areas, especially on farms. They *are* allowed to live in villages like Gap, Intercourse, and Bird-in Hand, but it's not really what the bishops prefer because it's thought there are many evil temptations there too.

One day Dad came home from Lancaster and surprised all of us. To our delight, he had bought a badminton set with four rackets, four birdies, and a net with posts. Of all places, he had bought it at Pep Boys for three dollars. He did occasionally play badminton with us on Sunday afternoons, but only briefly because of his bad legs. He also sometimes played croquet or horseshoes with us in the front yard. The only other sporting activity that I can recall him doing was occasionally hunting small game in the fields with us boys.

When each of my brothers and I reached twelve years of age Dad bought a shotgun for us, since hunting deer and small game was quite popular and was one of the few "worldly" activities that the Amish do not prohibit. Whenever any Lancaster County Amish went deer hunting, it was usually to the northern counties, which had a lot of deer, unlike Lancaster County. When John turned twelve, Dad bought him a twelve-gauge shotgun. When I turned twelve, Dad bought me a Remington twenty-gauge shotgun, which had less power. I don't know why he bought me a "smaller" gun, but I didn't complain. We hunted ring-necked pheasants and rabbits in the hay fields and cornfields and hunted squirrels in the woods. In the 1960s, small game was far more plentiful in Lancaster County than later on. I think the legal limit for rabbits was four per day. I am sure that the limit for pheasants was only two. However, a certain young Amish man who was a neighbor of ours, shot eight pheasants in one day. He should have been arrested for that, but I know for a fact that he was not.

When I was growing up, deer were nonexistent in northern and central Lancaster County where we lived and were even very scarce in southern Lancaster County, twelve or fifteen miles away. We had never seen or heard of a deer having been seen on our farm, or at any of our neighbor's farms. However, on a typical hot summer day when the neighborhood men were at our farm helping with the annual wheat threshing, something very surprising happened. Stevie Esh had been out in the field, forking wheat bundles onto the wagon when he looked way out across neighbor Henry's hayfield, quite a distance away. What he saw made him drop his fork and run in toward our barn where the other men were working. He was waving his arms and yelling, obviously extremely excited, so much that his brother Jesse jokingly wondered if Stevie had been choking on his wad of chewing tobacco. What Stevie had seen was a full-grown deer standing out in Henry's field, which might be considered equivalent to seeing Bigfoot or Sasquatch. That certainly provided for some excited conversation a little later during the lunch meal.

Life in the Lancaster County Amish community in the 1960s was generally quite peaceful and tranquil. It was not uncommon for Amish boys, who were at least twelve years old and had a valid hunting license, to walk through the fields hunting with their shotguns on their way to school in the morning. Of course, when they arrived, they would keep the guns at school, although safely unloaded and properly put away. Imagine any English student bringing a shotgun to school nowadays! And, that it was actually okay for him to do that!

Small game hunting season only lasted for the month of November each year, plus an additional week over the New Year holidays. During my teenage years, my brothers and I sometimes were involved with another "sport," trapping muskrats along the little stream that flowed through Henry's south meadow.

An old man named Ferree Erb lived at the one-horse town of Vintage on the south side of Harristown Hill. He always bought whatever muskrats that my brothers or other Amish boys caught. He had been doing that for about fifty or sixty years. His name surely was more familiar to many local Amish, including myself, then the names of John Kennedy or Lyndon Johnson. Of course, Mr. Erb's first name was always mispronounced Free, rather than Ferree.

Brother John once trapped a raccoon, from which he made a genuine coonskin cap, just like Daniel Boone had done. He did the whole procedure very carefully and precisely and was quite pleased with the result, as he had a right to be. Before we were old enough to have guns, we had homemade bows and arrows and slingshots. We'd shoot at birds or rabbits with them, but I don't think we ever killed any rabbits that way.

One Sunday afternoon, my parents and I were visiting some friends in the New Holland area. While hanging out in the woods with their boys, I saw a branch on a cherry tree that I thought would make a good bow. I climbed up and broke it off and took it home in Dad's carriage and made an excellent bow from it and it served me well for a long time.

In the summertime, John and I would often walk three-quarters of a mile to Pequea Creek and swim there, along with Leroy Esh's boys, Dave and Sam. Usually, it was on a Saturday evening and our swim there was considered to be our "bath" for the week, even though Leroy's cows had already befouled and contaminated the water by doing what cows do while wading in creeks which is, using it for their own personal bathroom! We also fished there at times, using our homemade "tree-branch" fishing rods to catch bluegills, catfish and sunnies. We'd take them home and clean them and Mom would cook them for the family supper. Dale Frankhouser, an English boy who lived by Osceola Mill, fished with us sometimes. We were envious of his modern fishing rod and reel but we never had similar ones during all of our childhood and teenage years because we were Amish and we were poor!

CHAPTER SEVENTEEN

Wheat Threshing
and the Forbidden Tractor

THE ENTIRE DAY AND night of November 22, 1963, and well into the next day was, for our family, very normal and mundane. It may seem almost unbelievable, but we didn't know anything about the assassination of President John F. Kennedy until twenty-two hours later at about 9:30 A.M. the next day. Even though we were at school when it happened, there was nothing there that could inform us of that tragic event, no radio, no television, no telephone, no car radio, no cell phone, and certainly no Internet. Even Willis, our friendly English neighbor who only lived about two hundred yards away, did not come to our house to tell us. He probably thought it would not be of major importance to us.

The next morning, George Steffy, the truck driver who picked up our milk every day, told Dad about the assassination, in the milk house by the end of the barn. We were all very shocked about it, of course. We were at home because it was a Saturday. Most of us, including myself, didn't even know who the vice president was. Someone asked Brother Aaron, who was considered to be the history or political buff in our family, and he said some guy named Lyndon Johnson was already the new president. We were surprised that such an important transition could have occurred so quickly when, in reality, he had already been sworn in nineteen hours earlier. Since we were all very curious about it, Dad, at our urging, immediately started a subscription to the daily newspaper, the Lancaster Intelligencer Journal.

Of course, we never saw or heard any coverage of it whatsoever on TV or radio. At that time, no one at our house even *had* a radio because Brother Amy had passed away the previous year and my three oldest brothers were now all married and not living at home any longer. Brother John and I were still so young that neither of us had yet purchased our first radio. We were all shocked that President Kennedy's assassination could have happened the way it did in the modern era of the sixties. However, because of our sheltered nature and lifestyle it was not considered to be nearly as big an event in the Amish community as it was to English people.

Back then it was quite common for milk truck drivers who hauled Amish farmer's milk to be the bearer of important news. There was another morning when George Steffy had done that when Dad and Mom's first grandchild was born to Brother Jake and sister- in- law Arie. George had stopped there earlier to pick up Jake's milk. Since none of us had phones, Jake told him to be sure to tell Dad when he arrived at our farm later, about the baby's birth. When George arrived, he greeted Dad in our milk house, saying "Hi, Grandpa." Of course, Dad and the rest of us were excited and pleased to hear about the new baby. I was also mildly excited that I was now already an uncle at only nine years of age.

Something else that interested me was George's big milk truck, and how he expertly drove it and backed it around the barnyard. At the time, I doubted that I would ever drive something that big. In fact, it was not till several years later that I first felt fairly certain that I would someday drive a car, even if perhaps for just a few moments. I had an obsession to watch TV before I became obsessed with driving a car, undoubtedly because I thought that was far more likely to happen.

One Sunday afternoon when I was eleven years old, my parents and sister and I went to visit some friends in Kirkwood. My school classmate, Ben, and his parents were visiting there also. Our friend, David, whose family we were visiting, had promised Ben and me that there was an older, single English lady who lived close by, who would let us come to watch TV at her house if we wanted to. Well, of course, we wanted to. There was no question about that. Especially, since we had all been emphatically taught that it is always unquestionably wrong and even sinful for any Amish person to watch TV So, it didn't even matter what we might watch, because we knew watching anything on TV would be exciting, even commercials. Of course, we had no knowledge whatsoever of the programming schedule. Without any of our parents knowing, we walked to her house and David eagerly rang her doorbell. When we told her why we were there, she seemed a bit surprised. She declined and told us no, even though we tried some mild pleading. We were slightly perplexed and more than slightly disappointed that she would deny us a little bit of innocent pleasure like that, as we trudged glumly back to David's house.

According to folklore handed down through our family, my grandfather, Benuel Fisher, bought two acres of woodland in the Welsh Mountains more than one hundred years ago, for one dollar per acre. The Welsh Mountains were five miles north of our farm and almost all of its few residents were poor black people. Every few years when I was growing up, Dad and John and I would, on a fine summer day, hitch up two of the draft horses to the big flatbed farm wagon. Then we'd go over to that woodland to cut small trees to use for fence posts on the farm. It was certainly more fun than working in the fields in the hot sun, and overall was a neat experience, although Dad would have trouble remembering exactly where the little parcel of woodland was located. It was not far from where Ike "Peggy" Boots lived in his shabby old tarpaper shack. Peggy was an older black man who had a wooden leg and that's why he had that nickname. He had lost his leg at the age of fifteen when a freight train had run over it as he tried to climb aboard the moving train. Peggy would sometimes drive down from the mountains into our neighborhood, and to our house with his pony and two-wheeled cart, peddling the wild huckleberries and blackberries that he had found on the mountain.

The most famous (or infamous) residents of the mountain were the notorious Buzzard brothers who often victimized Amish farmers by stealing their horses and chickens during their nocturnal forays. Even though they were caught and jailed several times, it seemed they were always able and willing to *come back for more!*

In the summertime, Dad raised chickens in a field about a quarter of a mile from the barn. They'd be kept at that distance so they wouldn't wander back to the barn. There were two moveable tin covered shacks called rain shelters which they stayed in at night. During the day, the chickens roamed around the fields. About three hundred little chicks were initially put out, and later in the year, they'd be brought into the henhouse and would start providing eggs for our family. While they were still out in the field, one of us would go out and feed them every day. Several times, some wild marauding dogs attacked and killed a lot of them at night and left a bloody carnage. There were also a few times when a lot of them got sick and died of disease.

Life on an Amish dairy farm involves a lot of extremely hard and boring work. I think the worst of it is milking and taking care of all the cows. Even though the Amish now have milking machines, there's still a lot of lifting required, pouring the milk buckets into a large container. When you factor in the cows switching their tails as much as they do, and the strong and bad smell of the manure, and all the work involved cleaning it out regularly, it's definitely not a job for the weak or faint hearted. We had to clean out the gutter behind the cows the Amish way, which was loading the manure onto a big steel wheelbarrow with a shovel. There was a sloping wooden ramp on which we'd wheel the heavy wheelbarrow loads of manure up high enough so that it could be dumped directly into a manure spreader.

One day as I was doing that, something very disgusting happened. I was pushing hard on the wheelbarrow handles and going as fast as I could, so I'd have enough momentum to get it to the top of the ramp. The ramp was slippery from rain and suddenly, while pushing so hard, my feet flew out behind me. You guessed it, my face went forward and straight down into the heavily loaded wheelbarrow that was piled high with fresh cow manure. I immediately found out that smelling cow manure from a few feet away is nothing compared to dunking your face in it, which is what I had just done. It was an almost over-powering and nauseating smell. With manure all over my eyes, nose and mouth, I was furiously cursing a mixture of Amish and English. I hurried over to the milk house, groping and fumbling my way as best I could because I couldn't see very well. I can unequivocally assure you I used plenty of water and paper towels to get that horrid stuff off my face and was also more careful pushing the wheelbarrow later!

When I "graduated" from eighth grade in 1965, I helped at our farm and at other neighbor's farms for the first time with the annual wheat threshing that summer. There were teams of four, loading the bundles of wheat onto the wagon with pitchforks, with two loading and two stacking. Of course, we were barefoot and always wore long black pants. Sometimes there were lots of horse nettles and jagged, thorny, weeds that we stepped on which would really hurt our feet.

An example of cruelty from an Amish "boss" against his hired boy was when Johnny B. made Brother Jake shock wheat by himself for three straight days while lazy Johnny sat on the horse-pulled weeder all that time. Shocking wheat is very hard and hot work, stacking thousands of wheat bundles in the field, while always wearing long sleeves. On the third night while lying in bed and rejoicing that he was finally done, Jake heard Johnny and a neighbor farmer down on the porch, planning for him to shock wheat at the neighbors farm the next day! *Four straight days* working by himself, doing such brutal labor was genuine cruelty which even slaves should never be forced to do.

The wheat harvest took about ten days at five or six different Amish farms. The host farmer would have to be up in the straw mow with about three or four horses and mules. They had to keep walking around to pack the straw down as it came flying out of the blower at the top of the antique threshing machine.

When the straw mow was so full that the horses were practically touching the rafters of the barn with their backs, it then became time to get them down to the barn floor again. A huge amount of straw would be pushed down on the floor and they would be pushed, prodded and "encouraged" to take about a twenty-foot slide on their haunches down to the floor. Since they were tired, hot and extremely dusty, it did not take much coaxing for them to do that.

Pappy Dave Esh's old steel wheeled Huber tractor would be roaring away outside the barn, supplying power to the thresher by a long thick belt about forty feet long. My brothers and I dreaded when the threshing was done at Brother Aaron's farm. One of the straw mows in his barn was a despised and horrendous place that everybody called the Dungeon. That's because it had a flat roof and was cramped and hard to walk around in, while at the same time chasing the horses and mules, always in extremely dusty conditions.

Whenever I helped with the threshing at the neighbors, they paid Dad directly for the work I did. In 1965, they paid him fifty cents per hour for my services and I didn't get any of it. Several benefits that I *did* get were the hard work that kept me in tremendous physical shape, and the scrumptious meals we always got when threshing wheat or filling the silos.

There often were several plastic gallon containers of homemade iced tea placed along the edge of the field that we could drink from. But there were also similar looking plastic jugs which contained gasoline for the tractor or the engine on the corn binder. One day Jesse Esh's hired boy, Ammon, grabbed a jug that he thought had tea in it, and took a big gulp. Unfortunately, it was not tea, it was gasoline instead. He said it tasted terrible and it took a long time before he could get rid of that awful taste. He soon found out he didn't perform nearly as well on unleaded gas as he did on iced tea!

Since I had had a major obsession with all things self-propelled since my childhood, Pappy Dave's big green tractor fascinated me immensely. Dave was the patriarch of the threshing crew. His three sons, Stevie, Leroy, and Jesse all had farms along East Pequea Lane, about a mile south of us. They were all congenial and well-liked and were considered model neighbors. Dave was about seventy years old and was the only one who drove the tractor, pulling the thresher from one farm to the next. He'd drive extremely slowly and carefully, always easing that hand clutch into gear very gently. I always yearned for the opportunity to drive the tractor, even if perhaps for just a few feet. So, one day when Pappy was not there, Stevie asked me to move the tractor ahead a little bit. I literally jumped at the chance, and in a few seconds, I was up on the tractor. I put it into gear, revved it up quite a bit and quickly pushed that hand clutch forward, forgetting how slowly Pappy always did it. That tractor undoubtedly had the surprise of its life, as it sprang forward. Stevie yelled at me and told me I was lucky Pappy wasn't watching because he would have really scolded me.

One evening Pappy drove the tractor and thresher to Aaron's farm, and set it up in preparation for threshing the next day. I was staying there overnight, since I was his hired boy at the time. I was really hoping Pappy would just let the tractor by itself and not connect it to the belt yet that evening. Pappy probably expected me to drive it or mess around with it so, possibly to discourage me, he *did* connect the forty-foot-long belt to the thresher before he left. Early the next morning when I should have been helping Aaron with the milking, I was secretly back behind the barn messing around with the tractor. I was happy that I could at least start it up because Pappy always left the key in the ignition. I fully planned on undoing the belt and driving it around, if only for just a minute or so. I can't possibly describe how hard it was to overcome that temptation, but eventually I reluctantly decided not to. It was only because I was very much afraid I wouldn't be able to connect the tractor to the belt again by myself. And I sure didn't want anybody to know what I had been doing.

Most Amish farmers are not nearly as careful and concerned about safety with horse-drawn equipment as they should be. There have been many instances when very young boys and teenagers have been killed or seriously injured in various runaway horse accidents. And, also in accidents involving engine powered and semi-mechanical ground driven farm equipment.

Something that occasionally happened to Brother Benuel, as an eleven-year-old, was both dangerous and cruel. At Uncle Eli Miller's farm, where he worked as a hired boy, he had to stand alone inside the fifty-foot-tall silo and walk on and pack down the silage as it flew out of the steel pipe, far above him and down around and on top of him. As the men fed the bundles of corn into the cutting machine outside, he could not see or hear them, and they could not see or hear him, because of the loud noise of the machinery. This went on for a period of several hours. Had he fainted or lost consciousness for any reason during that time, he would soon have been buried alive under the silage and would surely have suffocated. If any boss made a hired boy do that nowadays, he should be prosecuted for child endangerment and cruelty.

My cousin, Willie, lost his right hand when it was almost torn off in a corn picker accident. Sadly, it had to be amputated at the wrist and he always wore a prosthesis after that. Our neighbor, Jesse Esh, was hurt very seriously and almost died after falling from high up inside his barn late one evening while hanging tobacco. His grandfather, Stephen Esh, a bishop, was killed many years ago after falling from the top of a silo during corn harvesting season. Another man, Eli, from Kirkwood, was terribly mutilated and killed in a most horrifying accident when he was pulled partly into the corn chopper at the silo, where they were filling it with corn. He was pulled into the cutting machine, feet first, all the way to his groin area before he could push the handle that stopped the machine. There seemed to be no possibility he could survive such a dreadful accident. An ambulance was called, but because of being so far away in a rural area, about forty minutes had passed before it arrived. Sadly, by then he had passed away. He left behind his wife and seven young children. In another tragic and heartbreaking incident, two Amish teenage brothers died inside a corn silo after breathing in toxic silage gases. Their father almost died too, as he was trying to rescue them.

CHAPTER EIGHTEEN

Analyzing the Ordnung and Craving Freedom

WHEN I WAS STILL VERY young, of course, I realized that we Amish people were very different from the English folks. In our culture, everybody except the Amish and Mennonites are called English. This goes back to when the Amish first arrived in America, in the early 1700s. Possibly, many of the non-Amish then *were* of English origin. So, three hundred years later, the Amish still call them English, whether they really are or not. For simplicity's sake, I also do that in this book. Whenever I talk about English people, I simply mean non-Amish or non-Mennonite. We were told that all of the Amish themselves, are of German, Swiss or French origin. I believe the ancestors of our immediate family came from Germany or France.

Mom often used the ancient term, "Das alt landt," [The Old Land] when referring to the European homeland of our ancestors. She also called it Deutsch-land, which is Germany. We believe two of our ancestors arrived in Philadelphia aboard the ship, Charming Nancy, on Oct. 8, 1737. Mom told us that our great-great-great grandfather Christian Miller, along with five brothers [one of whom was named Pierre, while the others' names are unknown] arrived in America about 1790. Christian was the only brother who settled in Pennsylvania and the others all moved to Ohio or Indiana. That's why there are not many Amish named Miller living in Pa., and why Miller is a very common Amish name in Ohio and Indiana. The brother's parent's, Louis and Mary [Sommers] Muller [Miller] stayed in Europe and apparently never came to America at all.

As a young boy, I naturally assumed that I'd grow up and join the Amish church and stay Amish my whole life, just like all my relatives. Of course, I knew that was certainly expected of me. But I was never thrilled by that prospect, even at a young age. I started to grasp what life would be like if one had all the modern conveniences that we didn't have, and I was very intrigued by those thoughts. I remember as a young child sitting in the cramped back seat of my parent's horse-drawn carriage, with two of my siblings, looking out the open back window. We'd see a car approaching us from the rear, and in an amazingly short time, it would be whizzing past us. Also, in an amazingly short time, it would be far ahead of us. Meanwhile we would be plodding along at about seven or eight miles per hour, accompanied to the boring, clip, clop sound of the horse's hoofs on the road.

At a young age, I was very much intrigued by the idea of having a radio. By the time I was ten, I was sure that someday I'd have a radio, even though it would have to be a battery-operated model, since we didn't have electricity. I probably also knew, at least subconsciously, that I would someday drive a car, a thought that occupied my mind much of the time! As far as being daring enough to plan on someday *owning* a car, that was not until several years later.

The Amish call cars machines. One car is called a machine, while two or more cars (plural) are called "machina." Sometimes you'd hear the term "machina geisht," which meant someone with that condition was obsessed with cars. I suppose I got the machina geisht pretty early in life. Of course, I had to keep those thoughts well hidden. My parents would have been horrified if they knew I was thinking like that. And, if any of us kids had ever dared to ask why we don't have cars and TVs and electricity like English people, the answer would simply have been, "Because we're Amish," implying that there's nothing more to discuss. And if we had pressed the issue, we'd have been sternly rebuked. And, of course, we never, ever talked about whether the Ordnung and the Amish way of life was necessary and legitimate. We just *knew* that it was absolutely right and necessary for all of us.

I believe most Amish parent's top priority is to see all their children join the Amish church and stay Amish for the rest of their lives. They are taught in a subtle way that since they were born Amish, they have a permanent absolute, unarguable, distinct, and definite duty and responsibility to stay Amish throughout their whole life. They are taught that anyone not born Amish is exempted from that requirement. Never mind that no one has any control over what situation they are born into!

On rare occasions, a non- Amish orphan child has been raised by an Amish family. If that child decided to never join their church, the parents would be disappointed, even sad, but they would not consider that decision to be sinful, only because the child had not been born Amish. But, Amish-born children are taught to believe that it *is* sinful if *they* don't join. Still, if the orphan child *does* decide to join and later leaves, he would still be shunned and excommunicated. How can such twisted "reasoning" really be fair?

A certain Amish father had the tragic misfortune of five of his children dying in various ways. He had another child who had left the Amish church. The father told an English friend that burying the five children who had died, did not cause him and his wife as much grief as losing the one who had "strayed" and gone "English."

Most English people would be shocked and appalled that any parent could feel that way and make that statement. It illustrates to what totally irrational degree some Amish consider the importance of their children staying Amish. I think that statement is almost the same as him saying he would prefer to have even *more* of his children die than to see them leave the church. If he really felt that way, someone should tell him, "BE CAREFUL WHAT YOU WISH FOR." And that God just might allow that to happen as his punishment for saying that.

Even though I don't have six children, I would rather see *five* children leave the Amish, than to have *one* child die. Especially, if the five who left were all devoted Christians, and especially if the one who died was not saved.

I believe one strategy that Amish parents use to keep their children "in the fold," is to avoid ever talking with them whether leaving the Amish might be a legitimate option. This way the parents can appear completely horrified if and when the wayward one has enough nerve to bring it up for discussion. Certainly, parents feel that it's a "saeya," or blessing when children meekly and willingly join the church without requiring any persuasion. Personally, during my preteen years I never dared to seriously consider "going English" because that was thought to be extremely sinful and radical.

Amish parents often beg wayward and unwilling teenage sons to become baptized and to join the church. Of course, you *can't do one without the other*, so it becomes an *extremely* important decision. Parents will sometimes offer rewards if they join but threaten punishment if they don't. And, many parents think that when a son leaves the Amish church, it is practically the worst thing that could happen to him. Ironically, on the other hand, the son usually thinks it is the best thing that's ever happened to him!

There are several reasons why parents become very distraught when a son leaves. One is, they're afraid that he will live a wicked and sinful life and will probably go to hell when he dies, even though the vast majority of ex-Amish go on and live exemplary Christian lives. It's also humiliating to the parents, knowing that many others will privately blame them and think they had not been strict enough with the straying one. And if they don't shun him as much as some people think they should, they will at least privately be criticized for that.

When I eventually started to have serious thoughts of leaving the Amish, there were some very sobering thoughts I had to consider. For one thing, none of my brothers or sisters have ever left the Amish church, and I'm sure that none ever will. In fact, none of my thirty-five cousins on Mom's side of the family has ever left the Amish either. Even more amazingly, none (other than me) of Grandad Jacob Miller's total of approximately two thousand descendants (and counting) has ever left the Amish church, as far as I know. Of course, nobody likes to be considered evil or a renegade among such a large family group which, of course, happened to me when I left. I'm sure they have long considered me to be the black sheep, not only of my immediate family, but also of the entire family tree.

My parents always tried their best to raise all of us to be faithful and devout Amish, as they were. Dad had a very fine reputation for obeying the Ordnung faithfully, although he was not faultless. At his funeral sermon in 2002, he was called a post, or pillar, of the church and that certainly was considered to be high praise.

As small children, we were taught to say a little prayer to the "Gute Mann," (Good Man) Jesus, when we went to bed at night. And we were taught to greatly fear the "Veesht Mann," (wicked man) Satan, and to do our best to not yield to his evil temptations.

Family prayer time consisted of us kneeling at chairs or at the sofa before going to bed. Dad would get his little old black German prayer book out of the third drawer of the combine, where it was always kept. He'd read aloud the same prayer each time. It would take about three or four minutes. Often, some of us children would fall asleep while he was reading it. Also, there were many times when Dad came remarkably close to falling asleep himself. His voice would trail off drastically and become extremely slow and weak and faint. But he always managed to finish it! I don't fault him at all for the times he almost fell asleep, because he was a hard-working Amish farmer.

However, while I'm on the subject of praying out loud, I'll mention something that I remember very well. It's something that has always bothered me.

The bishop in our home church district had a very unusual way of reading the closing prayer in church. While the whole congregation was kneeling, he'd read aloud a certain German prayer. It was always the same prayer, as according to church traditions. It should have taken about five minutes to read. Soon after he began, he'd always start to read extremely fast and would continue like that until the end. He would literally read absolutely as fast as he could, faster even than the swiftest and most gifted auctioneers could speak. I always thought it was very rude and irreverent, especially since he also did it in a very loud tone of voice. I understand that at the end of a three-hour long church service, everybody would be more than ready for it to end. But, to end it like that was shameful and surely not pleasing to God. It was like speed reading out loud. When I think of it nowadays, it reminds me of the "compressed speed read" radio ads we sometimes hear which are spoken so fast that they're literally impossible to understand. Also, it's important to recognize that he was the bishop in that church district. The bishop is literally the leader of the congregation and is looked up to, even more than the other ministers. I wonder if anybody ever complained to him about his "speed-reading." Maybe nobody dared to *because* he was the bishop. However, he was disciplined several times by the church "elders" for other times that he misbehaved.

There was at least one time that this bishop (who is now deceased) had to confess on his knees, while crying with great contrition and remorsefulness in front of the church congregation, that he had failed. I remember hearing him dramatically shouting," "Schmysset mich nauss mitt de hunda vonn dah vellet!" ["Throw me out with the dogs if you want to!"] The event where he had misbehaved happened at a Sunday night singing at his house for the young folks in Rumspringa. Some uninvited boys from another gang came and started misbehaving. I don't know what they did, but the bishop reacted very badly. He ran out and, during the ensuing argument, struck one boy in his eye with a metal flashlight, causing a very serious eye injury. There was great fear that he'd have permanent eye damage, but he eventually fully recovered.

There was another incident when this bishop used extremely poor judgement which resulted in one of his driver horses almost dying. One Sunday morning, he and his family were going to be very late at church. So, he yelled loudly and really whipped the Palomino horse and made him run at full speed. They had traveled a long way and when they arrived the horse was beyond exhausted and possibly near death. He collapsed on the ground and had a lot of foamy white sweat over his body, while heaving and gasping huge breaths of air into his lungs. Even though I was just a young lad, I vividly remember seeing two men pouring bucketsful of water over him to cool him down. Fortunately, he soon appeared to be okay. I doubt if anyone even scolded the bishop for that.

On a lighter note, he took his preaching very seriously and sometimes practiced it on the road. One Sunday morning, he and his wife were traveling in their carriage to a church service in another district, at his brother-in-law's house. As is Amish custom, when a minister is visiting at another district, he knows he will be preaching there later that morning. As they drove along, an unseen Amish man was in a cornfield close to the road, searching for a missing calf that had wandered away from the barn. He was astonished to hear the bishop loudly practicing his sermon as he drove by. I don't know if the bishop ever found out that someone had secretly heard his sermon rehearsal!

I often wondered if any of my brothers, who were all older than me, had ever been as obsessed with cars as I was. One day, Brother Jake, who was twenty-eight years old at the time, told me that he had never moved a car an inch, and that he was glad he hadn't. I'm sure he felt that if he had, he'd have become addicted to driving cars and he certainly didn't want that to happen. As for myself, I felt as though I might almost go crazy if I never drove a car, so strong was the "machina geisht" in me. I wondered if I was just inherently eviler than him, for being as "car-crazy" as I was. I sometimes wonder if now, more than fifty years later, he has always continued to be glad about never moving a car even an inch. An interesting comparison is that I, on the other hand, have driven approximately four million miles in my lifetime. That's because I drove a tractor-trailer truck for quite a long time.

Dad told us the only time he had any control of a moving car was when he, as a teenager, was riding with a neighbor boy, Gene. He was the son of Ed Fenninger, who my grandfather, Benuel, had bought the farm from many years ago. Gene was driving his old Tin Lizzie Model T, or whatever it was, into the driveway. He let Dad reach over and hold the steering wheel for a few moments and may have even let him turn it a little. I doubt that Dad was a member of the church yet, as that surely would have been very much frowned upon.

I remember something else that Dad told me when I was still Amish. I'm sure he fully expected me to always stay Amish or he wouldn't have told it to me. He said an elderly Amish friend of his, Stephen, had told him that, by his own experience, even when an Amish person gets much older in life, the temptation and desire to have "worldly" things does not diminish. Dad didn't say if he himself agreed with that, but I certainly have always agreed.

When I was fifteen, on a Sunday afternoon while visiting at my cousin Johnny Miller's house, he told me there was a packer parked along the road by their hay field with the key in the ignition. I thought he said Packard, meaning the car model Packard, from the 1940s era. I immediately had fond hopes of starting it up and driving it. At my urging, we walked out to where it was parked. I was extremely disappointed to see that it was a packer, and not a Packard. It was a small engine-driven road paving machine with smooth round rollers to roll over and pack new pavement. Apparently, it had been left there by some township workers. "O, bummer," I thought, "no illicit car driving for me today." And, no, I was not tempted to take it for a "joy ride" because its top speed was probably only about three miles per hour.

Due to recent amazing advances in technology, it is now widely expected that self-driving cars will be fairly common in the not-too-distant future. Is it possible that the Amish bishops would allow those, since no one would be driving? An interesting idea, but I would caution them to not get their hopes up. Could it also be that someday there may be genetically modified and enhanced horses capable of much higher than normal speeds? If so, it seems the bishops would hardly dare to prohibit those either, as there would be no logical rationale for that. The "super-horse" idea may not be as far-fetched as it sounds, considering that scientists have already "created" various cloned animals. Since the difference between a horse and a car's top speed is a "quantum leap," (to say the least) that might seem to be the most "workable" solution for the future, so long as the bishops continue to prohibit cars.

In addition to my pervasive interest in cars, I was interested in an even faster mode of transportation. Yes, that would be airplanes. One Saturday we went to the Philadelphia Zoo, on a fine summer day when I was eleven years old. An English driver took us that day, of course. We talked about stopping near Philadelphia International Airport on the way home, to watch some jet planes taking off or coming in for a landing. I was excited about that, of course. Unfortunately, we did not go that way after all, so I didn't get to watch any jet planes up close. I was disappointed but we did have a lot of fun at the zoo that day.

That day at the zoo was considered to be our summer "vacation." Amish people largely reject the idea of vacations because they're thought to be worldly and unnecessary and any farmer who took a week's vacation might be considered naughty and undisciplined. And, besides, Amish people seem to be obsessed with doing a huge amount of hard work, as long as their health permits it. Otherwise, relatives and neighbors would consider them lazy (or FAUL, in Amish lingo) and that would be hugely damaging to their reputation. They often think they should work at a frenetic pace even during their "golden" retirement years. An Amish friend in his seventies, Abe, had worked diligently at a lumber yard for *fifty-two* years and wanted to continue, but his family finally persuaded him to quit. It was reliably claimed he had not a single lazy bone in his body! And, as my seventy-six-year-old cousin morosely said, while still working fulltime in an Amish "factory," "What else would I do, anyway?" Most Amish feel the same way, because the Ordnung prohibits much of what many retired Americans do, such as playing golf and other sports, traveling, watching TV, internet surfing and attending cultural, educational and civic events. Or, just doing what they WANT to do, a "luxury option" that the Amish don't have! And, speaking of vacations, I think possibly the best vacation/staycation that Amish parents could arrange for their teenagers would be to have them stay with a typical non-Amish family for a week. Then they'd realize how *amazingly* different the two lifestyles really are!

A typical Amish farmer spends many thousands of hours working in his fields during his lifetime, planting, weeding, cultivating, and harvesting crops such as corn, tobacco, hay, wheat and potatoes. The church forbids them to use the modern machinery that non-Amish farmers use. Therefore, the machinery and methods they use for planting and harvesting are much slower and much more labor intensive.

My parents bought the old Yonie Beiler (Coony) farm just south of Intercourse in 1959, so my oldest brother, Jake and his family lived and farmed there from 1960 to 1966. Then, Jake and Arie bought a farm of their own near Christiana, about ten miles away, and moved there. My next brother, Aaron and his family then lived and farmed at the Intercourse farm.

I worked there as a hired boy for Aaron during the years 1967 to 1971, except for the year 1969, when I worked at the home farm with Dad. Even though Aaron was a good boss and treated me fairly, it was extremely hard work. Also, it was extremely boring, which should be expected at any Amish farm. And, to make things worse, Dad never paid me, praised me, or thanked me for all the work I did at either of the farms. I never even knew how much Aaron paid him for my services. And I surely was taught to believe that hard, menial Amish farm work was more appropriate and more honorable than the easy, "city-fied" life of the English folks. Also, because the Amish lifestyle is so restricted, they feel that *work* is a good form of "entertainment!" But, of course, all that extra work makes their lives even more busy and burdensome. It's sad and astonishing that almost all Amish farmers "willingly" forego modern machinery, and then must exert an enormous amount of physical energy to plant, cultivate and harvest all their crops.

While growing up Amish, it seemed the three most important things in life to my dad were that we would all stay Amish, we'd work hard every day, and that he could be and would be an "effective" Amish role model to us. Indeed, he always seemed to be fully content living the Amish lifestyle. But if any of us siblings ever even *considered* leaving the Amish, that alone would surely have been considered radical and sinful.

The farm just north of Aaron's farm was owned by an ex-Amish farmer, Gid Stoltzfus. Of course, he used all the modern farming machinery that was available while we always used horses hitched to very primitive machinery. We never saw Gid or any of his family hoeing weeds in his fields like we constantly seemed to be doing. He sprayed his fields with modern weed killer which, of course, we didn't do. That's why we had so many weeds in our fields.

I believe it is Amish farmers' philosophy that it's good to have so many weeds to hoe because that would tend to keep the boys busy and out of trouble, and not following worldly pursuits like cars and radios. I often watched Gid drive rapidly through his fields on his tractor at a much faster speed than we ever could with our slow old work horses. I calculated that farming the modern way like Gid did, required only about ten to twenty % as much labor and physical energy as doing it the Amish way. I grimly told myself that our Amish style of farming was just so much foolish, self-inflicted torture. And, surely, the hardest working farmers in history, indeed, *are* Amish farmers!

The Amish must always wear long black pants, no matter how hot the weather is. Sometimes I pondered what might be the best solution for that onerous requirement. So, one sweltering day after lunch, I had a most welcome epiphany moment. I soaked my shirt and long black pants in the horses watering trough, and it felt wonderful when I then wore them soaking wet, out in the fields. Brother Aaron was astonished when I did that, but he did not object. We were never allowed to wear shorts, and always went barefoot in the summertime, except on Sundays at church.

I think the worst part of Amish farming was the interminable long days, weeks, and months that we spent out in the fields in the hot sun. All my brothers and I had to start working in the fields when we were about seven years old. Along with Dad, we'd be hoeing weeds, and pulling weeds by hand and planting and harvesting all the crops. Often it would be in ninety-degree heat or higher. Even the ground and loose soil that we walked on with our bare feet would be uncomfortably warm. The family dog wouldn't even accompany us on such boring occasions, unless horse-drawn wagons and farm implements were being used. Once in a great while I'd find an Indian arrowhead to add to my collection.

On a scorching, sweltering day, Dad, Lydia, and I were spearing tobacco at the Coony farm, where Aaron's lived. We had no water and eventually I got so hot I thought I might have a heatstroke. Lydia and I begged Dad to go to Push's John's house for water, only about a hundred yards away. Eventually, he did so and when Sarah came out with that pitcher full of precious, life-sustaining water, I was annoyed that instead of "guzzling" directly from it as I had planned, we had to take turns and drink from a cup. Those extra few seconds seemed like a long wait for me!

Sometimes, very dry weather in the springtime would make it hard to disk and harrow the soil finely enough to properly plant the crops. The dry weather would turn some of the soil into huge clumps of extremely hard earth, or "groont shulla," as we called them. They were sometimes as large as a person's head.

One day when John and I were working near Henry's fields we saw two of his sons, Henry, Jr and Moses attacking and waging war on those detestable "groont shulla" with a sledgehammer and a pickax. We called over to them and teasingly asked if they were mining for gold. They merely grinned at us and shook their heads in frustration.

Whenever we were hoeing weeds, we'd very slowly progress through long rows of corn and tobacco, and the shimmering heat waves would almost obscure the far end of the field, about a half mile away. It would have helped if I had been allowed a pocket radio but, of course, that was taboo. When a car went by in the distance, I'd wish I was in it and not hoeing weeds out in the hot sun. Sometimes I wondered if there might be a much better and more pleasant lifestyle awaiting me, far beyond the horizon. But how would I ever find out about that? Occasionally, when an airplane flew far overhead, predictably, I wished I was flying in it. Sometimes I'd see the long trailing plumes of wispy white smoke from a jet plane far, far up in the sky. On a very clear day you could see the tiny silver colored jet plane at the front of the smoke plumes. Of course, I had no clue at what altitude the plane was flying. The idea of flying many thousands of feet in the air intrigued me, even though I'd have been very afraid. After all, if the plane crashed, I had no idea if I would go to Heaven or hell, I just knew I would go to one or the other.

Years later, I learned that a relative of mine, Gideon Miller, was an airplane pilot. He grew up in Bird-in-Hand, about five miles away, and his dad was a cousin to Mom. He was the oldest child in his family and had seven younger sisters but no brothers. I suppose he was very disappointed about that. At a young age, he left the Amish and got the schooling and training he needed to become an airplane pilot, while working and paying all the expenses himself. I only ever met him once, at his sister's wedding, who married a good friend of mine. I didn't have a good opportunity to speak to him but later often wished I had talked with him about me possibly becoming a pilot myself someday.

Gideon was a veteran pilot with 33 years of experience with TWA. Sadly, he was killed in a tragic plane accident in 1996. He was on a flight from New York City to Paris when the jet plane he was in exploded and crashed over New York Harbor, under very mysterious circumstances, killing all 230 passengers. I don't believe it was ever really determined what caused the explosion. There was speculation that terrorism was involved and that a bomb had been put in the plane. In any case, it was a huge event that was in the spotlight of the national media for quite some time.

During the winter of 1969, when I was eighteen, I worked at H. M. Stauffer's in Leola making wooden building components, since work was slow on the farm at the time. A friend of mine, Ray Stoltzfus, also worked there. His parents were from the Amish, but Ray was a high-spirited guy who had a new souped-up 1969 Dodge Demon, and he drove it almost like a demon. He gave me a ride in it once in which I literally feared for my life.

What really excited and interested me was that Ray had recently gotten his pilot's license. Of course, we soon made plans to rent a small Piper Cub plane at New Holland Airport one Sunday afternoon. The cost was only $20.00 to fly it for one hour, which we split between us. Of course, I didn't tell my parents about going flying with him. They'd have been horrified and would have begged me not to do it.

My Amish buddies were at Jay Beiler's house in Bird-in-Hand that afternoon. I made sure to tell them that Ray and I would fly down low over the house and "buzz" them at a certain time. I told them to be sure to watch for us. When we took off from New Holland Airport, I was extremely excited, but also scared. Ray told me it was actually a lot safer than riding in a car, and I quickly agreed that it would be safer than riding in *his* car while *he* was driving. He merely grinned appreciatively at that remark.

I tried not to panic as the earth dropped far, far below us and soon we were thousands of feet in the air. There was some type of handhold inside the plane near the window, which I held to tightly for quite some time. I knew that wouldn't provide any safety if anything bad happened but holding on to it seemed to calm my nerves somewhat.

We headed west about ten miles to Bird-in-Hand and saw the house where I knew my buddies were. Ray took the plane down to an altitude of about three hundred feet and, sure enough, they came out of the house and waved at us. It was all very exciting, especially when Ray soon took the plane much higher. Then he did several heart-stopping dives with it, which caused me major fright for a few moments. Ray thought it was all quite funny, me not so much so. Then we headed east over Intercourse and soon were flying directly over our house and barn which was most fascinating, as I looked down. Then we continued east to the Parkesburg area and flew over the farm where Ray lived.

Then, it was back to the New Holland Airport and I was a little nervous as Ray landed the plane, but everything went fine. As we walked away from the plane, I had a distinct feeling of exhilaration as I realized that, at the tender age of eighteen, I had just done something that nobody in my family had ever done and probably also would never do in their entire lifetime!

CHAPTER NINETEEN

The Unwillingness
of the Amish Preachers

FROM MY EARLIEST MEMORIES, Uncle Ike and Aunt Emma Smoker fascinated me. That's because when they visited us, they'd be driving a car instead of a horse and buggy. When we went to visit them when I was a small child, I was intrigued by the electric lights and modern appliances in their house. One Sunday when we were there, John, Lydia, and I were playing down in the basement and I started pushing buttons on the washing machine even though I didn't even know what it was. Predictably, it started up and my siblings immediately ran upstairs to tell the grown-ups. Aunt Emma came down and turned it off and some of the folks had a good laugh about that.

Aunt Emma was Dad's oldest sister. Ike and she were Amish church members for many years before they left and joined the Beachy church or the "John A" church, as I believe it was called. Since they didn't have any children of their own, they adopted a daughter, Elsie, who later married a Mennonite man, Reuben, (Herbie) and they had a family of their own. When Ike was about fifty-five years old, he retired from his farm and started inventing and building several different types of farm machinery, including the biggest seller which was the Smoker bale elevator. He had a small factory building near their house in Intercourse, while employing twelve men, and I believe most of them were Amish.

Ike and Emma were close friends of Abe and Priscilla Stoltzfus. Abe was the oldest of six brothers, who were all Amish farmers in the Intercourse area. The brother next in line after Abe was Dan E. Stoltzfus, who happened to be the bishop in our church district. When Ike's business became much more profitable than what the bishops preferred, he was thought to have gotten "too big

124

for his britches" and Bishop Dan demanded he sell the entire business. When Ike refused to do that, a major "Sits-Gma" was called, with many bishops and ministers from other districts attending and providing their own special "advice." About twelve men from our district strongly supported Ike's refusal to sell his business. After several hours of arguing, Bishop Dan emphatically told Ike that he's ex-communicating him from the church. At that time, Abe yelled to Dan that he'd have to ex-communicate him and the whole "gang of twelve" as well, which a shocked and dismayed Dan immediately did. So, Ike and Emma and Abe and Priscilla and ten other men were ex-communicated, which was thought to be a record number for one day. It was also thought that may have been the last time Dan and Abe ever spoke to each other.

After a while, all the men "repented" and rejoined the church, except for Ike and Emma and Abe and Priscilla, and their son Gid, (our neighbor next to the Coony farm) who never rejoined. Of course, they all had cars and electricity and other modern conveniences for the rest of their lives. They always had black cars because that was a requirement of the Beachy church, which they became members of, after having been ex-communicated from the Amish church.

Aunt Emma was the oldest sibling in her family, and she had four sisters and three brothers, all of whom were always faithful members of the Amish church. Since Emma was very close to all her siblings, it must have been very painful for her to endure the life-long punishment of excommunication and shunning that she received. Especially since it is considered even more shameful when the oldest in a family "strays," as they are expected to set a proper example for the younger ones.

When an Amish person is ex-communicated and shunned it means he will no longer be allowed to eat at the same table with church members. They will refuse to ride with him in any vehicle that he is driving, even a horse-drawn buggy. They also will not accept anything that he physically tries to hand to them, even in an urgent situation. Business dealings also are not allowed. Sexual relations between husband and wife are prohibited. There are also many other forms of punishment that are practiced against the shunned one, so much that many non-Amish consider it all to be heartless, cruel and shameful. One example was when a shunned teen-age cousin of mine was not allowed to eat with his family on the day of his mother's funeral and burial. Even worse was when an ex-Amish man was not allowed to attend his older brothers' funeral!

Of course, whenever permanent ex-communication and shunning is practiced against errant church members, it creates much anger, remorse, disagreement and other mental strife, not only with the ones being ex-communicated, but also for the bishops and ministers who are "required" to impose that punishment. One reason that shunning is practiced so much, is that if those required to do it, fail to do so, they probably would be shunned or at least ostracized themselves to a certain extent. A former Amish man said that shunning works somewhat like an electric fence around a cow pasture. It keeps the animals inside and hurts them if they try to escape.

Many Amish people stay Amish for their whole life, not because they really want to but because it would be extremely painful to be permanently ex-communicated and shunned by their families, parents, siblings and others. And they often seem willing to forego the good (English) life and stay Amish, thinking that the children would then also be much less likely to leave. But if the parents themselves decided to leave, the children would likely consider them evil for doing so. And, it is incalculable how much anger and rage and shame and sorrow has occurred over the years between parents and teenagers and between bishops and church members because of the many dictatorial and senseless rules of the Ordnung. Yet there is rarely, if ever, any effort made by any bishops to reduce them or to lessen the frequency of the ugly and heartbreaking practice of shunning and ex-communication.

An Amish bishop's life is not an easy one, considering how much time and effort is often required trying to hold the congregation together and obeying all the rules and the Ordnung. It can be a very challenging and depressing role for him. Many years ago, an Amish bishop committed suicide by hanging himself in his barn one night, because of all the disciplinary problems he was facing with some church members.

When I was growing up there were five bishops in Lancaster County who were extremely well known. I believe some folks referred to them as the Famous Five. They were Bishop Dan E. Stoltzfus, from Intercourse, who ruled over our home district, Bishop "Buck" Sam Stoltzfus, who was Dad's cousin, from White Horse, Bishop Aaron Esh, from Bird-in-Hand, who preached at one hundred years of age and who baptized my mother in 1932, Bishop David Z. Fisher, the strictest bishop of all, from Nine Points and Bishop D. Ira Stoltzfus, who was my buddy Ira's grandfather, from Spring Garden. They were all grizzled and gray and far advanced in years, but all were highly respected and completely entrusted to be dedicated teachers and enforcers of the Amish Ordnung. They probably considered their life's most important duty was to preach obedience to the Ordnung in the most convincing fashion.

Uncle Ike and Aunt Emma still had a cordial, casual, relationship with our family after Bishop Dan ex-communicated them. Despite being permanently shunned, they never seemed bitter about it but were always pleasant and friendly with us. In fact, Ike was quite a jovial fellow and I liked him a lot. I envied him and Emma because of the cars and other conveniences they had. During my growing up years, the rumor in our house was that Uncle Ike was a millionaire because of his elevator manufacturing business. They had a house in Florida where they always spent their winters. I also envied them because of that.

There was another church, which was stricter than the Beachy church, that not only required all their members' cars to be black, but also the bumpers and chrome to be black. It was said, half seriously, that the black paint was required to keep the devil from shining through! Several of the Black Bumpers, as they were called, who frequently passed by our house, were "Stacky" Bawell, in his ancient 1937 Packard, and "Shorty" Lapp, in his 1961 Ford Falcon. Even though the Beachy's strongly disapproved of any tobacco usage, Shorty Aaron would frequently open his car door and spit tobacco juice out as he drove along. When asked about that, he said that when he did it that way, he could spit straight down on the road, and it would not get on the side of his car. However, I don't think any of the Beachy's grew tobacco, because they considered it to be evil.

The Canadian Amish could appear righteous and condemn tobacco, probably because their climate was too cold to grow it profitably anyway. One Canadian Amish writer complained about the tobacco that the Pennsylvania Amish grew so much of. He said, "What a useless plant, it has no branches with fruit on them, and no potatoes under the ground, so what good is it." However, it was an excellent cash crop for the Pennsylvania farmers, and they were not deterred. They grew huge amounts of it. One New Holland farmer grew about thirty acres of tobacco each year, which required a tremendous amount of work. I wonder if all that work might have had anything to do with the fact that his three sons all eventually left the Amish. I also wonder if the reason the Pennsylvania Amish bishops never condemned tobacco or prohibited growing or using it might have been because it was such a profitable cash crop! They have always considered it acceptable to chew tobacco and smoke cigars, whereas smoking a pipe was somewhat frowned upon. Cigarettes were considered even worse, unless they had dark paper on them, like the "All" brand cigarettes that the more liberal Amish often smoked. A typical cigarette with white paper wrapping was considered very worldly and hardly any Amish smoked them, except for some of the wilder single guys.

Nobody in our family ever had a smoking habit and the only time I ever saw Dad smoke was sometimes when one of us had an earache and he'd light a cigar and blow the smoke into our ears. I highly doubt that was effective!

The church Ordnung was deeply ingrained into us at a very early age and attending church was considered essentially as important as eating. A typical church service lasts three hours, and I doubt that many Amish people are even aware that is more than twice as long as non-Amish services. They are always held in the people's homes and fortunately they are held bi-weekly, not weekly. Apparently, centuries ago, Amish communities were sparsely settled and many homes were located far apart from each other. And, like now, they went by horse and buggy although sometimes then by horseback or oxcart. So, the church service back then was almost an all-day affair and only having it biweekly was certainly a logical idea.

I have never heard of an Amish person complaining about the fact that the services are only held bi-weekly. At the end of each service, Deacon Davey would always announce at who's home the next service would be held. However, he would not call them by their nickname, such as Push or Barney or Coony. He'd use their proper names and it would sound strange because otherwise, everyone always called them by their nicknames. On an "off" Sunday, the Amish are encouraged to read the German "leider buch," if they're at home. Or they can visit friends or go to a church service in another district if they want to.

Because the Ordnung allows so few forms of entertainment, Amish people probably visit each other more than any other people in the world. They feel that the strong comradery and affection they have for each other easily outweighs the inconvenience of not having modern things. But if cars and TV and "artificial" music are ever allowed, I'm sure they would then visit each other much less.

On "off-Sundays," Mom often tried to get us to read the German leider-buch after our morning barn chores were done. But my brothers and I would flee to the refuge of our upstairs bedroom to read Outdoor Life (a hunting magazine) or The Sporting News, or listen to our radios (turned very low, of course, so our parents couldn't hear them through the large heat register in the ceiling. We had the secret code word "moop" for our radios, so if our parents happened to hear us say that word, they wouldn't know what it meant!

Possibly because of their plain appearance, many non-Amish people think the Amish are stronger Christians and have a closer relationship with God than other people. But I don't believe that, as I have gotten to know many Amish and non-Amish families quite well. The fact that Amish people have far fewer possessions and less access to a worldly lifestyle, certainly doesn't mean they will necessarily be closer to God. The Amish people who are "content" with their church and its Ordnung, might not dream and obsess very much about the forbidden things they cannot have. But many crave and think a lot about other things, such as that expensive farm they're hoping to buy, those high-yielding farm crops they grow, and the carefully bred dairy herd which is constantly being pushed to produce as much as possible. And for those who are not farmers, many practically "worship" some things that they do have, as much as "English" people might worship English things. Like English people, many also have objection-able habits such as drinking, smoking and indulging in boisterous and crude language, although there would seldom be actual profanity. And, some have for many years disregarded, disobeyed and circumvented municipal laws such as ensuring adequate visibility and lighting for their buggies and having proper sewage disposal facilities where they live, in addition to many other infractions of various local ordinances. In fact, many who flout those laws, seem to think they're justified in doing that just *because* they're Amish!

I believe that many Amish fathers do kneel down with their family at bedtime while he reads from the German prayer book, as Dad did. But, other than the "silent grace" that Amish families observe at mealtimes, I've never known of any Amish families who have family prayer time in the morning, although some have claimed to do that. In any case, I really don't think that Amish people typically are closer to God than non-Amish people. And they certainly don't have a monopoly on spirituality either, as some fawning English admirers seem to think.

Secular writers almost unanimously favor, romanticize, and even "glorify" the Amish and almost never suggest or admit that Amish parents systematically brainwash their children with the desperate hope they'll always stay Amish. But most non-Amish people, especially those who have Amish neighbors, strongly agree that it happens all the time.

The Amish have a remarkably interesting way of selecting their ministers and it is known as doing it by the "lot." On that day, all the church members vote for a certain man. They do so by whispering their choice's name into an ordained person's ear in a private room. That person tabulates the votes by writing the totals on a piece of paper. Of course, everyone always votes for a man, as women are never eligible to be candidates. It has been decided beforehand how many votes each man needs to be in the "lot." Often the number is three, although sometimes it is more and sometimes less. All the men with at least the required number of votes are then in the lot and are now eligible to become the new minister. They may not excuse or recuse themselves, that is, they do not have the option of not participating in this strange "election/selection" process. Almost always, however, they all very strongly hope they will not be chosen, so the likelihood of voter "fraud" is essentially non-existent. Predictably, when the results are announced, congratulations are never in order and are never spoken, although there will be sympathetic handshakes. Interestingly, I believe they are the only culture or society anywhere who choses their ministers this way.

Each person in the lot selects a book for himself from the stack on the table. In only one book, the bishops have secretly placed a special piece of paper. They then check the books until it is found. The bishop then points at that "candidate/victim" to let him know that he has now instantly, unwittingly, and unwillingly become the new preacher! Even though his heart seems to have sunk to his shoes, a few moments later he needs to struggle to his feet and receive the holy kiss and "blessing" from the lead bishop.

Some ministers become extremely distraught, agitated and even despondent and desperate when they are chosen. The most extreme example probably was when one who had just been ordained was missing later that evening. The searchers eventually found him lying across a railroad track, obviously in the depths of mental anguish and despair and contemplating suicide. He may have required much counseling, but he did later accept his "responsibility" and served as a preacher for a long time. On a different occasion, a newly ordained man became so depressed that he also became suicidal and had to be "watched" for quite some time. Another man who had been in the "lot" (but had not been chosen as minister) reportedly decided to become a virtual drunkard so he would be much less likely to be chosen to be in the lot again. Predictably, he was never again voted to be in another "lot."

It does seem sad and unfair that, at such a solemn ceremony as the ordination of a minister, the chosen one will often be sobbing and weeping. Also, he usually feels such crushing sadness that he is tempted to simply collapse on the floor in despair. His wife will also be crying as other women try to console her and assure her that this surely is God's will. Meanwhile, the men who "escaped" and were not chosen are inwardly joyful and can scarcely conceal their jubilation. In fact, they probably will be crying tears of joy and relief. A rather awkward situation that does seem to be, indeed.

Many people find it surprising that Amish ministers typically are so distraught when they are ordained. It is understandable, though, when one considers all the negatives they face. First and foremost, it is a lifetime obligation. They are required to enforce the Ordnung roles, especially the bishops. Also, they have no formal Bible education and training. They do not receive any pay or other reimbursement. They may not have the necessary skill or aptitude for such "public speaking," especially given the relatively small number of *familiar* German words in their vocabulary. They have no *bible or any other written material at all that they can refer to while preaching!* They are required to continue preaching even if they suffer personal tragedies like their wife or children dying. There is no pulpit or chair or anything similar that they can sit upon or lean against. They are required to always keep their mutza on, even in stifling heat. And they are always required to preach for about forty minutes if they are the first preacher and almost twice that long if they are the second preacher.

They are taught to believe that when the words seemingly will not come, God will provide the proper words for them. That thought can be very comforting to them, especially if it's their first sermon or anytime early in their ministry. Nevertheless, because they have no written material, there surely are many times when they are desperately searching for the right thoughts and words. Everyone knows how, in certain stressful situations, a few seconds or a few minutes can seem like many minutes or even hours. And it seems like the hands on the watch or the clock have completely stopped moving. That's when an Amish preacher surely deserves some sympathy.

Some may wonder if there are any benefits, or "perks" of being an Amish bishop. One benefit is that they are almost always highly respected by their people. But there are a few who get very little respect, with the simple reason being that they hardly deserve any! Another benefit they have is, immense power within the church, which allows them to exercise strictness *or* leniency toward the Ordnung laws. They can even establish new rules, including allowing previously forbidden things or prohibiting things which *had* previously been allowed!

Many preachers are fairly fluent in the unique mixed German/Pennsylvania Dutch/ Amish dialect and speak at a normal pace. Others often desperately search for anything they think is interesting, relevant, and helpful while still being *permitted* to be spoken, as dictated by the rules and restrictions of the Ordnung.

At times like that it must be very tempting for preachers to not preach as long as usual. While many do not seem bothered by it, for others it is a struggle of courage and dedication. They know if they significantly shortened their sermon, some would be very perturbed and would be highly critical, although many others would be delighted. Nevertheless, it is very unlikely that the "official" time length for sermons will ever be shortened. And, it is almost inconceivable that they will ever adopt a different method of selecting their ministers. I'm sure they feel that is their only logical choice. Still, many non-Amish people wonder why that system is not dispensed with, since it is so unpopular. But, really, what other system could they logically use while still properly obeying the Ordnung?

On very rare occasions, I have heard an Amish minister speak, in his sermon, in a longing and wistful tone of voice of how much easier and more comfortable it was when he, as a teen-ager, was still on the "boova bunk" (boy's bench) and didn't have the major duty and responsibility of preaching. Other than that, I don't think I've ever heard any preacher complain about being forced to preach. And, amazingly, I have never heard any complain about the harsh and repressive demands of the Ordnung!

Several power-hungry men reportedly have cried tears of sorrow because they were *never* chosen as minister. This illustrates how, like society in general, even in insular sects like the Amish, there are those who greatly crave power and authority. Those men might consider the "lot" system of ordination to be a type of popularity contest rather than having a sincere hope of finding and ordaining the most qualified man!

It would seem to be much preferable and more humane if there were "term limits" and preaching was not a life-long requirement. That is also very unlikely to ever change. Of course, there is no such thing as running for "re-election." Very few would ever have any interest in that. And, of course, the women are completely content in never being eligible to become ministers. In fact, I've never heard of any Amish women who were bothered at all about that.

Because of the lifelong preaching requirement, certain members may become increasingly unhappy and dissatisfied with listening to the same preachers for up to fifty years or more. This sometimes is a very legitimate concern since the record apparently is held by Enos B., who preached for seventy-six years and was still "active" when he died at age one hundred one! One "solution" for such dissatisfaction might be for those to attend at other districts and only listen to those preachers. But I have never heard of anyone doing that on a regular basis. It would be a real challenge for the home district bishop to decide how to discipline that! Another option would be for disgruntled members to *move* to another church district. But what if they can't afford that or there are other compelling reasons to stay? There often are no easy solutions. And, no, impeaching an unpopular preacher is not a valid option!

The Amish are encouraged to only vote for men who already have at least one child. And, in a very subtle way, church members are encouraged to not vote for men who have any "English" children. So, on the few occasions when that happens, it is considered to be sad and even shameful.

As the population in any Amish church district normally increases, eventually it becomes necessary to divide it into two districts. That will then require three new ministers and, eventually, also a new bishop. Since so many men absolutely dread the thought of possibly being elected and "forced" to preach, many would hope that the establishment of a new church district is delayed for a long time.

A desperate ploy that some men might be tempted to use would be to stay home on ordination day, pretending to be sick. The most fearful could even arrange to BE sick by eating spoiled food beforehand. Or they could plan an "accident" upon themselves, causing injury so serious that they could not attend. However, I have not heard of that ever happening. I think their fear of being thought of as rebellious and unwilling might be even greater than their fear of becoming a preacher!

In reality, though, even if they were sick or injured and stayed home that day, they would still be eligible to be "made" a minister at that time! The Ordnung proclaims that members may still vote for them and, indeed, on at least one occasion a man was chosen that way, in "absentia!"

Understandably, most Amish churchgoers would *love* to see the services reduced from three hours to two hours. But very few, if any, would ever seriously and publicly petition the bishops for that because of fear their reputations would be tarnished. And, if anyone *did* try that, the bishop probably would say that it's always been three hours and it must continue that way. Of course, he strongly hopes such a disappointing answer would be meekly accepted! That kind of "reasoning" is very prevalent in their culture.

According to Amish legend, the lot once fell on a certain man who refused to accept it and he never did actually preach. It is said that, years later when he died, the kerosene lamp in the room at his viewing would not stay lit, to everyone's consternation. That incident was sometimes mentioned later as a subtle warning to others who also might be unwilling to preach. On exceedingly rare occasions, an Amish minister has fled his "calling" and left the church. But, almost always, he then joined an evangelical Christian church and became an important part of its ministry. I don't know of any instance of an Amish minister leaving the church and then living a heathen lifestyle.

I suppose Amish preachers are happy they didn't live during the time of biblical patriarchs like Methuselah and Noah who lived to ages 969 and 950, respectively. Since the Amish require lifetime servitude of their preachers, it's unthinkable that *anyone* would ever agree to preach for hundreds and hundreds of years, and possibly almost a millennium!

At Amish ordination services, all those who are in the lot will sit at a table, and two presiding bishop's place identical German Ausbund song books in front of them. The number of books equals the number of men who are in the lot. The bishops have already secretly put a piece of paper with a certain Bible verse in one book, at page 770 where the "lob-leid" is located. That is *always* the second song sung at every Amish church service. At the proper time, each candidate picks a book for himself. The bishops then check which man's book has the piece of paper in it and that man will be the new minister. There are literally no qualifications required, other than he be a married member in good standing with the church. This strange method could be thought of as a combination of democracy and divine intervention. The rumor in our family was that when Eli King was ordained minister in 1959, he had first chosen our neighbor Henry's book, and then they traded books with each other, which resulted in Eli becoming the new minister instead of Henry.

I remember well the day that the three ministers in our church district faced the sure reality that one of them would be "elected" as our new bishop. Whenever a bishop is elected the other members do not vote at all because only the three men who are already ministers are eligible to become the new bishop. So, unlike when a minister is elected, they are the only men in the house who are extremely nervous and fearful at that time.

On that particular day, the three ministers Eli King, Moses Esh, and Stevie Esh sat down at the table and, with trembling hands, palpitating hearts, and sweat on their brow, each selected one of the three books that had been placed there. Bishop Dan E. Stoltzfus was presiding and he was accompanied by another minister, Stephen [Steff] Esh. Bishop Dan then opened the first book and that extremely important piece of paper was not in it. He then opened the next book and looked inside. When he then immediately looked up and directly into Steff's eyes, it was fairly obvious that the piece of paper had been found in the second book. Bishop Dan then slowly spoke in a clear and solemn voice "Ess isht gefunna varre und siss in da Moses Esh sie buch." That meant it had been found in Moses Esh's book.

Immediately, there came from Moses, a loud moaning wail as he realized the full gravity and solemnity of what had just occurred. I was rather surprised when I heard that. But I was even more surprised when, simultaneously, we heard almost precisely the same wailing sound from his twenty-two-year-old son, who was seated directly next to me. It seemed I also heard, more faintly, a female voice which I assumed was Moses' wife, Katie.

Happily, and understandably, that exact method of electing Amish clergy is not used in all of their church districts. In just a few districts, an extra book is placed on the table and if that book contains the piece of paper and it happens to not be chosen, the "election" is canceled until a future date, which is usually a huge relief to all those who were in the "lot."

It's my understanding that Aaron and John were the only brothers of mine who were ever in the "lot." But, somehow, neither was ever elected to be preacher, even though John was in the "lot" four different times.

If there was ever an authoritative study done which claimed the Amish method of ordaining ministers was not "inspired by God" and therefore not legitimate, I believe very few, if any, of the bishops and ministers would want to know about that study. It does seem that the vast majority have no doubt that it is completely valid and legitimate. But there may be quite a few who are somewhat doubtful. Even so, I suppose none would ever want to be *completely convinced* that it's not legitimate, because then they would regret even more having been ordained and forced to accept the drudgery of being an Amish preacher for the rest of their life.

There are no minimum age requirements for Amish men to be elected as minister. Probably the youngest one to ever be elected was Mervin Bontrager of the East Johnson district in Indiana in 1993. Amazingly, he was only twenty years old. Another man, Leroy Miller, from Ohio was ordained minister at the age of twenty-one and became a bishop just one year later.

I believe that most non-Amish people would agree that the Amish people's method of selecting bishops and ministers could often be problematic at best. Are they not concerned about whether all the candidates are really qualified for such a serious and important role? One event which happened fairly recently should certainly give them pause. It involved an Amish man who was not only a minister, but also a bishop. That title carries with it the most solemn and serious responsibilities of anyone in the church. This bishop had shown a shockingly rude, callous, and uncaring attitude toward a young man who was a member in his church district. The young man had come to the bishop for counseling because he was very depressed and had told him that he was considering committing suicide by hanging himself. The bishop then told the young man that he was willing to provide the rope for him, so he could do that. Soon afterward, a group of eight men, including two ministers, went to pay the bishop a visit. It was decided that the bishop should be "schtill geschtelled" or "silenced" for a period of about three months. That meant he was not allowed to preach at all during that time.

Actually, some preachers might *prefer* being silenced sometimes, given all the negatives they face while preaching, as mentioned before. In any case, would not everyone agree that the rope-offering man was not qualified to be a bishop, or even a minister? But, nevertheless, no one should expect that their method of choosing ministers will ever change.

Each family is required to host the church service at their house when it is their turn, unless their house isn't big enough. Or, if the barn isn't big enough to hold all the horses, especially in wintertime. A big enclosed wagon is used to transport all the benches, songbooks, dishes, glasses and silverware from one house to the next, on a bi-weekly basis. After the service is over, there's a lunch of bread and peanut butter jelly, red beets, pickles, coffee and water. And even cheese if you're lucky enough. Of course, there are always lots of the famous snitz pies, made of dried apples.

After lunch, most families stay for an hour or two engaging in very simple and mundane conversation. Very seldom would it be about secular or worldly topics. It likely would be about gardening and farming or something funny such as when Farmer Zook's straw hat accidentally went through the corn chopper and up the pipe into the silo, to later, unknowingly, be eaten by his cows!

Whenever the church service was held at our house, Bishop Dan E. Stoltzfus and his wife, Lavina, were always the first to arrive, sometimes by 8:00 A.M. or earlier. John and I would hustle around outside, helping to unhitch the people's horses and tying them inside the barn.

The women immediately go into the house and visit with each other for a while. The men stand in the forebay at the front of the barn and shake hands and chat with each other. Ministers and bishops greet each other with the holy kiss. Rumspringa, teenage and pre-teen boys lounge around somewhere in a separate area until the service starts. They are always the last ones to come inside.

The Amish probably shake hands with each other more than any other culture. However, there's something quite odd that frequently happens. When a person has already shaken hands with another but then forgets or isn't sure, he'll probably try to shake his hand later. But the other one, remembering that they had already shook, sometimes will not shake his hand and will simply say "Meah henn katt," meaning "We already have." This even happens between men and women. It would certainly seem less rude if they simply shook hands again, even if it was the second time!

At Amish church services, everyone except the preachers, goes into the house in single file and in order of their age. It's important that those sitting next to each other are on good terms because they probably will be doing that over the course of many, many years! Unless one gets "elected" as preacher, in which case he'll then sit with the other preachers. The men and women always sit on opposite sides of the room. Even though I've never heard an explanation for that, I suppose it is to avoid being distracted by each other. By about 8:30, everyone is inside, and the service begins.

There are never any public opening remarks. The very first event is when a certain man, who probably feels he is *chosen*, calls out the page number of a certain song. Then he starts singing all by himself for about ten seconds, before the rest of the congregation joins in. They sing extremely slowly, almost like a 6th century Gregorian chant. The tunes are mournful, ponderous, swelling and melancholy. The Amish consider them to also be peaceful, melodious, harmonious, and inspirational and they absolutely want those songs to be preserved and sung at their church services until the end of time. A six-line verse takes about five minutes to sing. It's been said that in the 1500s, when many European Anabaptist Christians were being martyred for their faith, their oppressors would dance mockingly while they were being killed, while the Christians would be singing. Apparently, they decided to sing very slowly to discourage the executioners from dancing at that time.

The second song at Amish church services is always the Loeb song, or Praise song, number 770 in the ancient German Ausbund, which dates back to the year 1564. They then sing one additional song before the first minister preaches for about forty minutes. Then everybody kneels for about five minutes while the deacon reads from the German prayer book. The second preacher then preaches for about one hour. Time usually passes very slowly, as he drones on, while about 90% of the people sit on wooden backless benches which have no cushioning at all. The preachers and the old, sick and physically incapacitated people sit on chairs or rockers. When I was growing up it was almost unheard of for the boys and girls in Rumspringa to "take a break" and go outside for a while, midway through the service. It seems that is much more common nowadays.

In a very subtle way, we were taught that crossing one's legs at the knees during the service, while not being completely "oppschtelled," was unbecoming and even somewhat indecent. So, I don't recall ever doing that or seeing anyone else doing it. Since we were crammed in fairly tightly, space certainly was also a deterrent factor.

While trying to endure the torture of three-hour long church services, my mind often idly wandered, with many abstract thoughts. One day I tried to decide which people would be most uncomfortable sitting on the hard wooden benches for so long. Would it be the skinny people or the chubby people? I thought that it was probably more tolerable for skinny folks like me, because we weighed less. Then I realized that obese people's extra padding on their "bottom" should somewhat alleviate the stress of sitting there for so long. So, it really might all wind up a draw!

At the end of the second preacher's hour-long sermon the people are, mercifully, allowed to kneel on the floor with their elbows on the bench, and everyone's posterior blood starts to flow again. At that time, the deacon reads from the German prayer book for about five minutes. Then, everyone stands up for the benediction before sitting down again. Finally, the closing hymm is sung and the service is concluded.

At Amish church services in the summertime, it becomes very warm inside the house, even with the windows open, because there are no fans or air conditioning. People *could* bring "hand-fans" to wave in front of their faces but I've never seen that done at any church services. I'm sure it would be very much frowned upon. *Everyone* always wears long sleeves, and no one would ever dare to roll them up. The boys and most of the men are allowed to take off their black mutza, which is a suit jacket with hooks on the front instead of buttons. But no one would ever dare to take off their vest. The preachers and the deacon are not allowed to even take their mutza off. There really is no *written* law about that, but I have never, in any church service, seen a preacher preach without his mutza on or seen any other men or boys without a vest on. I guess the preachers' deeply ingrained respect and reverence for the Ordnung gives them the mental fortitude to do that. In any case, the ministers sometimes are sweating profusely, especially the one who's preaching. Sometimes, an emphatically waving hand will have a sweat-soaked white handkerchief clutched in it. And they always have a very sober and somber demeanor and never joke or smile or laugh at all while preaching. They rarely make eye contact with anyone and some will often have their eyes closed. They usually speak slowly, haltingly and laboriously and since there's never a microphone or other amplification they also need to speak quite loudly. And, of course, there is never any electrical or mechanical device of any sort that they can use. Fortunately, the host always hands a glass of water to him at that time, although there's rarely, if ever, any ice in it.

Of course, there are some Amish traditions that make a lot of sense and which nobody should object to. But the tradition of requiring the ministers to always wear a mutza at that time is, frankly, very puzzling and even inhumane. Especially inside a stiflingly warm house. Surely nobody would consider it immodest if he took it off. It seems to me that tradition makes no more sense than if they required him to wear knee-high rubber boots while preaching.

I don't think any preachers were ever praised by anyone if and when they had preached a "good" sermon. I think that would be allowed, but maybe it never occurs to anyone that the preacher might really appreciate those kind words. They'd think it would be inappropriate or that no praise is deserved. And, most certainly, no preacher is *ever* applauded while he's preaching. Nor is any preacher ever interrupted or subjected to derogatory remarks at that time. There is true Amish decorum from start to finish (except for lots of sleeping by many of the congregants!) At the end of the second sermon there is always a short time of "zeignus," or testimony from several men who the preacher calls upon. They usually say they are "aynich mit de lehr," meaning they are in agreement. They normally also do a "mini-sermon" of their own that lasts just a few minutes.

When an Amish couple hosts the church service at their house, the parents always attend, even if they're from another district. The father knows that he almost surely will be asked for "zeignus," as it is considered an honor when the minister requests that from him. Many, however, dread such public speaking, especially in a "foreign" district!

Since the second sermon is much longer than the first, people will then be more likely to fall asleep. At that time, many men and boys (and also some women) lean forward with their elbows on their knees and eyes closed, obviously trying to sleep while they sit there. While leaning forward they often rest their forehead against the back of the person in front of them, who then might also have his head propped against the person sitting in front of him. There may be quite a few rows of people all sleeping or nearly asleep, with many having their heads propped against the back of the person in front of them. Since the benches have no backs on them, there is nothing to impede such head resting. At any time, though, anyone in the "sequence" could move sideways or lean forward, thereby possibly causing a near domino effect and suddenly awakening the sleepy headresters as they lurch forward. There was at least one occasion I know of when a teen-aged "sleeper" fell off the bench unto the floor! Very likely, he'd been trying to "sleep off" a serious hangover from a liquor laden Rumspringa party the night before.

Since so many in the congregation try to sleep while the sermon is being preached, I suppose some occasionally try counting sheep. Or take sleeping pills beforehand. Certainly, I would have done that sometimes, but we never had any at our house. We never needed sleeping pills at home because at bedtime we were already very tired from working so hard on the farm. I do remember at least one time when I skipped church and stayed home on the pretense of having an upset stomach.

Surprisingly, I rarely skipped church, probably a half-dozen times during my Rumspringa years. Not that I feared huge unpleasant consequences from my parents, but attending church was so deeply ingrained into our psyche that we rarely even considered not going. Certainly, my parents always attended unless they were sick or attending at another district.

I suppose if the church benches had any cushioning on them, the "headresters" would more often sit up properly. And would not be as quick to "headrest" against the person in front of them, which from my own personal experience, can be rather annoying. But, for the true optimist, the person's head against one's back could also be considered a welcome prop! As far as putting cushioning on the benches, that probably will never happen because the bishops would fear that the people would then become too comfortable and be even more likely to fall asleep.

Since Amish sermons often lack a coherent message, they are usually very boring. At least, that is *my* opinion! The first four words are the most predictable in any preachers' sermon. Almost always, they are "Leevy mitt-fersammelty sehla" [Beloved gathered-together souls]. Many preachers have their own favorite verses, quotes, and "stories" that they like to preach about. There surely also is lots of ad-libbing. Some preachers spend a lot of time expounding on the Ordnung, which makes it even more boring. And, I believe the opportunity and likelihood for genuine spiritual growth while listening to Amish sermons is both sparse and remote!

One day at a church service I decided to do a survey and see how much interest there really seemed to be in the sermon being preached. I looked at as many of the men and women as I could see, a total of about fifty, and only two were looking directly at the preacher, and seemed to really be listening. Surely it would be more interesting if the preacher used a Bible and preached from a specific chapter or section or topic rather than in a way that could often be described as rambling along haphazardly. If he did that, he would be more effective, more interesting, and it would also be much easier for him. But who would ever initiate such a seemingly radical idea? Probably, nobody. So, I strongly doubt that will ever change.

An interesting "trade-off" that always seems to occur in Amish church services is that the congregants never criticize the preachers for uninspiring and ineffective preaching and, conversely, the preachers never criticize them for all their sleeping while he's preaching!

Did I ever come away from hearing an Amish sermon feeling more informed and enlightened about the Scripture? Rarely. However, there was always a distinct sense of comradery and a feeling that I really belonged there with all those relatives, friends and acquaintances who I knew extremely well and had worshipped with for my entire life.

A typical Amish sermon consists of a mixture of Pennsylvania Dutch, "high German" or original German along with an occasional English word added. Since many Amish, especially the young folks, have an extremely poor understanding of "high" German, it would be more productive if the sermons were preached in English. However, I'm sure there is no chance of that ever happening, either.

A very strange Amish custom is that the congregation is never told the name of the ministers who preach, even when it's a visiting preacher from another district. This also holds true for sermons at weddings and funerals. So, he preaches his whole sermon while many people have no idea who he is, which can be quite annoying. Of course, bulletins would provide that information but there are never any bulletins at all. So, it would be much appreciated if one of the "home district" ministers introduced the visiting minister when he starts preaching. Or he could introduce himself. And, by the way, he should also tell which church district he's from. But, like many other aspects of Amish life, upholding traditions is far more important than anyone's own personal convenience. So, I don't expect that to ever change, either.

Are there any Amish bishops who *might* agree that making that change would be perfectly okay and that it also would be much appreciated by the congregation? And that there are also many other simple little rules that could and should be changed without sacrificing the "authority or integrity" of the Ordnung? However, if anyone tried to "lobby" the bishops for such changes, he would probably be ridiculed and even considered a troublemaker.

Have any bishops ever caused some people major depression and possibly driven them almost to madness and suicidal thoughts because of all the harsh and unreasonable demands of the Ordnung? I think many bishops should ask themselves that, especially since depression is quite common among the Amish. I would implore the bishops to sincerely listen to the voice of reason and to at least honestly consider *what seems to make sense*, as they unendingly try to regulate their people's lives. They would say that obeying the Ordnung *does* make abundant sense because they have always been emphatically taught that is the right way and the *only* way for them. They would disregard the fact that almost all non-Amish people disagree with that thinking. Still, they continue to preach relentlessly about the need for permanent submission to the Ordnung. In fact, they obsessively preach on the theme of "obedience to the Ordnung," even more than on the doctrine of salvation!

There are never any bulletins provided even at major events such as, ordinations, baptisms and funerals. At those events, the preacher slowly and methodically goes through each step of those rituals, seemingly completely unconcerned about time. No one ever complains to him but there will be many impatient sighs. And even though he sees many people sleeping, that will not induce him to shorten his sermon at all!

Events of major national importance are never specifically mentioned in the preacher's sermons. For example, they never say the word "President." Even when President Kennedy was assassinated, that event was not mentioned at all. I only heard a very brief and vague reference to it, which was, "Leevy leit, de veldt iss in a hocher schwang" which essentially means, "Beloved people, the world is in a deplorable and sinful state."

At funeral sermons, the deceased person is referred to as a "brother" or "sister," but only if they are church members. A child is called a "kindt" (child) while a non-member is called a friend. Only at the end is their name mentioned at all. Their full name is spoken then, including their middle initial and last name. Their exact age is also stated, in terms of years, months and days.

Because staying Amish for one's entire life is considered extremely admirable and laudable, it would seem someone who's accomplished that might sometimes be thanked or praised for it. But, strangely, it seems that *never* happens, even when they've already passed away. I guess it's thought that having achieved that was not at all above and beyond the "call of duty!"

Most people would find it odd that if and when an Amish man has a serious physical problem, he is still eligible to be "elected" as a minister. One man who I knew very well had a badly crippled leg which was the result of polio when he was young. Nevertheless, even he became a preacher, almost surely unwillingly, and has been one for a very long time. I believe that he always wore a metal leg brace. Nevertheless, for someone like that, standing and preaching for a long time is especially difficult without having a pulpit or anything similar that they can lean against.

In our home church district, there was a large family with two brothers who were both midgets. Their adult height was only about one-half that of other adults. I would hope, because of that, no one would ever vote for them to be in the "lot." Nevertheless, on various ordination days that they attended, they still may have been very fearful of being "elected" because their father was already a bishop and he had a reputation of being a "strong" preacher. And, if a midget did have to preach, it would be especially problematic because Amish preachers, no matter their height, do not stand on a raised area but simply stand on the floor at the same level as everyone else.

A specific negative that often happens is some people being unable to even *see* the preacher! Even though Amish houses often have at least one movable wall partition, overall visibility often leaves much to be desired. The "listeners" affected that way, however, can take comfort in knowing that the preacher can't see them sleeping "on his watch!"

There are no Sunday School classes at any Amish church services. Nor is there any nursery or children's church of any kind. So, small children always sit with their parents. They know that the only "change of scenery" that they might see would be if the parent they're with takes them to sit with the other parent. Nevertheless, small Amish children are amazingly well-behaved during the three-hour long church services. If they eventually become restless, there might be one or two small toys that their father provides for them. The most likely ones would be a tiny pair of magnetic "tricky dogs," one white and one black.

In very warm summertime weather, the church service is sometimes held in the upper floor of the barn where it is much cooler than in the house. The ceilings in the house trap the heat, while in the upper barn there is a large, wide-open space all the way to the roof of the barn about forty feet overhead. Also, the large barn doors are open, which makes the area even cooler.

Sometimes a lot of horses are tied in the upper barn floor and are quite close to where the singing and preaching is being done. Some people will smell various horse "odors" at times. Cats can sometimes be seen furtively slinking nearby, which provides welcome entertainment for children. And, there often are pigeons cooing sleepily in the rafters overhead. The pigeons, however, have no concern about the people sitting below and do not observe proper pigeon etiquette.

I recall a specific incident during a church service when I happened to be sitting behind our neighbor, "Push's" Rueben. Suddenly, with no warning, I saw a large glob of fresh pigeon dung land directly on the shoulder of Rueben's mutza. When he turned his head and saw it there, the look on his face showed disgust and possibly also some amusement. In any case, he ignored the incident for the time being.

A similar event occurred when a naughty pigeon ejected a glob of steaming dung directly on top of John M's bare head during a service in the South Intercourse district. I don't know if he, like Reuben, continued to just quietly sit there. He certainly could have immediately gone downstairs to the milk house and used water and paper towels to clean his hair and head. But, given the traditional and time-honored Amish philosophy and practice of non-resistance, stoicism and acceptance [gelassenheit], he may very well have decided to just sit there until the service was over. Of course, the men and boys *could* wear their big black hats for protection from the pigeons overhead but, unfortunately, the Ordnung forbids that during church services. Not surprisingly, many events similar to what happened to Reuben and John have occurred to other Amish people over the years. I guess that's considered an environmental hazard of attending a church service with pigeons perched in the rafters overhead!

When I was a teenager, Amish boys from the plainer groups wore little black bow ties at church, but the worldlier boys did not, which might seem somewhat strange. Also, the plainer boys had longer hair, almost covering their ears, while the wilder boy's hair might only reach the tops of their ears. At the beginning of each church service, all the single boys above the age of eight or nine, walk past the preachers and shake hands with them. That gives the preachers a good opportunity to check the length and style of their hair and decide if they were obedient or rebellious.

When I was ten years old, my parents gave me a jackknife for Christmas. I carried it proudly in my pocket wherever I went. One day at church, I did a very foolish thing with it. A teenage boy, Push's Sammy, was sitting in front of me and I decided to test my knife on his mutza while he was sleeping. I cut a piece off the tail of his mutza about two inches wide and one inch long. Just after I had done it, the boy next to me saw it, and later told the victim about it. I had not had any reason to do it. I guess it was just out of boredom and being naughty and rebellious. My parents were told about it and they were very upset with me. They said I would have to pay for the damage, even if that meant paying for a brand new mutza. Also, I would have to go to the boy's father and personally apologize for what I had done. Which I did as he was milking the cows in his barn one evening. I was so ashamed and embarrassed by what I had done that I had tears in my eyes and was almost sobbing at the time.

One evening, a few weeks later, Push drove his horse and buggy into our driveway and saw me mowing grass in the back yard with our old reel-type push mower. He came up to me and simply handed me a piece of paper. All that was written on it was, "Mutza, $22.50." Then, without saying one word to me, he abruptly turned around and left. I was shocked and horrified that a new mutza would cost that much. They had indeed ordered a brand new mutza, which are always handmade by an Amish seamstress. My parents told me if I don't have enough money to pay for it, I would have to earn it by pulling weeds in Push's cornfields. As it turned out I could pay for it, but only by raiding my meager savings account at the Intercourse bank. That drastic withdrawal almost put my account into bankruptcy. I learned a valuable lesson, and never did such a foolish thing again.

My mom would cut the shirt pockets off our English shirts, whenever my brothers or I had one. That would anger us considerably. However, I certainly can't use that as an excuse to cut and ruin Sammy's mutza. Mom, at least felt she had a good reason to cut the shirt pockets off, and that it would be too worldly to leave them on. She would have loved the current trend of pocketless dress shirts and not having to cut them off. But, partly out of rebellion, I think we might have only bought shirts *with* pockets. By the way, Amish men also are not allowed to have hip pockets on their pants or outside pockets on their mutzas.

One summer evening when I was thirteen, Great-uncles Danny and Mikey Kauffman from Chester County, came to visit us and Uncle Benny. They were two of my grandmother Suvilla's brothers and they had both long ago joined the Mennonite church at Millwood. Uncle Mikey parked the 1960 Chevy Nova way up at the north end of the house where Benny lived. During their visit, of course, I went to check out their car, since they couldn't see me snooping around there. I was excited to see the key in the ignition, so I quickly got in and started it up. Even though it ran very quietly, I was nervous, thinking they might hear it running and come to investigate. I played with the radio and cigarette lighter and windshield wipers, but I didn't dare try to move the car even though I really wanted to.

Finally, when I was about fourteen, I accomplished what I had been yearning to do for years. One Sunday afternoon, while walking home from church with my friend, Dave Esh, we took the scenic route through the fields. We stopped at Belmont Quarries and briefly rolled some big rocks down the side of the huge rock pile there, which was about seventy feet high.

Then we decided to snoop around the buildings to satisfy our typical Amish curiosity. Soon, I saw an old yellow pickup truck and, of course, I immediately hurried up to it. Not only was it unlocked, but to my delight, the key was in the ignition. I quickly climbed in and turned the key. The truck jerked forward a few inches but didn't start. It was a manual shift model and had been parked in gear. Since I hadn't put the clutch in, *of course*, it jerked forward! I tinkered around and experimented for a few moments, and soon I found the right combination. Or, at least a combination that enabled me to move the truck. While holding the clutch down, I turned the key, and, bingo, it started right up. My heart was pounding with excitement as I contemplated driving a real motor vehicle for the first time.

I wasn't worried about getting caught, as it was on a Sunday, and there were no employees anywhere. Also, the quarry property was in an isolated area, and I certainly didn't take the pickup on a public road. Of course, not knowing which first gear was, I stalled it several times. Finally, after grinding gears briefly I got it moving. I *think* it was in first or second gear, but I wasn't sure which. Since I didn't know how to shift gears, I left it in the same gear. I happily drove around in circles for a few minutes, while Dave watched with a big grin on his face. I was probably more excited than most people are on their first date. I parked the truck and as we walked home, I realized that I likely had just experienced the most thrilling few moments in my young life. I even dreamed about it later that night!

CHAPTER TWENTY

My Hopeless Dream
of Higher Education

DAD OFTEN COMPLAINED ABOUT the big tractor trailer trucks from Lester Summers Trucking Company, that went speeding past our house at near break-neck speed, loaded with crushed stone. It was especially dangerous since Newport Road had more than its fair share of slow-moving Amish buggies and wagons on it. And, also because our house was very close to the road. The north end of the house where Uncle Benny lived was only about eight feet from the road. A huge stone-filled runaway truck crashing into it would have almost reduced that rickety structure to kindling wood.

Dad would have been horrified if he'd known that I often wished I had been one of Lester's truck drivers. Interestingly, it turned out that later in life, I did drive an eighteen-wheeler for quite a few years. Dad also complained about the high school students racing by, often far above the speed limit. Of course, I would have liked to do that too. Pequea Valley High School was located just one mile east of our farm and, not surprisingly, I would have liked to become a student there and continue my education like the English folks. And, because of my near obsession with sports, I feel certain I would have fulfilled my dream of being on the school baseball and basketball teams. Instead, I spent those very important years slaving away on the farm, doing everything the old fashioned, sweat-inducing and boring Amish way. And, as far as my playing sports at Pequea Valley, the only time that ever happened was occasional impromptu baseball and basketball games outside on the playground on Sunday afternoons with some Amish buddies during Rumspringa.

Even if I had attended Pequea Valley School and been on the baseball and basketball teams, I can't imagine Dad ever attending any of those games. After all, he had very little involvement in my life ever, other than the many, many hours we spent *working* together in the fields or in the barn. In fact, Amish parents on farms usually neglect their children terribly because they are always extremely busy at work. That's because of being forced to do almost everything the slow burdensome Amish way. As for his personal recreation, a certain Amish boy didn't know what that word meant, when asked by a sympathetic English man!

I don't know of any kids from bonafide Amish families who were ever students at any of the local high schools. Of course, such an idea was rarely, if ever, even discussed between any Amish parents and their kids. It surely was never discussed in our household. If we had questioned that, we'd have been told in a disparaging tone "Meah sinn Amish und henn unsahr aagniy shoola. Meah bracha kenn fahfeerishe Englishe shoolla." ["We are Amish and have our own schools. We don't need any deceitful English schools."] Almost all parents would have been horrified if their kids were interested in that. And, of course, the kids were so indoctrinated in the Amish culture, that they just meekly accepted the status quo. It is sad to know they probably will continue to be educationally and culturally deprived on a permanent basis.

I've often wondered what would have happened if some Amish kids had insisted on getting a high school education. In fact, I have often wished I had tried it at that age. Surely, any kid who tried that would have been scolded and criticized and made to feel very guilty by the Amish, but it certainly should not have been denied them. Certainly, some English folks would be willing to help and accommodate them, but unless the kids specifically asked them for help, very few would want to get involved in a meaningful way.

One such instance involved a high-school age Amish student who desperately wanted to attend. So, his friends tried to help him enroll at the local high school but were unable to because school policy required his parents to sign for him. Which, of course, they refused to do. So, sadly, as it turned out, he never did attend high school at all. Can anyone fully comprehend how unfair that really was?

As a young lad, I tremendously craved knowledge about a vast spectrum of things, especially the many modern, "worldly" forbidden things that we did not and could not have. It seemed that because they were forbidden, I only craved them more. How could I explain to my parents that I had this insatiable quest and desire to learn many things that they surely didn't want me to know about?

How could I convince them I should be allowed to freely explore the strange, exciting and alluring but yet forbidden world of the English people? I absolutely knew I didn't want to be held back and to remain as ignorant as most of my people were. And I certainly didn't want the English world to consider me a second-class citizen or to think that I actually *belonged* on the bottom rung of society's ladder! If any Amish teen-ager dared to express a desire for "worldly" forbidden things, the parents and bishops probably would have tersely responded, "We don't need that stuff in *our* lives."

In many ways, we were segregated from normal American society. We were denied the knowledge of a vast amount of important information that every American citizen should have. But, of course, bishops and parents throughout the Amish community desperately hoped and prayed that we would just blissfully and willingly accept the status quo and always be content with this repressive Amish lifestyle.

I believe the Supreme Court made a huge mistake in 1972 when they ruled that Amish kids need not attend school past eighth grade. I doubt that the justices who made that decision fully understood the ramifications of it. Did they stop and realize how many thousands of Amish youth would be adversely affected by it, not only at that time but also far more so in the future, considering the continuing and dramatically increasing availability of excellent jobs, for those who have the necessary education and qualifications? How would those justices themselves have liked to be denied all the advantages of receiving a high school education? Would they also, like the Amish, have denied that to their own children? I DON'T THINK SO. Perhaps they would have ruled differently if some eighth-grade Amish school students would actually have been in the courtroom, earnestly and desperately pleading for the opportunity to attend high school. But, predictably, that didn't happen. I suppose the parents made absolutely sure that it did not happen. Probably, even the justices preferred that no Amish students be there to plead their own case. So, their absence obviously made it very easy and convenient for the justices to make the unfair ruling that they did.

What about the hopes and dreams and aspirations of the Amish students? What about certain ones who, instead of becoming farmers and carpenters, wanted to become a surgeon or a scientist or the CEO of a large corporation? Or any one of many different careers that require a high school education? If they had the opportunity to attend high school, many would also have attended college later, which would have enabled them to escape the drudgery and boredom of the Amish lifestyle. To me, the Supreme Court's decision shows a baffling and infuriating lack of concern about the rights of Amish eighth graders. When the Court made its ruling in that momentous case, were there even any children's advocates or attorneys who argued on behalf of Amish students? Or were the students considered to be little more than chattel? Or slaves?

In Shawn Francis Peters' lengthy and well-written book, [The Yoder Case] Peters provides a vast amount of information about William Ball, a prominent and leading attorney who argued vehemently and vociferously (pro bono, *of course*) on behalf of the Amish parents in that case. Yet astonishingly, (but, predictably) there is *no mention* of Mr. Ball ever addressing the *rights* of the Amish students, whose lives would be tremendously and harmfully impacted by the Courts' verdict in that infamous ruling!

The Supreme Court justices, who clearly admired the Amish and sympathized with the parents' plight, (based on their Court arguments) apparently let those feelings cloud their judgement and caused them to make the unfair ruling that they did. So, the Amish parents were given *special rights and privileges*, while their children were deprived of their Constitutional right to attend high school, apparently only because the justices favored the parents and felt sorry for them. They should have felt much *sorrier* about the ensuing plight of the children!

One justice tried to make the pathetic, feeble and disingenuous argument that Amish students could still attend college when they became adults, even if they hadn't attended high school. Of course, they *could*, but it's very unlikely that they *would*. That justice must have known that in such a case, they wouldn't be nearly as interested and inspired and motivated as if they had already attended high school. Also, they would probably still be as uninformed as ever about what college is all about and how much it could benefit them. So, of course, they would be far less likely to even want to attend college.

In the 1970's, most Amish kids grew up on farms and expected to have a "career" in farming. However, several very important things happened between then and now. One was that because of the huge increase in the Amish population, few farms are available, and most are unaffordable. Also, because of the amazing advances in science and technology, there are now many more excellent jobs available in many different types of occupations than there were in the seventies. That's why the issue of Amish education is so much more important now than it was then, especially since the Amish population is expected to continue to increase greatly. Yet sadly, because of being denied high school, Amish students surely will miss out on many terrific opportunities. It's very troubling to see my people blissfully strolling through the valleys of ignorance and apathy, seemingly completely unconcerned about that. I strongly believe it is now time to relitigate that infamous Supreme Court decision that deprives so many Amish youth of the further education that they surely deserve to have. Indeed, if it WAS relitigated in the current "modern" era, the decision would almost surely be struck down and reversed, according to a brilliant and well-educated lady attorney whose area of expertise specifically and accurately covers such matters.

I would have *loved* to go to high school and get a good start in life and not have that unfair Supreme Court decision hinder me and snatch away my right to a proper education. But, of course, the Amish bishops were ecstatic and even gleeful about it. And, they most certainly did not care a whit about the unfairness of it all!

The bishops and parents may be dismayed when they find out that I have already contacted my Congressman and Senators on the issue of reversing the Court's decision. The bishops will, however, smugly and confidently claim that nothing will change and that it has been settled law for a very long time. Still, I feel it is my duty to pursue this, especially since no other former Amish have, as far as I know. It appears to be a lonely road ahead but I'm hopeful I can rally others to the cause. I certainly believe the vast majority of the American people would agree that Amish children have as much right to a high school education as anyone else. In fact, many non-Amish people are saddened and dismayed that Amish parents willfully and deliberately sabotage their children's education by not allowing them to attend high school.

So, I think Amish kids, after they've completed eighth grade, should be required to attend an official meeting at the local high school where an unbiased, well-informed person, such as the superintendent, would clearly explain to them all the advantages of a high school education. The parents should be strongly encouraged to attend the meeting also.

Even more importantly, I think a very logical idea would be for the Supreme Court to rule that Amish youth must attend high school for one year after they've completed eighth grade. Would that not be a very fair compromise? Even a few Amish parents might inwardly agree, but very few would dare to verbalize it. They would correctly realize that, for many kids, attending for one year would greatly increase their desire to continue attending, even until graduation in many cases. Most parents, however, would worry that requiring just one year's attendance would be like allowing the "camel to get his nose under the bottom edge of the tent." Of course, the Amish school system is cleverly designed to keep the students as ignorant as possible to the "ways of the world."

While growing up, I was told that the Amish lifestyle was far more peaceful, predictable, and stable (and therefore better) than the English lifestyle which, presumably, consisted of major immorality and crime and greed. But, since Amish life also features major hardship, deprivation and ignorance, it certainly is *not* better or happier than a typical English lifestyle.

In certain ultra conservative Amish communities, parents deliberately neglect to report newborn children's births to the proper authorities, with the desperate hope that the child's subsequent lack of having a birth certificate and Social Security card will eventually help to deter him from leaving the Amish. Some parents have even pretended ignorance of the lawful requirement of reporting those births. Indeed, anyone not having those forms of identification, will usually have much difficulty procuring them later in life.

So, to all Amish parents I ask, "Where is your sense of fairness and equality? Where is your concern for the betterment of your children's lives? Where is the courage you need to stand out boldly and help to *enhance* rather than to *hinder* your child's learning abilities?"

But I'm sure most Amish parents and bishops strongly hope that the status quo will continue on a permanent basis. The more progressive ones might privately admit that a high school education would be good in some ways. But, because they themselves "toughed" it out without that, they prefer that current day Amish youth also only get an eighth-grade education. This way the parents would benefit if the young folks, during that time, provided free or low-cost labor on the farm for them instead. Of course, the parents would very much fear that high school attendance would contribute greatly to leading the young folks astray. In fact, I believe if they *were* required to attend, eighty to ninety percent of them would go "English" at that time, or later. So, it's understandable that the parents are so desperate to not let them attend.

In retrospect, I'm sure if I had an inkling back then of how much I could have benefitted from high school and college education, I would have been even far more interested in attending than I was. But, sadly and understandably, I had no idea of how much I was missing out on. My ignorance about that, of course, is a direct consequence of having been born and raised Amish.

I believe I make a very valid point, as I admit with great embarrassment, that I was at least seventeen years old before I even knew what college attendance was really for. Until then I had always thought that people go there just to acquire lots of *general* knowledge of many different topics and issues. So, that's when I found out that colleges offer many different *majors* which enable someone to acquire the necessary knowledge required for *specific* jobs and careers. I sincerely hope Amish youth will learn about the many, many careers featuring hundreds of different types of jobs that are available in the English world. Including well-paying jobs which are far more interesting and satisfying than what the Amish world offers them. But, of course, the bishops don't want them to know all that, for fear they'd leave the Amish church.

Will the Amish people ever realize that ignorance and deprivation are not the answer to life's problems and that a typical high school education would not be the end of the world for their teenagers but would, instead, be hugely beneficial for them?

I wish Amish parents were aware of how many non-Amish people think that it's both cruel and selfish that they don't allow their children to attend high school. Most people would agree that life is challenging enough without the benefit of a high school education, and that intentionally prohibiting that is absurd, especially since the Amish still have to pay school taxes just like everyone else.

Since Amish parents are extremely reluctant and unwilling to send their children to a secular high school because of the perceived worldliness there, they should consider sending them to a Christian school. Probably, very few would consider that, though, because they would have to pay the tuition expense. Also, they surely would worry that the child might be led astray there, even in a Christian school. Indeed, if those students then became devout Christians, many Amish parents would think they had been "tragically" deceived.

On the topic of school education, Amish people's main interest is rote (memorization) learning and few of them apply critical thinking or even know what that term means. Many are also very uninformed about lots of import-ant things, some of which even involve serious legal issues. This is especially true on certain matters concerning Amish teen-agers. As most people know, ignorance of the law does not protect one from the consequences of breaking the law. When I was growing up, most Amish youth, including myself, were well informed as to what was forbidden and wrong in a moral sense. However, for certain offenses, we didn't even know it was actually a crime and could get someone into serious legal trouble.

For instance, a teen-age friend of mine told me that, just out of curiosity, he was seriously considering "sneaking" into his uncle's house while they were at church. He said it would be easy because he knew they didn't lock their doors. He told me that he certainly wouldn't steal anything, but just wanted to "check things out." When I told him that would almost surely be considered burglary, a criminal act, he was surprised and decided not to do it after all.

On a much more serious level were sexual acts which many Amish youth up to the age of twenty or more, did not even know were illegal. For instance, they didn't know that such things as having child pornography or men exposing themselves or unwanted groping and sexual acts involving underage girls were criminal offenses. In fact, I think the only sexual acts or behavior that we *knew* was illegal was the crime of forcible rape. Of course, we should have known all that stuff, but we didn't. Who would tell us? Our only source would have been unreliable "gossip" from other Amish boys. We certainly never learned even *one thing* pertaining to sexual matters from our parents. Or from our teachers or any books at school. We did have a weekly "health" class at school, but it was completely asexual and did not remotely compare with modern sex-ed classes in public schools. And, even nowadays, many Amish adults gloss over and pretend they don't know what constitutes various sexual crimes, or the seriousness thereof. By the way, we didn't have a clue as to what sexual harassment was and undoubtedly would have assumed that it did not even exist!

The Swartzentruber branch of the Amish are thought to be the plainest and strictest and most uneducated of all the Amish people. Nevertheless, it's amazing how uninformed one newly married man really was. Only upon getting married did he learn of the reality of women having menstrual cycles!

A seventeen-year-old Amish teen-ager who had attended Harristown School when I did, asked his mother a question one day which must have embarrassed her greatly. He had just read a newspaper headline which stated that an eleven-year-old Amish girl had been raped by an English man. He then asked his mother what the word "raped" meant because he actually didn't know! I'm sure she did not explain it to him, and I suspect she did not even answer him at all.

While many might find this amusing, for me it is also embarrassing and sad that such a level of ignorance existed among Amish youth at that time. I strongly hope that today they are much better informed. My main point in writing this is to illustrate that, had these young folks attended high school, they would surely have known about such things. In addition, they would have received a valuable "English" education to augment their sparse total of eight years of Amish schooling. My sincere hope is that, somehow or other, they will attain a proper perspective and understanding of all the pros and cons of English life versus Amish life and will not just meekly accept the biased, slanted and one-sided viewpoints of the Amish bishops.

"We don't know what we don't know" is an old saying that most people have heard, and it applies dramatically to the Amish people. Having grown up Amish as I did, I didn't realize at the time how extremely uninformed I also was to the "things of the world." And as greater and greater strides are constantly being made in the fields of technology, science and general knowledge, I am increasingly dismayed and frustrated that "my people," the Amish, willingly choose to stay shockingly ignorant about many very important things. However, in some ways, maybe it's just as well they don't know how much they are missing out on.

When I was growing up, I thought that a computer was simply an adding machine, or at best, a calculator. Sadly, there may be many Amish even today who generally think that too, and have no concept of the miraculous things it can do.

The Amish bishops fear, probably correctly, that smartphones are most likely of all devices to lead the young folks astray. So, they are desperately begging them to not get one and warning them that owning one would put them on the road to destruction. The reality, however, is that it puts them on the road to knowledge and freedom and a much better way of life.

If the Amish were clearly informed of the amazing capability and convenience of computers, smartphones and the Internet, I'm sure they would be in disbelief. I wish they knew that not having a smartphone and Internet access is, arguably, as disadvantageous and as much of a hindrance in life as *not knowing how to add, subtract, multiply or divide!* Of course, if they didn't know how to do that and they DID have a smart phone or computer, they could simply have that device do it for them! And, with an astonishing degree of speed and accuracy, including ten-digit numbers (billions) being correctly divided by seven-digit numbers (millions) in less than two seconds! Surely, they also would be interested to know that smartphones can be made to "sing" (simply by voice command) hundreds of thousands of different songs, including even the Amish Lob-leid!

I wish they knew that by simply typing a few words on a computer search engine or smartphone they could almost instantly access a vast amount of information on virtually any subject or topic. Including all the best ways to treat a sick cow or horse. Or how to get maximum milk production from the herd of cows. Or how to get that balky baler engine going again. And all kinds of information about millions of other things. Literally. For free. *Amazing!*

I don't mean to sound glib or condescending when I say these things. I really do wish they knew how convenient a microwave oven is in comparison to any other way of heating food. And that electric hair dryers provide lots of *instant* heat for many different purposes, including warming cold hands or providing relief for arthritic limbs. And the myriad other ways in which electricity is a most convenient and valuable servant. I wish they knew that cars and telephones and radios are far more often a force for good than for evil. I wish they knew how inexpensive many modern things are, especially with Internet access. I guess many Amish, especially the bishops, don't even want to know how cheaply someone can buy a good used car, usually for a small fraction of the average cost of a horse and buggy. Or that color television sets, even large ones in excellent working condition, are often available for *free* on Craigslist. I wish they knew how eagerly non-Amish society welcomes them with open arms to the world of the twenty first century which offers such a convenient and pleasant and modern standard of living. I don't say these things to anger or tease them, but only to inform and help them if I can.

CHAPTER TWENTY-ONE

The Amish Version of High School

THERE ACTUALLY IS A small amount of schooling required for the Amish beyond eighth grade, but it is so unfocused and unhelpful that it seems silly to have it. In the fall, each student who had "graduated" from eighth grade the previous spring, begins to attend vocational school, or Dutch school as it is called. The fact that it is called a vocational school was laughable because there are no vocations taught there at all. Perhaps it was called that to try to mollify those who thought the Amish students deserved more schooling. It also seemed silly because the few subjects that were taught there, we had already learned in earlier grades. The students only attend on Saturday afternoons for one school term and then their education is complete, whether they are satisfied with that or not. Then, more than likely, they face a life of hard work and drudgery on the farm.

I did eagerly anticipate attending Dutch school, even if for only three hours per week. I knew it'd be interesting because everyone was of the same age, and there were guys from other neighborhoods who I hadn't met before. Also, some liberal guys would talk about older brothers who had cars, and about getting cars themselves during Rumspringa and, of course, I was also thinking of doing that then.

Dutch school attendance involved my buddy Ira and me riding together and taking turns, driving a family driver horse and picking up a neighbor girl along the way. Ira was my best friend before I was in Rumspringa and he was only nine days younger than me. He lived at the farm on the hill, just a quarter of a mile north of us. The old fashioned one seat open buggy we used back then was really only meant for two people, so when there were more than that they would sit on each other's lap. It was also commonly done that way during Rumspringa.

On the morning of my first day at Dutch school, I was working on the farm at Brother Jake's. About 11:00 A.M., Dad drove over and told me I better get on home and get ready for Dutch school. He was supposed to also tell me about a sad accident involving our family dog, Lassie. She was a white Eskimo and I basically considered her to be my dog. She was only half grown, about seven months old, and by far my most favorite pet I ever had. I loved that dog so much, because I felt that I got more love and affection from her then from the members of my family.

That morning, Dad did not tell me what had happened to Lassie, because he later said he just couldn't bring himself to tell me the bad news. So, I walked home in a happy frame of mind, excited about going to Dutch school for the first time and getting to meet a lot of teen-agers who I might become friends with.

When I walked into the house, and Suvilla saw me, she assumed Dad had already told me about Lassie. She turned to me and sorrowfully told me that Lassie was laying out behind the pump house, by the edge of the garden. Fear struck my heart, as I noticed her sad tone of voice, and I asked anxiously, "What do you mean"? She looked at me blankly and asked, "Didn't Dad tell you about Lassie being hit and killed out on the road by a car this morning?"

"No," I yelled in an anguished tone. Then, horrified, I ran out behind the pump house, even though I really didn't want to. When I saw Lassie's lifeless body lying there, I walked up and stared down at her in horror and disbelief, as the hot tears stung my eyes. Then Suvilla came up behind me and told me that Tommy Lefever's wife, a neighbor, had accidentally hit Lassie with her car. Mrs. Lefever, of course, had come back to our house to tell someone and that she was very sorry. Everyone knew it had not been her fault but, of course, we were still very sad, especially me. I took it harder than anyone else.

Then Suvilla quickly remembered to tell me, "There's a new puppy out in the barn already." As I listened in near disbelief, she told me they had quickly thought to look in the newspaper to see if anyone nearby had pups advertised. Lo and behold, our neighbor Henry had pups to sell. It was decided that some-one quickly go there and buy one before I got home that morning, to lessen my grief over Lassie's death.

I walked out to the barn, still in deep sadness, feeling sure I would never love the new puppy as much as I had loved Lassie. I opened the cow-stable door and saw the new puppy lying on her stomach with her chin down on her front paws, over by the horse feed bin, a few feet away. She was looking mournfully up at me and shivering in fright. She was a Sheltie Border collie mix and at first I really wasn't much attracted to her. Then I felt sorry for her and I went over and said, "Hi, Puppy," and picked her up, and held her close and petted her. Then the little tail started wagging and a happy look came over her face and from that moment on, we were friends for life. She was also named Lassie and was a faithful and beloved companion on our farm for many years.

Suddenly, I remembered that I had to get ready for my first session of Dutch school. Soon, Ira arrived with his horse and buggy and I climbed in and we rode over to the schoolhouse, about three miles away. Ira warned me there would be some "hard guys" there from the public school at Intercourse where he had attended. That term was often used for guys who were arrogant and rebellious and "gross-hensich," (elitist snobs). Indeed, some did meet that description and were also dressed quite worldly and using rather risqué language. We briefly lounged around outside before classes started, engaging in idle chatter. One boy, Elmer, from Dry Hill complained about how much money he had lost playing poker with his friends the previous weekend. I thought I would like to just be IN a poker game, or at least watch one. I didn't know the first thing about how to play poker. Another boy, Levi, from Hatville, proudly told about how his older brother, Abe, who was no longer Amish, had recently bought a brand new 1965 Pontiac Bonneville, and had paid $4000.00 for it. I marveled at that because it seemed like an enormous amount of money to me.

Suddenly, the Amish lady teacher's horse got loose from where it had been tied at the hitching post. Still hitched to the buggy, the horse ran out through the open gate and bolted straight across the road, fortunately without getting hit by any traffic. Uncle Levi and Aunt Annie Fisher's farm was straight ahead, and the horse galloped wildly down their long driveway with the buggy careening from side to side. Just as it went over the lawn and passed by the house, Cousin John dashed out the back door of the house in hot pursuit. Soon both he and the horse were in the cornfield behind the house and running through the broken-down corn stubble. That slowed the horse down considerably and John soon caught up and jumped into the buggy and turned the horse around. Then he saw us running in the driveway and we told him it was the teacher's horse and buggy, so we brought it back to the schoolhouse. The teacher, of course, was very grateful for what Cousin John had done. When it was all over, one of the Intercourse boys disdainfully remarked, "Well, you wouldn't have to worry about a car running away like that," as most of us chuckled or provided an obligatory laugh.

Ironically, Cousin John was involved in an interesting situation himself when he attended Dutch school, as a fourteen-year-old in 1953. At that time, the Amish people were involved in a huge controversy with local government officials, who insisted that Amish youth go to high school like English students did. Or at least attend school until age sixteen. Amish bishops and parents had been totally opposed to that idea for an exceedingly long time. Uncle Levi himself had been arrested four separate times because of his refusal to send John to high school. He had spent five days in jail and many other Amish fathers were also arrested and imprisoned for a few days. Some men were arrested as many as ten different times. Authorities in the Lancaster area had arrested approximately one hundred different Amish people during that time. In fact, Dad probably would also have been arrested and jailed, but it was during the time that he was recuperating from the broken back he'd suffered in the farm wagon and car accident on Newport Road. So, the Amish fathers' stubbornness and their willingness to wait out the opposing officials served them very well during that time.

Many non-Amish people thought the Amish men's willingness to go to jail for that cause was admirable, even heroic. But there were also many who were horrified that they showed such desperation and determination to sabotage their children's further education. At a 1937 protest meeting between the disputing factions, the Amish grandly and proudly unfurled a 130-foot long letter with *three thousand* signatures on it, hoping to impress and convince their opponents. Eventually, the Amish reached an agreement with the school boards and government officials and the "vocational" Dutch school program was initiated.

We didn't learn anything in school that first day that we didn't already know. We had a boring German reading class, some German singing, some English spelling and a little bit of arithmetic. I did find the spelling class interesting, as that was something I had always excelled at. Each student was given about twenty-five words to spell every Saturday afternoon. I do remember that I correctly spelled every word that was assigned to me throughout the entire school year.

Sometimes, Ira and I would have some extracurricular fun after school while driving home. Either he would be driving his horse that day or I would be driving my horse, Blackie. We got into some seriously competitive horse and buggy races with Elmer, the poker playing boy from Dry Hill. In each buggy, there'd be one or more girl passengers riding with us. The race would be on Clearview Road and, indeed, it did provide what we needed, a clear view on a straight road which was about a mile long. As the horses would be wildly galloping along, the reaction from the girls would be anything from near enjoyment and amusement, to scolding us and possibly being almost terrified. However, they were braver than non-Amish girls would have been, because they had all grown up on horse occupied farms and knew what it was all about. Fortunately, there wasn't much traffic on Clearview Road, which allowed us many passing opportunities and added to the fun of it all.

One afternoon I made a "serious" driving mistake, as we got to the stop sign at the corner of Harvest Drive and South Queen Road in Intercourse. Elmer and his passengers were already stopped there and were properly on the right-hand side of the road. I thought I would get a slight advantage by pulling directly alongside them, on the left side, even though that was for oncoming traffic. While we were all briefly stopped there, Sarah, a passenger in Elmer's buggy, yelled at me, "What if a car comes?" Well, I hadn't thought about that. Fortunately, there was no car turning into where my horse and buggy were blocking that lane. I then quickly pulled out and since I was turning left, I did have an advantage over Elmer and was now ahead of him. However, since we were now on a busy street, the racing needed to stop immediately and, indeed, it did stop. At least until the next Saturday afternoon!

One afternoon at Dutch school, when the school term was almost over, I was feeling rebellious and sorry for myself. Sorry that in just a few weeks my formal "education" would come to a grinding halt. I had no hope or expectation that I'd ever go on to high school or college, both of which appealed to me greatly. That afternoon I became so disruptive that the teacher, Miss Beiler, and the Amish man who was visiting that day, became annoyed with me.

The visitor was a sour and dour man from a neighboring church district, who I knew fairly well. Seven of his thirteen children had attended Newport school when I had. It was almost time for school to end for the day, and I was ready to get out of there and go home. Maybe there would be another horse and buggy race on the way home. However, just before we were dismissed, the sour, dour man spoke up and said, "Ich vet venich schvetza mit da Yonie schpaydah" meaning, "I would like to talk a little with Yonie later." I was surprised at that but stayed at my desk while the others filed out. Two of the Intercourse boys slammed the door extremely hard behind them as they left. I considered that to be a show of support for me.

After everyone else had left, the visitor and Miss Beiler both gave me a severe scolding. They said we should all be glad that this "special" school class had been approved for Amish kids. They went on and on about how important it was to have this silly (my word, not theirs) Dutch school. I certainly felt that they overdid it. I resented that they talked to me as though I was a young child. I didn't argue with them, but before I left, I had a nearly overwhelming urge to tie about fifteen or twenty knots in the Amish man's horses' harness reins, which he'd have to undo before driving home. I reluctantly decided not to, only because I was afraid he might catch me doing it. Also, I knew Ira was waiting for me for our ride home together. On the way home, I was thinking about how my life would soon become even more boring since it would still be a long time, about fifteen months, before I would be in Rumspringa. Since Brother John was already in Rumspringa, Sunday afternoons were especially boring for me, unless Ira and I would get together and hang out, which we often did.

At the end of the school term, the teacher gave each of us a white folded card with an "optimistic" message, [*Congratulations, Graduate!*] in neatly flowing letters which we accepted with wry but grim humor. However, any congratulations spoken to each other would have been with a heavy dose of sarcasm because we knew that, from an educational standpoint, this was essentially the end of the road for us!

Fourteen-year old Amish boys such as me and the boys at Dutch school, are usually quite shy and reserved among girls. I suppose I might have been the shyest of them all. At the time, I didn't know why since I was always very much at ease with any group of boys. Later, I attributed it to the fact that during my growing up years, there was often criticism and scorn amongst our family members. Also, it seemed there usually was a distinct lack of praise and appreciation or "thank you's." Appropriate displays of manners were often in short supply, even at mealtimes. Since we had a big family and a big table, food often was passed back and forth. Whenever someone wanted something, they'd just say one word, such as bread or potatoes or pie. Or, quite likely it'd be homemade applesauce, since we had that at every meal, year around. The person requesting something would never say "Please," unless he just wanted to be dramatic. Sometimes the person closest to the desired item would just say "lung foss" meaning, "reach for it," if he thought the person requesting it was close enough. Whenever an item was passed from one to another, the person receiving it would never say "thank you." But all that was not considered rude, except for the statement "lung foss." It was just considered normal and I suspect had been like that for generations, not just in our family, but in most other Amish families as well.

Something else that is very common in Amish households at mealtime is belching. It is actually expected and is always accepted as being perfectly normal and no apology is ever required, even for major "belches." In fact, the cook, who is usually the wife and mother, might feel increasingly honored based on the loudness and frequency of the belching, because that could indicate that she had prepared an exceptionally large and appetizing meal!

As far as girls were concerned, I was just as attracted to them as anyone else, despite my shyness. But I didn't have any confidence and had a low self-esteem when I wanted to strike up a conversation with them. I often felt awkward, bumbling and tongue-tied around them. Still, when I was about fifteen years old, the three things in life that I most wanted to do was drive a car, watch TV, and to not be nervous, but to feel comfortable when chatting with girls. Especially looking ahead to the not too distant future when I'd start Rumspringa at age sixteen. I really didn't even know how to flirt and was too nervous to try.

In many of the western Amish settlements, when a boy wants a first date with a certain girl, he gets one of his friends to ask her for him. As far as I know, no Lancaster County youth do it that way but always directly ask the girl themselves. And, in some church districts, the young folks must be church members before they're even allowed to date. This gives the bishops even more control over their lives and makes it likely they'll become members sooner, which is the bishops major goal!

The Amish teacher at the Dutch school was an unmarried fifty-year old and she was known as an old maid. All the Amish used that term toward women who had never married and were over thirty years old and it was not considered derogatory or insulting. All the unmarried men of that age were called bachelors. Because of shyness being quite common among Amish girls, even more than with the boys, there usually were a disproportionately high percentage of them who became old maids. Rumspringa would end when anyone got married or when they turned thirty or soon after. The unmarried girls who turned thirty continued to look the same as before, that is, there was no change in how they dressed. Unmarried men who reached that age, would soon be required to grow a full beard. At that point they would stop Rumspringa completely, because if they showed up at the single folk's gangs or singings as a bachelor and wearing a beard, they might be ridiculed. However, they were free to date and marry an old maid or widow if it worked out that way. In comparison to English society, Amish courtships are more often successful because of the narrow confines and similar habits and lifestyle of their culture. Pertaining to beards, a recent phenomenon is that a few rebellious forty to fifty-year old bachelors still don't have beards, which displeases and frustrates the bishops greatly. To all the newly married men's "credit," I've never heard of any who refused to grow a beard. If any ever did, they'd better have a very convincing excuse for the bishop. And, even those who can only grow "fuzz," are still absolutely required to grow what they can!

During my growing up years there was only one unmarried young man in Rumspringa who wore a beard. That was considered very strange, even among his buddies. His name was "Pepper" Ammon and he was with the plainest group, the Kirkwooders. However, the bishops didn't mind, as having the beard was actually considered to be an act of humility on his part.

Rumspringa comprises a huge part of young Amish people's social life, so when it ends because of their having gotten too old (reaching old maid or bachelor age) their lives usually become much more boring. So, it's much better if the "forced" ending to Rumspringa happened because they got married.

Amish teen-agers, both boys and girls, are rarely overweight because of all the hard physical work they do. And, despite never wearing jewelry or make-up, a lot of Amish girls are quite attractive. Many of them (but not all of them!) are as innocent and pure as the wind driven snow. But, from birth till death, they are not allowed to cut one hair on their body, according to the Ordnung. They also are taught in a subtle way, that make-up makes girls *less* pretty, not more so. And, that perfume stinks!

In the old days, when a bachelor or a widowed man was interested in an old maid or a widow, he'd go to her house in the evening and secretly peek in the window. If he saw her inside, he would tap on the window to get her attention. Then she'd definitely know he was romantically interested in her. But it seems to me the proper way would have been to send her a letter first. Then she would not be as startled at hearing the tap on the window, and would have time to prepare for his visit.

Certain older and widowed Amish men were quite tactless when pursuing a woman that way and sometimes they were desperate. One man practically begged the woman he was pursuing, saying "nem mich usht," which means, "Just take me." I don't know what resulted from that plea. Another man, Levi, who is now deceased, emphatically told an Amish lady that he would not take no for an answer to his marriage proposal. Believe it or not, she consented, and they got married. I never heard if they had a good marriage or not.

One well known story involved an old maid and a bachelor who were good friends, and for him it was only platonic. The lady was, however, romantically interested, so she said to him, "Why don't we get married"? He stoically replied, "Who would want us?" She then was too shy to provide the necessary clarification and it never went any further.

One advantage that an older couple has over a young couple who are marrying for the first time, is that the older couple may get married at any time of the year. For many, many years, until just recently, the young couple would be virtually prohibited from marrying at any time other than in the fall "marrying season." One exception would be if the girl was pregnant, and then it was hoped and expected that she would soon get married to her boyfriend. Of course, there have been instances over the years, when unmarried Amish girls became pregnant, although on a percentage basis it is far less than in non-Amish society. There have been a few rare cases when an unmarried Amish girl had a baby and for some reason the father would not marry her. She would then likely raise the child with the help of her parents. I have never heard of an Amish girl giving up a baby for adoption. I don't know if the church would allow that. I have never heard it mentioned in the church Ordnung by any Amish bishops or ministers.

Of course, divorce is totally prohibited in the Amish community, and I don't know of any instance when an Amish couple actually were divorced. That's certainly not to say or imply that there are not a lot of unhappy Amish marriages, because there surely are. Amish women may be the most submissive and subservient women in the world. Even so, I'm sure there are many who think their marriage *should* have ended in divorce. There have been a few times when Amish couples have separated, and when they have, it often was for many years, and sometimes until one spouse died. One Amish man I knew who had been excommunicated from the church, and then "became" English, was separated from his wife and family for many years. Eventually, he committed suicide by hanging himself.

Many years ago, it was unheard of for Amish people to get professional marriage counseling but now it happens frequently. I suppose most Amish couples who are in unhappy marriages might feel more trapped and more desperate than a non-Amish couple in similar circumstances because the Amish church totally forbids divorce. Still, since they don't have the option of divorcing, I think it's likely that they might try harder to nurture their marriage and get along then a non-Amish couple would.

CHAPTER TWENTY-TWO

Working for Jake as His Hired Boy

IN THE SPRING OF 1966, my oldest brother Jake and his wife, Arie, bought a ninety-acre dairy farm near Christiana for $130,000. It was all of ten miles away, quite a jaunt for horse and buggy travel. They had been farming on Dad's other farm just south of Intercourse for the past six years. Now, Brother Aaron and Katie wanted to farm there, so it was decided that Jake's should buy their own farm and move to it. It was quite a momentous event and involved traveling over both Harristown Hill and Wolfrock Mountain, a formidable section of mountain range, four miles south of our farm. They would now be living on the eastern edge of an Amish community that was sparsely populated, quite different from the heavily populated Amish church district they were moving away from.

Life at the new farm would certainly be a step, or two, or three, back in time. There were usually only about five vehicles per day that traveled past their farm on Lower Valley Road, along with about that many Amish buggies. About a quarter of a mile away was the spot where a famous house had stood many years ago. It had been used to hide slaves during the days of the Underground Railroad, more than one hundred years earlier. The famous Christiana Riot had happened there in 1859, when slave holder advocate Edward Goresuch was killed during a fierce gun fight. The house had been a famous American historical site for many years.

Along the north edge of the farm, just a short distance away, several freight trains traveled on the Low-Grade Railroad every day. A small stream ran through the south pasture and it was home to catfish and blue gills along with an occasional garter snake lurking nearby. Unlike in the Intercourse area, they now saw deer frequently which was exciting, especially at first. The farm was quite secluded, so John and I sometimes took our shirts off while working in the summer heat in the southern fields, which was far from the road and the house. We wouldn't have dared to do that at the Intercourse farm or at our home farm.

At the west end of Jake's farm was the Walter Shaeffer farm. Even though Mr. and Mrs. Shaeffer were "English," their lifestyle and their farming methods were quite primitive. Walter's bachelor brother, John, lived with them and was their permanent hired man. When they eventually retired, the farm was sold to Jake and Arie.

The Shaeffer house and barn and the old wooden silo were all quite shabby and run-down. One memorable thing about the house was that at the time of the sale there were a lot of pigeons and birds that had been living in the attic for a very long time. They'd fly in and out through broken windows. There was an enormous and almost unbelievable accumulation of about a foot of hardened pigeon and bird dung all over the steps of the attic stairway.

A lot of work was involved in moving all of Jake and Arie's belongings to their new farm. It included trucking all the horses and cows over the mountain range along with all the heavy farm implements. The cows were quite stressed by the move, so they didn't give much milk the first time afterwards. The farm had been owned by non-Amish people, so there was electric power in all the buildings. The young boys, Eli and Johnny, were fascinated by the electric lights in the house and kept switching them off and on a lot during the first day or two. Of course, it was explained to them that the lights would soon stop working when the electric power to all the buildings would be permanently disconnected, in obedience to the rules of the church. Never mind the convenience factor. Continuing to use electric power there was never even considered at all!

The first big project at the farm involved building a new silo. It would be filled with corn silage to feed the cows in wintertime. It would require about a thousand concrete stave blocks weighing about fifty pounds each, which were made at Cousin Omar Stoltzfus' block plant near Lancaster. The silo would be twelve feet wide and sixty feet tall, which was considered huge at that time. Nowadays, it's considered to only be about average size.

During the first summer that Jake's lived there, in 1966, Brother John and I took turns working for him as hired boys, on a weekly basis. I felt lucky that I happened to be there during the week that all the new silo blocks were brought from Omar's block plant. They were loaded on a flatbed tractor trailer truck and the driver hauled them to the new farm. Brother Jake and I rode along, and I made sure that I got to sit in the middle between Jake and the driver, so I could better watch how he drove the truck. Eventually, we approached the mountain range that we had to cross over. The driver grimly told us, "This should be fun, getting over this big mountain." Long before we even started up the mountain, he was speeding up the truck as much as possible. I watched with great interest as he expertly shifted gears, using all the power of the truck's mighty diesel engine. As we started up the mountain, he had to downshift many times as we went slower and slower. Finally, he shifted into the lowest possible (granny) gear and we were actually going slower than normal walking speed. Jake and I nervously wondered if we would make it to the top as we timidly expressed our concerns. The driver shouted, "Don't worry, we'll make it, but it's going to take a while," as he kept the accelerator pressed fully to the floor and the steady loud roar of the engine filled the air. Still going very slowly, we finally made it to the top. I wondered if the truck's strenuous workout might have been hard on the engine. I asked my buddy Ira about it later and he said that if it was in the right gear it should not have harmed it.

When we got to the farm, an English neighbor, Lenny Smoker, unloaded all the pallets of silo blocks with his forklift, for which we were most grateful. A few weeks later a crew of four Amish men, along with Jake and I, built the silo and it was a lot of extremely hard work. The Amish men worked fast and efficiently and didn't seem to mind all that strenuous labor in the hot sun. I remember one of them, Henry Lapp, sometimes loudly singing German songs while he worked. I privately thought a battery-operated radio would have been more interesting, but I wouldn't have dared to suggest that even if I had one, which I did not. When the silo was fully built, I felt proud, as a fourteen-year-old lad to have helped build that mighty concrete structure to its completion.

When Jake and Arie and their three young boys moved to the farm that spring they felt like pioneers because they had moved such a long distance into an area where very few other Amish families lived. Shortly after they moved, three-year-old Johnny became sad and started crying one day. When asked what was wrong, he just said, "hame gaye," meaning he wanted to go home. They gently explained to him that they were at home now and this would always be their home. He seemed to accept that and didn't seem bothered about it anymore.

The pasture fence at Jake's new farm was "worn out" which occasionally resulted in some very unwanted and frustrating night-time activity for Jake and me. That was jumping out of bed and running out to the cornfield and chasing his whole herd of thirty cows out of the seven-foot-tall corn and back into the pasture. And, with absolutely no light except what the moon and stars provided. Not a pleasant or easy task after having been sound asleep, just moments earlier! And, every morning at 4:30 A.M., I would be wakened by Arie cheerfully calling up the stairway to me, "Yonie, bisht ready fah uch schtay" [Are you ready to get up?] To which I would sleepily and dutifully, but untruthfully, reply "Yah" [Yes]

Each Monday morning, Adam Nolt, an elderly man from Intercourse, drove his van loaded with Amish teenage boys and girls to the various farms where they worked. Brother John and I rode along on a weekly basis as we took our turns working at Jake's farm. The mood of the young folks would be very glum as everybody knew there was another week of hard farm work ahead for them. Their mood was certainly much better upon returning home on Saturday eve, especially for the ones who were in Rumspringa. Since I was not yet in Rumspringa, even my Sundays were very boring.

One evening we hired Adam to take us to Jake's to celebrate someone's birthday with homemade ice cream. Having often ridden in Adam's van before, I was very aware of how accessible the accelerator was to anyone sitting next to him. When we boarded the van at our house, I quickly sat beside him. Anyone sitting there could easily have accidently pushed the accelerator just from stretching their left leg. However, when I did it, it certainly was not accidental because I had planned it all along. As Adam was driving along and looking straight ahead, I pushed down momentarily with my foot on the edge of the accelerator that his foot was not covering. The van speeded up noticeably faster for a moment, while I acted surprised and pretended it had been accidental.

"Hey, be careful there," Adam said to me, then chuckled, obviously thinking I had not planned it.

Some in my family probably were suspicious, although they didn't question me about it. The way I had planned and done that proved that I surely had already been smitten with the "machina geisht!"

On the east side of Brother Jake's farm was Levi Pownall's farm. He was an older English gentleman farmer who was rarely seen outside. That emboldened me to go through the pasture fence one day and snoop around a trash heap in his meadow. I only found one item that I thought was worth taking, a "holey" pair of brown men's jeans. I thought I would wash them and hide them somewhere at home and wear them occasionally at baseball games during Rumspringa.

That Saturday evening while riding home in Adam's van, I had the jeans hidden in my bag underneath some Amish clothes. When I got home, I put the bag upstairs in my room. I either forgot to hide the English jeans, or I didn't think Mom would root through my bag. Later she said to me, "I think you accidentally took somebody else's bag of clothes because your bag has a pair of English pants in it." She had planned on washing my Amish clothes and that's why she had checked my bag.

"Uh-oh, what do I say now," I wondered. I acted surprised that the jeans were in my bag. I pretended they probably belonged to someone else, and I'm sure I never fully explained it to her. She seemed suspicious but, surprisingly, I don't think she told Dad about it. Or, if she did, Dad didn't confront me about it. By the way, I never did wear the jeans to Rumspringa, or anywhere else because they were really quite ratty and literally worn out already.

CHAPTER TWENTY-THREE

Rumspringa,
The Great Liberator

FINALLY, AT LONG LAST, in August of 1967, with much excitement and anticipation, I entered into the long awaited and glorious era of Rumspringa, as I reached my 16th birthday. All Amish youth, both boys and girls, eagerly welcome this unique rite of passage because their previous stiflingly boring lifestyle will now become much more exciting and "glamorous" than before. They now join their peers on weekends without supervision and are even allowed to date if they're daring enough. They will now have exposure to lots of worldly prohibited things that their friends have and do, and will be tempted to do the same. All of which causes the parents a great deal of worry and concern.

Dad had bought a horse for me from Aquilla Stoltzfus two years earlier when I was in Dutch school. He was an old nag named Blackie, had accumulated "high mileage," and was not as fast as I would have liked. However, he was gentle and safe and I'm sure that was more important to Dad. I was anxious to get going though, because to me getting there slowly was a lot better than not getting there at all, as far as attending the Rumspringa events!

When Amish boys and girls reach the age of sixteen, then and only then are they first allowed to participate in Rumspringa. On Sunday afternoons, large groups of young folks in their teens and early twenties gather at some Amish home and socialize. In the summertime there would be a large flatbed farm wagon in the front yard loaded with food. The food consisted of whatever the young folks brought, usually hot dogs, baked beans, potato salad, watermelon, apples, pretzels, snacks, cookies, etc. And, of course, lots of homemade root beer and lemonade. Those Sunday afternoon events were called "pound suppers," because most people brought a pound of food, more or less. When groups meet at someone's house on a Saturday night, it is called a gang. Often, at homes where the church service has been held on Sunday morning, there will also be a singing in the evening. There might be a total of about one hundred or more young folks there. They'd all be single, with some dating and some planning to get married in the fall. I joined the Keffah (Bugs) gang which all my siblings had been with before me.

When I started Rumspringa, there were only six different gangs. There were two gangs that were more liberal than ours, the Groffies from the Groffdale area, and the Ummies, or Upper Mill Creekers. There were three other gangs who were plainer and more conservative than ours, the Happy Jacks, the Lemons, and the Kirkwooders. Before John and I were in Rumspringa, Mom would sometimes encourage us to join the Lemons when that time arrived. But they were a lot plainer than we wanted to be, so we joined the Keffahs instead. By the way, when someone starts Rumspringa there are no initiation rites or hazing or "signing on" required. Nor are they officially invited there, they just go and "blend in" like everyone else before them had done. And, even though no one had GPS devices back then, it seemed we had "homing pigeon" instincts that reliably directed us to all those exciting Rumspringa events that we eagerly "flocked" to!

On Sunday afternoons, at least one baseball game was played at the farms where the young folks met. The more liberal gangs frequently played at baseball fields at local high schools. The bishops and ministers abhorred that because it was in a much more public place. The only groups who didn't play baseball on Sundays were the Lemons and the Kirkwooders. They were, however, allowed to play baseball on weekdays if it was on an Amish holiday, which was about three or four times a year.

A lot of the Groffies and Ummies had cars, a few of the Keffahs had cars, but none of the Lemons or Kirkwooders had any cars. A very small number of Happy Jacks might have had cars at that time. Brother Jake told me once that the first Keffah to ever have a car was Hossy's Jonas when they were both in Rumspringa in the fifties. Jake warned me in an ominous tone that Jonas isn't Amish anymore either, seemingly implying that owning that car was a factor in Jonas going astray and also that that was a most sad and regrettable event. He may have had a valid point because I've never heard of any member of the far more conservative Lemon and Kirkwooder gangs having a car or going English.

When I was in Rumspringa, the three most liberal gangs usually had hoe-downs on the upper floor of the barn or the tobacco shed after the Saturday night gangs and Sunday night singings. Three guys would stand on a large flat-bed farm wagon playing a guitar, a banjo, and a fiddle, with one of them singing country and bluegrass songs. After playing for about an hour they'd get down off the wagon for the much-anticipated break known as "liquor mission." [Read, intermission] They'd go to their booze cooler and swig beer for a while before continuing with the music. Someone would pass the hat [literally, a big black Amish hat] and take up a collection for the musicians, with most guys contributing a dollar and the girls contributing nothing. I remember a friend once regretfully and mournfully telling me that he thinks he had accidently contributed a ten-dollar bill instead of one dollar as he had planned. The reason was that he probably was quite drunk at the time. Sometimes there would only be a battery-operated record player providing music as the young folks danced away. When I started Rumspringa, the music was all country and bluegrass but within six or eight years there was also some rock and roll.

In the more conservative gangs, all the girls always participate in the singings as well as most of the boys, especially the ones who want to impress the girls. In the wilder gangs, many boys would not participate at all and instead would be outside smoking, drinking, and playing poker. All Rumspringa youth usually stay extremely late at the Sunday night singings, often till midnight or later. And because of having to get up very early the next morning, and many boys suffering from hangovers, Monday has long been known as "blue Monday!"

The Lemons and the Kirkwooders were the only gangs that didn't use the afore-mentioned worldly musical instruments. But they were allowed to dance and, in fact, were often encouraged to dance if they only used harmonicas, or mouth organs, as we always called them.

What's wrong with this picture? Dancing was frowned upon when worldly instruments were being used but encouraged when only harmonicas were used! Rather strange indeed.

Brother Jake was undoubtedly the most conservative and well behaved and sedate of all of us six brothers during Rumspringa, although the rest of us were also quite shy around girls during that time. So, it is surprising that John and I made the discovery that we did one day while snooping in our brother's dresser drawers when we were about eleven and nine years old. We found what we thought was a white balloon which had an unusually wide opening.

After trying unsuccessfully to inflate it, we took it downstairs and showed it to Mom and told her we could hardly blow up this odd-looking balloon. In retrospect, it's surprising that, to the best of my memory she did not even seem shocked or horrified. Maybe she didn't even realize at that time, as John and I did much later, that the funny looking "balloon" was actually a condom. She did, however, immediately confiscate it from us. We were puzzled about that and thought we should have taken it back up to our brothers' bedroom. I suppose Mom quickly disposed of it somewhere. Had John and I known at that time it was a condom, we would have been very curious which brother it belonged to but would have been too embarrassed to ask. I'm certain they wouldn't have told us anyway.

There was another occasion when Mom must have been horrified with John and me. One night when he and I were about nine and seven years old, we were having an interesting discussion while lying in bed in our upstairs bedroom when we should have been asleep. The topic was about certain childish sexual fantasies we had about some girls at Hatville School. Suddenly the door swung open and Mom appeared, angrily brandishing her famous rawhide whip. Of course, she had overheard our conversation. She then gave us both a severe scolding and whipping. If John and I had any similar bedroom talk later, we surely were much quieter and more discreet!

About three or four months before my 16th birthday, I discovered to my great dismay and frustration that my birthday fell on a Monday. What lousy luck, I thought, waiting all this time and then missing out on my first time at Rumspringa by one day. The pound supper was at Kizer Jakes' that Sunday afternoon and I desperately wanted to go and I wished later I had. It would have been a good day to be my first attendance too, as three boys, Roy's Ivan, Elam Ebersol, and Jakey Y. had just returned from touring the western states in their red 1960 Chevy Impala, as Brother John reported to me. They had lots to tell and all were sporting full beards and mustaches, undoubtedly as a sign of rebellion.

The next Sunday when I did attend a pound supper for the first time, at Elam Zook's, one guy got extremely drunk, after having drank about a quart of hard liquor. He was staggering, lurching, and wobbling down a steep hill and obviously didn't even see a corn shed that he banged into, while taking a heavy blow to his head from it. Down he went, but he soon got up again. Later he became extremely aggressive, which required about five or six guys to hold him down. He apparently had what we called "poker," and what is also known

175

as a delirium tremens. That happened very rarely, probably about two or three times that I saw it during my Rumspringa career.

At the end of a gang or pound supper, there would be lots of empty beer cans strewn about the lawn and barnyard, often about two or three hundred, especially if it had been at a liberal group's gang. Certainly, none of the guys ever took their empties home with them. When I started Rumspringa very few girls drank at all, although seven or eight years later a fair amount of them did at times. I was never a big drinker but did become rather inebriated at times, along with my buddies.

During one of those times, I had a narrow escape one night while returning home from a gang in my buggy. Soon after I got over the mountain range at Wolf Rock Road, I fell sound asleep. Before long I was approaching the heavily traveled Lincoln Highway. The Good Lord must have been watching over me because, unexpectedly, I woke up only about one hundred fifty feet before I got to the highway, allowing me to stop if necessary, before I crossed it. Certainly, my horse was not going to stop on his own. It was at the same location where another Amish boy had been killed by a car years ago when he apparently had been sleeping as his horse crossed the highway.

There was another time when I fell asleep for about forty minutes while coming home from a singing. When I woke up, I found that the horse had gone about five miles further than I had planned, and in a somewhat different direction. There was another horse that I never had to worry about falling asleep whenever I drove him, because he was a lugger. That means he clenched the bit firmly with his teeth and ran much too fast as I had to constantly pull back hard on the reins and my arms would get very tired.

When I started Rumspringa, I soon became good friends with a group of seven other boys who had a baseball team which I eagerly joined immediately. I became the regular third baseman on our team. My cousin, Sammy Miller, also joined the team and completed the nine-player requirement. We played against other Amish teams on Sunday afternoons in the cow pastures where the gang was being held at, or in a hayfield if it had been cut recently. Sometimes we played on baseball fields at local high schools. A few years later, I joined another Amish team, and we had custom made "worldly" white baseball uniforms with red trim and red lettering, which read "All Stars" on the front. My uniform was never washed with any of my mom's regular laundry at home, for good reason. Mom and Dad, of course, did not know about it and I knew better than to try to have it washed with the family laundry. We occasionally washed our uniforms at the local Laundromat in Smoketown, although not nearly as often as we should have.

Our original group of eight friends would get together at someone's homes every weekend. Half of them always played bridge, or what we called five hundred. The other four, including myself, always played poker. My best friend from that group was John G., whose nickname was Beatle, because he had a simulated Beatles style haircut. To complement the two little radios that we had, I soon bought a small ancient battery powered record player from another Amish boy. Part of its history was that it had been owned by at least eight different Amish boys before me. Incredibly, it had somehow escaped the wrath and inevitable destruction from any of those boys' fathers during all that time. When I eventually sold it, of course, I sold it to another Amish boy. Unquestionably, it had the poorest sound of any record player I've ever heard, as it was extremely scratchy and "tinny." I bought a box of about 50 LP country and bluegrass records for 25¢ each from Elam Ebersol, who had to sell them because he was getting married soon. I kept them well hidden along with my radio in a secret place in the barn during the week.

Amish boys usually start cutting their own hair when they turn sixteen, unless they are with a plain group, in which case the parents probably would still cut it. The wilder boys won't have bangs anymore and their hair will be shorter along the sides than before. One day, soon after I became liberated that way and obviously feeling quite rebellious, I cut a shockingly large amount of my hair off, especially along the sides. So much that one of the ministers asked me in a scolding tone of voice if I had gotten my ears lowered. I chuckled but didn't bother to answer! Lots of boys would also grow fairly long sideburns and start shingling their hair. Shingled hair meant that it was layered or tapered, like English boys had, but usually only on the back of their head. That was considered to be very worldly and sinful. If it was extremely tapered, that was said to be a "hard" shingle.

Since it's very important for all Amish males to have bangs, one might suspect that bald Amish men would be required to have an extreme frontal-flowing comb-over (like Donald Trump) to substitute for the missing bangs. Thankfully, however that has never been required by the Ordnung.

One Sunday afternoon when my parents were away, a neighbor boy, Moses, came to our house to play poker with my brother. Moses was a member of the plainer Lemon gang. None of the Lemon boys wore shingled hair and I knew that. However, I was feeling naughty and cantankerous, and just happened to have the haircutting scissors with me at the time. I occasionally would playfully and teasingly snip some of Moses' hair off the back of his head, giving him a crude shingling. He warned me several times not to do it, but I didn't obey. Suddenly, he jumped up and tackled me and since he was much bigger and stronger than me, he soon overpowered me and started strangling me until I was really scared. When he finally let me go, I was most willing to stop shingling his hair!

The most serious hair offense among the Amish is when someone parts their hair along the side rather than in the middle. That is called a "side-shaydle." They usually only do that when they consider themselves to be English or are planning to become English. The next most serious "hair offence" is shingling, so it is certainly understandable that Moses punished me the way he did.

Before I turned sixteen, I longed for the day when I'd be allowed to cut my own hair. I'd sometimes check to see how well my whiskers grew, hoping to be able to grow long sideburns, once I was in Rumspringa. My brothers and I not only always cut our own hair but were very fussy and meticulous about it. We'd never let another brother cut it, not even one hair. And we certainly would not let Dad or Mom cut it, either, even though they'd have been most willing to do that. Of course, they'd have wanted to cut it in the plain Amish style with a full row of bangs.

One day when I was seventeen, we all went to Cousin Naomi Millers' wedding near Bird- in- Hand. Mom thought my sideburns were definitely too long. She had recently asked me to shorten them but, of course, I had not. Early that morning while I was still sleeping, Mom quietly crept into my bedroom with the hair-cutting scissors and started cutting and shortening my sideburns. Since I was a light sleeper I quickly woke up after about the first or second snip, before she had damaged them much. Of course, I immediately stopped her and was slightly perturbed at her for doing that.

At Amish church services, the women and girls are the first ones to go inside and sit down. Soon, they are followed by the ministers and other married men and young boys. The last group to come in are all the single boys above the age of eight. Just before they enter, they all put their hats in a pile somewhere, except for several older, fussier boys who would carefully put theirs separately somewhere. Later, the boys whose hats were in the pile could identify them surprisingly quickly by each hat's unique upward tilt of the brim (or lack thereof) and by looking for the owner's three initials which old Harry Haas had perforated into the leather inside hat band. At the beginning of the church service, after the boys have all put their hats down, they file past the ministers and shake their hands. This gives the ministers a good opportunity to briefly inspect them if they want to. And they often do want to!

What gets scrutinized most is the various aspects of their hairstyles, involving different degrees of conformity. Mutzas usually did not draw much attention because most of the boys wore the plain style. Hardly anyone wore the worldly "herringbone" style except for some Groffie boys. Fortunately, the vests that all the boys were wearing would cover and hide the "schnalla gallusa" that some would surely be wearing. Schnalla gallusa are suspenders that have the worldly little metal clamps which are used to adjust the suspenders' length. They are very much frowned upon unless the clamps have been removed and substituted with safety pins. The only type of suspenders that are fully approved are the ones that have no adjustment mechanism at all!

Other items of clothing also draw attention, especially anything that is considered worldly or verboten. This would certainly include the color of socks. In the 1960s and early 1970s, boys from the plainer groups would only wear black socks. The other groups would wear colors ranging from dark blue to white. The lighter the color, the worldlier it was thought to be. Therefore, the colors were progressively worldlier. Black, dark blue, solid blue, light blue and finally the ultimate, white, which was considered extremely worldly and sinful. The most liberal boys would wear loafer style shoes whereas the plainer groups would never wear them. My brothers and I were never allowed to have loafers. We always had to wear the low-cut string-tied shoes, which we called slippers. Also, until I was about twelve years old, I had to wear my brothers used "hand-me-down" shoes that I inherited from them. So, I certainly was proud of my first pair of new Sunday shoes the first time I wore them to church. Older married men are expected to wear high topped black leather shoes on Sundays, even in warm summer weather.

One cold winter day when the church service was at our house, my buddy, John Z., who was from another church district, came to visit. He was wearing a bright blue turtleneck sweater, with the collar or neck of it reaching up to his chin. He was also sporting thick black sideburns that were at least four inches long, something that's totally Verboten. When he strolled past the preachers, innocently shaking their hand, they stared at him in horror and disbelief. But since he was from a different district and they didn't know him, they didn't dare complain to him about it.

Up until about the late sixties, the shorter the boys wore their hair, the world-lier and more sinful it was considered to be. Conversely, the longer they wore their hair, the more they were in conformity, so long as it was not an extreme length. With the arrival of the Beatles encouraging longer hair in general society, the wilder Amish boys also started wearing their hair longer than before. This became quite confusing to the ministers and anyone else who wanted to enforce the Amish rules. Whereas before they never had to worry about someone's hair being too long, now it was a real concern with some of the wilder boys.

One Saturday night, shortly before my seventeenth birthday, I got to do something I had never done before. That was seeing a movie at the old Ritz Theatre in New Holland, about five miles away. I drove my horse and buggy and went by myself, but I didn't mind. I went with great anticipation because I had often been told how much fun it would be. I paid the 50¢ admission fee and went in and sat with all the other people. The movie was about an African safari and I found it all to be very interesting and exciting. Of course, I didn't tell my parents where I had been that night.

Of course, going to movie theaters and secular sporting events is totally forbidden among the Amish and is punishable with ex-communication. No doubt that increases the allure and temptation for Amish teenagers to go to such places. During our Rumspringa years, whenever John and I left the house on weekends, Mom would ask where we were going. If it was a place that was Verboten, we would simply say, "Away." Then she would, of course, assume it was somewhere that she would not want us to go to.

Shortly after my first movie experience I also got to go to Hershey Park which has long been an immensely popular tourist attraction. Dad gave me five dollars for spending money, and I went with my buddy, John G. We hired an English driver and our parents even paid for that. The thing that I found most interesting and exciting was riding the old wooden roller coaster called the Jack Rabbit. It seemed quite scary but was small in comparison to today's modern roller coasters around the country.

Later that summer I saw the Atlantic Ocean for the first time and was in awe and much amazed by the magnitude and grandness of it all. I went down to Rehoboth Beach in Delaware with some friends on a Saturday morning and we only stayed till dark, but we all had a great time. Imagine anyone nowadays who lives only about one hundred miles from the ocean, and not ever seeing it till they are seventeen years old!

For at least the first two years of my Rumspringa, our group of eight close friends got together virtually every weekend and often it was both Saturday night and Sunday afternoon and evening. Something that we all were definitely addicted to was playing cards. Danny, Amos, Elam and Junie always played bridge, or "500" together. John Z., John G., Dan K. and I always played poker. We even used real money, although the bets were small. Each would put a nickel to start, and the maximum bet after that was one dollar, which was a shockingly large bet.

Meanwhile, my little old blue record player would be playing next to us. Also, there was often a small radio playing at the other table, both of which were battery operated, of course. The parents were never present at that time, having planned to go visit friends, or having been asked to do so by their son, so that the radios could play freely and undeterred. Also, so we could play poker, which the parents would not allow. The parents would, however, allow us to play bridge or 500.

One Sunday afternoon in September, 1968 when our little gang of eight were together at someone's house, I had a mishap which put me in the hospital. As my friend, John Z was leading his horse through the barn to tie it in the stable, I snuck up behind him and set off a firecracker, hoping to give him a huge scare. Expecting him to chase me, I turned and ran through the cow stable and jumped about four feet down onto a concrete walkway. There was a board that had been put across the opening which I didn't see. When I hit the board, I was flipped horizontally in midair and landed flat on my back on the concrete floor below. The back of my head hit the floor and I was knocked unconscious.

As I was regaining consciousness, I dazedly saw all of them standing around me, but I still thought I would be okay. However, I soon felt a lot of pain in my back and it was decided that I go to Lancaster General Hospital. An English neighbor was summoned to take us in his car. At LGH, they took X-rays and I was told I had a broken vertebra in my back. I was fitted with a back brace to keep it straight, and I had to stay there for six days. I had three English roommates and the TV was on almost all the time, which I thought was great. It would have been much better, however, as my friends later reminded me, if it had happened a week later. Then we'd have been watching the Detroit Tigers and the St. Louis Cardinals playing in the World Series. I certainly agreed that would have been much better. In any case, I quickly recovered from my injury but had to wear a back brace for several months. Of course, I didn't let that slow down my Rumspringa activities at all!

In the 1960s, in Lancaster County, probably only about fifteen different Amish male names, made up 90% or more of all the first names. The most common names were John, David, Amos, Samuel, Levi, Jacob, Henry and Daniel. The most common girls' names were Mary, Katie, Rebecca, Annie, Lydia, Rachel, Sarah and Lizzie. The most common last names were Stoltzfus, Fisher, Beiler, King, Lapp, Esh and Zook. In 1967, there were fifteen boys named John in our Keffah gang out of a total of about sixty boys. Fortunately, many Amish have nicknames, or use middle initials, or several of the previous generation's first names, such as Seth's Johnny's Danny's Henry. That would mean that Seth is Johnny's father, Johnny is Danny's father and Danny is Henry's father. I think sometimes as many as five consecutive first names were used to identify some-one. Most Amish people have their mother's maiden surname as their middle name. Many Amish go by their first name, plus their middle initial. Some are partly identified by their father's middle initial even if it's different from their own. Often, people are identified by simply saying their first name preceded by their father's first name without saying the mother's name at all. For instance, Henry and Becky's son, Danny, would simply be referred to as Henry's Danny. Often the children of a widow would be identified by their mother's first name followed by the word "eehr" and their own name, such as Katie eehr Levi or Becky eehr Sammy. The word "eehr" meant that she was the mother of that child. A woman named Sarah whose husbands name was John, would be known as John "sei" Sarah, meaning she belonged to him! Confused yet?

Another very common occurrence is for sons to inherit their father's nickname. Dad was nicknamed Barney when he was very young, after a comic strip character, Barney Google, from that era. He was then known as Barney throughout his whole life. Each of my brothers and sisters and I were also nicknamed Barney, plus our first name. Of course, I was also called Yonie, which is German and short for Jonathan.

Because so many Amish have similar first and last names, it is very helpful that there are so many nicknames. Among Amish people's nicknames that I remember, besides Dad's, were Hossy [Rabbit], Homly [Calf], Hingle [Chicken], Micely [Mouse], Shipley [Sheep], Buffalo, Porky, Dog, Hansy, Corny, Shep, Fats, Kicky, Chockey, Wacky, Zip, Cactus, Termite, Turkey, Parrot, Squirrelly, Piggy, Spider, Bully, Coony, Peanut, Wooden, Proudy, Hump, Buck, Kizer, Friendly, Happy, Preach, Hick, Blocky, Push, Fat, Pumpkin, Pepper, Moldy, Ready, Rhymey, Squeaky, Chewing Gum, Beany, Popper, Chubby, Wiry, Rags, Bootsy, Pudd,

Rail, Black, Stacky, Shtuppy, Poutsy, Giggles, Cookie, Beatle, Messy, Swifty, Jiggers and Pioneer. Some had nicknames which revealed their occupation such as Butcher, Baker, (although I don't recall a candle-stick maker) Plumber, Carpenter, Sadler, Butter and Straw. Certainly, many of them had a right to be offended because of the nickname they were stuck with. And, yes, there were also many women who had nicknames. And, overall, there are many, many more, surely hundreds more that I haven't mentioned.

In the 2009 Fisher Family History Amish Register, there are 266 John Stoltz-fus' listed as heads of households, including 39 with the middle initial S. That total does include many who are deceased and goes back to about 1730. Because it's almost unheard of for any English people to become Amish, the list of last names almost never expands.

There were seven Amish men named Moses who lived within about a square mile of us when I was growing up. Also, there were fifteen people named David Esh who lived within our Gordonville mail district, including two who for *years*, regularly sat on each side of me at church. This can be verified by my relatives! Maybe Walter, the mailman should have lobbied our Congressman for a Limitation of Names Bill.

It has always been exceedingly rare for people who were born and raised outside of the Amish community, to become Amish and join the church. In Lancaster County, where we lived, only two of those ever joined the church since about 1900, and even both of them eventually left. Up until about 1985, I was aware of only one such person from another area who had done that. His name was Warren F. and I think he was from Ohio. He was a member for a long time but even he eventually decided to leave the church after all.

About 1970 a young English man named Davey Fidler appeared to be making a genuine transition from non-Amish to Amish. He lived with "Black" Jakes, a few miles away in Byerstown and we often saw him driving by with his horse and buggy. He was with one of the plainest groups, the Lemons, and he was taking the membership class to join the Amish church, or "following the church," as that is called. Brother John and I sometimes teased our sisters that he might want to start courting one of them.

One Sunday afternoon when Davey was swimming with some Amish friends in the Pequea Creek, the others decided to search his clothes which were laying there unguarded. They found some papers which made them suspicious that he was a spy. I don't know if they confronted him about that, but in any case, he did not join the Amish church and soon moved out of the area, and I never heard any more about him.

My mom's great-grandmother, Catherine Bollinger, was born into a non-Amish family in 1830 but because the family was very poor, she was raised by an Amish family [Speicher]. I believe she may have come from Ireland with her twin sister during the famous potato famine. She later joined the Amish church and married my great-great grandfather Abram Stoltzfus. As far as we know that is the only "English" blood in our family ancestry.

Even though our Amish blood strain was so close to being "pure," I still had this wicked obsession with worldly things like watching TV. One place that John G. and I and other friends often went to on Sunday evenings, was to Dave and Helen Chambers' house, in Smoketown. They were an older English couple and were neighbors to John G.'s family. Of course, John's parents never knew we went there to watch TV as that is a major violation of the Amish Ordnung. Sometimes as many as a dozen of us guys would be there watching football or baseball or some movie on TV. For those of us who were obsessed with watching TV, (which, really, was *all* of us!) it was a place we could reliably plan on going to on Sunday nights, if everyone was well-behaved.

In July of 1969 I finally did something that I had wanted to do for a long time. One Sunday morning, ten Amish boys and I hired an English man to take us to a major-league baseball doubleheader in Baltimore to watch my beloved Orioles. We went with Earl Walker and his son Doug in Earl's van, which he often used to haul Amish. There were thirteen of us and we were packed in like sardines. We pulled off of Loch Raven Boulevard and stopped at a "Geno's" restaurant for some fried chicken. Some of the guys were rather amused when I went inside in my bare feet. I didn't think it was a big deal and, indeed, I think that was allowed at many fast food restaurants back then. The Orioles were playing a doubleheader against the Detroit Tigers, who had won the World Series the previous fall. The Orioles lost the first game, to my disappointment. But they won the second game on a base hit by my hero, Hall of Famer Brooks Robinson, in the last of the ninth inning. So, I was happy about that and we all had a lot of fun that day.

A year later, my buddy Dave Zook and I were planning to go with his English friend one evening, to a baseball game at ancient Connie Mack Stadium in Philadelphia. I had never been to a Phillies game before and was really anticipating it. Of course, I had not told my parent's or asked their permission. Dad was not around, but Mom certainly was there when she saw the sleek green 1966 Ford convertible with the top down, waiting in the driveway to pick me up. I was upstairs in my room, hurrying to get ready. I told Mom where we were going, and she was horrified about that and begged me not to go. If she knew how badly I wanted to go, I wonder if she would have relented. While I was still undecided, she dramatically made her point, no pun intended. She jabbed me in the arm with a pin from her apron. Even though that angered me considerably, I somehow made the decision to obey her wish, even though it was an extremely difficult decision to make. When I went out to the car to tell them I wasn't going along, they seemed puzzled and disappointed that I would obey her rather than go with them. It turned out to be a beautiful evening at the game and, in all honesty, I later really wished I had gone along, despite Mom's disapproval.

About a year later, in the spring of 1971, the Phillies opened their brand-new baseball stadium called Veterans Stadium. I was working as a hired boy for Brother Aaron on Dad's other farm. My buddy, Manny K., had a gorgeous yellow 1966 Pontiac GTO and we decided to go to the new stadium for a Saturday afternoon game. I was working with Aaron that morning, and when I told him I was going to the game, he disapproved very strongly. That didn't matter to me because this time my mind was definitely made up. I was planning on going no matter what anybody said or did. This time they would have had to tackle me and tie me up to keep me from going. Fortunately, it didn't come to that, and I doubt that Mom ever even found out about it. I rode with Manny to the new stadium and we had a lot of fun that day watching the game and exploring the new stadium. Strangely, I don't even remember if the Phillies won or lost that day.

During the rest of my Rumspringa days, my buddies and I went to watch baseball games at Philadelphia and Baltimore about four or five times each year. One year we went to Philadelphia four separate times to watch three doubleheaders and a single game and the Phillies won all seven games. Later we saw a Philadelphia Eagle's football game, and several Philadelphia 76ers' basketball games. Of course, that was all without any of our parent's knowledge or permission.

In the fall of 1969, the Orioles were in the World Series against the New York Mets. During one game, Dad and I were working together out in the cornfield, husking corn by hand that afternoon. I had a little seven transistor radio in my pocket which, of course, he was not aware of. It was not the one I had bought from Willis, as that one wouldn't fit in my pocket. I desperately wanted to tune in to the game and check the score, but I couldn't do that with Dad working right beside me. Eventually, I decided to excuse myself and pretend to Dad that I needed a bathroom break. Without benefit of an actual bathroom, of course. I went through the tall corn to a spot about one hundred feet away, and eagerly got the radio out of my pocket and tuned it to the game, on station 1090 AM Baltimore. I was dismayed to find out the Orioles were losing a game that they certainly should have won. And when I finally went back to join Dad, he wanted to know why it took so long and if I had been constipated! I told him not to worry about it and we continued our work. I sometimes wondered if he suspected what I had really been doing.

I was disappointed that the Orioles lost the World Series to the underdog New York Mets that year. But things were much better the following year when they were in the World Series again, and this time they beat the Cincinnati Reds in five games. That certainly worked for me because I had betted a total of about one hundred dollars with my buddies that the Orioles would win, and that was a huge amount of money to me at the time.

For quite a few years at World Series time there was a lottery at Flick's Bar in the town of Kinzers, a few miles away. All the participants were Amish boys who had initiated the lottery and who frequented the bar. For a bet of ten dollars everyone had a chance to win five hundred dollars or more. The winner would later throw a big beer party somewhere for all the participants. When my buddy, John G., won it one year, Christ Fisher dumped a lot of beer on his head in celebration and he seemed a little annoyed about that. Nevertheless, he was really thrilled at having won the five-hundred-dollar World Series lottery that night.

CHAPTER TWENTY-FOUR

Where Do I Hide
My Forty Dollar Chevy?

ONE SATURDAY AFTERNOON, IN April of 1969, three of my buddies and I went to visit some friends at the Amish community at Gettysburg, about sixty miles away. We got on the bus in Lancaster and when we arrived in Gettysburg one of our friends, Jake, came to get us. That evening there was a gang at somebody's house where we hung out but most of the time we were riding around in Jake's old green 1954 Chevy. We were fairly close to the Mason Dixon line, so we went down into Maryland to the one-horse town of Harney to get a supply of adult beverages. In Maryland, the legal drinking age was eighteen and that's why we went there to get it, because we were all underage. In fact, I was not even eighteen yet. Jake was the only one of us who had a driver's license but that didn't stop any of us from taking our turn at the wheel of the old Chevy. We stayed mostly on rural farm roads and dirt roads and by mid-night we were rather inebriated. We named the car the old green puddle jumper, after a car in a 1960s era comic strip. Jake told us about the experiences he'd had with it, and that it had 172,000 miles on it. Back then there were not many cars that lasted that long.

After a while he told us something that really got my attention. He said the old green Chevy was for sale and he was only asking forty dollars for it. Of course, I immediately started thinking very seriously about buying it and that this was a car I could actually afford. That was the main thing on my mind for the rest of the night and the next day. By morning, I had made up my mind to buy it. I pondered the various logistics that were involved. The fact that it was sixty miles from home was only a minor issue, as I saw it. After all, it was a car and it was meant to be driven, so I thought I might as well drive it home. I decided I would have to wait until the following weekend, however.

What was, of course, a concern to me was that I didn't have either a driver's license or a permit. None of the other boys who were with me had a license either. I planned to come back the following Saturday and get a title and a license plate at the local notary and drive the car home. The reason I had not gotten my license yet was that my parents would have had to sign for me since I was only seventeen, still four months away from my 18th birthday. I had never asked them to sign for me, because I absolutely knew that they never would. I thought that since I didn't have a license, I probably wouldn't be able to get car insurance either. Of course, I would never dream of telling my parents about the car, which meant I'd have to hide it somewhere in the neighborhood back home, like other Amish boys did. Several of them parked their cars at Granny [Granville] Wenger's car lot at the intersection of New Holland Pike and Peters Road but that was much too far away for me. Even the most "desperate" Amish boys would not park that far away and have to walk to it each time. They would rather take a chance and hide it in their father's cornfield, even though he would probably vandalize it and flatten its tires if he found it. One example of such paternal punishment involved breaking off the car's radio antenna and stuffing an ear of corn into the car's exhaust pipe. As for myself, I was hopeful that I would be allowed to park at Stauffer's Diesel Shop in Hatville, which was only about a half mile away, if you walked across the fields. I knew that my cousin Melvin and Dan Zook and some other Amish boys already parked their cars there.

A specific dilemma that I had was where to have my license and registration sent to. Surely not to our family mailbox out by the road at our house. A family member would likely see those items when they arrived in the mail and would tell my parents, who would undoubtedly confiscate them. Despite all these issues that had to be dealt with, the thought of actually having my own car, along with the freedom and mobility that it would give me, and all the fun that my buddies and I would have, was very exciting and enticing. After all, wasn't this exactly what I had been dreaming about and longing for, for years? I told myself that yes, it was, although a newer car would have been even better. However, with the old Chevy, certainly the price was right, and it would have to do as my first car.

My buddies were excited about me buying the car and agreed that having it would be wonderful fun. Plus, it would be so much faster and more convenient, then being in a buggy and looking at the tail end of an old plodding horse and being bored almost to tears. I told Jake that I wanted to buy it, and we sealed the deal with a handshake. I certainly didn't have $40.00 with me but I gave him most of what I had. We agreed that I would pay him the rest when I came back the following Saturday to take the car home.

Meanwhile, at the first Gettysburg visit, my exciting plans almost came to a "crashing" halt. At the Sunday afternoon gang, Mike Hershberger, who had been Amish but was now borderline English and drunk at the time, begged Jake to let him take the Chevy for a spin. About five of us were in the car as Mike took the wheel, with me strongly disapproving. He went down a narrow gravel road, and I became increasingly more nervous the faster he went because he was laughing and yelling and was very drunk. When he topped out at about sixty-five miles per hour, I was afraid he would wreck it and I literally feared for my life as there were no seat belts in the car. My thoughts of owning the car were secondary to the fear I felt at the time, as Mike was driving very recklessly. Of course, I was also concerned because he had no license and the cars inspection had expired. Soon he stopped the car without incident, and I was greatly relieved. A few hours later we all had to leave so we went to Gettysburg and took the bus back home.

All week I was excited and thinking about going back to get the car. When Saturday finally came, I took the bus out to Gettysburg again with two of my buddies. Jake met us at the bus station with the old Chevy puddle jumper. I paid him what I still owed him, and we went to a notary to change the title and get a license plate. And now, believe it or not, that ugly green heap was all mine!

We headed home on Route 30 East which is the famous coast-to-coast Lincoln Highway. I was extremely nervous and literally sweating most of the time. Fortunately, the car was an automatic, because it would have been a lot more challenging if it had been a stick shift. Our initial destination was Dave Haldeman's garage in Bird-in-Hand, to get the car inspected. Eventually, we were only a few miles away and I felt sure that we'd make it there without any misfortune.

However, about three miles before our arrival, the right front tire suddenly blew out with a loud bang. The steering wheel jerked to the right and it all startled me so much, I think I almost had a coronary. We pulled in at some business place to change the tire because we didn't want to do it out along the highway in case a state trooper came along. Since this was the first time any of us had ever changed a car tire, it took quite some time till we had it done correctly. Then we took it to Haldeman's Garage. After he had inspected it, he parked it across Beechdale Road on the hill near the railroad track. John Z, who lived about a mile away, paid the bill for me for the time being. Later, when he told me, I was horrified to learn it had cost sixty-nine dollars, which in 1969 was almost like a king's ransom to me.

That Saturday evening, I hitchhiked the five miles up to Bird-in-Hand to get the car and go out with my buddies. I had an extra key made so I was all set to go. My heart was pounding with excitement as I walked up to it an unlocked it and got in. The idea of "catting" around in my own car with my buddies on a Saturday night was immensely exciting. As soon as I started it up, I gleefully threw my big black Amish hat down on the seat beside me, partly out of rebellion and partly because it was warm inside the car from having been in the sun all day. I felt wonderfully free and liberated. I drove through Bird-in-Hand and over to Smoketown to pick up John G and four other boys. Then we headed over to New Holland, about seven miles away, to the Ritz theatre.

After the movie was over we headed back and they all begged me to let them drive a little. I refused, since none of them had a driver's license either. I also would not allow any beer or drinking in the car that night as I didn't want to push my luck. By the time we got back to John G's house the car had started to overheat, apparently from a small leak in the radiator. Someone went down to the barn and brought back some water which we put in and it was okay for the rest of the weekend.

The next day, on Sunday afternoon, we went to a Keffah gang at Danny Dienner's house, down near Millwood. By now I had become fairly good at remembering to hold my hand in front of my face whenever an Amish buggy approached from the opposite direction. This was standard procedure for any Amish boy driving a car so that whoever was in the buggy would not recognize him. It was especially important if he was already a member of the church, as driving a car was totally verboten and it would definitely get the offender expelled and shunned. Just owning a car or having any money invested in a car would also bring that result.

While we were at Dienner's house, a bunch of guys checked out the car and asked a lot of questions, of course. Then, with seven guys in the car, we headed back up the road to watch the Amish baseball game at the school yard. Suddenly two guys yelled at me to stop and back up. So, I did so, thinking something had fallen out the rear window. As anyone would agree, when a driver is backing up, it's a good idea to check your mirrors to see where you're going. But, as I was totally new to this, I seemed to have somewhat forgotten!

Remember, I didn't have a driver's license, and probably had never even read a driver's manual. Another problem was my rear-view vision being somewhat obscured by the four big black Amish hats bobbing around in the back seat. After I had backed up about ten feet I suddenly heard and felt my car bang into something behind me. To my utter horror, I realized I must have backed into another car. I immediately envisioned myself getting arrested and being in a huge amount of trouble. I jumped out and went back and when I saw who the driver of the other car was, I was greatly relieved. It was another Amish boy, Aaron F, who was a friend of mine and he had also been at the Keffah gang. He was driving his ugly old Plymouth Valiant and had been following me too closely. He said in a serious tone, "I hope you have insurance," and then we both laughed. Both cars had big heavy bumpers as most cars did back then and there was no damage other than his bumper being slightly bent. Of course, we didn't report it and I decided to be more careful backing up in the future.

That night I parked my car on the grass in the back corner of the Stauffer Diesel property, even though I hadn't gotten permission. Certainly, it seemed like the most logical place, right next to four other Amish boys' cars. I didn't enjoy the three-quarter mile walk home in the dark but at least now I didn't have to unhitch and unharness my horse and water and feed him and bed him down. I was not too concerned about my unauthorized parking at Stauffer's because I had never heard of any Amish boys having to pay to park there. So, I never even asked good old Mr. Stauffer about it and he never brought it up to me. He was a fairly liberal Mennonite and I guess he might have felt sorry for us poor, underprivileged Amish boys.

That summer each time I went for my car, I'd stop at the mobile home court next to Stauffer's at the water spigot in the middle of the courtyard and fill up my plastic jug with water for the radiator. I wasn't even aware there was such a thing as stop-leak that I could have used! During the time I owned the car, I usually only drove it on weekends and, overall, only put about two thousand miles on it. I admit that it was completely wrong for me to drive so long without out a driver's license and I am ashamed about that. But, at the time I was so rebellious that I just didn't care.

Now that I finally had a car, there was another important issue confronting me. That was how to earn enough money to keep it running, since Dad didn't pay me anything for working fulltime for him on the farm. One thing I had been successful at was playing poker with my buddies and with other guys at the gangs. But that was only enough for pocket change. My buddies tipped me for hauling them around, but I needed more than that.

Many Amish boys *love* to shoot pool and I certainly was no exception. No doubt part of the allure of shooting pool was that it was strictly verboten in the Amish church and would get the offender ex-communicated if the bishop found out. Still, we frequently shot pool at various hangouts, including the Snack-Bar in Bird-in-Hand, at Charlie's Juke Box in New Holland and at Walker's Garage in the town of Bart where we even played on Sunday afternoons. Of course, we always gambled while doing that, eagerly trying to take each other's money.

Another way of making money for desperate Amish boys was going over to Strasburg Railroad and Museum, a big tourist attraction, and give tourists buggy rides on Sunday afternoons. So, I decided to try that. The first Sunday I went there I was the first Amish boy to arrive. I parked in a good spot and soon some tourists came up and talked to me and I asked them if they wanted a ride. So, I left with a family of four. The parents sat in the narrow buggy seat with the kids on their laps. I had to squat on my knees on the floor up front. We went about a quarter mile down the road and came back and they gave me a dollar; I was pleased with that. Several other Amish boys came with their horses and buggies and also gave rides to tourists. I stayed for two hours and made about fifteen dollars. That seemed a lot better than slaving away on the farm for Aaron for nothing.

That summer I made enough money doing that to keep my car running but when winter came the tourist traffic dried up, and I had to try something else. My Rumspringa buddies told me that Bird-in-Hand Poultry Company had contracts with various farmers to raise chickens that would be slaughtered later. There were about five thousand chickens in each long chicken house that had to be caught and put in crates when they were big enough to sell. Art Brown would go out in the evening to pick up a van load of hard-up Amish boys who would catch all the chickens. So, I also did that occasionally. As anyone could imagine, it was vile, boring and disgusting work. At least we didn't have to chase the chickens. They were all sleeping and bunched together on the floor. There were a few dim red light bulbs giving off just enough light for the "catchers" to do their job, but not so much light that it would spook the chickens. There'd be about five guys grabbing them and carrying them upside down by their legs. We each made hundreds of trips back and forth from inside the chicken house to the tractor trailer truck parked outside, always carrying seven chickens, four with one hand and three with the other. We'd always have some painful claw scratches on our hands when we were done. Outside, on the truck were two guys grabbing those angry birds from us and jamming them into wooden crates. Inside the chicken house it was stuffy and warm and stinky.

To make matters worse, this was always done at night after I had already spent a whole day working hard on the farm. I was already tired when we started so it was total drudgery catching chickens for about five hours. I could think of about one thousand things I would rather do than that. But I desperately needed the money and because I was now used to the fun and convenience of having a car, I wasn't about to go back to driving a horse and buggy, come chickens or high water.

On a typical chicken catching excursion, I'd arrive back at Brother Aaron's house at about two in the morning. With the help of a flashlight I'd enter the completely dark house and try to make my way upstairs as quietly as possible so as not to wake Aaron and Katie and the kids. That wasn't easy because Amish people don't have lights OR carpet in their stairways. I knew I'd have to get up and go to work on the farm in about three hours. I'd be exhausted and bone tired and would collapse into my bed, too tired to even take a shower. In about one minute, I'd be sound asleep.

It was very quiet at the farm at that early morning hour. I'd still have my filthy shirt on that reeked of dirt, dust, sweat and chicken manure. For some strange reason, the Amish always wore their shirts to bed at night, no matter how warm it might be. My good sister-in-law, Katie, never complained to me about how bad the bed sheets must have smelled, and as for myself, I think I was too tired to notice. For what it's worth, I never caught chickens on two consecutive nights. I was never that desperate for car money!

CHAPTER TWENTY-FIVE

Amish Teens Robbed
at Gunpoint

DURING THOSE EXTREMELY CHALLENGING times when I never seemed to have enough money and yet felt like I was literally working myself to death, there were some very logical alternatives I could have chosen. Especially since I turned eighteen just a few months after I bought my car. Of course, now being of legal age, I could easily have just walked off the farm and gotten a well-paying job at the trailer (mobile home) factories in Leola. Or work at picking cherries and apples at Kauffman's Fruit Farm. Or something else that was suitable since jobs were plentiful and unemployment was very low at that time. And, no matter where I worked, I could legally keep all the money I earned!

I could even have done the ultimate evil, gotten an apartment in Intercourse and gone totally "English." I was vaguely aware that I could legally do all those things, although my parents would have been horrified. Apparently, I had not yet become so "hardened" that I seriously considered those choices. And, if I acted on them, my reputation among the Amish would suffer greatly, especially with certain girls I was enamored with. That would have been a classic example of having my "naama ferdarva," (name ruined) which most Amish seek to avoid at all costs. There is probably no other group of people in the world who are as concerned about their reputations amongst each other as the Amish, especially the most true-blue and faithful ones. So that, undoubtedly, was the biggest reason that I, meekly and dutifully, continued as an unpaid worker on the farm for Aaron.

Of course, Dad benefitted greatly from that arrangement because I had been very effectively indoctrinated to believe that all the money I earned (except my chicken catching money!) before I turned twenty-one, should go directly to him. I was taught to believe that was totally normal and reasonable for all Amish people. And because that was also done to all my friends, I came to accept it surprisingly well!

The old green Chevy was unique in several ways. It was the only car I've ever known that could stay running with no battery in it. Of course, it needed a battery to start it, but then it could be taken out of the car and it would still run. Don't try this at home with any modern car. Once we drove about one-half mile on the shoulder of a country road at night with no battery in it and, of course, no working headlights.

When guys go from one gang to another on a Saturday night, often they are not welcome, and certain guys there might do some mischief to their buggy or car if it's left unattended. One night we stopped at a Happy Jack gang and left my car unattended. When we came back to it, a Happy Jack who apparently was extra happy, meaning he was drunk, was urinating into the gas tank of my car. I had good reason to believe a few of his buddies had also done that. I yelled angrily at them and we got in and I nervously turned the key. It started okay and seemed to run as well as before. As I drove away, I wondered if what they had done had raised or lowered the octane level of the gas in the tank. Of course, back then no cars had locking or antitheft features for the gas tank, so anybody could access it at any time.

Another form of mischief was guys showing up uninvited in the evening at Amish weddings. Some guys who *were* invited and wanted to flaunt their authority would grab them and rub black shoe polish or coal black on their faces. That would prove to everyone that they were trespassing. Scouting was another thing that was done by the adventurous at heart. That involved some guys secretly going on Saturday nights to an Amish house where a guy was visiting his girlfriend. They would often hide something from the boyfriend's buggy or his horses' harness. One night we scouted (Israel's) Moses Stoltzfus while he was in the house with his girlfriend, Barbie, at preacher Eli King's house. I crept into the barn, found where Moses had tied his horse, then took the crupper off the harness, and put it into Eli's mailbox. The crupper is the leather piece that goes under the horse's tail and usually doesn't smell so nice. When our faithful mailman, Walter, opened the mailbox later and saw it, I'm sure he didn't take it along and deliver it, especially since it had no postage or address on it.

Sometimes, certain mischief occurred that could be considered "extreme scouting." One event featured a window being hurriedly jerked open and a cat, a chicken, and a goose thrown in at the startled couple. In another incident, the boyfriend went to the barn to hitch up his horse and go home. He was astonished to find that someone had already hitched the resident "bull of the barn" to his buggy. Another young suitor came out to find his buggy missing. He eventually found it perched high up on top of the barn.

About the time my oldest brothers were starting Rumspringa, my parents were seriously thinking of moving from the "worldly" Intercourse area and across the southern mountain range to the ultra-conservative Kirkwood area. When it's thought that certain areas are becoming too "wild," Amish parents often flee to remote areas where farms are cheaper and, more importantly, where other extremely conservative and Ordnung-obeying parents live. The ministers at Kirkwood and Nine Points were so strict that Bishop David Z. Fisher once excommunicated an Amish youth merely for drinking one quart of beer. So, the extreme level of strictness was thought to be a good thing and that my brothers would not be subjected to as many evil and "fahfeerish" temptations as back in the Intercourse area. Dad and Mom said that Grandad Miller somberly warned them, however, that "da diefel iss dott au," meaning the devil is there, too. As it turned out, they did not move there and stayed on the home farm for the rest of their lives.

But there was a far more sinister reason for their desire to move across the mountain range. A middle-aged unmarried Amish woman of ill repute who lived in our neighborhood sometimes practiced her immoral seductive charms on "innocent" and vulnerable teen-age Amish boys. So, of course, my parents were genuinely concerned about that for several years.

Sometimes a carload of inebriated Amish youth made a late Saturday night visit to a preacher's home; someone who they felt had been too strict with them. Once a group of angry boys surprised a preacher in his barn and tackled and overpowered him. Then they gave him a haircut which was extremely short and in total violation of the Ordnung. Of course, he had to live with it that way until it grew out. I'm sure he preferred that to them cutting off his beard. I doubt that he ever found out who did it because they had been wearing handkerchiefs over their faces. Probably the reason they had done something so extreme was because of him having wrongfully excommunicated them.

A more innocent event occurred when Sam F. and a carload of boys pulled into preacher Eli King's driveway late one Saturday night and drove across the yard and right up to their bedroom window. Then they blew the car horn nonstop for quite some time until flashlights were beaming out at them from various windows. At that time, Sam backed the car up and they all left. Some other boys were racing around in another car doing "doughnuts" in Eli's field nearby until they almost got stuck in the mud.

One Sunday afternoon some Groffie guys came to the Keffah gang at Aaron Miller's farm and they were looking for trouble. They drove their car through a field of fully-grown tobacco that was ready to harvest. My brother John then threw a rock at the car, and it just "happened" to break the windshield. Of course, the intruder got very angry and threatened to come to our farm some night and dump a lot of mud or rocks into John's milk tank, which would have ruined the whole tank full of milk. That's how he extorted the money from John to pay for the broken windshield.

Sometimes, Amish boys driving in their open buggies at night were accosted by rowdy English guys who threw rocks at them, occasionally causing injury. Once, I was driving alone in my open buggy at night when a car approached, and someone threw a big rock at me. It slammed into the buggy seat beside me, missing me by inches. Less ominous were the times when English youth surprised Amish boys and ran up behind the buggy and grabbed and stole their Amish hats. But that was certainly serious enough.

Some drivers become impatient following the slow-moving Amish buggies and that is understandable. Sometimes they'll shout or blow their horns. Once a driver behind me who apparently was drunk, yelled at me "If you can't drive it, park it!" Even though I was driving as well as anyone else could have!

Some Amish folks have even been robbed at gunpoint while traveling by horse and buggy. That happened to my buddy, Dave Zook, on a cold winter night when he was sixteen years old. His sisters, Mary and Dora, were with him on a lonely and remote road, Pond Road, two miles north of Intercourse. The horse had slowed to a walk while going up a hill. Suddenly, two long haired bearded thugs ran out from behind a corn shock in the field. One grabbed the horses' bridle to stop him. The other man had a shotgun and jabbed the business end directly into Dave's ribs and demanded his wallet, which Dave immediately handed to him. The robbers then ran to their car and drove away.

Dave and his sisters, shaken as they were, quickly drove to the closest "English" house and called the police. It took some time till they arrived and since the robbers had a huge head start, they were never apprehended. A burglary and theft had occurred the same night at Zimmerman's store in Intercourse and it was assumed the same people had done it. Later, Dave went to Lancaster Police Barracks to try to identify them from a lineup of inmates but was unable to, and they were never caught or punished.

During Rumspringa when Amish boys have hoedowns, the parents leave before it starts and go to visit friends or relatives. If they come home while the hoedown is still in progress, they discreetly do not interfere and go directly into the house. One exception was the hoedown at Uncle Sam Miller's farm when Sam went to investigate. When he saw the battery-powered record player blaring out the evil music, he grabbed a pitchfork and attacked and stabbed it until it died. Then the angry boys pelted him with ears of corn and apples that were stored in the barn. Sam then fled to the safety of the house. Later John S., the irate owner of the ruined device drove his car over the lawn to the window of Sam and Bertha's bedroom and blared his car horn in protest for quite some time.

Before John and I were in Rumspringa, whenever there was a singing at our house, followed by a hoedown in the barn, Mom would encourage us to stay in the house and not go out to the hoedown at all. That just made us more eager to go out and watch. I think each time we disregarded her advice and went out to watch.

We had lots of fun with the old Chevy that summer, going to hoe downs and other events. Occasionally, on Saturday nights, about six of us would go to the old Sky View Drive-in Theater. Since saving money and cutting corners was especially important to us, we came up with the idea of having two boys already hidden in the trunk upon arrival. That way we'd need to buy two less tickets. Once, at an extremely popular movie, a lot of cars were moving very slowly on the way in. Meanwhile the trunk was getting stuffy as the two guys inside were getting hot and sweaty from the summer heat. Occasionally, we'd hear their muffled yells. Finally, we got the tickets and drove in. We went to the back of the lot and cautiously and discreetly let them out, hoping nobody was watching. Of course, that was before there were any hatchback seats, in which case they could have climbed from the trunk into the back seat, and we wouldn't even need to open the trunk.

One Saturday night there was a hoedown in the Groffdale area, where a lot of plain Mennonites live. About six Mennonite girls came up to the barn to watch the dancing and they were quite shy and nervous. My buddies and I had been drinking and we were feeling our oats a little. We chatted with the girls and soon my buddy, Dave Z, told me privately that if I convinced a certain one of them to go into the green Chevy with me and if I kissed her, he would give me five dollars. That sounded pretty good to me, to be paid that much for achieving my first kiss. Unfortunately, it wasn't that easy. I was not a particularly good flirter, and even though I tried not to show it, I was probably just as nervous as her, so it just didn't happen. I really regretted that later, as I realized that catching the hated chickens only paid about that much *per hour*, and with no fun involved either. And, for what it's worth, I didn't have enough of nerve to even ask the Mennonite girl to sit in the car with me! I guess that shows how shy I was around girls back then!

In July, 1969, soon after I had bought my car, a few of us decided to go to the Potter County mountains in northern Pennsylvania for a week's vacation. In our group were Levi K., his brother Dan, John G, and me. The K brothers had relatives who had a deer hunting cabin that we stayed in. I didn't want to take my car that far for fear it might break down although, as it turned out, that would have been better than taking the car that we did. So, we borrowed a car from another Keffah guy, Dan S., who had a venerable old black 1956 Pontiac with extremely bad brakes and a convertible top, which certainly appealed to all of us. The convertible top, that is, not the bad brakes. Dan told us to be very careful with it. The brakes worked fine if you applied about thirty times the normal pressure to them. With that thought in mind, we started off on the one hundred sixty-mile trip.

Not far from the cabin, while going through the town of Coudersport, the driver, Dan K, suddenly had to stop quickly because of a car stopped at a red light. We were going about sixty miles per hour when he slammed on the brake extremely hard, then kept pushing it absolutely as hard as he could. At the same time, he had such a death grip on the steering wheel that he may have bent it slightly. To our great relief, the car stopped about one foot short of hitting the other car. Of course, we should have gotten the brakes fixed that week, but there was no garage close by, so we didn't bother.

Soon we got to the cabin, and unloaded our things and got comfortable and settled in. An old black and white TV got a lot of our attention, and we did our fair share of playing poker and drinking adult beverages. The cabin was in a remote area with a narrow winding road going past it, with very little traffic at any given time. Several times we went to the small general store a few miles away, but we really didn't drive the car much that week. Still, some of us wanted to see how fast we could drive on that narrow road, while still making allowance for the bad brakes. Of course, we kept the convertible top down all week.

One day, John G and I went for a spin, (literally!) with him behind the wheel. We were about one-half mile from the cabin and thought we were familiar with all the curves in the road. But this time was the fastest any of us had driven it in that exact area. We had become more and more daring as the week went by. That certainly was foolish, especially since the road was gravel instead of pavement. As we went around a curve much too fast, the back of the car fishtailed across to the other side and suddenly we realized it was completely out of control. John oversteered and we started to go up a steep embankment at a very dangerous angle. With the convertible top down, we were now in extreme danger, although I don't remember seeing my life flashing before my eyes during those heart-stopping moments.

We were almost at the point where the car would tip over and roll upside down, and it probably would have crushed both of us to death. At that last terrifying moment, and just in the nick of time, John swiftly and desperately spun the steering wheel to the right. Immediately, the car came down off the bank and was now sliding sideways across the gravel road. It had slowed down considerably but was still not under control. It went off the road at right angles, and suddenly we saw something we hadn't noticed before. Near the edge of the road stood an old wooden barn and we were heading directly toward its double doors.

Unfortunately, the barn doors were not open to accommodate the car's entry. We crashed through the wooden doors and came to a stop moments later with the car now completely inside the barn. We momentarily sat there in stunned disbelief as dust drifted down on top of our bare heads and suddenly it was quiet except for the surprised squawking of chickens somewhere in the barn. I was the first one to find my voice and I said in a tone of sheer incredulity, "I can't belieeeeve this really happened." Well, as the old saying goes, seeing is believing. We had barely gotten out of the car when the irate owner of the barn stormed up to us.

We sheepishly explained to him what had happened. He said we would have to fix the damage to his satisfaction or pay to have it done. He called the police and John was cited and had to pay a heavy fine. We were able to back the car out and drive back to the cabin, where we told Levi and Dan what had happened. At that moment they, literally, were not happy campers. The four of us spent most of a day fixing the barn doors. Oddly, it was on the same day that the first astronauts landed on the moon, but we couldn't watch that anyway because it wouldn't come in on the old TV set in the cabin. We, along with many other Amish people, had some doubt the moon landing had really occurred, anyway!

The car was not damaged much, just a few bumps and bruises. Later, on the way back to Lancaster County we sideswiped a guardrail, causing even more damage. Of course, we blamed that on the car's bad brakes. Needless to say, we had some explaining to do to the car's owner when we got back, not to mention paying him for the damage to his car.

That summer my old Chevy ran pretty well most of the time. I didn't put many miles on it since we only ran it on weekends. When I bought it, I didn't dare to have the title sent to my home address, so I arranged to have it sent to a friend's post office box in Smoketown. On my eighteenth birthday, August 23, I applied for a learner's permit. When it came in the mail, I was much relieved because now I could drive legally if a licensed driver was with me. So, on an Amish holiday in October, I decided to take my drivers' test at the State Police barracks in Lancaster. My buddy Dave already had his license so I was now driving legally, with him sitting next to me. When we arrived, I was a little nervous as I eagerly awaited my turn. I did fine on the written test and then a kindly older police officer and I got into the old Chevy for my big challenge. I passed with flying colors, or at least he didn't complain about my driving. We went back inside, and my permit was stamped and now I was in clover, a legal driver, and I was certainly thrilled and relieved about that.

One evening in November, which is Amish marrying season, Dave and I went to a friend's wedding over at the mountain range, near Nickel Mines. Amish wedding ceremonies and celebrations usually last till about 11:00 P.M. After staying there for a while, Dave and I went back to where I had parked the car in a field. For some reason, the battery was very weak and the car wouldn't start. There were no other cars there that we could get a jump start from. I doubt that I had jumper cables anyway. It was about 9:30 P.M. and getting cold, and we were faced with the very unpleasant prospect of staying in the car overnight with no heat. Even if we had been able to get a ride with someone else, I didn't want to leave the car there. So, we slept in the car that night. Or tried to, that is. It was very chilly, and we slept poorly. Of course, we didn't even bother to notify our folks at home where we were spending the night. There were no cell phones then and, of course, no phone at the Amish house where the wedding was.

In the morning we woke up, still tired, and decided to walk about one mile to the small town of Nickel Mines where we knew there was a general store and a telephone. Nickel Mines School was where five Amish schoolgirls were brutally murdered in 2006 which, of course, was in the national news for quite some time. Dave and I were in the phone booth outside the store, looking for someone to tow my car. Lo and behold, we saw an old tow truck pull up. There were three hairy bearded mountain men in it and quite unsavory looking they were, indeed. We told them our predicament and they agreed to drive back to my car while Dave and I stood on the back of the truck. Apparently, they didn't have any jumper cables either. They offered to push the car with the tow truck and get it started that way, even though it was an automatic. Modern cars with automatic transmissions will not start that way, but they said the old Chevy should start. They pushed us about a half mile to Wolf Rock Road at the top of the mountain range. From there we had a very long hill that we could coast down. After coasting a short distance, I turned on the ignition and put it into drive and to our delight, it started right up. The mountain men only charged a few dollars and I drove it about five miles to the corner of Uncle Sammy's field where I sometimes parked it.

I had only recently gotten bold enough to park it there, along Newport Road, about a quarter mile from home. That was much closer than walking to Stauffer's Diesel Shop every time. It was also much more likely that the car might be vandalized. One Saturday evening when I got to the car, I found that somebody had thrown a big rock through the windshield. Of course, I was very upset, but I decided it probably wasn't worth fixing, especially since the car had overheated badly recently and didn't run well anymore. Besides, I had been hoping to get a newer car soon, anyway. But I wasn't sure what I should do with the old Chevy because I didn't think anyone would want to buy it. So, I let it sit there for a few weeks. Dad must have known it was my car. I suppose Uncle Sammy had seen me go to it and had told him. So, Dad told me I might as well call Gap Auto Salvage to come and get it. So, probably to his surprise, I agreed. The next day they came and took it, and just like that it was gone from my life forever. I have always fondly remembered it, my very first car, the old green $40.00 puddle jumper. Unfortunately, I have no pictures of it because I did not yet have a camera then. The only memento I have of it was the round glass like horn button with the old green Chevy logo on it. For the past fifty years, it has resided in an old White Owl cigar box with my collection of Indian arrowheads, some 1950s-era metal dog license tags and various other childhood treasures.

CHAPTER TWENTY-SIX

Misadventures with Forbidden Cars

AFTER THE CHEVY DIED, I was faced with the unhappy reality of again having to ride in a boring and slow-moving horse and buggy. Dad wanted me to work at tobacco giant, P. Lorillard's huge brick warehouses in Lancaster that winter, along with about ten other Amish boys, and I readily agreed. It was hard work, unloading truckloads of tobacco bales that the Amish farmers had grown, and stacking them in the warehouse by hand. A couple of the boys had cars that we all rode back and forth in. A former schoolmate of mine, Aaron, had a black 1959 Ford convertible and he picked me and some other boys up each day. During lunch break at the warehouses, we'd all play poker while eating our lunch.

When each Amish farmer's crop was unloaded and weighed, and the tobacco company gave him that big check, we knew that was the best time to hit him up for a big tip. We'd all divide the tips amongst us at quitting time. The stingiest farmers only gave about a dollar while the most generous ones gave up to five dollars.

As spring approached, Dad had already dictated to me that I would be working for Brother Aaron again on Dad's other farm. I was, of course, hankering for another car, and was trying to save money for that. One would think that should be easy since I was working at the tobacco warehouses. However, most of us had to turn our paychecks over to the "old man," as most of us referred to our Dads. Since the checks were, of course, made out in our own name, legally they would have been ours to keep. But we were afraid if we kept them our Dads' wouldn't let us work there anymore. I guess none of us realized how much we were like indentured (but still willing) slaves at the warehouses and at home on the farms. I do remember keeping one check for myself that winter, and Dad didn't complain about that. I was being paid two dollars per hour which was the minimum wage at the time.

One of the English tobacco workers, Harry, a brash old curmudgeon, had a big red 1959 Buick that he wanted to sell for $150.00. It had huge long flaring "fins" from the back fenders to the taillights. I almost bought it, but the deal fell through because I could hardly afford to pay that much for it. Plus, I really didn't like the way it looked. Instead, I wound up buying a two-tone pink and cream colored 1957 Buick Special for $100.00 from Clair Wizzel, a suspicious looking bearded character who lived at Round Top Road, over on the mountain range. The car had a very strange ignition system. In order to start it, you turned the key on all the way and pushed the accelerator down until the starter engaged and that's how it would start.

Most of our original group of eight close friends were now more interested in girls than cars, except for John G. and me. He and I, along with Dave Zook, now hung out together regularly on weekends and some called us the Freesome Threesome, as we proudly tooled around to various hoedowns in my "new" car. Unfortunately, two weeks after I bought it, the transmission started going crazy.

One evening, Dave and I went over to Strasburg to buy some baseball equipment at the sporting goods store. I noticed that when the shifter on the column indicated it was in park, the car would then start to back up. Or when it indicated it was in neutral, the car might be moving forward. Or some other weird combination. Of course, we should have parked it and gotten it fixed before driving any further. After considering our options we decided to drive it home. Or, at least try to. On the way back, we were desperately hoping it would keep going as it had become totally erratic. Eventually we got to Leon Hess's farm on the east side of Intercourse and that was all she wrote. It wouldn't budge an inch in any gear. I parked along the side of the road and locked it up and both of us walked to our respective homes in total disgust, a distance of about one and a half miles. The next day I called Landis Transmission Company in Leola to come and get the car.

When I went to get it a week later, I was horrified to learn the bill was $139.00, which would be the equivalent of about $800.00 today. I had to borrow most of the money from Dave to pay for it. I went back to Clair Wizzel, hoping he would refund some of my money but he totally refused. Of course, I was very unhappy about that because I presumed he knew the car's transmission was going bad when he sold me the car, even though he denied that.

It was now summertime and I was working full-time for Brother Aaron again so I had to resort to hauling tourists and catching chickens at night, as virtually my only source of income. All the money that I earned working for Aaron went directly to my dad and I didn't get a cent of it. I've heard that quite a few Amish boys' and girls' parents gave them 10% of the money they earned working on Amish farms, but I wasn't that lucky. During all the years I worked for Dad and Aaron, the only money I ever got was a tip of fifty cents. It was from Aaron, one Saturday evening when I worked late, raking hay out in his field for a couple of hours.

One day, Ralph, the truck driver who delivered our cattle feed from Clem Hoober's feed mill in Intercourse, asked if I would help him for about two hours, unloading bags of feed at the mill in Bird-in-Hand. I was a little surprised that Dad consented to it, and even more surprised that he allowed me to keep all of what Ralph paid me, the princely sum of one dollar and thirty-five cents. I doubt if Mom knew about it. She would have objected to me having all that money, because she'd be afraid I would spend it on "dumm sach."

I needed a closer place to park the Buick and I thought I found the perfect place at Elam J's apartment house, about five hundred feet from Aaron's house. Elam J, an Amish man, had bought the house and barn from Christ R. a few years earlier and had converted them into apartments. Since Elam did not live there himself, I thought I could park my car there with the tenant's cars and he wouldn't know it was mine. Unfortunately, it didn't work out that way. He confronted me at Aaron's barn one day and asked me if I was parking a car at his apartment building. When I admitted that I was, he immediately asked if I was a member of the church, and I told him I wasn't. Did he think I would tell him if I *had* been a member, and risk ex-communication? In any case, he told me I couldn't park there. So, I started parking at Stauffer's again, which was more than a mile away.

I felt as though I had now moved up the ladder a few rungs, as owner of the '57 Buick, instead of the humble old '54 Chevy. While certainly not a fashion plate, either, it was more reliable, and obviously miles ahead of a horse and buggy, no pun intended. I did have to replace the gas tank for some reason, so we went to Leidy's junkyard over at the mountain range for a replacement gas tank. We found just the right one on a junked car and removed it and installed it on the Buick, without even dumping out the old gas that was in it. So, sometimes it ran very poorly while jerking and shaking ominously. Then Dave would say,

"Is this thing yooksin again?" I dreaded when it did that, afraid that it would let us sit. Eventually, the old gas worked its way through, and it seemed to be okay. I guess my idea of leaving the old gas in the tank showed the degree of frugality (stinginess?) that prevailed in my family and in our culture.

Another problem I experienced was a defective hood latch on the Buick. It is not a pleasant or calming event when, while driving a car at highway speed, suddenly the hood flies up all the way and comes back almost against the windshield. Since driving visibility is then immediately reduced to zero, one needs to apply the brakes very quickly and decisively, better known as a "panic stop." This happened twice before we got the hood latch fixed.

The grass "parking lot" at Stauffer's Diesel shop seemed to be a safe place for the other Amish boys and me to park our cars, although there was one incident of mischief that happened to my car. One Saturday evening when I arrived, I saw some shelled corn laying on the ground by the car's gas tank opening. It was obvious that some had been put into the filler opening. I seemingly had no way to know how much might have been put in. I was greatly relieved that the car apparently still ran as well as before. I suppose whoever did that considered it to be a Halloween "joke."

One Sunday afternoon while playing baseball at Witmer School in Smoketown, Sam Fisher was pestering me to let him take the Buick for a spin. I should never have allowed that because I knew he was somewhat drunk. But he said he would only drive it a little around the school yard and he'd be very careful. So, he and all his buddies got in and he started off. Predictably, he got carried away, while his buddies were whooping it up and egging him on. Just as I was running up to stop him, he came around the driveway and onto the grass where a parked school bus stood. To my horror, he banged right into the back corner of the bus. The car's left headlight was smashed, and the front fender was badly crumpled. The bus was not damaged, only because it had been hit on its big heavy back bumper. Of course, I was furious and demanded that he pay for all the damage to my car. But he was such a cheapskate that he only ever gave me a total of ten dollars. I took the Buick to a local body shop and spent about seventy-five dollars to get it fixed. I wished later I had sued Sam in small claims court, but for some reason I did not. Maybe it was because I knew the Amish were extremely averse to suing anybody. Sam could easily have paid for it too, because he was at least twenty-two years old, which meant he kept all the money he earned instead of his dad confiscating it. Also, since he was already a member of the Amish church, I'm sure he would have been willing to pay me the proper amount if I had threatened to tell his bishop about the incident. Since I have always been a peace-loving individual, I decided to not go that route. But I have often thought I probably should have.

John's friend, Ephraim, had an older brother, Peter, who had been married for a few years and he and his wife had several young children. Of course, when an Amish person marries, any more Rumspringa with the young folks is strictly Verboten. Peter was very bored at home on Sunday afternoons and sometimes went with Ephraim and the others in his car, which Peter had helped him to buy. It was a beautiful, red 1960 Chevy Impala with a white convertible top.

One Sunday morning, while they were nursing serious hangovers from the night before, Peter had a not so brilliant idea. There was a long stretch of straight roadway that went by the house where they were staying. Peter wanted to give them a thrill and impress them by driving the car dangerously fast past them as they stood out along the road watching. He drove alone in the car to the far end, about a half mile away, then turned around and started back. Soon he was traveling at well over one hundred miles per hour. He blissfully waved at them as he raced by. Everyone knew there was a T-road ahead with some big trees at the far side of the intersection. When Peter thought the time was right he stepped firmly on the brake, confident that he would get stopped in time. However, he soon realized to his horror he had seriously underestimated the amount of space he needed to get stopped. To make things worse, there were no seat belts in the car. Now frantically pumping the brake, he gripped the steering wheel with a death grip, and braced himself as best he could. As he bore down on the intersection, the trees were just a few feet ahead. With a sickening crash the car slammed into the trees head on, as the boys behind him watched in horror and disbelief. As they ran up, they were greatly relieved to see him climbing out of the wrecked car, apparently unhurt. He was, however, physically and emotionally shaken up and certainly also feeling quite foolish. That beautiful car was demolished and was now ready for the salvage yard. I suppose there was a lesson very well learned that day!

Another foolish car "accident" involved two Amish teenage boys, one of whom was a cousin of mine. One Sunday afternoon at a gang, they decided to play "chicken" with their cars. No doubt, they were both drunk at the time. They dared each other to start some distance apart and then drove toward each other at a very dangerous speed. Whoever veered away first would be the "chicken." Unfortunately, neither one veered away soon enough, and there was a very serious head-on crash. My cousin was almost killed, as he had suffered very serious injuries, but he eventually fully recovered.

During the time I had the Buick I never told my parents that I had a car, similar to when I had the Chevy. I suppose they must have known or at least strongly suspected that I had a car again. They often reminded me that by the next year, 1971, I would turn twenty years old and they'd really like to see me get baptized and join the Amish church. I had absolutely no desire to do so, although I didn't tell them that. Except for Brother Amy, all my siblings had joined the church by about age eighteen. I was feeling some pressure from them as well as from my parents. I really didn't want to give serious consideration to the idea of never owning or driving a car again and being permanently stuck behind a slow-moving horse and buggy. But, of course, that is what is required of all Amish church members.

When winter came, I was working at the tobacco warehouses in Lancaster again. Now, instead of riding with someone else, I was driving my own car every day. My latest acquisition was a black 1962 Pontiac Bonneville that I had bought from my cousin, Melvin, for $200.00. He had to sell it because he was planning to get married soon. Every day I picked up five other guys who rode with me. That worked well except for one guy who seemed to think that he should ride for free. Like the previous winter, working at the warehouses was a lot of hard work and not enough pay but overall, it was a fun experience, certainly much better than staying home and stripping tobacco.

One morning there was a lot of fresh snow on the roads. I had just picked up the last guy, and we were going down a hill on a narrow country road. There was a car stopped up ahead that was stuck in the snow. It had partly slid around and was at somewhat of an angle. Belatedly, I realized I was going down the hill too fast and I slammed on the brakes. All four wheels were locked up and just sliding on the snowy, icy road. I was unable to steer away from the other car at all. With my heart in my throat, I could only hope I would get stopped in time. Incredibly, when I finally got stopped my front bumper was about six inches from his driver's door! It seems I can still hear Chocky, one of my passengers, yelling "Boy, are you ever lucky." My car was so close to the other car that the driver couldn't even open his car door until my riders got out and pushed my car backward.

In the spring of 1971, I was back at Dad's other farm, working for Brother Aaron again. My life seemed to be programmed for another boring summer of hard Amish farm work, along with much more of the dreaded chicken catching. I was now almost twenty years old and still with virtually no clue as to what lay ahead, on my life's journey. My parents were now pleading more frequently than ever for me to become a church member that summer. So, every day I struggled mightily with that all-important question, "Should I join the Amish church or not?" Many times, I wondered disconsolately to myself, "Why, oh why, was I destined to be born Amish and eventually be forced to make this seemingly impossible decision"? Often, while working alone hoeing weeds in the tobacco and cornfields, I would desperately cry out to God for the wisdom I needed to make the right choice. We had all been taught to believe that if someone was a member of the church, they would be much more likely to go to Heaven if they died, than if they were not a member. Also, the preachers would empha- size how eternity is not measured by time, but that it actually transcends the concept of time, and that everyone either goes to Heaven or hell when they die. We were taught that it would be sinful and dangerous to consider joining any other church or even just visiting one. So, here I was, facing what was surely the biggest and most important decision in my life and not knowing what to do or who to turn to. Even if I had known an English pastor, I wouldn't have dared to ask him for advice, for fear of probably being deceived.

One day my friends and I had a rare theological discussion about people being saved or lost when they die. John Z solemnly declared that people know where they'll go when they die, either to Heaven or to hell. He meant that we all intuitively "know" if we had been good enough to get to Heaven. At the time, I tended to mostly agree with him. However, later I realized that, no, I had absolutely no idea where I would go, and that was very scary for me sometimes.

I vividly remember one hot summer night, when a mighty thunderstorm arose at the farmhouse. I was sound asleep in my upstairs bedroom when suddenly there was a tremendous crash of thunder. It seemed to be much, much louder than anything I'd ever heard before. It was especially loud with all the windows being open on that hot summer night. It seemed as though I shot straight up in bed, certainly more frightened then I had ever been before in my life. I was sure that unbelievably loud noise must surely mean that this was now the end of the world. I ran to the window, desperately praying it was not the end, because I knew I was not ready. I still was not aware that tremendous noise had only been a mighty crash of thunder. As I stood there trembling and shaking in abject fear, I realized with indescribable relief that it was a powerful thunderstorm, and not the end of the world as I had feared. As my heart resumed a normal rhythm, I watched in awe, as many brilliant flashes of lightning illuminated the sky, accompanied by more mighty crashes of thunder. Then the heavens opened up and torrential sheets of rain poured down on the ground. I watched for a while, then went back to bed, my mind still troubled, and thinking of how frightened I had been. It seemed like several hours before I was able to fall asleep again.

CHAPTER TWENTY-SEVEN

My Escape From the Amish Lifestyle

IN THE SPRING OF 1971, a major event occurred in my life which would have profound implications on how the rest of my life would unfold. It also would allow me to postpone for several years, the extremely important and difficult decision confronting me about whether to join the Amish church or not. Moreover, and happily, now almost everyone would agree that I was justified in postponing that decision. Also, it seemed as though I still was not any closer to knowing what that decision eventually would be.

When I turned eighteen in the summer of 1969, the Vietnam War was raging and had been for a very long time. In fact, that year was thought to have been the bloodiest year of the entire conflict. A large proportion of the American people, including the Amish, thought the war was unjustified and probably unwinnable. People everywhere were horrified at the shocking toll in human lives of many thousands of heroic, brave, young men and everyone wondered when this awful war would finally end.

During that time, there was a nationwide draft in effect. A unique lottery system was also used in conjunction with the draft for a period of three years. The lottery applied to each young man for the year in which he turned eighteen. Everyone was assigned a random number from one to 365, or 366 if it was a leap year, coinciding with the date of his birthday. The ones who had the lower numbers were most likely to be drafted, while the ones with the higher numbers were least likely to be.

When I became aware that the number ten had been selected and applied to my birth date, August 23, I felt certain I would eventually be drafted. I doubt that my parents were even aware of the draft lottery and that I had such a low number. I decided to not tell them anything about it because I thought it probably would just cause them a lot of worry.

Shortly after turning eighteen I registered with Selective Service in Lancaster, as required. Later, in a large examining room, in a group of about fifty young men, we had to take off every stitch of clothing for our physical examinations. Included in that large group of English guys were four Amish guys, besides myself. We had to stand in two long lines, according to our ages. I was very glad I didn't have to stand next to Melvin B., although that almost happened as there was only one guy between us. Melvin and I were not on good terms with each other. I strongly suspected it was him and his buddies who had put the shelled corn in my car's gas tank, and later painted some peace symbols on the Buick.

One of the English guys, a short young guy named Kenny, said in a resigned and fatalistic tone of voice that he wasn't going to fight the system and was going to Vietnam and get it over with. I was somewhat shocked and wondered if he actually expected to die over there. I suppose no one really wanted to go to Vietnam and I didn't want to, either. But I knew that, whether right or wrong, I would not have to fight in military service, because Amish people never have to do that. The United States government has always given exemptions for Amish people to not serve in the military, because of their religious and anti-war beliefs. I knew that many others who served were just as anti-war as the Amish, so I certainly understand if they feel that exemptions for the Amish are unfair. In fact, I largely agree with that thinking. Whenever Amish have been drafted, however, they have always been required to serve several years of non-military duty at a government approved facility or location. Among these were civilian work camps, government sponsored farms, and psychiatric or general hospitals, each of which would have to be at least seventy-five miles from home. It would also have to be for a term of at least two years.

In addition to not telling my parents about the draft lottery and the implications it had for me, I also didn't tell them that I actually hoped I would be drafted. I knew that if I was, I would be required to move out of the Amish community during that time. I could then live the much-coveted English lifestyle for at least a few years while I served the required time. And, being the Amish rebel that I was, that seemed so much better than this boring farming lifestyle that I had endured for so long.

What also appealed to me was that several Amish buddies of mine who had been drafted earlier, were already serving their terms at Morristown Memorial Hospital, (MMH), in Morristown, New Jersey, which was about one hundred thirty miles from home. I decided that if I was drafted, I would try to serve my term there also.

The more I thought about being away for two years, the more I yearned to get away from the Amish lifestyle. So much that I soon came up with what the Amish would consider an evil and diabolical scheme. I decided I needed to increase the odds that I would be drafted. So, I secretly, but truthfully, notified a lady named Irene at the draft board in Lancaster that I was not currently working on the farm, but was working at the tobacco warehouses instead. I also told her that, as I understood it, that would put me in the classification where I'd be most likely to be drafted and that I actually hoped for that.

Surely, my parents would have been horrified if they'd known about that letter I sent to the draft board. The reason I thought the letter was a good idea is that the Amish thought their boys were less likely to be drafted if they were working full-time on a farm. Because of that, Dad *was* nervous about my tobacco warehouse employment, but he liked that extra income so much that he apparently thought it was worth the risk.

So, I didn't leave the Amish by running away at night as quite a few others have done, but instead concocted this elaborate scheme and sent that letter. I suppose my letter may have been "one of a kind," that is, probably the only letter the draft board ever received where someone actually requested to be drafted, which must have astonished them!

For a long time, I felt somewhat guilty about having sent that letter. I certainly was never proud of it. In fact, I never told anyone at all for at least forty years! But my craving for a few years of the strongly alluring "English" lifestyle, plus being able to avoid the decision about joining the Amish church, convinced me I was justified in doing that.

About four months later, on a warm spring evening, while plowing a field with the mules at Brother Aaron's farm, I saw Dad pulling off the road with his horse and buggy. He tied his horse at the pasture fence and wearily trudged over to meet me in the field about a quarter of a mile away. As he walked up to me, I yelled whoa to the mules and they were happy to stop immediately. With a troubled look on his face, Dad grimly told me that the draft board must have found out about my wintertime warehouse employment because they'd sent a letter notifying me that I had been drafted, and that I would soon have to start serving my term of alternative service, as it was called. He, of course, was upset about that because he surely was afraid that when I did, I would be even less likely to ever join the Amish church. Especially with me being far away from the Amish community during that time. While he was upset I, on the other hand, was excited to hear the news, although I tried to appear nonchalant. In fact, I was more than excited, I was tremendously pleased to hear this specific news which I had been strongly hoping for. I knew that this would now effectively allow me to "go English" without anyone even trying to make me feel guilty or considering me evil.

When Dad asked me where I would go to serve my time, he probably was hoping I would go to Spring City, where there was some type of government sponsored farming operation that we had heard about. I had no desire to go there because I wanted to get away from farming, not to continue it. So, I told him about the guys already serving at Morristown, and that I would prefer to go there, too. Predictably, he asked me about joining the church. I didn't give him a definite answer, but I already knew in my mind that I would not, while I was away for several years. Even if I had been willing to join, it certainly would have been impractical, because I wanted and needed a car for my everyday use, and also to come home occasionally to visit. I'm sure Dad and Mom were extremely unhappy that I had been drafted at that exact time, when I might otherwise actually have soon started to "join the church." In fact, the day on which the draft notice letter arrived in the mail was less than a month before the formal church baptismal class started. I was still completely undecided as to whether I would join at that time or not. I presume that it surely was God's will that the letter arrived at such a critical time.

I wrote to the personnel department at Morristown Memorial Hospital, inquiring if they had any job openings. In their reply letter, they said they have openings in the building services department, which essentially meant I could be a janitor there. I decided to apply for that, thinking I could probably transfer to the maintenance department later, as some of my buddies there had already done. The pay was two dollars and fifty cents per hour, which seemed fantastic to me, considering that I had never had a regular fulltime paycheck. And, of course, it was exciting to think that I could keep it all for myself. I guess Dad sensed it would be useless for him to try to confiscate any of *that* money. But, of course, I would also have a lot more expenses than before.

I told my parents and Aaron that I would be going to Morristown in two weeks to serve the required two-year term. Mom was very sad about that and said she doesn't think she'll make it through the two years I'd be gone. She no doubt assumed I would dress English and get a car and live a totally English lifestyle. I reassured her that things would work out fine, and I reminded her that I had been drafted and really had to serve those two years somewhere, whether I wanted to or not.

There were nine Amish boys working at MMH, who were conscientious objectors. They were also known as "conscies" or c.o.s, like I would be if I joined them. Seven of those nine boys were living in a two and one-half story rented house in Morris Plains, about three miles from the hospital. I was hoping to join them there when I was hired.

The next two weeks passed slowly, during which time I was extremely excited, contemplating how much my lifestyle would soon change. No more spending dreadfully long boring hours, days, and weeks, hoeing and pulling weeds in the hot sun, always wearing long black pants. No more strenuous backbreaking work harvesting all the crops the old-fashioned labor-intensive "Amish" way. No more looking at the tail end of a plodding old horse while slowly meandering down the road in a buggy, with cars tantalizingly whizzing by. No more being nagged to join the Amish church. And last but not least, no more of the dreaded chicken catching. At least not for the next two years!

Some of my siblings expressed concern about the move I would soon make. Could it be that, in reality, they somewhat envied me? Of course, I did not ask them that, but I can't help but think that a lot of Amish are probably extremely bored and unhappy with their lifestyle. And I'm sure that many of them were really envious that I would soon be blissfully waltzing off to a distant English community and living a totally worldly lifestyle for two years. But I guess there were also some who were quite content with the Amish way of life. It is utterly amazing how many Amish people can and do train and program their minds to almost completely accept a lifestyle that has so many inherent disadvantages.

Since I didn't have a car of my own at the time, I had arranged to ride to Morristown with Toby and Christ, two Amish boys who I knew who already lived and worked there. Toby was driving his 1965 Chevy Impala that Sunday night and I was more than ready when he pulled into our driveway, at about 11:45 P.M.. We had been at a hoedown and that's why we left so late. Of course, my parents were already in bed, so they didn't see me off.

I eagerly climbed into the back seat of the car with my bags and we started on the 130-mile trip. Even though it was well past my usual bedtime, I was so excited that I slept very little. Morristown had a population of about 15,000 people and is located thirty miles west of New York City. Of course, I had never been to NYC, but I knew that I would surely go there sometime soon. I tried to imagine how different my new lifestyle would be from the slow-paced primitive farm life I had always known. I thought about Christopher Columbus embarking on his first trip to the New World. While I knew it was silly to compare his situation with mine, nevertheless, it did seem as though I was also going to a new world!

For years I had been yearning to explore the strange, alluring, and exciting, but forbidden world which existed right outside our tightly boxed in Amish Community, but I could not. Now, suddenly and astonishingly, it seemed to be thrown right into my lap and I could explore it to my heart's content!

We arrived at the house in Morris Plains at about 2:00 A.M. There were seven Amish and two English boys already living there. I had been told that I would have to live in the basement until Steve moved out in about four months. His two-year term at MMH would end then, and he would go back home and join the Amish again. So, after Toby and Christ had gone to bed, I eagerly explored the unfinished basement, and discovered the pros and cons of living down there. I decided there was only one positive thing, and that was that it was quiet there. However, it was also rather damp, and there was no furniture except for a dilapidated old sofa which I would sleep on. All my belongings I either kept on the concrete floor or on two rough old wooden shelves built against the wall. I soon procured an old stuffed chair from the attic and, *voila*, my castle was now complete!

A solitary light bulb burned in the light fixture above my head and I quickly noticed there was an electrical receptacle with it. I eagerly plugged my radio cord into it and, for the first time, I had the luxury of my radio being powered by electricity instead of the expensive batteries that I always had to buy. I found there were far more stations to choose from in that heavily populated metropolitan area than back home in Lancaster County. With some amusement, I briefly listened to several worldly rock and roll stations from NYC.

I finally laid down on the old sofa but was still so excited that I didn't sleep well. In the morning, I got up and went upstairs. All the boys had already gone to work at the hospital, except for Toby who worked the night shift there.

While he was still sleeping, I wandered about, reminding myself that this was the first house I had ever lived in that had a TV, telephone, radios, electricity and, of course, electric lights. And, to my delight, a top-notch professional style pool table on the main floor. I thought it was all just wonderful and immensely exciting. Plus, when I would get a car soon, I could park it right there where I lived, unlike back at the farm, where I always had a long walk just to get to my car.

The one negative thing about my moving to Morristown was that I would not see my buddies back home much anymore because of my work schedule, which allowed me only two weekends off in each seven-week time period. However, that was an easy trade-off for me as I quickly and eagerly embraced this wonderful new English lifestyle.

That afternoon I rode with Toby to the hospital, and applied for a janitor's job and had an interview with John McKee. He hired me on the spot, and he would be my supervisor. He was a balding, white haired little seventy-two-year-old Scotch man with a beak nose, who reportedly had quite a taste for all things alcoholic. I started my new job two days later. I would be working the day shift from 7:00 A.M. to 3:30 P.M., mopping floors and collecting trash bags. Not overly exciting, but at least now I was living in a very interesting environment, where there were always lots of people around. Vastly different from back home on the farm. Not only was I no longer out in the hot sun, but the work pace was so much more leisurely than what I'd known before. I soon made various friends and settled into a regular routine at work.

One thing that soon caught my attention was all the pretty young nurses flitting around the hospital in their miniskirts. Of course, I was too shy and self-conscious to talk or flirt with them. In fact, I didn't really even know how to flirt. Nevertheless, when I saw Mary Ann Kraiger walking briskly down the hall toward me, I summoned up my courage and coolly said, "Hi." She gave me a half-smile and also said, "Hi," as she breezed on past me. Later I told the guys at the house about it and bragged that I had been talking with a pretty young nurse. Of course, I didn't tell them that I had only spoken that one word to her!

So, suddenly, here I was, a wide-eyed, innocent, and totally naïve country bumpkin, a nineteen-year old farm boy, newly transplanted off the Amish "reservation" and trying to, seamlessly and inauspiciously, blend in with all these well-educated modern day "English" folks, only a short distance from the great "evil" metropolis of New York City! And, with practically no social skills whatsoever. So, of course, I felt intimidated and out of place. But, still extremely excited and happy to be there!

Toby took me to a department store where I eagerly "improved" my meager wardrobe with an orange shirt and a pair of maroon-colored corduroy bell-bottom pants which I thought looked *so* cool! Finally, I could walk around with society in general without anyone staring at the weird Amish clothing and haircut I'd always worn before! I had made sure to get a bona-fide English haircut the first day I was there, so now I felt as though I fit right in. Especially, when I also grew long mutton chop sideburns, which was the style back then. While working at our jobs, we had to wear blue cotton pants and shirts that the hospital issued to all the janitors. I would have preferred shorts, though, since the hospital didn't have air conditioning. But, hey, even in the English world you can't have everything!

Two of my co-workers, Toby and Dave F., were from my church district back home. When Deacon Davey Esh found out that we all were required to wear those blue English work pants, he suggested we wear Amish pants in addition to the required blue pants. I presume he meant the Amish pants would be on the outside, but I'm not sure. I wonder if he gave any thought as to how warm that would have been, wearing two pairs of pants. Understandably, we never even considered obeying such silly advice!

The monthly rent for the house was $250.00. With ten guys dividing it, that came to $25.00 per month each, which was certainly cheap enough. We were really a rather docile and sedate group, with very little drinking and partying going on at the house. In fact, I only remember one party of any significance during all that time, when one of the guy's term was up and he would move back home and join the Amish church again. There was a lot of liquor flowing that night, and a group of friends from the hospital there to help drink it.

I think that was also the first time I asked an "English" girl for a date. But Sophie M. quickly turned me down, probably for these three reasons. I was somewhat drunk, she suspected I was ex-Amish, and (*of all things*) my wanting to go to a night-time Yankees game in New York City on a first date! Of course, she said no!

Several of the guys occasionally had casual girlfriends, but nothing serious except for one guy who had a girlfriend for several years. It was generally agreed that what happens in Vegas stays in Vegas, meaning Morristown. Most of the guys, including myself, were somewhat shy and self-conscious around English girls, especially at first. After all, we had not been taught English social graces back home. We did enjoy the time we shared there together, and all got along with each other very well. We kept our noses clean and, to the best of my memory, none of us ever really got into any trouble during that time.

Remarkably, all the guys except for two of us, obediently went back to the Amish community when their term was up and have been faithful Amish church members since then, throughout their entire lives. I guess that somewhat illustrates the immense power of the brainwashing that we had all received while growing up.

I needed a car, so I checked out two cars that were advertised in the paper. The first one was an absolute nonstarter, or almost a nonstarter, no pun intended. It was an old 1958 Plymouth, which would sputter, shake, jump and jerk more than any car I'd ever seen, even while just sitting there "idling." It was almost like having the benefit of a back massage if you sat in it at that time. The second car was more suitable, a big 1963 Pontiac Grand Prix, which I bought for $300.00. It was bigger than I needed, but with gas costing only about 30¢ per gallon, fuel economy was not a big concern. Now, there were ten cars parked at the house. Fortunately, there was enough room for all of us to park there.

The eight Amish guys who lived there were Amos, (Amy) Steve, Aaron, Dave, Jake, Toby, Christ and me. The two English guys were Barry and Curt. There were also about twenty-five other C.O.s working at the hospital who were serving two-year terms like us. They included five longhaired bearded hippies from the New York City area. One of them was Owen from the Bronx, who I was fairly friendly with. He went back home to NYC when his term was up. He said he had been taught to believe that he was a Jew and I suspect he was also an atheist. I didn't expect to ever see him or hear from him again.

Imagine my surprise when one day, thirty-four years later, in 2005, I accidentally happened to see his name in my phone book in Lancaster. I knew it almost surely had to be him. After all, I thought, how many Owen Kaminoffs' are there? So, I called that number and sure enough it was him, and we chatted for a while. When he told me where he worked, I was amazed again. He said he worked at the Lancaster Post Office, which is exactly where I was working as a truck driver at the time. I met him and his wife later one evening for pizza and we had a nice chat and reunion.

At MMH, I was casually friendly with Owen and his hippie buddies but was never invited and never cared to be invited to their pot smoking parties. They probably thought we were a bunch of Amish squares. One of them got one of the kitchen girls pregnant and she had the baby, but I don't know if they ever got married.

On one of my first days there, one of the hippies, Phil, and I along with two maintenance men were moving furniture out of a residence building. Phil's girlfriend came along and as soon as he saw her, they engaged in the longest kissing session I had ever seen, right out on the sidewalk. I had hardly ever even seen anybody kiss someone at all before that except when the Amish preachers kissed each other at church on Sunday mornings. So, I watched intently to see when Phil and his girlfriend would finally stop for some air. John Luzetski, the old maintenance man who was with us, winked at me and privately told me to ask the girl if she had any left for me. I merely chuckled at that thought!

Some people at MMH considered John Rogers a hippie because he had a full beard and shoulder length hair. But he was quite different from the others because he was a Christian and would willingly share his faith, so the hippies referred to him as a Jesus freak. John was a C.O. like us, and he was very pleasant, and certainly an all-around good guy. He told me that he was in a group who was having regular Bible study meetings and he invited me to come and join them. That immediately sent up my radar, for I had been told by the Amish that going to "English" Bible studies is stepping into very dangerous territory, because so many who had started doing that, were then soon obviously "deceived," and eventually left the Amish.

Since the Amish only have church services every other Sunday, I'd like to ask the preachers if they would allow their people to attend an English church on the "off" Sunday. I'm sure they would not allow that, fearing they'd become deceived. If each Amish minister and bishop would just at least once attend a sincere Bible-teaching evangelical church, I'm sure they would be amazed and might even be favorably impressed. That is, if they were able to evaluate it from an unbiased perspective, which would be unlikely. I'd also like to ask the Amish, if you don't trust yourself to study all of the Bible, why you would trust any of it? Focusing only on certain chapters or verses that seemed to substantiate your viewpoints seems very biased, and even hypocritical to me. Could it be that there are more verses in the Bible that seem to advise against excommunication and shunning then advise in favor of such? I am sure that is the case. The Amish bishops and ministers might be interested to know that, in the modern NIV version of the New Testament, the word "love" appears two hundred thirty-two times and the word "hate" only appears seventeen times. If they knew that, they might not be so quick to practice ex-communication and shunning against "straying" members.

Because of what I had been told since my childhood by the Amish, I declined John Rogers's invitation to come to their Bible study group, even though I really wanted to. Throughout my lifetime I have often regretted that I never went to it. I think if I had attended several times, it's very unlikely I would have ever made the major decision in my life that I did a few years later.

I soon found out that none of my buddies at the house were really sports fans, as far as playing sports themselves. So, I bought a basketball and went to a nearby outside court and practiced by myself. The hospital had a basketball team and a softball team that played in local industrial leagues. I went to watch sometimes and became extremely interested in joining those teams. I resolved that I would at least play on the softball team the following year. I had no doubt that I would do well as that was the sport I was most skilled at. In fact, I did play on the softball team the next year and finished the season with the second-best batting average on the team. What was really neat was that now we played on real softball fields and had paid umpires who really knew the rules, so it was a lot more fun than Amish softball! Also, we had proper equipment, including top quality balls and bats, unlike when we played in the cow pastures and hayfields back home. I always played the catcher position for our team at MMH. I also played sparingly on the hospital's basketball team, but because of being so "green" and my lack of experience, I didn't play well and only contributed marginally to the team's success.

Amy G. had a neat blue and white motorboat that we took to Lake Hopatcong sometimes. I soon learned to water ski with the best of them, although I never learned to ski with only one ski. Well, neither did any of the other guys! The first time I went boating with them on a hot Saturday afternoon, I got the sunburn of my life. Growing up Amish, we weren't allowed to have our shirts off in public, so I'd never had a sunburn on my back and chest before. So, I shouldn't have been surprised that I got a major sunburn. I had been shirtless on the lake in the hot sun all afternoon, without having used any sunscreen.

I became friends with two English "conscies" who worked at MMH and who were also from Lancaster County. They were John Futer and Rich Knauer, who was married to John's sister. They lived in an ugly black residence building on the hospital grounds, in which my supervisor, McKee, also lived. Everyone else derisively and scornfully called it "the barn," but McKee, dutifully and affectionately, called it D'Olieh. That was its proper name, which apparently was of Irish origin. It was for men only, and most of them were Hispanic janitors and kitchen workers. The barn was torn down, appropriately so, several years later.

McKee had acquired the nickname "Scotch" because of his excessive drinking. His high time for the day was each afternoon after work, driving up town to the Washington Bar, and getting drunk while eating his evening meal. Eventually, he'd go back to his dreary and pathetic room in the barn. He'd drive his big old black 1959 Oldsmobile down Franklin Street, while weaving from side to side. He'd be trying hard not to hit anything, while peering anxiously ahead and his eyes being barely higher than the steering wheel.

During the latter part of my term at MMH, I also lived at the barn. My room was upstairs and across the hall from Scotch's room. I'd know when he got back to his room at night when I heard the slamming of the screen door. Then he'd sit in his drab old chair till quite late, with the TV blaring, before finally going to bed.

One morning at MMH, I was assigned to vacuum the carpet in the front lobby at the main entrance of the hospital. Of course, there were a lot of people walking by at the time. I thought the electric vacuum cleaner didn't work very well so I decided to use a broom, since that was something I was more familiar with and had always been successful with back on the farm! It did work better than the vacuum cleaner but, unfortunately, also created a "small" cloud of dust. Someone notified Scotch, who ran up to me and angrily berated me for sweeping the carpet with a broom. He asked me if I had grown up on a farm and I told him, yes, indeed, I *had* grown up on a farm. He seemed doubtful, and a surly scowl crossed his face as he scampered away. As one might assume, that was the last time I "cleaned" that carpet with a broom!

One Saturday morning, John, Rich and I decided to go to the shore at Asbury Park in Rich's 1965 Plymouth Barracuda. Asbury Park is about twenty miles south of NYC, and we endured a major traffic jam along the way, but later had lots of fun at the shore. This was the first time I had ever seen New York City's famous skyline and I was quite impressed. The World Trade Center Towers were being built at that time and were at about one half of their finished height. None of us could imagine then of the horrifying and tragic events that would happen there almost exactly thirty years later.

Later that evening, after our day at the shore, we went north almost as far as the Big Apple and stopped at a nightclub girlie bar. I was shocked at how little the dancers were wearing as we watched through the open door. They were trying to lure these three wide-eyed young country bumpkins inside and have us throw money at them, as others were doing, but I wasn't about to fall for that!

Liz Smith was a young nurse at MMH who worked on the same floor where John worked as a janitor. After John, Rich and I changed the spark plugs in Liz's car one day, she took us out for pizza along with her friend, Lynn, who was also a nurse at MMH. Both girls were from western Maryland and somewhat countrified like us. Lynn and I became friends, and eventually I had enough of nerve to ask her for a date. We went to New York City one evening to watch a baseball game between the Yankees and the Minnesota Twins. In retrospect, I think it was sort of weird to go that far on a first date, and she probably thought so too, but she didn't object. We didn't do a whole lot of talking, and I don't think I even asked her anything about her family, which is also rather weird. Nor did I ever tell her anything about my Amish background. I didn't want any of the girls at the hospital to know about that, thinking they'd probably be less likely to go out with me if they knew.

On the thirty-mile trip back to Morristown, we listened to Buck Owens, Merle Haggard and Charley Pride on my car's eight track tape player. A week or so later, Lynn and I went bowling one evening. By the end of that date, she was probably wondering about me since I hadn't yet even tried to do as much as kiss her. Have I mentioned yet that I was *somewhat* on the shy side? The next time I asked her out, I suggested we go to the beach one Saturday morning. She turned me down and claimed that she was sick. I doubted very much that she was sick. Maybe I wasn't amorous enough for her style! In any case, we never went out together again. About a year later, she and Ken B. took off for Florida, and as far as I know, they never came back. Ken was a married man who worked in the maintenance department at MMH. I believe he was about fifteen years older than her.

After a while, I wanted a smaller and nicer looking car, so I sold the 1963 Grand Prix to Leroy F. back home for $150.00. He is now an Amish preacher so, of course, he's driving a horse instead of a car these days. I bought a sky blue 1966 Pontiac Lemans with white racing stripes, from Aaron K for $900. He had to sell it because he was moving back home and re-joining the Amish church. Now, for the first time in my life, I owned a car that I was really proud of, as it was a very nice- looking car.

After a while I decided to get a motorcycle because I thought I would probably go back and be Amish after my time at MMH was up. So, I thought if I ever wanted to have a motorcycle, now would be the best time. I bought a 1967 Suzuki from a guy in Morristown for $300.00. It was the old style that had to have oil mixed with the gas. I had never driven a motorcycle before, but I taught myself how to do it on the back streets behind the house. None of my buddies had a motorcycle during the time we lived there, which seemed surprising to me.

CHAPTER TWENTY-EIGHT

My Life as a "Conscie" At MMH

IN THE SUMMER OF 1972, a monstrous storm, Hurricane Agnes, roared up the East Coast, killing 128 people and causing tremendous flooding and massive damage in Pennsylvania, especially on the Susquehanna River from Scranton to Harrisburg. There was extremely heavy flooding throughout Lancaster County as well. It was probably the worst flooding caused by a hurricane in the history of Pennsylvania. It wasn't nearly as bad in Morristown where I was. So, I was shocked when Brother John called me that evening and told me that one of his best friends, Sam Kauffman, who was 23 years old, had tragically drowned in the flood, along with his infant son. Sam, his wife and ten-month old baby boy had been traveling by horse and buggy when they encountered extremely high water by the Pequea creek bridge near the Frogtown Road intersection. The water was so high and swift that it upset the buggy. His wife, Sarah, who was six months pregnant, managed to hold on to a tree till rescuers arrived, but her husband and baby son were swept away by the raging waters. Their bodies were found much farther downstream the next day.

The sad and untimely death of Sam and his infant son reminded me of how brief and uncertain one's life can be. Of course, I had often been struggling with the dilemma of trying to decide if I would join the Amish church when my term at MMH was over. By now I was completely accustomed to having the constant joy and convenience of many worldly things such as a car, TV, radio, telephone, pool table, electricity and English clothes, all of which the Amish totally forbid. I tried to calculate how hard it would be to not have any of these things for the rest of my life if I joined the Amish church. I thought that since

I had not had those things while growing up, it might not be too hard to go back to the Amish lifestyle. Especially if I then found a nice Amish girl to marry and raise a family with. I knew if I did that, I would be loved and accepted and admired and adored, despite my two years of being English at Morristown. Some would consider me almost a hero because I could be and would be living proof that it's possible to make the change from being full-fledged English to permanent Amish status.

On the other hand, if I never came back and joined the church, I would still be considered a rebellious renegade, and a black sheep, and at least to some extent, I would always be scorned and ridiculed. Such a situation could be thought of as "shunning-lite." It just would not be as intense as if I had joined the church and later left it. All my siblings were already faithful church members and I was absolutely sure that none of them would ever leave the church. That would mean that I'd always be the only one in my immediate family to be a pariah and a social outcast.

By now I had almost fully decided that I didn't want to stay in the Morristown area after my term was up. I knew I wanted to live somewhere in Lancaster County on a permanent basis. But, by far my biggest question was, would I be Amish or not? And, if so, would I really be able to again endure a lifestyle that is devoid of most of life's normal pleasures and conveniences?

I only had two weekends off in each seven-week time period. Of course, I'd be with my family and buddies at those times. I'd park my car at the Flame Right Gas Company about a third of a mile from the farmhouse, just up the road from Uncle Sammy's house. I'd go to church and I would be welcomed and treated courteously. Of course, my folks were all strongly hoping I would join the church after my term at MMH was over.

Several times on Sunday nights after the Rumspringa event, I was daring enough to park behind our tobacco shed where my car was not visible from the house. I'd leave early the next morning while Dad was still in the barn milking. I'd take the dirt field lane down to Henry's long lane where no one could see me, and then out to the main road when heading back to Morristown.

Meanwhile, at MMH, I had a lot of idle time in the evenings and on weekends so I worked at several different part time jobs. One was pumping gas at Bogart's gas station on Ford Avenue on weekday evenings. I knew John Bogart's wife, Linda, a very pleasant lady, a nurse, who worked at MMH. I also briefly worked at a part-time evening job at a factory building, taking thousands of cans of Right

Guard deodorant off a conveyor belt and putting them in cardboard cases. There were a lot of bored, tired, and unhappy looking women who also worked there next to me. I very soon became likewise and I quit that job after two nights.

A much better part time job was working on Saturdays in the summer time at two wealthy retired gentlemen farmer's estates, about ten miles south of Morristown. They were Mr. Linen and Mr. Richardson. I did garden, yard, and farm work for them, but it was leisurely and certainly was not hard work. I enjoyed mowing Mr. Richardson's grass and hay field with his tractor and mowing machine.

Another part time job I had was working for Ed Woodward, who had an office cleaning business. His regular day job was working in the receiving department at MMH. I often worked evenings for Ed, along with Ivan Hurst, who was a "conscie" from Ephrata and who lived in the barn at MMH. Ivan was a very strait-laced Old Order Mennonite, who like the Amish, also was not allowed to have a car. He had a girlfriend back home who he was engaged to. She had told him firmly, that even if she just heard one rumor that he was involved with another girl at MMH, she would end their relationship immediately. Ivan made very sure that didn't happen. They got married while he was still working at MMH, so he was an "absentee" husband for several months before he moved back home when his term was up.

Ivan was the only one of the Amish or Mennonite C.O.'s who ever talked Dutch while at MMH. Sometimes he would unintentionally embarrass and bother me by talking Dutch to me while we were in a hospital elevator or elsewhere when other employees were present. I certainly didn't want those people to know that I was Amish!

Ivan told me several things which indicated how frugal his people were back home. One example was how they lit their lanterns when working in the barn on winter evenings. Ivan's father had warned him and his brothers that they better not use more than one match to light all of the five lanterns. After all, the father had demonstrated that if the lanterns were already "pumped up" and properly lined up in a row, they could all be lit with one match if one was skillful and quick enough.

Ivan also told me about a more liberal Mennonite who owned a car but was nevertheless quite frugal. Apparently, when he came to a left-hand curve in the road, he had a unique strategy which he thought would save him a few cents if he did it often enough. He would, of course, check for oncoming traffic and if there was none, he would go to the other side of the road and navigate the curve that way. Presumably, that took less gas because the car had a shorter distance to travel. I suspect that he would also, at the top of a hill, turn off the engine and coast down to the bottom!

One night while cleaning offices, I saw a tape recorder on someone's desk. I was intrigued and very curious to find out for the first time ever what I sounded like. So, I turned it on and gave my best rendition of a certain country music song that I had memorized. Of course, I was fascinated and amused when I immediately played it back and listened to it. I did not erase it, because I didn't quite know how to. The next night while cleaning there, I found a note someone had left for me, which kindly requested me to not mess around with the tape recorder again.

Another night while Ivan and I were cleaning offices, I found a cabinet with about fifteen different bottles of whiskey in it. I sampled quite a few bottles of it, while trying to impress Ivan. I poured myself a full styrofoam cup of whiskey and "chugged" all of it without stopping. By then, it seemed as though my throat was almost on fire. I guess Ivan had the last laugh on me though, because soon I was so drunk that I was lying face down in the snow just outside the front door. Ivan had to finish the cleaning by himself, and then rouse me up to drive him home in my car, since he didn't have a driver's license. Somehow, I made it home safely, a distance of about four miles, with Ivan nervously directing me all the way. The next morning, I noticed that I had parked the car strangely in the back yard, about five feet further ahead than usual. I soon regretted having drank all that whiskey, while working at the hospital that day. I couldn't eat anything or keep anything down and had an extremely bad hangover. Of course, what I had done was completely wrong in every way, whether I got sick or not. But I did appreciate that Ivan didn't scold me at all for getting so drunk that night.

Several times while I was at MMH, some buddies from back home came to visit me on the weekend. We'd go into New York City for some sightseeing and once went to a New York Mets baseball game out on Long Island. One weekend, Ray Stoltzfus, who had taken me on the plane ride a few years earlier, rode up on his motorcycle to visit me. This was soon after I had gotten my motorcycle, and I had not yet learned the correct way to do a "wheelie." That evening, after we stopped for gas at the Texaco station, I got the foolish idea to show off for Ray and do what I hoped would be a really impressive wheelie. I revved the motorcycle up fairly high, then popped the clutch. Like magic, the front wheel instantly came way up high and it did a magnificent wheelie, all right. It shot ahead like a streak of light, with me desperately trying to hold on. It literally took off and just went out from under me. I was violently thrown ahead and was sliding on the pavement on my stomach. My chin and knuckles were dragging painfully on the pavement, and I had major brush burns on them. My neat blue plastic racing shirt was torn and had major scuff marks on it and was essentially ruined. Meanwhile, the motorcycle was hurtling ahead on its side for about forty feet. Fortunately, it didn't hit anything, but it also had a considerable number of scrapes on it, along with a damaged mirror. Of course, I was very embarrassed and upset and never did that again, at least not till I could do it properly!

One weekend back home, Dave Z. and I went to Sample's Bar in New Holland on a Saturday night. We were shooting pool with two English guys who might have belonged to a motorcycle gang. At first everything was fine then it all went downhill. They got more and more belligerent as they got more and more drunk. Dave and I were dressed Amish and were winning money from them and they were mad about that. Eventually, it got so late that we were the only customers there and we belatedly realized we should have left earlier. They started quietly threatening us, saying they were going to beat us up when we left and would cut our eyes and tongues out. Of course, we should have told the management or called the police but were reluctant to do that because I had been drinking and was still underage and would probably be in trouble because of that. So, Dave and I went into the bathroom to plot our escape. After starting up our game of pool again, we strategically just happened to be near the door at the same time. Suddenly, we both dropped our pool sticks and were out the door like a flash. We sprinted past the old Ritz Theater, and down into the theater parking lot where my car was parked about a hundred feet away. The two guys were hot on our tails, with all four of us running at full speed. I already had my car key in my hand, ready to unlock it and jump in the instant I got there. I was running so fast that I ran into the side of the car and bruised my knee but that was the least of my worries. I immediately unlocked the car and jumped in, then quickly pushed the lock button down. Then I pulled the lock up on Dave's side and he scrambled in and locked it right away. A split second later they were at both doors grabbing the handles and trying to get inside. As I hurriedly and nervously started the car, and it roared to life, the guy on my side hit the window as hard as he could with his fist. Later we saw streaks of skin from his knuckles on the car window. While turning the steering wheel, I backed up extremely fast and almost knocked one of them to the ground. I sped out onto New Holland Pike and headed west, briefly going at about twice the speed limit, in case they followed us. Happily, they did not and we never saw them again.

One Saturday night, a gang of us were having a "private" beer party at an Amish farm near Kirkwood. We were all drinking, out in the woods by the creek and not bothering anybody. Suddenly we saw two police cars coming down the dirt lane directly toward us. Most of us, including myself, were still underage. Some guys quickly waded through the creek with their shoes and black Amish pants still on and hid in the woods on the other side. That's how they avoided being cited for underage drinking. I had not followed their example and was caught red-handed along with the others and had to pay a fine of about $25.00. What made it especially annoying was that it was only about two weeks before my twenty-first birthday when I could legally drink, and I would not have been fined at all.

I was among the last of the Lancaster County "conscies," who'd lived at the house in Morris Plains. Therefore, as each guys' term ended and he went back home, there were fewer of us and each had to pay a higher percentage of the rent. So, by the fall of 1972, it was no longer financially feasible for us to stay there. There were some rooms available at hospital residence buildings, which the other guys took. I had to settle for a room in the barn, being the last guy on the seniority totem pole. Scotch also lived at the barn and his room was almost directly underneath mine. When he found out I was moving in there, he almost snarled at me, while warning me emphatically that if I was involved in any foolishness, out I would go. I told him not to worry and that I was not the partying type. In fact, during the eight months that I lived there, I only brought one girl up to my room, other than my sisters who came to see me. Brother John also visited me once. No Amish preachers ever visited any of us at Morristown, even though they wanted us to think they were extremely concerned about our spiritual health. But I often got letters from Mom and Dad and occasionally a friendly letter from Rueb's Barb, a kind-hearted elderly widow from our church.

Even though I was now living at the barn, I had one of the best rooms there, because it was larger than the others and because it was upstairs, where it was quiet. My rent there was only $10.00 per month which included electric and heat. That expense was deducted each month from my hospital paycheck. As I expected, it was more boring and not as much fun as it had been at the house in Morris Plains with the other guys. Other than my part time cleaning job, most of my spare time was spent reading and watching TV.

One negative thing about living in the barn was the squirrels living in the attic that sometimes ran across the ceiling and woke me up. I complained to the maintenance men several times, but they never did anything about it.

That time in my life would have been an excellent time for me to extend my education by studying and getting my G.E.D. But I'm not sure I knew such a thing even existed or that I might really want and need that later in life. Unsurprisingly, such ignorance and lack of concern is common with people who were born and raised Amish!

There was an electric hot plate downstairs in the hallway that was shared by us four guys who lived there. I often used it to heat food for my evening meal. One night I heated up some chicken on it, then went back upstairs and soon fell sound asleep in my easy chair. Suddenly, I woke up as Scotch was pounding on my door and yelling that the "bloody" chicken I was cooking was smoking up the whole hallway. And, indeed it was. I apologized profusely, and hurried downstairs to dispose of the burnt and ruined chicken, and opened the door to let all the smoke out. Scotch had just come home from the bar and that smoking chicken had sent him into a drunken rage. He certainly was not one bit amused by it like I was! He even badgered me about it the next day at work.

Dave Fisher was one of the Amish guys who had recently moved back home because his term at MMH was over. He'd had a cushy job that I had applied for and was now assigned to do. It involved working outside of the hospital building with another janitor, pushing a linen cart and supplying the hospital workers at the four resident buildings with bed sheets, pillowcases and towels. It was the easiest job I ever had, and allowed me and Will, my partner, lots of time to goof off. Sometimes we'd take a nap or watch TV in an empty room.

One of those times, I happened to fall sound asleep, then was suddenly awakened when I heard a key turning in the door. Before I could get up, Scotch and Mr. Truex had come inside and were both glaring angrily at me. Truex was the head supervisor of our department and he dramatically told me that if I'm caught sleeping on the job again, I would be fired. I took that very seriously and did not let it happen again. Ironically, a few months later, he himself was fired for theft and embezzling money from MMH.

Since I now had the job of distributing linen to the residents, I was given a grand master key, or "grond moster," as Scotch called it. It allowed me to open any door on the MMH grounds, including even the residents' own rooms. I had always been curious about what it looked like inside Scotch's room to see if the rumors I'd heard were true. It was said that he'd wear his hospital assigned shirts and pants until they smelled quite bad and then he'd throw them into a pile in the middle of his room. But, instead of washing them, he'd eventually burn them in the burn barrel outside. The rumors apparently were true, because one day I secretly checked his room. I really wasn't authorized, since he always supplied his own linen, but I did it anyway. There was indeed a big pile of such dirty, smelly clothing on the floor, waiting to be burned. Of course, I would never have dared to tell him that I had been in his room and seen that.

One Sunday afternoon in November, 1972, when I was bored as usual while watching TV in my room, I happened to see a program that interested me greatly. Rev. Billy Graham, who I had heard a little about and who I knew was famous, was preaching. I had never heard him or seen him on TV before. I had been taught that listening to evangelists like him, or reading his books, was dangerous and could easily lead Amish people astray. Nevertheless, I decided to watch, largely out of curiosity. I was soon very impressed with how emphatic and sincere he obviously was. He certainly was preaching with great conviction. More importantly, he preached that even the most evil sinner could be saved by faith in Jesus Christ and repentance of their sins, and that they could have full assurance that they were saved. He also said that it was not dependent on any good works they did or how well they followed the *Rules* and *Regulations* of any church!

That was vastly different from what I had been taught. I had always been taught that we need to do our best and obey the rules and regulations of the Amish church, and then we could have a "good" hope of getting to Heaven. I had been taught that anyone who said they knew they were saved were putting themselves in a very wrong and dangerous position. And, that it was very conceited and presumptuous and arrogant for anyone to think that.

However, Rev. Graham seemed to be so much more knowledgeable and eloquent than the "self-educated" Amish preachers I had always listened to. In fact, the only sermons I had ever listened to before, were by Amish preachers. We were told that because we were born Amish, we should only listen to Amish preachers.

Once I asked Dad about the worship practices of another branch of Amish, whose settlement was at the Big Valley, near Mifflinburg, Pa. We always called them the "Valleyers." A unique thing about them is that the men and boys only wear one suspender on their pants. Even though the Valleyers were just as plain as our Lancaster County Amish were, and probably even plainer, Dad just calmly and dismissively said "Meah deena nett mitt cee," meaning, "We don't worship with them." I wondered why not and thought it must be only because they had a slightly different church Ordnung than we did.

When I asked Dad if English folks can be saved, he told me their responsibility is to work out their salvation in the way they are taught, and our responsibility is to do it the way we are taught. So, while I very much admired Rev. Graham as I listened to his preaching, I thought that it was fine for English people, but it still didn't really apply to me, because I had been born Amish. I was still not fully aware, even at that time, how strong the power of the brainwashing was that I had received while growing up. So, sadly and amazingly, I felt almost as strongly as before, that the right thing for me to do was to join the Amish church when my term at MMH was over, even though having all the "worldly" things for the rest of my life was tremendously alluring. Also, I knew that if I did join, I might bitterly regret it later and be haunted by that decision for the rest of my life. If only a helpful, well-meaning English person would have told me and reinforced in my mind the many, many advantages of the English lifestyle and also really explained the Gospel to me and correctly answered all those questions I had, I'm sure my life would have unfolded much differently than it did. But, of course, I'll never know exactly how it would have been different.

In January, 1973, while still living at Morristown, my two best friends, Dave Z., John G., and I went to Florida in my car for a weeks' vacation. I had never been to Florida before. We went to Disney World, Sea World and Busch gardens, among other places. We also visited the Amish community in the Pinecraft area of Sarasota, which is quite a hot spot for Amish, young and old, especially in the wintertime. We were at an Amish hoedown that Saturday night, and it was quite a wild one. There was a lot of drinking by many actual Amish, a lot of "pretend to be" Amish and some "used to be" Amish youths. One of our best friends from Lancaster County was staying there for the winter. He got drunk and crashed and wrecked his beautiful red 1955 Chevy into a tree that night. Fortunately, he and his buddies escaped with only a few bumps and bruises.

The Miami Dolphins beat the Washington Redskins in the Super Bowl that year and finished the season with an unbeaten 17-0 record, the only time that an N.F.L. team has had an unbeaten record throughout the whole season. We just happened to be vacationing in Miami that very day, and we watched the game on TV in our motel room. After the game, we along with hundreds of other drivers drove around the city honking the horn and celebrating, even though we were not Miami Dolphins fans. We blew the horn so much that it stopped working but by the next day it had recovered and was working again.

One Sunday night while riding with Amy G. to Morristown, I experienced the ride of my lifetime. While traveling on Route 287, about twenty miles south of Morristown, he opened up his 1969 Plymouth GTX 440 to full throttle. Soon it seemed like we were almost flying and he told me we were going one hundred twenty-eight miles per hour. That was much faster than I had ever ridden before. He maxed out at one hundred thirty miles per hour and then slowed down to sixty-five where he "leveled" it out.

In April, 1973, Dave G. and I took a weekend trip from Morristown to Boston and went as far north as Vermont. Dave was one of the few remaining Amish boys still at MMH. That Sunday morning, while in Boston, we went to Fenway Park, the famous old stadium where the Red Sox play. Even though the team was away that day, there were some workers there. I managed to sneak inside and saw the inside of the stadium as some employees were working down on the field. It was built in 1912 and is now the oldest major league baseball stadium still in use.

I met a charming auburn-haired girl at MMH, Mary Etta Murphy, who I became friends with. One thing that we did, at my suggestion, of course, was [you guessed it] we went to see a Yankees baseball game in NYC. Her mom seemed a bit apprehensive about us being in the Big Apple at night like that, but everything went fine. I guess I had not quite yet learned that a typical eighteen-year-old girl might not be as interested in going into New York City for a nighttime baseball game as I was, although she was fine with that idea.

Once, after having been to a movie together, I showed her where I lived in the barn. We tiptoed quietly passed Scotch's doorway and up the steps so as not to waken him. Later, she was a little squeamish when she heard the squirrels running across the ceiling of my room. After all, it might have been rats instead of squirrels!

Mary Etta and I decided to go to my home in Lancaster County one weekend. She had a girlfriend in Lancaster with whom she stayed that weekend. When we arrived in my home neighborhood, I drove past our farmhouse and told her what my life there had been like. I told her that I was seriously considering returning to my former lifestyle and joining the Amish church. Understandably, she seemed skeptical about the wisdom of my doing that. I told her I didn't dare take her inside to meet my folks. I had no idea how Dad would react. She seemed to understand. So, we parked at the end of Henry's long lane about a quarter of a mile away, looking at our house and barn as we talked for a long time.

I spent that weekend with my Amish buddies, as planned. While driving back to Morristown that Sunday night with Mary Etta, there was a lot more talk about the Amish lifestyle. Of course, we also talked about her religion, which was Catholic. As most everyone would agree, the two religions are very different, although both have a disproportionately strong emphasis on upholding the church traditions. She was planning on entering her freshman year at West Chester University in the fall, and I was seriously thinking of joining the Amish church, so our lives were heading in diametrically opposite directions. We said our goodbyes a few days later, as I was getting ready to move back home. I did see her once more two years later, when I went back up to Morristown to visit. She seemed unimpressed and even somewhat bothered that I had actually joined the Amish church.

During my last three months at MMH, I worked regularly at cleaning offices at Bell Labs in the evenings. I decided I would give all that money to my parents, plus some of my regular earnings. I knew that I had caused them a lot of heart ache and concern during the two years I was gone, but I still loved and respected them. On the weekend that I moved back home, I put the checks totaling over $900.00 on their bedroom dresser. They were very grateful and thanked me sincerely.

As the end of my two-year term and *decision time* had drawn relentlessly closer, I experienced increasingly more mental and emotional stress, because of my seeming inability to *make* that scary decision. I felt sure it would be the most important and most difficult decision I'd ever have to make in my life. Many times, while driving back home to visit, I would plaintively cry out to God to help me make the right decision, even though I knew almost nothing about effective prayer. Now, in retrospect, it seems very odd that it was such a difficult decision for me. Why could I not and why did I not realize then, that the new modern lifestyle I was experiencing was so much better than going back to the Amish church? Of course, it was because of the amazing power of the brainwashing I had received while growing up. Because of the long-enduring and intensive manner in which that had been done to me, I strongly doubt anyone else understands the immense power of effective and strategic brainwashing better than I do. In any case, I eventually decided that I would join the Amish church even though God had not clearly revealed to me that I should. That momentous decision seemed reasonably logical at the time, although I realized later, to my regret, that it had been poorly thought out. For some time, I'd had a nagging "gut feeling" that I dared not ignore, and it clearly seemed to be demanding baptism and Amish church membership for me. Still, as anyone would understand, it was extremely difficult to convince myself to give up my cushy job at MMH. Especially since I had no idea what I'd be working when I moved back home. More importantly, I'd be facing the very daunting challenge of trying to live the Amish lifestyle again in the way I had always been taught it should be done. Nevertheless, the day came when I sadly said goodbye to my friends and co-workers at MMH, and on Saturday, June 2, 1973, I packed up my things and drove back home to Lancaster County, fully determined to put forth my best efforts at re-adapting to and being happy in the lifestyle that I had grown up in during my childhood and teenage years.

CHAPTER TWENTY-NINE

Becoming an Amish Church Member

SOMEHOW, I HAD MANAGED TO convince myself to move back home and to sell my car and begin attending the church's baptismal instruction class, which would culminate in me being baptized and becoming a member of the Amish church. Of course, Mom and Dad were totally thrilled that I had decided to do that. The baptismal class had already started before I moved back, so I missed one session but the preachers didn't seem to mind that at all. I'm sure they were extremely happy that I was actually willing to join, and I suspect that was quite surprising to them.

There were three other boys and two girls in the class, all of whom were at least three years younger than me. I was older than the typical age because of having been away for two years. Nevertheless, everyone was happy, even delighted that I had decided to move back home and join. They probably thought my situation was like the parable story in the Bible of the prodigal son coming back home to his father's farm after having lived a wild and sinful lifestyle in a faraway distant land.

In each Amish church district, services are held bi-weekly, not weekly. I'm sure that's the biggest reason the services are so long, about three hours. At the beginning of each service, those attending the class for baptism are privately given instructions by the ministers in a separate room. Eventually, in late September, it's expected they'll all be baptized and be faithful members of the church for the rest of their lives. One strange requirement that the Amish church has which other churches, understandably, don't have is that before they can be baptized, they must promise to always be faithful members and never leave the Amish church. And if they ever stop attending or are "kicked out" for committing other "qualifying" sins, they will be permanently ex-communicated and shunned. Of course, they can always repent and rejoin later, but that would simply bring them back to "square one."

It was not till years later that I first pondered these questions, "Did Jesus really intend for there to be a requirement such as that, for someone to be baptized or saved? Did Jesus Himself require new believers to promise to always be members of a specific denomination before they could be baptized or saved? *No, He did not.* The Amish Bishops, of course, know that if they did not require that specific promise, it's certain that many *would* be baptized but would never actually join the church. Especially, since then there would not be the reality or the threat of permanent ex-communication and shunning. Also, for an Amish couple to get married, they must both currently be members of the church. If it were not for that requirement, many would probably get married without first becoming members, and then decide to never become members at all. Was that requirement put in place in an attempt to slyly coerce any doubters into becoming members first? When I started the baptismal instruction class, I was not fully aware of certain realities. If I had been, I'm certain I would not even have attended the class at all or become a member.

Another reality of life was that I needed to find a job, since I was now living back home with my parents again. I had no interest in going back to working on a farm somewhere. And I most certainly wasn't going to catch any more of those dreadful chickens. I had heard there were several mobile home factories that were hiring in Leola, about five miles away. I became extremely interested when I was told that some of my old friends worked there, at Liberty Homes. I drove over with my horse and buggy and met one of the foremen, a young Amish man named Sylvan. He had also worked as a C.O. at MMH, although it was several years before me. However, we knew each other, and he hired me on the spot.

I started working there the next day, riding along with a van load of Amish workers. The Amish buddies that I worked with there, in addition to Sylvan, were Manny, Sam and "Pancho," who was ex Amish. There were also two cousins of mine, Jonas and Elam, who had left the Amish years ago. They were two of Uncle Sammy and Aunt Mary's eight sons.

Since I was now "following the church" in preparation for membership and baptism, I had to always wear the plainest Amish clothing and the most "Dutchified" haircut which included a full row of bangs, hair well over my ears and hardly even a trace of sideburns which, of course, were very popular at the time. I hated looking like that among all those English workers, especially after having been full-fledged English all the time I was at MMH. Perhaps that should have given me pause about the wisdom of joining the Amish church!

The mobile homes, or trailers as they were called, were built in an assembly line operation by English and Amish workers. My cousin, Manny Miller, and I were at the very beginning of the line. We nailed long sections of two by six lumber pieces together and installed the floor insulation and fastened the heavy metal frame underneath. Sam, Poncho and Larry did the next thing, applying floor glue and putting linoleum on the floors. It was much harder work than the easy job I had left at MMH, but I was making a lot more money now and we enjoyed working together.

We sometimes played pranks on each other, including when they lured me into running onto a freshly glued mobile home floor without my knowing about all the wet glue. I immediately fell and slid about fifteen feet and had glue smeared all over my clothes. Another "prank" was when someone put a strip of nails into another guy's sandwich, then at lunchtime watched him bite into it. Manny once put a small turtle into my sandwich, then was eagerly watching, hoping I would bite into it. Fortunately, I saw its head sticking out before I took that first bite.

One evening I was bold and daring enough to drive the company pick-up and take Sam King to his house twelve miles away because he needed a ride home. If the bishops had found out, they surely would have harshly interrogated me and might even have put me on "probation" or suspended me from the baptismal class.

During the summer we were extremely busy at the mobile home factory but by late fall things had slowed down drastically. The economy was also slowing down, coinciding with the events of the Watergate hearings and rumors of President Nixon possibly being impeached.

Earlier in the year, when I was still at MMH, and unsure about going back to the Amish, I had inquired for details about a car auction in the Morristown area. Apparently because of a long delay, the postcard reply they sent to my address at MMH, came instead to the farmhouse at home. As luck would have it, Dad saw the postcard before I did, and he confronted me with a very worried tone and demanded an explanation. I explained the situation to him, and he accepted it but still seemed somewhat troubled. No doubt, we both wondered if I would be able to endure the life-long inconvenience of driving a horse instead of a car!

As the day that I would be baptized drew closer, it was certainly hoped that I would get rid of everything I had that was verboten. I had already sold my car to an Amish boy, Dan, but I still had a wristwatch and a radio, both of which I kept well hidden.

I don't think I ever left any incriminating evidence of having worn a forbidden wristwatch, which happened to an Amish friend of mine, a church member. One day at a construction site with some older Amish men, Mike F. stopped by. I noticed specific marks on his wrist which clearly indicated he had been wearing a wristwatch with a metal expansion band. Obviously, he had just taken it off moments earlier so the Amish men wouldn't see it. So, Mike was embarrassed and did not have a good answer when one of the men, a minister, asked him in a very solemn tone about those marks on his wrist. But, of course, he couldn't punish him because just the appearance of a crime is not *proof* of a crime!

Another Amish friend of mine still owned a radio on the morning he was to be baptized and his dad knew about it. The boy seemed to think that maybe he shouldn't be baptized that day because he still owned the radio. Also, he probably didn't want to be baptized. His dad, of course, very much wanted him to be baptized. He offered to buy the radio and begged him to sell it to him. In fact, that is what happened, and he was baptized that afternoon. I'm sure the father did not use the radio but quickly disposed of it in some way. He may have stabbed it to death with a pitchfork as my father had done to my brother's radio years ago.

By late September I had completed the church membership instruction class, along with the five others in our group. The day we would all be baptized was September 23, 1973. During the summer months, my attitude toward that had mostly been one of stoic resignation. I can certainly say that I never eagerly anticipated it. I tried to console myself by thinking that after I was a church member, I might be fortunate enough to soon start dating some wonderful young Amish girl and she would become the love of my life and we'd get married and start raising a family. I thought that by being baptized and being a new church member, I surely would be considered more eligible to the girls then if I had not done that. Would that not surely indicate to all the girls that I was now done with the worldly and sinful English life, and was truly ready to settle down? That made sense to me. However, after having had all the independence and conveniences that I had at MMH I really didn't like living back home at the farmhouse with my family again. I thought that getting married and moving to our own house somewhere with my new wife would be so much better, even if I didn't have all the modern conveniences that I had at MMH.

All summer I tried to convince myself that, surely such a huge group of "righteous" people as the Amish, were not wrong in insisting on such a "humble and peaceful" lifestyle for their people. And that they were fully justified in demanding that of their children as well. *Or were they?*

For many teen-agers, the decision about joining or not joining the Amish church is not a difficult one. For those who willingly joined as they had *always* planned, and for those who always knew they would *never* join, it is often a very easy decision. But, for many others like myself who were at the apex of uncertainty for a very long time, it is usually an agonizing and tortuous decision.

Many people might wonder why I didn't simply delay for another year or two my decision about joining the church if I was still so doubtful. For one thing, it seemed that delaying it still wouldn't make the decision any easier later. Also, if I did that, many people would have really started to doubt my sincerity and thus would have formed extremely negative opinions of me. That would have included many girls who I was trying to impress into having very *favorable* opinions of me. After all, I was absolutely sure I didn't want to be both an Amish church member *and* a bachelor for the rest of my life like poor old Uncle Benny!

I'm sure Mom and Dad were elated almost beyond measure that I had somehow "endured" and successfully survived all the evil temptations that surrounded me every day at MMH. They must have been overjoyed that I had finally decided to abandon the "English" lifestyle and come back and join the church and live my life the way they had always hoped I would. No doubt that hope had often been very dim while I was at MMH. And, of course, they would have worried far, far less about me if I had never been at MMH at all, but instead stayed home and dutifully joined the church at about eighteen years of age as all of my siblings had done. I'm sure they had faithfully and fervently prayed many times for that and also that I would soon find just the right girl who would become my wife and that we would always be faithful and happy members of the Amish church.

Because I respected and admired my parents so much, I really wanted to obey and please them by joining the church. And I knew that if I did, I would almost achieve "hero" status with all of my friends, uncles, aunts, cousins and other relatives, some of whom were carefully watching my "progress" in the baptismal class. Still, I had this huge struggle of fighting my total addiction to cars, TV, radios, musical instruments and so many other forbidden things. And

I just didn't know how much I might still crave and yearn for all those things throughout my lifetime, if I did join.

How does one respond when his parents are desperately pleading for him to join the Amish church and he knows that they're as sure as they could ever be that that's the only right choice for him? How can he permanently put aside his love and desire for all the thrilling and wonderful things he's had and done and now knows he can never experience those things again? Only if he had a vast amount of love and respect for his parents would he be able to make that enormous sacrifice.

In retrospect, now many years later, it really is sad and unfortunate that this huge gulf had come to exist in how my parents and I thought so differently about the necessity of being Amish and obeying the Ordnung. It was a gulf that, seemingly, never could be bridged. Someone is either born Amish or they are not. Someone is either a member of the Amish church or they are not. It seemed there never was a "middle-ground" solution available that would have really allowed us to accept and agree with each other on the Ordnung issues. However, over the years we largely agreed with each other on almost all issues that were not related to the Ordnung and the Amish way of life. My point is that, had we always been a non-Amish family, I believe our lifetime relationship with each other would have been quite happy and harmonious.

There are two specific times in most young Amish people's lives when an event occurs which brings the parents great happiness. The first is when the young person is baptized, the second is when he gets married. Each event is considered a major steppingstone to his expected permanent allegiance and adherence to the Amish church. Once that person is both baptized and married, it's far, far, less likely that he will ever break away than if he had never been baptized and joined the church at all.

A particularly important part of the baptismal classes is discussing and studying the ancient Dordrecht Confession of Faith that our Anabaptist forefathers, along with certain Mennonite leaders, adopted at Dordrecht, Holland in 1632. There are eighteen articles of which two are studied at each class. Of course, it's strongly hoped that those studies will convince us to eagerly embrace and obey the Amish Ordnung, which was partially originated at the Dordrecht meetings.

There have been quite a few instances when an Amish person attended and completed all the new members baptismal instruction classes, but on the day he was to be baptized, he decided to stay home and not even go to church at all. That thought entered my mind briefly on the morning of that fateful and memorable day but with grim resolve, I decided to go through with it. I felt certain that if I gave it my absolute best effort, I could somehow force myself to re-adapt to and possibly even "like" this previously familiar lifestyle.

At the final instruction class that morning, the bishops and ministers solemnly admonished and reminded us that the vows we made later would be extremely important and would be completely valid and binding for the rest of our lives. We were told that it would be far better to not make them at all than to make them and break them at some later time. The other boys and I were required to promise that if we were ever selected by the "lot" system to be a minister, we would faithfully and dutifully yield to that calling for the rest of our life. The bishop told us that our vows would be made, not to them, but to God. Later, as the church service progressed and the preachers droned on, I still wasn't sure if this was the right thing for me to do. One minister said in his "zeignus" testimony, with an ill-concealed tone of satisfaction, "What a wonderful thing it is, that these young folks still want to do what is right." Well, of course, *he* thought it was the right thing for us to do. I was not so sure!

I have often wondered if I had refused to promise to "accept" the Amish ministry if it were ever thrust upon me by the lot system, would the bishops still have been willing to baptize me and accept me as a "bonafide" church member? I am quite certain they would not have. In any case, it's a moot point now, since I have never been and never will be in any Amish "lot."

All summer during the baptismal classes, my parents had never questioned me as to whether I was confident I could make this monumental transformation from English life to permanent Amish status while still properly obeying the Ordnung. They certainly may have had grave concerns because of my having lived the worldly English lifestyle at MMH for two years. Nevertheless, I'm sure they were thankful and inwardly rejoicing that, at the advanced age of twenty-two, their youngest and most rebellious child had now finally decided to fully yield and humble himself to God and the church and to be baptized. It must have been a huge relief to them to finally be able to consider me safely "in the fold" as all my siblings had already been for years.

Eventually, the time came when we were all told to kneel on the floor. The bishops' wife then carefully untied and removed the girls white coverings (kapps) in preparation for their baptisms. It has long been Amish custom for the ministers to remind the ones being baptized that they are making those vows on their bent knees. The reminders are made in the most earnest and solemn tones, implying that because of the knees being bent, the vows are not only extremely important, but are actually more important than if the knees were not bent. And, to some in the congregation, our vows promising to always stay Amish, specifically, may have been more important than our profession of faith in Jesus Christ!

I would be baptized first, since I was the oldest one in our group. The three other boys were Danny Esh, Samuel Esh, and Elam Esh. The two girls were Annie King and Savilla Fisher. Bishop Dan E. Stoltzfus was the one who would baptize each one of us. He was a most familiar old patriarch with flowing white hair and beard, and he had been the spiritual leader in our church district for a very long time. He first asked me if I believed that Jesus Christ was God's Son and I told him I did. He asked me if I would always obey and support the Amish doctrines and the Ordnung and I promised him I would. Then I was required to promise that I would renounce the devil and the world and my sinful desires, which I did. To everything else I, of course, answered the way they expected me to. Then, as Deacon Davey stood next to him with a pitcher of water and a cup, Bishop Dan solemnly said "Yonie, durich dein geshprechten Glauben, siesht du Gedauft. In Der Nauma Der Vater, Der Sohnes, und Der Heilegen Geishtes. Schtande auf und sie eine Getreue Bruder bie de Gmay" ["Yonie, in accordance with your professed beliefs, you are now being baptized. In the Name of The Father and of The Son and of The Holy Ghost. Arise and be a humble brother with the church."] Suddenly, the moment had come when I realized it was too late to change my mind, as I felt the water being poured on top of my head. I felt a moment of near panic but tried to suppress it. Somehow, I endured that last final convulsive moment of mental resignation and surrender, even as I fully realized the gravity of what had just happened. Then Bishop Dan and Deacon Davey proceeded to the other three boys and two girls and baptized each one of them in turn, as the whole congregation watched with rapt attention.

There was something that somewhat drew my attention away from the seriousness of what had just occurred. That was the pain in my knees from having had to kneel on the hardwood floor for quite a few minutes. Of course, we probably would not have been allowed to put our hands on the floor for support. Or, at least it would have been seen with much disapproval. At another similar baptismal event, a girl had kneeled for so long that she couldn't get up by herself and had to be helped up by the bishop's wife.

Finally, the bishop extended the hand of fellowship and the holy kiss to all of us boys while his wife did likewise to the girls as we all stood up. Now, suddenly we were all, not only baptized, but also full members of the Old Order Amish church. And, of course, it was very much hoped and expected that we would all remain so for the rest of our lives.

I stayed at home with my parents all that afternoon, evening, and night as they had requested. They surely didn't want me to go to Rumspringa that evening and possibly lose my focus on the day's events. That afternoon Mom said to me she supposes that today I probably was closer to God than I had ever been before. She probably also thought that I should be and would be happy at that time. In reality, I did not feel happy at all. Instead, I felt a pervading and growing sense of sadness and gloom and near-despair because of everything I had agreed to do without for the rest of my life. As the full impact of what I had just done *really* hit me, I sadly and pensively brooded in my upstairs bedroom that evening, as waves of doubt and dismay swept over me like giant ocean waves. I wondered how I could possibly have thought this to be a wise decision. What was I getting for having made this enormous sacrifice? Certainly, no one had even congratulated me, thanked me, or praised me for it. I asked myself in near disbelief how I could have practically "signed my life away," like that. How could I have, like many thousands of other Amish youth at their "appointed" time, just meekly and foolishly gone like sheep to the slaughter, as some might characterize it. And agree to never have many, many modern conveniences that would make my life so much easier and more pleasant. I wondered if Bishop Dan and all the other adults at the baptismal service were actually happy that I now also had to endure a lifetime of hardship and deprivation and gut-wrenching boredom, just like them. Or did some possibly feel sorry for me? Had some possibly thought they should warn me not to do it? Even if they did, surely none would have dared to express that to me. I remember thinking that I would have been very willing to simply have a sincere and proper Christian baptism without having to, at the same time, join the Amish church with all its restrictions. But, of course, that's not the Amish way. They fully believe that the two must go "hand in hand" and that you can't do one without the other.

The next few days were difficult for me as I realized that, in addition to doing without many modern conveniences, I would also be deprived of many *future* inventions which would undoubtedly provide unfathomable benefits to society. I tried to imagine what it would be like to never have a TV or radio or telephone or pool table again. And to never own or drive a car again for the rest of my life. I thought about Brother Jake having told me that he'd never moved a car even an inch, and that he was glad he hadn't. At least, he had the advantage of never having suffered major withdrawal symptoms like I surely would!

A few months later at a Sunday church service, I did something that probably surprised everybody. I decided to lead the Loeb song, as it is called in German. It means the praise song and it is always the second song that's sung at every church service. The person leading it never announces the page number, because everyone knows it is on page 770, in the old German Ausbund, circa 1564. So, "out of the blue," he courageously begins and sings the first syllable all by himself, which takes about ten seconds. If someone is doing it for the first time, and if he's on the shy side, it can be quite scary. Especially, since there are *no musical notes!* So, it's very easy to "run off track," that is, to lose the right pitch or cadence or inflection. When that happens, it usually all comes to an embarrassing halt. Then, a self-appointed "expert" will often take over and try to get it going again, which can be quite humiliating to the one who had botched it. The congregation joins in at the second syllable, and when they do, it is a huge relief to a first-time song leader. There are four verses which take a total of about twenty minutes to sing, with the lead singer singing the first syllable of each line by himself. Only men who are already members lead the singing because women are never permitted to do that. Interestingly, hardly any children or teenagers, either boys or girls, ever participate in the singing at Amish church services, even though the older folks would be delighted if they did. I presume it has been that way for decades, possibly centuries. As for myself, I rarely joined in the singing, even once I became a member. I suppose many adults, including parents, don't really want to sing that way either, but they know they'd lose a huge amount of credibility with their children if they didn't.

Twice a year there is Ordnung church, followed two weeks later by Communion church, both of which are attended only by church members. At Ordnung church, the deacon tells the congregation what is "oppschtelled," meaning the things that are prohibited. There is no actual "Rule" book from which he can read those things. If he forgets to mention some things, which he always will, that doesn't mean that having those things is now permitted. If it was said to be forbidden last year, you need to remember that, and realize that it is still forbidden. Since there are now so many modern things that are forbidden, the deacon usually doesn't even try to remember and mention all of them.

He might, however, ask the other preachers to mention various things that he had not, if they want to.

So, nobody knows how many "rules" and restrictions there really are. Even though there are hundreds, sometimes it seems they number in the *thousands!* And, there are many things that are *never* mentioned as being "oppschtelled," but yet the members are expected to simply "know" they're prohibited. That would include flying in an airplane or having rubber tires on any buggies or farm equipment or going to college. So, it all can be quite bewildering.

During my first Ordnung Church attendance, Deacon Davey was trying to recite by memory, the things that were prohibited. In a disparaging tone of voice, he said he doesn't think bathtubs are necessary and he thinks the Amish who have them are worldly and conceited, or "hoch-mutich," as he called it. That's when Christ R, the man with the golden front tooth that had fascinated me as a young boy, protested in an indignant tone, "We don't have our bathtub for that reason. We have it because we like it, and it's much better than using a bucket." Deacon Davey quickly backpedaled and said, "Excuse me" which was considered to be a semi-apology.

Apparently, Deacon Davey was not convinced that what Christ R. had told him about his bathtub was true, as far as it being much better than using a bucket. His own method of bathing continued to be the traditional and time-honored Amish ritual of using a bucket of hot water with a bar of soap and a small wash-cloth. However, even this fully acceptable form of bathing had its drawbacks. Because of the modesty factor, it was often done in an area of the house that was not heated, which presented a problem at wintertime. That problem was a reluctance to bathe as often as one should. That's when Deacon Davey must have set a dubious Amish record of historic proportion, during one cold winter season.

Mom once told us a story that Davey's wife, Katie, had told her. She said that Davey had such an aversion to bathing that he often failed to do it, even at the prescribed and recommended frequency of once a week on Saturday evenings. During wintertime there would often be much longer intervals that he didn't take a bath. Especially when Katie once decided to not nag him at all about it anymore. Of course, she also was curious to see how long it really would turn out to be. So, she was greatly relieved (I suppose her nose was also greatly relieved!) when he finally took his familiar "bucket bath" after, remarkably, having abstained from that for a full six weeks. In fairness, it is possible that he "dry-toweled" himself occasionally during that time.

By the way, it seems that not bathing for six weeks would require enormous mental will-power and endurance because of the itch factor. I've never heard of any other Amish person even coming close to matching Davey's amazing record.

Deacon Davey also seemed to have an exaggerated opinion of how much authority he really had. That was especially true when it was decided that his home church district should be divided into two separate districts. That usually happens about every twenty-five years because of normal population increases.

Of course, the bishop, the two other ministers and the deacon are considered to have more authority than the other church members in deciding how the district should be geographically divided. Even so, Deacon Davey clearly overstepped his authority when he insisted that it be done his way. If one used a topography map, his version of the geographical land shapes of the two new districts were very contorted and odd-looking. In fact, it was quite similar to an extremely "Gerrymandered" congressional district that politicians sometimes devise. It was obvious he wanted it done that way because that would keep all his relatives in his own district. Because he was an "elder statesman" and was older than the bishop and the two other ministers, it was grudgingly decided to do it his way. [In the interest of full disclosure, Deacon Davey passed away many years ago].

The Amish Ordnung church service lasts about seven hours. Two weeks after Ordnung church is Communion church, also known by the Amish as "GROSSGMA," or Big Church. It is the marathon of all Amish church services and it lasts about eight hours. At those events, only church members attend, so children and non-member teenagers are, mercifully, allowed to stay at home. On that day, it is especially important that all members are in a submissive and obedient frame of mind so they can (mitthalda), that is, in good conscience, partake of Communion. The preachers lecture at great length through the contents of the Bible, with most of the preaching focused on the Old Testament. When it's finally over, all church members wash each other's feet, using warm water in a metal bucket. Of course, it is always gender specific, with men only washing other men's feet and women washing each other's feet. After the feet were dried, the two individuals were required to kiss each other on their lips. I found it to be quite *repulsive* to do that to another man!

Next, everyone eats a bite of homemade bread and drinks a sip of real homemade grape wine, passed out by Deacon Davey. He then walks up and down the rows of members and collects their alms money. That is the money they want to contribute to the widows and poor people. They just hand him whatever amount of cash they want to contribute. He stuffs all of it into his inside mutza pocket, for the time being, without looking at it at all. He is *trusted* to fully divest himself of it later. And, no, the donors are never given a receipt for tax purposes.

It was rumored that a wealthy man from the New Holland area usually gave one hundred dollars, which was presumed to be much more than anyone else gave. I suppose he could easily afford that because each year he grew about thirty acres of tobacco, which was considered to be an enormous amount. And, yes, tobacco was a very lucrative cash crop.

There usually was quite a disparity in the amount of alms money that people gave during the Communion Service. I remember several times that the guy next to me, who was in his mid-twenties, apparently only gave some coins, because I heard them jingling as he handed them to Deacon Davey. Observing those paltry offerings made me think of the Bible story of the widow's mite, although she surely was much poorer than him!

Each church member is required to fast during two separate mornings each year. Specifically, they are not allowed to eat anything until noon that day. It is always on Good Friday morning and on the second Friday in October, usually two days before Communion Sunday.

Dad told us about a liberal Amish man, Elias, who apparently would get quite hungry on the morning of the "fast." His solution was to go fishing at a local creek the evening before, with a few friends and relatives. Then they would make a bonfire and have a late night-time fish-fry before returning home. So, technically, he was not violating the Ordnung. But, surely, it resulted in some clucking and shaking of heads from some of the stricter brethren.

I was laid off from my job at the mobile home factory in late November, and was soon hired by our Amish neighbor, "Push" John Esh, and his partner, Cliff Martin. They had about eight carpenters working for them, building and remodeling houses. All of us were Amish, except for one English driver. Of course, I immediately noticed that everyone always talked English, by necessity, because the English man couldn't speak Pennsylvania Dutch. Nevertheless, it seemed strange and almost "sinful" for even Preacher Stevie to always speak English, even to us Amish folks.

It certainly was a worthwhile and interesting experience, learning the tricks of the trade of home construction. Everybody got along very well and we all had a lot of fun. There were six boys who were roughly the same age as me. Dave,

Manny and Simeon belonged to the Happy Jack gang, which was an "up and coming" group. My old gang, the Keffahs, were slowly dying out and becoming extinct. Thinking that the three Happy Jacks wouldn't mind, I decided to run around with their gang because they had a lot more girls that were of interest to me than in the stodgy old Keffah gang. But I suppose a lot of Happy Jack boys were quite concerned about me coming to their gangs. No doubt, they were afraid I would "steal" one of their girls. They needn't have worried because nothing really worked out between me and any of the Happy Jack girls.

I had a few dates with several Keffah girls, including Aquilla's Sarah, an interesting young lady who I had met at a recent "hoedown." When I arrived in my horse-drawn buggy at her house that Saturday evening, I was pleasantly surprised to see there an old friend, Dave F., who had been a "barn dweller" like me at MMH, during our time there. He was having a date with Sarah's older sister, Annie and, as it turned out, they got married about a year later. As for myself, Sarah dumped me after that first date even though we had gotten along very well. I assume it was because I was about five years older than her, which is a lot by Amish standards. Many would have considered that to be a bold attempt to "rob the cradle."

My next date was with Lizzie B., a friendly, dark-haired gal from Groffdale. All evening we played some board game which "bored" me considerably. A welcome interlude came when the "forbidden" phone hidden in the kitchen cabinet started ringing and she guiltily got up and went over to turn it off. But, of course, she made no mention of it to me and, in fact, she hadn't even answered the phone.

Another date I had was with Katie G., a cute young maiden from Upper Mill Creek. She was a sister to Amy G., a former MMH compadre who had once thrilled me with a one hundred thirty mph ride to Morristown in his powerful 1969 Plymouth GTX. My ride with Katie to the singing at Strasburg was much slower, however, as that happened to be with my slow and boring old horse and buggy!

I had a great opportunity to ask the prettiest girl in the Keffah gang, Anna B., for a date. It was at a Sunday afternoon pound-supper as she and her friend, Barbie, sat in my buggy chatting with me. As it turned out, I was too shy to ask her, but I think I just *might* have if Barbie hadn't been there!

In the summer of 1974, some deadly tornadoes ripped through the southern states, causing considerable death and destruction, especially in Alabama. My bosses, John and Cliff, decided to go there and help out for a week, along with any of us who also wanted to volunteer our services. Our entire crew went along, except for one older man, Ike D.

On our first morning there, a Mennonite man was coordinating the volunteer worker's relief efforts. He said, half seriously, that we could consider this to be a vacation, and that the only difference was that we had to work! Later, we worked at replacing some roofs that had blown off houses, as well as doing other repairs to storm damaged homes. It was an interesting experience, even though we did not get paid and the weather was extremely hot.

Later, back home, I occasionally dated several different Amish girls from the Keffah and Happy Jack gangs, but nothing became serious. On three different occasions I asked a different Happy Jack girl, late on a Sunday night, for a date the next weekend. No matter whether the girl agreed or not, by the next morning my Happy Jack co-worker buddies were pestering me and asking me about it at work. Apparently, the night before, the girl I had asked, quickly told her friends and the news spread like wildfire. I thought that was very strange and would not have happened that way in the Keffah gang that I'd been with before. Apparently, the Happy Jack boys really were genuinely concerned about me possibly "stealing" one of their girls.

After about a year of being Amish again, I started to become increasingly more restless and bored with this stifling and hauntingly familiar lifestyle. I began having serious doubts about whether I would ever be able to again properly fit myself into the tiny, constricted world of the Amish. Especially to the satisfaction of the bishops, who still seemed to watch me closely, almost as though I was on probation. Every day, I wondered with increasingly more doubt and dismay if I had made a huge mistake by coming back from MMH and joining the Amish church. Every day I tried extremely hard to be content with that decision, but it seemed virtually impossible. With increasing bewilderment, I wondered how I could have been so naïve as to think becoming Amish again could possibly be a good idea. I asked myself if I really wanted to permanently associate with people who were totally unconcerned about ever improving their standard of living, and experiencing a much more pleasant and rewarding lifestyle. And, even though I was now living the way the bishops and my family and other Amish wanted me to, they all seemed to take for granted that I would just naturally continue to do so. Even though a lot of them had encouraged me, even pleaded with me to join, none ever thanked me for doing so. They also never encouraged me to just "hang in there," no matter what, and that it eventually should get easier.

No one ever even asked me if I was happy that I had decided to join. Maybe they thought if they asked me that, it might make me consider leaving the church. While I was not actually considering that at the time, I certainly was very bored and unhappy. Even so, I did not confide that to anyone and certainly not to my friends, siblings or parents. Like Amish people usually do during periods of major trials and adversity, I grimly and stoically struggled through those many long days, weeks and months of unrelenting boredom and mental turmoil and misery. And, of course, I had no idea how long it all would continue.

In the winter of 1974, Dave and John G., both of whom were also extremely bored, decided to go to Florida for a lengthy period of R and R, and to pal around with other rebellious Amish youth at Pinecraft. They very much wanted me to go along and I can't possibly describe how badly I wanted to do just that. But I thought I would make a much better impression on certain Amish girls I had my eyes on if I did not, so I stayed home. Predictably, with my two best friends in Florida for those four long winter months, I became desperately and almost indescribably lonely and bored. And, to make things worse, nothing worked out between me and any of the girls I had been pursuing anyway.

As it turned out, I never did marry an Amish girl. I'm sure my parents were very sad and frustrated about that because that would, presumably, have greatly increased the likelihood I would always stay Amish. A few years later, when my eventual marriage decision had been made, I was very happy that I had *not* married an Amish girl, but I never had the heart to tell my parents that.

Also, it seems that every day now, I have an intense feeling of thankfulness and happiness that I did not stay Amish. Increasingly more throughout my lifetime, I have always been glad that I made the permanent decision to leave the Amish church. I have never regretted that at all, despite having been ex-communicated for all these years. Many Amish people, especially certain bishops, would say that is because my heart has become wicked and calloused and hardened. But, no, I insist it's because I have become much more enlightened and better informed during all this time. And I have become more and more aware of the many, many excellent and logical reasons to *not* be a member of the Amish church. Still, I assume some bishops *hope* that I have a huge fear of going to hell because I left the church. Happily, I can say that I do not.

Many years ago, while I was struggling to accept my status as an Amish church member, an elderly Amish friend told me something that he hoped would comfort me. He said that if I just fully and properly yielded myself to the Ordnung, gradually and eventually a feeling of serenity and contentment would come over me and I would be at peace. But, as it turned out, I did not experience that until *after* I left the Amish church!

On a bright, sunny, day in the spring of 1975, I decided to go back to MMH to visit, two years after I had left there. It was on an Amish holiday, Ascension Day, which is always on a weekday. I thought that would be a good day to do it, even though I expected it to be a bittersweet event for me. I decided to make the one hundred thirty mile trip there by hitch-hiking, even though I had little idea of how that would go. I was fairly successful at getting rides despite having walked about five miles. I guess I made a strange sight, wearing my big black Amish hat while hitch-hiking on busy interstate Route 78 East. Later, I ate at the hospital cafeteria with some of my former friends. I'm sure a lot of old acquaintances were surprised to see me dressed Amish, as I had always been very secretive about that. That evening I took the train to Newark, N.J., then rode the Amtrak train to Lancaster, and finally, a taxicab to my house at 9:00 P.M. that evening. And, yes, the visit to MMH was a bittersweet experience (mostly bitter) as, over the next few days, I regretfully and sorrowfully mourned that wonderfully exciting lifestyle I had "willingly" given up two years earlier.

My old buddy, Dave Z, had gotten a car again and that seemed a lot more appealing to me then my horse and buggy. I started riding around with him regularly again on weekends, along with our old friend, John G. As I think anyone would agree, when someone has been accustomed to owning and driving a car every day for two years, it's very, very hard to completely give that up and go back to a horse and buggy as one's normal mode of transportation. And to no longer be surrounded by music and heat and air-conditioning and the many other luxuries that modern cars provide. For me, it really is hard to overstate the joy and convenience of owning and driving a car instead of a horse and buggy.

Still, there are actually a few *advantages* to driving a horse instead of a car. In addition to no carbon footprint being created, there are no expenses for gasoline, car insurance, registration and license. Also, unlike with cars, one never has to worry about a horse "spinning out" on icy roads or having a deadly high-speed crash with another horse. Still, every buggy driver *does* need to worry about other traffic as car/ buggy accidents are common. As an Amish driver pointedly stated, though, "It's the cars that do the killing, not the buggies!"

On Saturday nights and Sunday afternoons, I'd walk to where Dave and I had arranged to meet. I didn't want him to pick me up at my house, because then my parents would surely know that I was traveling in a car. And, at the same time, Dave didn't want them to see him driving, because he was now also a church member.

Dave's car was a white, 1960 Chevy Impala, with a three-speed manual transmission. One Saturday night we were at the Bullfrog Inn at Bart, about ten miles away, when something broke in the clutch linkage. To our utter dismay we discovered that, while it would drive properly in first gear, we couldn't shift into any other gear. So, we could only go at about the same speed as a driver horse on a good day. Some Amish would have laughed and said it serves us right because we should have been driving a horse instead of a car, anyway. In any case, it was a long, boring, nighttime ride all the way to Brackbill's Garage in Intercourse. That slow ride back made us again greatly appreciate the convenience of owning and driving a car instead of being stuck behind a slow-moving horse and buggy.

CHAPTER THIRTY

Shunned Because of
The West Coast Trip

DAVE, JOHN G., AND I had for a long time been hoping to take a cross country trip to the West Coast someday. Finally, in the summer of 1975, those plans came to fruition. Of course, we would take our own vehicle and take turns driving, since we all had a driver's license, although mine had expired after I had joined the church. At that time, I didn't think I would ever need it again. So, I did get my license renewed. We had eagerly been anticipating this trip and correctly thought it would be a great adventure. At the time, we were all in relatively flexible job situations, and thought our jobs would all be secure until we came back in about six or eight weeks.

There had been a previous occasion when six Amish boys from the Keffah gang and a young English friend named Allen went on a similar western trip. All of them except Allen were church members, so the Amish parents were assured that he would do all the driving. No doubt the boys thought that what the parents didn't know wouldn't hurt them. So, it's laughable and ludicrous to think that Allen really did all of the driving on that trip of many thousands of miles. Especially when the other boys often really wanted to drive, whether they had a driver's license or not. In fact, they must have thought that this was a great opportunity to do lots of forbidden driving. Of course, they needed to be careful that no incriminating evidence circulated back to the Bishop, such as photographs of them driving the van.

As for Dave, John G. and myself, our parents were not happy when we told them about our plan to go on the western trip. Especially when we told them we'd be going in a van but didn't tell them who would be driving. They, no doubt, correctly assumed that the three of us would share the driving.

We had a 1972 Dodge van with which we accumulated over 14,000 miles during our trip. We started out in early July, 1975 and our first stop was at an Amish settlement in western Pennsylvania, where John's sister and her husband lived. We visited them while, of course, still wearing our Amish clothes. We stayed overnight and left the next morning. About one mile up the road we stopped the van and "un-Amished" for good. Of course, by doing that we had committed the major sin of "rumm dressa" that is, dressing around, which means wearing English clothes, with belts and zippers and bright colors and all. Well, it sure felt good to be wearing shorts, tank tops and sandals instead of hot black Amish pants and suspenders and all that uncomfortable stuff. Then we headed for Detroit and saw a baseball game at Tiger Stadium that night. During our entire trip, we only slept in a motel three times. Every night one of us would sleep in the van and the others slept outside on the ground or on an air mattress. It usually was in a park or some other rural location.

From Detroit, we headed to Chicago and did some sightseeing there and saw a Chicago Cubs baseball game at Wrigley field. From there we went through Wisconsin and Minnesota and into North Dakota and South Dakota, where we saw various attractions, including Mt. Rushmore. Then, into Wyoming where we saw Grand Teton National Park, Yellowstone National Park, and a famous annual national rodeo in Cheyenne.

There were two separate occasions, when we picked up a young hitchhiker and they were both heading to Alaska, hoping to get high paying jobs on the Alaska pipeline. Their names were Bob and Denny and they rode with us for several hundred miles. Since they talked glowingly of all the "filthy lucre" (as the Amish would consider it) that could be earned in Alaska, we thought maybe, just *maybe*, we might someday also wind up there with a pipeline job. So, we asked them to write to us and let us know how they made out but, predictably, neither of them did. We couldn't tell them to call us, because we didn't have telephones at home, although I doubt they would have anyway.

We went from Montana into Alberta, Canada and visited Banff National Park, which is an exceptionally large park consisting of 1,640,000 acres. Next was British Columbia and Jasper National Park. We briefly thought about going on up to Alaska, but after discovering that it was about a thousand miles further, we quickly agreed not to. We took a ferry from Vancouver over to Vancouver Island, and later drove through Washington State and down the Pacific Coast. In Seattle, we saw the Space Needle Tower and Mount Rainier National Park. Then, down through Oregon and into Northern California to Redwood National Forest, and on to San Francisco. There we did some sightseeing and saw, yes, yet another baseball game. Had I mentioned yet that we were all huge baseball fans? There would be more visits to other baseball stadiums during our trip. The nighttime game at San Francisco was between the Giants and the Cincinnati Reds, and the famous chill and mist that Candlestick Park was known for, permeated the park as usual.

The next day we went to Yosemite National Park. After that it was Kings Canyon National Park, Sequoia National Park and Death Valley National Park. That's where I encountered the hottest outside temperature I have ever felt, at about 122°. From there it was on to Los Angeles where we saw a game between the Dodgers and the Atlanta Braves. Then on to Las Vegas, Nevada. We got there after midnight and it was all lit up as though it was evening hours. We went into several different casinos and played blackjack for a while. That night we stayed in a motel room for the first time on our trip because it was sweltering hot.

We got up late the next morning and had breakfast and then spent all day in Las Vegas. When we got back to the van, we noticed that someone had pried open the one front vent window and unlocked the door and stolen all our eight track tapes. That is, all except the one that was already inserted into the tape player. Even though the front of it was visible, it was held securely in place because the van's ignition was turned off. There were about twenty-five tapes in a case that had been stolen. The one that was stuck in the player, however, was Dave and John's favorite tape, as luck would have it. We didn't even report the theft to the police because we thought there was no chance of getting them back. We belatedly realized that Las Vegas would probably be the most likely place for us to be robbed and we should have made sure the little vent window was locked.

The next day we went to Hoover Dam, a mighty structure 776 feet tall and 660 feet thick at its base, with 6,600,000 tons of concrete having been used to build it. We later drove east into Tucson and visited an ex-Amish acquaintance who lived there, Christ [Hurst] King. It was great to sleep in his air-conditioned house and swim in the pool. He was interested in hearing about recent news from Lancaster County.

The next night we were at a minor-league baseball game in Phoenix, and it was their annual 5¢ beer night. Predictably, we drank more than we should have and got rather intoxicated.

During the trip, we got our fair share of exercise, walking around the national Parks and other places we visited. But it was still not nearly as much as if we had been at home working, so we often played basketball at various school playgrounds.

The next stop after Phoenix was Petrified Forest National Park, followed by the Grand Canyon, which was magnificent and awe-inspiring. Undoubtedly, it was the highlight of our whole trip. Next, we went east to the famous Four Corners site where a corner of each of the four states of Arizona, New Mexico, Colorado, and Utah all come together at precisely the same spot. We took pictures of us standing on a corner of each of those states simultaneously. We next went into Utah and saw Canyonlands National Park and Arches National Park.

The van was doing quite well with all the miles we were putting on it, in the hot summer weather. It did overheat once and we had to get the radiator repaired but it was not a major problem. Soon we arrived in Colorado, where we saw Rocky Mountain National Park followed by famous Pikes Peak. We drove all the way to the top, about twelve miles, and when we got there it was snowing. It was late July and, of course, we were dressed in shorts and sandals, but it wasn't uncomfortably cold. When we left there, we went south through New Mexico to the border town of El Paso in Texas. When we crossed a bridge over the Rio de Janeiro into Mexico, there were a lot of Mexican kids standing about twenty feet below, holding up sticks with baskets on top. They were hoping the tourists would throw money down to them. On the other side, in the Mexican town of Juarez, the drivers drove more recklessly than any place I'd ever been. Most of the cars they drove were older American cars.

Our next destination was Carlsbad Caverns and it was a remarkably interesting and memorable experience. After that we went to Houston and saw a baseball game in the Astrodome which was then known as the eighth wonder of the world. We slept in a motel that night because of extremely hot weather. The next stop was New Orleans, with sightseeing at various places, including the French Quarter. Then, north into Tennessee to Nashville to various record shops where our favorite types of music, country and bluegrass, filled the air. St. Louis was next, where we saw a baseball game at Busch Stadium and took a ride to the top of the Steel Arch. After that we really became homeward bound, making the long drive on Route 70 East, past Indianapolis and Columbus, Ohio to Pittsburgh, and finally the home stretch on the Pennsylvania Turnpike.

When we arrived back home in Lancaster County, we had been gone for seven weeks and four days. I had spent about $1200.00, which included my share of the gas expense, which had cost about eighty cents per gallon. We had all gotten along very well and there had only been one major argument during the whole trip. It was a truly memorable and worthwhile trip and none of us have ever regretted doing it.

We arrived home at nighttime and Mom was both happy and horrified when she saw me the next morning. She was happy that I was safely back home but horrified at how I looked. None of us had shaved at all or gotten haircuts during the trip. Mom begged me to shave my beard and mustache, which I did, although I did sport some long sideburns for a while. It felt good to be clean shaven again, and I felt that now I knew what it would be like to wear a beard for the rest of my life and I certainly was not enamored with that idea. In fact, it seemed repulsive to me, especially since, according to the Amish "laws," I really didn't have a choice. But, of course, that is what my family would eventually expect from me.

On my first day back, they were busy harvesting tobacco in the fields, and I joined in and helped them in the hot August sunlight. It felt good to be active and doing some real work again, but it also reminded me of how much drudgery and hard work is inevitably involved in farming the Amish way.

My folks didn't really badger me with a lot of questions pertaining to the western trip. Nevertheless, I expected the bishop to pay me a visit very soon and demand details about what we had done and who had been driving. Since none of us could deny that we had all driven thousands of miles, I fully expected that I would be expelled and excommunicated, and that it would just be a matter of time until that happened. So, I decided to simply "plead guilty" to being dressed English and doing all that driving. I thought that would make a much more favorable impression, rather than wait for the Amish bishop's "indictment" that would surely have occurred anyway. So, I went to see Stevie, who was my favorite preacher and confessed to him that I had done a lot of driving and had been dressed English the whole time. I actually requested to be expelled. He solemnly agreed that they would do that, but he said that he really hopes I would immediately do the required penance and would rejoin the church again as soon as possible. I told him that was my plan.

When I told my parents about it, they seemed relieved that I had done that. They did, however, remind me that they'd have to practice shunning toward me during the six-week time period that was required until I could become a member again. I accepted that but, of course, it seemed very strange eating at a little folding table all by myself at mealtimes. It was even more embarrassing during several days when I worked for one of my married brothers on his farm. His young children, of course, noticed and wondered why I was sitting by myself at the little table to eat. Thankfully, however, everybody was tactful, and nobody tried to embarrass me.

Some Amish church districts have a requirement that is designed to cause the shunned person major embarrassment at mealtimes. That person is served last but then later his plate, glass and silverware are washed before anyone else's, presumably to avoid "contaminating" anyone else. However, I don't recall that ever being done toward me in our district.

During the time that I was shunned, I was required to meet with the ministers in the "counsel" room upstairs each time before the church service started. Later, I'd go downstairs and would have to walk in alone to the service, which was already in progress. Almost everybody would be staring at me at that time. After I sat down, I had to put my head down very low and put my hands along the sides of my head as a sign of humility. Eventually, the preachers came down and only after one had preached a sermon was it proper for me to sit up straight like the others.

I was not allowed to go to any of the Rumspringa gangs or singings during the six-week period I was ex-communicated. However, I bent that rule slightly once when I went to visit a friend, Dave Fisher, one Sunday afternoon at his farm near Mile-Long Hill, south of Paradise.

During the time that I was in the "ban," I was not familiar with what was involved in "rejoining" the church. I wondered to myself if I would be re-baptized. It does seem strange that I didn't know that, but it's understandable because there is no Amish rulebook pertaining to that, and, certainly, no one had ever told me. So, I asked Brother John and he told me that baptism is only done when someone first becomes a member.

After having been in the "ban" and shunned for six weeks, I was reunited and became a member again during Sits-Gma, the special meeting which is for members only, at the end of the church service. I received the hand of fellowship and the "holy" kiss from Bishop Moses, who admonished me to strive faithfully to abide by the laws and Ordnung of the church.

Of course, ex-communication is the most serious disciplinary punishment that's done at Amish church services. It's also very serious when a member is "aus de roete" (out of the counsel) meaning he cannot participate during "Sits-Gma."

"Failah bekenna," (admitting one has failed and sinned), is the least serious of those three disciplinary events. When that happens, the guilty person must kneel among the congregation during Sits-Gma, and describe and admit his wrongdoing and ask forgiveness. However, all non-members and children are prohibited from witnessing that event. This process has always been a strict part of Ordnung law.

Because there is no building or location known as the "Central Governing Authority" of the Amish, it is not a quick or easy process to pass new disciplinary Ordnung legislation. Or, even simply to "touch base" with the thousands of bishops. Especially, since they don't have telephones, e-mail, or other similar devices. (Actually, many Amish people do now have telephones, but the least likely ones *are the Bishops!*) They *can* be contacted by "snail-mail" but few bishops would use such a slow, two-way process to resolve any serious church discipline matters. So, the other option would be to schedule it for Sits-Gma.

Dave and John G., who lived in other church districts, were also expelled for doing all that driving and dressing English during our trip, but both were soon reunited in the same way I had been. So, the day after we arrived back home from the western trip, I went to my boss, John Esh, and told him I was back and ready to start working for him and Cliff again. He told me that he has no work for me anymore and it seemed obvious that he was firing me because he was upset that I had been gone so long on the Western trip.

In any case, I now needed to find another job again. A few days later I was hired at H.M Stauffer's, where I had worked six years earlier. There I built wooden floor and roof trusses the same as before. It was more boring and not as much fun as it had been working with the Amish carpenter gang. Still, we had our moments of fun playing jokes on each other. Benuel King, who had been a schoolmate of mine at Harristown School sixteen years earlier, had "gone English" and was now Stauffer's regular truck driver. He delivered the products that we made to their customers. His dad, old hunchback "Tippy" Sam King was the floor sweeper and clean-up man. Abe Petersheim, a notoriously hard worker, labored on the floor "truss table" with me. A unique "claim to fame" in his family, was his *three* sisters being married to three brothers, who were cousins of mine. They were sons of Uncle Sam and Aunt Bertha Miller. John Lapp, who was a bachelor and who had been in Rumspringa with my older brothers back in the fifties, was the top "saw man". He was about four feet, eight inches tall and had been given the nickname Son (substitute for John) as a teenager, but at Stauffer's he was now called Shorty. He had a hearty appetite for chewing tobacco and always kept a supply of it in his wooden locker in the lunchroom.

At Stauffer's, we used steel plates to fasten the various pieces of the wooden trusses together. Each plate has many sharp jagged steel protrusions on one side, and when it's pressed into the lumber with the heavy electric roller press, it becomes fastened as securely as if it had been heavily nailed.

One day, I took a new, unopened pack of tobacco from Shorty's locker and secretly bent a plate around both sides of it and then pressed it extremely tightly with the big press. The pouch of tobacco was now only about a quarter of an inch thick. It was completely covered and trapped on both sides by the jagged steel plate, making it virtually unsalvageable and useless. I then put it back in his locker and told some of the others what I had done.

Later, at lunchtime we all watched as Shorty went to his locker and reached up into it for a new pack of tobacco. Unwittingly, and to his astonishment, he grabbed the pack that was now encased in the steel plate. He then immediately looked over at me with a very accusatory look in his eyes as though he knew I had done it. Probably, someone had told him that I'd done it. I was just calmly eating my lunch and pretended to be innocent. He didn't say anything, but I knew he would get even. He then disgustedly tossed his steel-plated pack of tobacco into the trash can.

The next day while we were eating in the lunchroom, I opened my thermos bottle to pour chocolate milk into my cup, when out floated a dead drowned mouse into the cup. I immediately looked over at Shorty, and he had been gleefully watching me and now he was laughing hysterically. By now, everybody else was also laughing, including myself. Shorty and I then willingly admitted that we had played those pranks on each other.

CHAPTER THIRTY-ONE

Finally,
Seeing the Light

JONAS KAUFFMAN, WHO I AM distantly related to, also worked at Stauffer's. He had previously been an Amish church member and later left the church so now he was excommunicated and shunned. Because of that, none of the other Amish who worked there ate at the same table where he did. He was now a devout Mennonite, or Beachy, and would always bow his head and silently pray before he ate his lunch. There was nobody else there who did that. He was a quiet and Godly man, and everybody respected him. He did not go around proselytizing, but he was willing to share his faith and his beliefs about the Bible and how we not only can be saved, but that we can know we are saved. Eventually, I became daring enough to chat with him about such things and I found it all very interesting.

Of course, whenever we had these discussions, we made sure none of the other Amish men overheard us. Dad also worked at Stauffer's but always in another building. If he knew of all the things Jonas told me, he'd have been very upset. When I told Dad months later, predictably, he was very unhappy about it and warned me that Jonas was deceiving me. By then, however, I was completely convinced that everything Jonas had told me was true and I very much wished I had known it years earlier.

The Amish think that nobody should feel sure they are saved, but that they should do their best, and then should only *hope* that they are saved. They think it is very arrogant and presumptuous for anyone to feel sure they are saved. They should read the following Bible verses. First John, Chapter 5, verses 11-13 in the Bible reads, "And this is the record that God has given to us eternal life, and this life is in His Son. He that hath the Son hath life, and he that hath not the Son hath not life. These things have I written unto you that believe on the name of the Son of God. That ye may know that you have eternal life and that you may believe in the name of the Son of God." The last verse, verse 13, seems to clearly show that the Amish viewpoint here is wrong.

Because of all the warnings I had been given and all the Amish indoctrination and brainwashing I had received throughout my life, I had never allowed myself, not even during the two years at MMH, to consider from a completely unbiased viewpoint, how valid the Amish doctrine might seem to be in comparison to what the Bible teaches. The reason was that I think I virtually knew, at least subconsciously, that if I did, I would soon conclude that the Amish doctrine is not really as valid or as important as the Scripture. It would seem that I'd eagerly embrace such thinking. Strangely, however, I was hesitant to do so because I think I knew that if I was strongly convinced of it, I would inevitably soon leave the Amish church, and then I would surely be excommunicated and shunned.

I believe it's safe to say that I was now more confused than ever about the religious beliefs I had been taught. On the one hand, I knew that if I left the Amish church, I would have the religious freedom to listen to and learn from genuine, well-educated Christian pastors. They would be *truly* concerned about my spiritual wellbeing, without requiring me to be a member of a specific church denomination for the rest of my life, which is what the Amish require. On the other hand, of course, I was fully aware of the excommunication and shunning the Amish would surely always practice toward me and I knew that would be a very steep price to pay. Only people like myself who have experienced a lifetime of ex-communication and shunning can fully know and understand the extent of heartache and heartbreak that occurs in such situations.

After much praying and soul searching, finally, one day when I was twenty-four years old, I allowed myself to take the very daring step of trying to determine, in a completely honest and unbiased way, if the Amish doctrine was proper and legitimate and necessary for me in order to be saved. I compared it in a completely impartial way to what limited knowledge and understanding I had of what the Bible seemed to teach. To my surprise, by the next day I was completely convinced that the Amish doctrine and lifestyle was not necessary for me or for anyone else who had been born Amish!

It had taken a great deal of courage for me to try to think of all the reasons, [both Biblical and non-Biblical] which would seem to justify my leaving the

Amish church. And it was especially important and necessary for me to search for and to find those reasons, so that I would never have to doubt that I did the right thing by leaving. I strongly doubt I would ever have allowed myself to do such thinking if I had already been married Amish. Also, I'm sure there are very few married Amish people who ever allow themselves to think that way, even though it must often be very tempting. The Amish, of course, are taught to never, Never, *never* yield to the temptation of questioning or trying to decide whether to stay Amish or not. As for myself, now that I had taken that audacious step and come to the conclusions that I did, I could finally shed the heavy, stifling blanket of doubt, indecision, and fear that had haunted me for a very long time.

Most true-blue Amish think it's both evil and sinful for a church member to try to find as many valid reasons as possible to leave the church. The Amish bishops would say that once I crossed that line and allowed myself to think those wicked thoughts, I would quickly become influenced by the allure and anticipation of having all the worldly things that the bishops prohibit. To that I would honestly say that, of course, having modern conveniences appealed to me, as they would to anyone, but it was other things that really swayed my decision. My first question to the Amish bishops would be, "Would they agree that the most important thing for everybody should be whether or not they will go to heaven when they die." I hope they would agree with that. If they do agree, they'd probably say it's possible to be Amish and also go to heaven and I would agree. Then I'd ask them if a young Amish person wanted the bishop to baptize him, and he did exactly what God (*not the Amish church*) requires for a Christian baptism, but that young person didn't want to join the Amish church at that time, would the bishop still be willing to baptize him? I'm sure he would not be willing, and I'd demand to know why not. He'd probably say that if they didn't require the person being baptized to also join the church at the same time, then that person often would not join the church at all, which certainly is true. The bishop then might say that if they allowed that, eventually there might hardly be any Amish members left, and there would be a possibility of the church becoming extinct. While it's true that possibility would exist, what we all need to realize is that the most important thing to everybody should be whether they are saved or not when they die. So, to the Amish I ask, "Which is more important to them, that Amish people are saved and go to heaven when they die, or that they are Amish church members when they die?" That should require a very thoughtful and serious answer.

Amish youth are strictly taught that it would be terribly sad if the Amish church became extinct. But, is it not also very sad that so many thousands of Amish people willingly and needlessly deprive themselves of so many modern conveniences that would tremendously enhance their standard of living? How unfortunate it is that so many Amish have little knowledge of the vast number of enjoyable, exciting and inexpensive activities that modern society offers which are not in any way sinful. And how sad that they think simply owning and using many modern things *is actually sinful!*

The Amish bishops need not worry about their church becoming extinct. Jakob Ammann was their founder and early leader and the word Amish is derived from his last name. Today, Jakob would be amazed to know the current Amish population is more than 340,000 which is up from about 5,000 in 1900. Obviously, it has been growing at an astonishing rate for an exceedingly long time, with a defection rate of only about ten percent. The bishops are troubled even by that low rate and strongly wish that none left at all. They would be horrified at my advice that Amish parents should not try to persuade their children to join the church. The parents should even tell them it is perfectly okay if they don't want to join. And that it's also okay for them to thoroughly explore what the "English" lifestyle has to offer. The parents should assure them that they won't shun them at all if they decide to not join the church. That would be much fairer than to put extreme pressure on them and try to "force" them against their will. If the young person joins unwillingly because of that and later in life bitterly regrets it and is very unhappy about it, would the parents not be largely responsible for that unhappiness? Really, the parents need to very seriously and soberly consider just *how much* they are depriving from their children if they convince them to join. How many parents who are desperately trying to persuade their children to stay Amish, really have the *child's* best interest at heart rather than their own *self-interest?* Certainly, if the child does *not* stay Amish, the parents will be permanently saddened and embarrassed and will suffer loss of stature and, to some extent, be shunned or at least be looked down upon by other Amish folks. In fact, sometimes people who failed to shun certain others as "required," were punished for that by being shunned and ex-communicated themselves. How sad when such a vicious cycle occurs!

Those are some major reasons why the parents hope so strongly that the children stay Amish. Most people would agree that it's perfectly okay if the parents want to stay Amish. But they cannot force that lifestyle on the children and the parents *must* recognize that the child's life is his own to live and that they cannot live it for him. And that the child does not have any obligation or duty whatsoever to stay Amish if he doesn't want to. The parents focus and emphasis really should be on teaching Christian principles to the young people, whether they join the Amish church or not. After all, would not everyone agree that it's better to be a Christian and not Amish than to be Amish and not a Christian?

Most Amish parents really don't have a good understanding of what the English lifestyle has to offer to their teen-agers in comparison to what their lives would be like if they stayed Amish. How could they when they've never experienced the good ("English") life themselves? The parents extreme and obsessive desire to see all the children stay Amish creates in the parents an unbalanced and irrational viewpoint of the Ordnung. Whereas most non-Amish people see the Ordnung as being unnecessary and even tyrannical, most Amish have been taught it is *very* necessary, even though it causes tremendous hardship in their lives.

A favorite tactic that Amish bishops and parents often use is to tell the young folks that if they leave the Amish church, they will greatly regret it later and that it surely wouldn't be worth all the shunning and guilt and shame and loneliness they would always feel. However, a recent survey showed that the vast majority of those who left, not only never regretted it, but were very happy that they had left. This seems to be proven by the fact that, of all the ones who did leave, virtually none ever went back and joined the Amish again. That is significant because doing that would have ended the pain and scorn and stigma of the shunning. Interestingly, I know of only one shunned man who rejoined the church and permanently stayed, and that was because his dying father told him he wouldn't get any of the family inheritance unless he does. On the other hand, there have been a *huge* number of Amish-born people who stayed Amish their whole life, but then greatly regretted it during their twilight years.

In my family, while my siblings and I were still youngsters, we never thought it odd or doubted at all that we absolutely needed to join the Amish church at about eighteen years of age, as we had been taught. We, along with most other Amish kids, just meekly accepted and believed that as earnestly and as steadfastly as everyone believes, for instance, that a universally effective remedy for hunger is eating!

Of course, the more rebellious Amish youth often have strong doubts about joining, during their late teen years, as I did. Most Amish parents fervently hope those doubts don't arise until after they are safely baptized and married and therefore presumed to be permanent and steadfast members of the Amish church. Most parents also strongly hope the children never ask them if *they* ever regretted having joined. I think probably all Amish church members regret that decision sometimes at least to some extent! Really, how many Amish parents can honestly say they have *always* been glad that they were born Amish and stayed Amish their whole life?

I guess there are a few "progressive" parents who do not actively encourage their children to join the Amish church. But I've only ever heard of one Amish couple who actually encouraged their children to *not* join and I think that is perfectly logical advice. Predictably, none of them did join and it's said that none ever regretted that decision.

Many Amish would say someone can be a very godly Christian and still be Amish and that certainly is true. However, doesn't it seem very strange that many Amish, especially the bishops, don't encourage studying the Bible, and even discourage Bible study if it is done with a group of English people? In fact, an ex-Amish friend of mine said his family was forced to move away because his teen-age sister was attending a formal Bible study. Whenever any Amish attend any such Bible study group, the Bishops get extremely nervous and will surely disapprove of it. They'll say that the reason for disapproving is they are afraid those people would become deceived and would decide to leave the church. I believe the Bishops actually want their people to be paranoid and to have an obsessive fear of listening to English pastors or attending Bible studies. It's true that many times when Amish people attend "English" Bible study groups, they do eventually leave the Amish church. But I would disagree with the bishops that they have been deceived. I would say that they have been enlightened instead and have been taught many wonderful Biblical truths that they would never have learned while listening to Amish preachers.

A certain seventeen-year-old Amish youth was dismayed with all the rowdiness that he saw in his Rumspringa gang, so he started meeting secretly with some friends for prayer and Bible study. When his mother found out, she told him, "We know it can't be the Lord's will for our young folks to come together like that to study the Bible."

It's shocking that anyone who professes to be a Christian could be so misguided as to make that statement. Perhaps the Amish should be reminded that in Europe many years ago the common people also were not allowed to read and study the Bible, which resulted in the persecution and torture and death of thousands of our Anabaptist forefathers over a very long period of time.

Whenever an Amish person becomes "Schriftich," that is, starts quoting Scripture extensively, his family becomes very concerned. But if he only does it on a Sunday it may not be cause for real alarm but is still somewhat worrisome. And they'll wonder if someone had been trying to "deceive" him.

It's sad that not only don't the Amish bishops read the Bible very much but they seldom try to interpret it or learn of the many meaningful insights and interpretations of the Scripture that have been done by various Godly and devout Christian pastors and scholars. Also, the bishops seldom, if ever, read any books written by such people.

If the Amish ever listened to the sermons of Rev. Billy Graham or Dr. Oliver B. Greene or Dr. Charles Stanley or some of the other giants of Christianity, they might be greatly impressed. Fortunately, those sermons have been recorded and will always be available for the Amish or anyone else to listen to, if they so desire. Have there ever been any Amish bishops or ministers who were also "giants" of Christianity? Should any of their sermons have been recorded? How many Amish people have ever learned what is really necessary, *and what is not necessary* for salvation while faithfully listening to Amish sermons? I suppose it would be rather few, considering that Amish preachers have no formal Bible education or training. And, of course, it's very troubling that they don't actually study the Bible, insofar as really trying to interpret its meaning. Sadly, just attending a formal Bible study group is forbidden, especially if English people are teaching it. In fact, over the years, quite a few Amish have been ex-communicated for doing just that and one has to wonder if the bishops don't see at least some hypocrisy and irony in that.

CHAPTER THIRTY-TWO

Important Advice for the Amish People

MY MOST IMPORTANT REASON for writing this book is to share many very sincere and honest thoughts with the Amish people. I strongly hope they will listen to my message and will trust that I am absolutely not trying to deceive them or lead them astray. In fact, I often pray to God for wisdom to be able to write the correct words and what is most helpful and necessary.

I very much hope that many thousands of Amish teenagers will not have to endure an enormous amount of emotional turmoil and torment and stress as I did, agonizing for a very long time about whether to join the Amish church or not. And that by reading this, they might be fully convinced that, no matter what the bishops tell them, they need not feel any obligation whatsoever to join the church. And if they have already joined, they may feel completely justified and guiltfree in leaving it at any time.

I remember when as a teenager myself, how desperately I wished for someone to give me clarity and accurate answers to the many questions I had about the Amish religion and the Ordnung. I hope that I can now provide the needed answers for many, many Amish people, especially the vast number of teenagers who I know are desperately seeking the truth, as I was at their age. And I sincerely and earnestly want them to also have the opportunity for a normal and proper education that has always been denied them.

I hope I can convince them and prove to them that there is no Biblical reason for them to feel obligated to live such a sparse and restrictive lifestyle. And to remind them that the Ordnung, which they think is so important, are *Amish rules* and not God's rules. Many highly respected religious leaders in Biblical times also followed lots of strange and restrictive rules. But Jesus warned the Sadducees and Pharisees that all their "righteousness" is as filthy rags, and He strongly criticized their sinful legalistic beliefs and practices and their attempts to "earn" their salvation by obeying their own man-made rules and regulations. Isn't that exactly what the Amish are doing by teaching that it's extremely important to obey their self-imposed Ordnung?

When I think of how much I struggled with the decision about joining or not joining the Amish church during my teen-age years, and especially during my two years at MMH, it seems absolutely amazing and almost incomprehensible that I never once visited an English church there and asked the pastor for advice. I certainly was often very tempted to do that. I now realize more than ever that, at least sub-consciously, I had this *huge* fear that the pastor would deceive me, as I had often been warned. That shows the tremendous power of the programming and mind control (brainwashing) that I and other Amish youth received while we were growing up. It was not daily admonishing and badgering, not at all, but it was very subtle and *it was there all the time*. It was like a strange, all-encompassing, invisible presence embedded in the atmosphere. No outsider can possibly comprehend how powerful it was. Only those of us who were born and raised Amish can fully know and understand it. And, of course, constantly being forced to listen to the long, arduous and Ordnung-saturated Amish sermons greatly increased its effectiveness.

Amish bishops are always horrified when any of their people challenge the validity of the Ordnung or of the necessity of obeying it. But I challenge them to show any Bible verse that requires or even suggests that anyone needs to live such a repressive and regressive lifestyle. In fact, they should sometimes be reminded that *all* people have a natural desire for freedom, not slavery!

Many people find it perplexing that the Ordnung permits certain seemingly "worldly" things, but then prohibits other things that appear to be similar or possibly even less worldly. Riding in a car as a passenger is completely acceptable but driving or owning one will surely bring ex-communication and shunning. Many Amish would be surprised to learn that English people consider it even more "worldly" to just be a rider in a car, or "chauffeured" than it is to drive it. That's because many wealthy people have their own chauffeurs.

A hay baler surely is just as "worldly" as a corn harvester, yet the baler is allowed, and the corn harvester is not. Forklifts and bulldozers are allowed but tractors used in the fields are not. They are, however, allowed to provide belt power if they're only in a stationary position. Rubber tires are not allowed at all except on wheelbarrows. There are many, many similar inconsistencies which cannot be adequately rationalized. Even the bishops would find it hard to explain and some might even privately agree that some of the rules don't seem to make sense. A familiar phrase they often use though, is, "Well, we can't just let you have anything and everything. We have to draw the line somewhere."

My adamant response is, "*No, you don't!* Just do away with all the silly and bothersome legalism and follow the commands and advice of Jesus Christ rather than those of Jakob Ammann." What Mr. Ammann apparently didn't understand was that the Biblical recommendations of ex-communication and shunning were meant for people who were guilty of *major* unrepented sins like murder, assault, theft and other serious offenses, not for petty and trifling violations of the Amish Ordnung.

There are specific Bible verses that the bishops say will justify their decision to ex-communicate and shun their "fallen" Amish brethren. They are First Corinthians, Chapter 5, verses 5 and 11, Matthew, Chapter 18, verses 15-18, Titus, Chapter 3, verses 10 and 11 and Second Thessalonians, Chapter 3, verses 14 and 15. But the bishops usually will misinterpret these verses and use them in inappropriate and abusive ways.

Sometimes, certain bishops ponder a new strategy of an even *stricter* Ordnung to keep the members properly obedient. But that is not the answer for the many disciplinary problems they face. Instead, they should become more *lenient!* Really, they need to get over their fear of what church members would think if they greatly relaxed the Ordnung rules. Even though they'd all feel guilty at first, soon everyone would greatly enjoy all their new "freedoms." Sadly, it's unlikely that will ever happen, so most members will continue to be just as slavishly obedient as before.

Even if the Ordnung was someday abolished (which I can't imagine ever happening) it should be understood that doing so would not give them license to practice a hedonistic and sinful lifestyle. It would simply lift the "ban" on the many, many, modern things they *think* are sinful, but which an honest interpretation of the Bible would clearly prove are not sinful in any way!

Some Amish seem to think that they are "set aside" and are special people and that perhaps the admonitions and commands of Jesus don't fully apply to them. But, since His life was *perfect*, they should follow His advice and examples, rather than focusing so strongly on the demands of Jakob Ammann who was a vastly *imperfect* man and who was often considered a troublemaker. In fact, he is famous for wrongfully excommunicating his counterpart, Hans Reist, because of a major dispute about the Ordnung. And, when Reist continued to hold church services as before, Amman expelled all his followers as well. Years later, Ammann admitted he was wrong and tried to return to Reist's church, but the desired reconciliation did not take place. According to a famous writer who is a well-educated authority on the matter, certain people who later read Ammann's letters, readily admitted that they were embarrassed by his rancorous tone and combative style. Apparently, his popularity diminished greatly in his later years because, strangely, even the year of his death and place of his burial *are actually unknown.*

Interestingly, I am sure I have never heard any Amish preacher mention Jakob Ammann's name in any of their sermons and I have no idea why that is. It would seem that if they greatly respected and admired him, they would want to sometimes speak favorably about him. I doubt that there is any other denomination which never speaks favorably about its founding leader and, in fact, never even mentions his name in any sermons. Despite this, the Amish apparently think Jakob Ammann's teachings should always be obeyed without question.

Considering all this, it's very strange and even astonishing that Jakob Ammann was somehow able to initiate and command near fanatical loyalty to his bizarre demands, with what eventually became a very large group of people over a time period of more than three centuries. Even though there have been many other successful indoctrinations of large groups of people throughout world history, I believe Jakob Ammann is unique in successfully persuading his people to wear long beards and strange clothing and to do without modern conveniences simply because that was considered "worldly" and therefore sinful. Do the Amish think that living that way provides an alternative route to Heaven? Or, is it thought to at least be an important and necessary stepping stone? Perhaps the Amish should be reminded that neither Jakob Ammann or his legalistic teachings can save them from their sins and get them to Heaven, but Jesus Christ certainly can!

The Amish fall into a legalistic trap because they think many modern or "worldly" things and practices are automatically sinful, even when they clearly are not. What they need to understand is that, *there is no biblical command or requirement to ban something just because it is modern, convenient, or "worldly!"* So, they should freely and boldly reach out and *joyfully* partake of all the material conveniences and blessings that God has lovingly made available to mankind.

The Amish should consider a hypothetical situation involving Jakob Ammann. Suppose that during Jakob's lifetime nobody rode horses because they had not yet been domesticated. Then, in a fairly short period of time it became quite common for people to ride them. That certainly could then have been considered modern or "worldly" because so many people were doing it. But surely nobody would think it to be sinful. In fact, almost everyone must have considered it a blessing when people were first able to do that. In the same way, all people now should be thankful that God has blessed the civilized world with modern technology that has greatly enhanced people's lives, *for those who avail themselves of it!* And, if Jakob Ammann had actually banned horse-riding it would have made no more sense than the current Amish practice of banning many modern things, especially things that are completely innocent and which can not in any logical way be considered sinful. So, it really is perplexing and seemingly impossible to explain how certain Amish "determine" what is worldly and sinful and what is not. A sad example is of an ex-Amish woman's heart being almost broken during her childhood when the bishop demanded her family's ponies be sold because he said owning them was too "worldly!" This, even though the Amish have always been allowed to own *all* kinds of *horses!*

For quite a few years, Brother John and I, as young boys, *begged* Dad to get us a pony, seemingly to no avail. Maybe we thought *our* begging would be more effective than that of our older brothers, who had never had one either. But, one day soon after Amy died, Dad surprised and overjoyed us by buying an adorable black and white pony from New Holland Sales Stable. But, sadly, it seemed it took Amy's death for him to finally decide to do that for us. Happily, *our* bishop didn't object at all to us having the pony!

The Bible says little, if anything, about people doing things *just for fun,* but it certainly does not forbid that. And, surely, neither Jesus or His disciples ever forbade it either. Meanwhile, the Amish forbid almost all types of fun that the modern world enjoys, including many things that, even under the strictest definition, could not logically be considered evil or sinful.

Pertaining to "worldliness," eating with a spoon *could* be considered "worldly" because everyone does it. Does that mean that it's sinful? Of course not. Surely, no one would want to go back to eating with their hands. Also, laughing is "worldly" because everyone does that, too. But, surely no one considers that to be sinful, either.

Speaking of laughing, a very plain and sober Amish man once told me that it's not necessary for anyone, especially Amish people, to seek worldly amusement and to engage in lots of frivolity and laughter. He pointedly told me there is no mention in the Bible of Jesus ever laughing. I told him I was aware of that. I also told him the Bible *does* make mention of other people laughing and it never says or implies that it's wrong to do so.

It's sad that Amish people rarely avail themselves of the many prohibited things that would make their lives vastly easier and more interesting. Certainly, most could not clearly explain (and would not want to explain) why they allow themselves to be lifelong victims to all their strange beliefs. So, it seems obvious the old saying that ignorance is bliss, really does strongly apply to them.

The Amish bishops say that if they don't "draw the line" on worldly things, the Amish wouldn't really be Amish anymore and, in a sense, they might be right. However, because human nature is what it is, most Amish would love to own many things that are prohibited, and they do without them *only* because they must. This seems to me to be a tyrannical form of legalistic slavery and it's sad that they don't have the freedom to live the way other people do. But, certainly, they have only themselves to blame. It would be very interesting to see how many or how few would continue to live the Amish lifestyle if there were no punishment for "straying" away. In fact, I think most would leave the Amish church if there was no shunning and ex-communication. Sadly, however, the ones who stay will never fully know how much life has to offer for those no longer enslaved to the unbiblical and unnecessary Ordnung of the Amish church.

Why have the Amish bishops insisted, for hundreds of years, that the ugly practice of shunning must continue? It is because they *know* that discontinuing it would result in a huge exodus of people from their church. The bishops think *that* would be far worse than dealing with the incalculable amount of anger and grief and broken hearts that all the shunning has caused. And if Jakob Ammann himself knew how bad it all has become I suppose he might almost be "spinning" in his grave! But I guess he never could have suspected that his Ordnung laws would cause so much anger and sadness, hundreds of years later. After all, he was known to be extremely poorly educated. So, it is the Amish bishops who really are to blame for the shameful situation that exists today. But even if they were somewhat willing to become more lenient and forgiving, it would still present a major "catch 22" situation for them, because many of the enslaved ones would strongly *oppose that!*

Many bishops think they are fully justified in excommunicating and shunning church members guilty of even relatively minor violations of the Ordnung. They realize that if the practice was ended, many Amish would soon have lots of prohibited things and live such a worldly lifestyle that they'd be considered Amish in name only! They'd say that would essentially be the end of the Amish church and that almost nothing would be sadder than that. And they'd be shocked and horrified if anyone suggested that ex-communication and shunning should end, especially if it resulted in the Amish church becoming extinct.

I have no realistic expectation that the bishops will ever abolish the Ordnung, because that is the bedrock of the Amish church and the theological "glue" that holds the community together, along with the dreaded shunning. I do have a faint hope that shunning may eventually be discontinued but many people would consider that to be an unrealistic "pipe dream!"

Despite all my criticism toward them, most Amish bishops are considered to be mild-mannered and congenial. I really don't think any of them want to be hated and despised and thought of as cruel and tyrannical dictators. But their limited education and intelligence along with their typical stubbornness, keeps them from realizing just how out of date and out of touch they are, with their strict and zealous enforcement of the Ordnung rules. Almost unanimously, they firmly believe it needs to be continued no matter how unwilling their "subjects" may be! They strongly feel they would be shirking their duty if they didn't. Many bishops seem to think that properly obeying the Ordnung is as important as being baptized. And, some of them actually believe the *act* of baptism is what brings salvation to that individual!

Many Amish people who pretend to be content with their lifestyle are secretly very frustrated that so many modern things are prohibited. Yet the most "true blue" and determined ones, with typical stoic acceptance and "gelassenheit," will convince themselves that it's only frustrating if they *allow* it to be frustrating! Some even try to console and convince themselves that they won't "miss" things that they've never had, which is quite a pathetic and disingenuous argument. Someone should tell them how much really IS missing from their lives!

Millions of people around the world can hardly fathom such a large group doing without so many modern things and living like the Amish do. But there are several major reasons for that. One is their ignorance of how much those prohibited things would really improve their lives (such as the Internet) and, at the same time fully believing that having them would even be sinful! Another reason is that when "worldly and sinful" things are invented, they are only *gradually* prohibited, that is, each item at the time it is invented or soon after.

No group of people would ever accept the *simultaneous* prohibition of all the things the Amish bishops disallow!

By the way, what strange rationale allows a bishop to, one day simply say it is now okay to have something that was forbidden yesterday? Suddenly, *his saying so* makes it right and now it is not a sin anymore? How convenient for him to have such power!

Every day, as the Amish struggle with their repressive lifestyle, they valiantly try to just "make do" and function as best they can. And each time they see an English person using and enjoying the many prohibited things, it is a grim and painful reminder of how much is missing from their own lives. Really, what better time could there be than *now*, for them to come out of the dark and grim reality of life without cars, electricity, computers, and many, many other modern things?

The Amish should adopt a unique strategy which, hopefully, would keep them from eventually falling completely "off the radar." As science and technology advance at an exponential rate the Amish bishops should, on a proportional scale, allow them to have more and more modern things that are presently forbidden. Otherwise, they might someday fall so far behind mainstream America that some would compare them to prehistoric cave people and would relegate them to the ash heap of history!

An interesting example would be if Bitcoin and other cryptocurrencies someday almost completely replace coin and paper money. With the Amish not having electricity, credit cards and similar items, that would be a particularly challenging and perplexing situation for them!

If the Amish people continue to stick their heads in the sand and ignore many wonderful new technologies, *they* will be the big losers and they will only have themselves to blame! A related topic is their opting out of Social Security for many years already and now many of them are left high and dry with very little income in their twilight years. And their practice of not participating in adequate health care programs and insurance has left many with huge financial burdens as well.

During Jakob Ammann's day there were very few problems with establishing and enforcing the Amish Ordnung. That's because Amish people lived and looked much like non-Amish people, since there were very few modern or "worldly" things in existence at that time. So, of course, the Amish way of life was much easier to tolerate then than it is now. However, because of the ensuing rapid growth and innovation of technology and science and because of the extremely strict and legalistic rules of the Ordnung, it was inevitable that there would be a continually widening gap in the standard of living between Amish and non-Amish people. Since the Ordnung is an unwritten set of rules and varies greatly from one district to another, there are now hundreds of things that are either completely prohibited, somewhat prohibited or, "should be" prohibited in this increasingly more confusing and complex ritual of rules.

I have long felt that a good comparison of Amish and non-Amish lifestyles is that the former is like being permanently limited to a diet of potatoes, bread, and water (with perhaps an occasional apple included) while the latter always enjoys a gourmet meal!

It's very instructive and revealing that very few adult English people ever join the Amish church. Undoubtedly, the biggest reason is because so many modern things are prohibited. Of course, all people, including the Amish, have a natural desire to have worldly and convenient things. And, even though quite a few claim to be glad they're Amish, I'm sure very few would ever join the Amish church had they been born English. In fact, a certain non-Amish man said he would rather always be a poor English man than to be an Amish millionaire. An even more startling remark was when a shunned ex-Amish man said he would rather commit suicide than to rejoin the Amish church!

When a rebellious teenage son abruptly tells his father he will no longer attend the Amish church because of being forced to sit on a hard-wooden bench for three hours, (along with many other valid reasons) what should the father's response be? Especially, if the father somewhat agrees with him and even *sympathizes* with his plight? If he does not encourage his son to stay Amish, he likely faces harsh criticism from his relatives. However, if he pleads with his son to stay Amish and to not forsake such a "peaceful and pleasant" life, he should be reminded that if it indeed was a peaceful and pleasant life, millions of non-Amish people would already have joined. But it is exceedingly rare for them to join, and when they do, they almost always eventually leave again. Among the biggest reasons are the drudgery of living such a repressive lifestyle, the prohibition of so many modern amenities and the necessity of learning a new language.

As a teenager, I once asked Dad and Mom if they would like to live their lives over. I asked it in the context of them still being Amish, as I'm sure they understood. Mom answered first and said that if everything went well, she supposes she wouldn't mind. Dad, however, grimly and somberly replied, *"once is enough!"* I suppose there are many other Amish people, however, who *would* like to live their lives over if it was as a non-Amish person.

The most honest Amish people will admit (at least to themselves) that their lifestyle leaves much to be desired. But they'll claim that the good still far outweighs the bad. However, if they factored in the high incidence of male sexual abuse that exists in their community, they might be less likely to feel that way. I think they will appreciate that I provide no further details about that in this book, even though it has long been a very serious problem. But, obviously, I've been very critical about many *other* things.

Because of my own experience of having been an Amish church member for three years, I absolutely know that a high percentage of Amish people really do have an intense longing for the many prohibited things throughout their entire lifetime, (although I would never have included my parents in that group!) A very few Amish might reluctantly admit that if they were asked by an unknown English person, such as a tourist. But I strongly doubt that any would knowingly admit it to an ex-Amish person like myself, who's been ex-communicated and shunned.

It is very easy and common for English people to just naturally assume the Amish are happy and content, "blissfully" living their lives of deprivation and hardship and ignorance. But there really are a vast number of them who are very unhappy living like that. Really, being Amish is not at all the charming, peaceful, idyllic lifestyle it often is portrayed to be! After all, for anyone in this day and age to do without major amenities like cars, electricity, television, and air-conditioning is tremendously inconvenient and frustrating! In fact, for those like myself who had those things while at MMH, it becomes excruciating if they are permanently denied those things.

I once wrote identical letters to ten different Amish bishops in Lancaster County, begging them to have mercy on their people and to at least let them have electricity and air-conditioning. The temperature was ninety-eight degrees that day so I thought maybe, *just maybe*, they might give it some serious thought. But, predictably, I never got a response from any of them, even though I provided all of them my address and phone number. And, of course, they didn't take my advice about allowing their people to have those things. If they had, or even if they do, anytime in the near future, it would be the biggest surprise I've ever had in my entire life.

If the government ever prohibited horses and buggies on all public roads, I'm sure many Amish people would be ecstatic. Especially if the bishops then grudgingly allowed them to own and drive cars instead. Many would *pretend* to be very upset about the law prohibiting horses and buggies, but would be inwardly rejoicing because of now being allowed to have cars. In fact, some of those might then start fantasizing and hoping that the government would become even more intrusive and would prohibit certain dangerous and antiquated farm implements, and that the bishops would then allow them to have more modern versions thereof. And, I guess some Amish people's ultimate *Nirvana* moment would be (although I'm sure it'll never happen) if the bishops decided to completely dispense with the Ordnung! Many church members would be excited and even overjoyed but would feel so guilty that they'd never actually acquire many previously forbidden things.

If ninety percent of the American people did not have cars but always drove horses instead, should that not be considered "worldly," because so many are doing it? Conversely, if the remaining ten percent, including all the Amish, always drove cars, *that should not be considered worldly,* because so *few* are doing it! So, if it's not worldly, it also should not be considered sinful, according to typical Amish thinking. And, in that context, they should be allowed to do it.

Since many Amish people have seemingly boundless patience, they accept the tyrannical demands of the Ordnung amazingly well. Still, even their patience has limits. And, many outsiders, especially tourists, feel genuine pity for them as they struggle daily with such a restrictive lifestyle.

Very few non-Amish people are fully aware of the vast number of things that the Amish church prohibits. Simply a *partial* list includes cars, trucks, motorcycles, motorboats and airplanes. It's uncertain whether flying in a glider off of a mountain top would be permitted because that's never been mentioned in the recitation of the Ordnung! There are many, many other things that have never been officially prohibited but you are just supposed to "know" that you shouldn't do them or have them. In fact, it seems that far more things are prohibited than are allowed!

Other prohibited items include electricity, television, radios, wrist watches, cameras, smartphones and computers with Internet access, along with a bewildering plethora of other modern things. Activities that are prohibited include driving motor vehicles, attending movie theaters and plays and professional sports events, owning and playing musical instruments such as guitars, banjos and fiddles, drinking alcohol at taverns, playing golf and billiards, gambling and playing cards, *unless* there are no kings, queens or jacks in the deck. Lots of things are only "partially" prohibited, or grudgingly allowed, such as "clamshell" type cellphones, engine-powered lawnmowers and battery powered electric converters. And it seems the more rapidly new things are invented, the more vigilant the bishops feel they need to become, to ward off all that evil influence. One wonders if the bishops don't envy their counterparts of three hundred years ago, who had virtually no such tough choices to make at all, as far as what should or should not be prohibited! To reduce this burden on the bishops, perhaps a full-time arbitrator/dictator should be hired to decide just *which* modern things should be prohibited!

Because so many things are only "partially" prohibited, even Amish people are sometimes unsure of what things they may own. A fairly reliable way to determine that would be to ask themselves whether a certain modern item is fun, convenient and inexpensive, and if it is, the Ordnung probably prohibits it!

When a group of Amish bishops decide, as they sometimes do, to allow ownership of a certain "sinful and worldly" item that had not been allowed before, do they think that now God also considers it to be less sinful than before? Surely, whatever God considered sinful yesterday, He still considers sinful today, since His laws are unchanging. So, is it not very obvious how foolish it is when mere men prohibit something simply because they think it is too modern and convenient? Interestingly, there's no evidence that Jesus and His disciples ever refrained from owning something just because it was modern or convenient. And, yes, there surely were lots of things that were considered "modern" even way back then!

Jesus also never taught that the predominant features of people's lives should be hardship and ignorance and deprivation, which many Amish obviously feel is necessary. If anyone thinks living that way holds the key to happiness, they are wrong in the extreme! And, in addition to not being allowed to own many, many modern things, it is even frowned upon and considered unseemly to simply *discuss* things like politics, religion, technology and sports along with many other popular contemporary topics. It's sad that the Amish delude themselves into thinking that their lives will be just as interesting and meaningful without any knowledge of such things.

If leaving the Amish church was a good idea twenty, or fifty, or a hundred years ago (and I firmly believe it was), it is an even better idea now because of all the modern technology that has evolved. Really, it's *fine* for Amish people to live humble and "unworldly" lifestyles, but not to the total exclusion of any modernism for them and their children!

While the Amish lifestyle does provide opportunities for many pleasant and happy family events shared together, they also share much misery because of the Ordnung forcing such a bleak lifestyle upon them. There has rarely, if ever, been any culture with so many inherently charming and appealing aspects to it, but also such a huge number of disturbing and distressing features which tremendously clash with the normalcy of modern society. I think many Amish people would even be suitable and willing candidates for communal living if the bishops demanded that of them. Especially since they strive so strongly for harmonious living with each other and are also hugely concerned about each other's reputations.

In all cultures and societies, parents naturally want their children to have access to modern conveniences and they hope those things will bring them satisfaction and enjoyment and fulfillment. But the Amish bishops don't mind when their people are denied all that and they actually want to deprive them of those things. I wish they knew how much easier and more interesting and rewarding life can be when one can enjoy all the conveniences that the modern world has to offer. But they cling to the tenets of their faith with a degree of tenacity and zeal that is probably unmatched by any other sect in the world. I suppose some who have striven daily to meet the requirements of the Ordnung, now believe they are almost as pure as the wind-driven snow. But when, and if, they get to Heaven, they will be greatly disappointed if God doesn't give them any credit for having so fervently obeyed the extremely legalistic Ordnung throughout their lifetime!

At the end of their life, even some very devout Amish people have major deathbed doubts and wonder if being Amish their whole life had been a huge mistake. But very few of those would dare to share such thoughts with their family, because if they did, their reputation would be ruined, even in death. Far better to feign complete happiness, retain their "hero" image, and die with dignity and always be remembered as a stalwart "pillar" of the Amish church.

Many non-Amish people are greatly perplexed and wonder why most Amish parents so desperately want their children to always be faithful Ordnung-obeying Amish. Of course, there are several reasons. One is that if they join the church and never *require* shunning and excommunication, that would be a huge source of comfort to the parents. Another reason is that many parents think the kids are hell-bound if they don't join the church. The parents yearn for them to join because then they'll share the same religious beliefs and have similar (cookie-cutter) appearances. And, if they all join, an idealistic comfort zone is created which has a distinct sense of family and togetherness and unanimity that the parents probably have long hoped and prayed for. They strongly hope that very little persuasion is required and that all the kids joined the church willingly.

More than likely, however, some were very unwilling, deep down inside, but still gave the appearance of being willing and decided to join for the sake of "the greater good." Many people join because throughout their whole life they have been taught, and by now they are completely convinced that by doing so, they are far more likely to get to heaven. For some, the biggest motivation to join is because they are in love and want to get married and, of course, to do that they must both be members.

Still, it is my firm belief that many of those don't really want to stay Amish. But their deep love for their spouse-to-be makes them ignore their better judgement and they join the church so they *can* get married. But later, there is often major regret that they ever did join. This shows how the requirement of being members *before* they're allowed to marry, is so effective in permanently "locking them in" to the Amish lifestyle.

There are many parents who feel sadness not only for the children, but also for themselves, because they decided, for whatever reasons, to live such an austere and deprived lifestyle. Some parents even feel guilty for having demanded that the children join the Amish church. How many of the parents are even aware that the Bible never requires people to join the same church denomination as their parents? It seems that is a requirement unique to the Amish people.

Although many parents feel some guilt about having deprived their children of a modern lifestyle, very few would ever admit that to anyone, because *that* would then often be considered sinful! I'm sure my parents never felt any such guilt. They thought their *absolute duty* was to convince us to always stay Amish!

Some Amish parents are envious of children who have never joined and even secretly applaud them for that. And are even tempted to tell them that they made a better choice than the parents did. Especially if those children's lives had been happier and more successful than their own lives. Yet some of those parents will unhappily think "*I'm still stuck* with always being Amish and it's really not fair that the kids now have a better life than me." Others, with the typical stoic and self-punishing mentality that Amish are famous for, will determinedly tell themselves, "Well, I'm sure I can somehow struggle through it. Eventually, I'll die anyway and then the temptations and trials will be over." Lastly, I suppose there are a few members who are completely happy and content and willing to be Amish for their entire life.

Still, many unhappily wonder for the rest of their life if they should have "gone English." Yet they desperately and valiantly cling to the belief that they MUST stay, while "courageously" refusing to consider any other way of life. They constantly put up with huge inconveniences throughout their lifetime, always with the faulty logic and misguided rationalization that, "No matter what happens, come what may, the bottom line is, *we can't leave the Amish church!*"

My sincere response is, "YES, YOU CAN! *Nowhere* in the Bible is it stated, or even implied, that anyone has to live the way the Amish do!" In fact, most non-Amish people find it astonishing and almost incomprehensible that, in the modern era of the twenty-first century, hundreds of thousands of Amish people "willingly" and permanently do without cars, electricity, computers and many other modern things that almost all other people have. Really, it does seem that if someone *wanted* to live as boring and regressive a lifestyle as possible, they just might choose to be Amish! Will it be many more years, and possibly even decades or centuries before the Amish bishops allow their people to have cars and electricity. Since none of them ever seem to even *consider* that, it really is anyone's guess as to when or if that wonderful day of liberation will ever arrive!

Many Amish people (and, possibly, many non-Amish people) will condemn me for so strongly encouraging them to leave their church. But I think many people around the world might greatly support my efforts. They may consider it similar to explorers and discoverers who have, in a different way, "rescued" previously unknown tribes of natives from remote jungles and told them about a much better way of life that is available to them. But I think quite a few Amish people would not in any way, shape, or form, even want to be "rescued" from their lifestyle.

After this book is published, I may become the most hated ex-Amish person in history. Hated by thousands of Amish parents who desperately want their children to always stay Amish. But I predict that many "soon to be enlightened" teenagers will be very thankful that I *did* write the book. It is for *their* sake, more than any other reason, that I wrote it. Nothing can convince me that they don't have a right to the information I've provided for them. And, I don't mind at all if, and when, they *do* join the Amish church, if that's what they *truly* want, and they haven't been subjected to extreme pressure and coercion from their parents. And, of course, my sincere hope is that the bishops will also read the book and will seriously consider my advice and recommendations.

Many Amish people have, with great effort, almost fully convinced themselves that they are quite happy living the primitive and deprived lifestyle that they do. Sadly, they just don't realize how much happier they'd probably be if they were allowed all the material things that the bishops prohibit. Especially, if they then somehow also became guilt-free and fully convinced that having those things would not put their salvation at risk!

Even though many Amish parents yearn to leave the church because of the extremely deprived lifestyle, very few actually do leave. That's because of the lifelong shunning they would face from virtually all of their relatives, friends, and acquaintances. Even their own children would consider them evil, especially the ones who are "true-blue" and fully dedicated to the Ordnung. Yet many Amish parents sometimes feel guilty (as they should) that they didn't allow their children to live a normal American lifestyle, but instead forced upon them a lifestyle of deprivation and hardship. And, the parents often secretly bemoan and lament to themselves of how much easier *all* their lives would have been if they had always been English instead of Amish. And, very importantly, the ones who had experienced the "luxury" of owning and driving a car during Rumspringa, *will never forget* how much better and more convenient that is than driving a horse. For them, it will be extremely hard to accept the enormous frustration of a lifetime without cars, radios, electricity and many, many other modern things.

A sad reality is that many Amish people, especially undecided teenagers, endure a huge amount of emotional stress, (as I did) thinking and debating with themselves for *years*, about whether to stay Amish or not. But, even after all those difficult struggles, the vast majority will eventually decide to join the church and stay Amish.

On the other hand, many who were fully indoctrinated and had *always* been willing to join and who were sure they would never be untrue to the "hallowed and revered" Ordnung, eventually found to their dismay and consternation that, later in life they had a gnawing and growing fear and realization that the Ordnung really WAS unnecessary and invalid and obsolete. And they grimly wondered if they had foolishly "squandered" their lifetime, trapped in such a primitive and self-denying system. How many Amish who are in their twilight years, greatly regret having stayed Amish for their whole lifetime? And how many of them sadly lament to themselves, "Well, I *thought* I was doing the right thing when I joined the church. Many times, I was told to just listen to, and obey my conscience and join, *as I surely know that i should!* So, *I did that* and now I bitterly regret it."

There really are many good things about the Amish lifestyle. But there are also many other things which seem positive and endearing but which, for the most part, only help to confuse the young people who have to make the enormous decision of whether to join the church or not. To most people who were born Amish, and especially to those who are still very young, staying Amish not only seems like such a noble thing to do, but it also *seems so right*. For one thing, they are peaceful and humble people who are extremely helpful and supportive of each other. The wearing of plain and simple clothing absolutely seems right and proper to them. Their family and friends live honorable and obedient lives of frugality and hard work. The vast majority of impressionable young children have parents who constantly exhibit an unwavering, unflinching acceptance and allegiance to the Amish religion and Ordnung. The children's well-trained conscience has almost fully convinced them to stay Amish. They have been led to believe that they are far more likely to get to heaven if they stay. They know they will always be loved and accepted and admired if they stay. The threat and reality of permanent ex-communication and shunning is a powerful inducement for them to stay. So, all these things convince many young Amish people that *staying* Amish is absolutely the *right* decision. In fact, it SEEMS so right to them that very many instinctively believe, as I once did, that even considering anything else would be sinful and foolish. *Nevertheless, just because a certain lifestyle seems absolutely right, that doesn't mean it actually is the right or the best choice!*

Since there is no physical violence (as far as I know) practiced by any bishops and parents toward the young folks if, and when, they're unwilling to join the church, it really is astonishing that so many actually do join. Especially, given the extreme degree of deprivation of knowledge and of modern technology that they must then endure. Of course, all the multiple forms and different aspects of Amish brainwashing are strategically combined to create what is probably the most powerful and effective formula for specific brainwashing and mind control in human history. Yet neither the ones administering it or the ones receiving it, realize that any brainwashing is even occurring!

The Amish have many different tools in their arsenal of brainwashing tactics. Besides shunning and ex-communication, they practice coercion, threats, shaming, and social exclusion toward their victims. Bestowing rewards on obedient members is also an effective strategy. But, instilling the fear of hell into them may be their most effective tool in keeping them "in the fold." The combination of all these tactics makes them surprisingly obedient and "willing" to live such a bleak and regressive lifestyle. I can and do fully understand how it happens that such an astonishingly high percentage of them (about ninety percent) stay Amish their whole life and do without so many modern conveniences. As most non-Amish people would agree, it really is an amazing phenomenon. But, having observed it throughout my lifetime, I'm very much aware that *all the necessary components and aspects* of unparalleled indoctrination and mind control are very effectively being utilized, so it doesn't really surprise me that it happens so much and that the success rate of the indoctrination is so high. It is truly astonishing how effective totally "immersive" brainwashing is when it begins in infancy and continues throughout one's lifetime. Especially, when the parents and all the siblings have experienced that as well!

Of course, it is painful for me to be permanently ex-communicated and shunned by all of my siblings, in addition to a vast number of other Amish people. A mitigating factor, however, is that, because of the *huge* cultural divide that now exists between us, I really don't have as much desire to associate with them as much as I would if they were English, in which case we would have much more similar viewpoints about religion and many other things. Certainly, I am very glad that I'm no longer being brainwashed on a daily basis like I was while growing up.

Sometimes now, when I think back more than forty years ago to when I so meekly and willingly accepted all that brainwashing, it all seems somewhat hazy and surreal. But the dramatic and persuasive power and influence it had on me, I will always vividly remember. I do feel extremely thankful and fortunate, however, that I was somehow able to get past it and eventually join the ranks of my non-Amish American peers. I'm inclined to think it was always God's will for me to write this book and to provide many excellent reasons for Amish people to leave their church and not even needing to feel any guilt about that. And, also, to expose to the world, so much that is little known about the Amish doctrines and religion.

Not only do I think that God planned for me to write this book, but for a very long time it has seemed that He was sending many of these thoughts and words and sentences into my mind. When I started the book seven years ago, I *never* thought it would get anywhere nearly as long as it has. I also never thought I would criticize the Ordnung and the Amish lifestyle as much as I have. It certainly was never a matter of eagerly and anxiously trying to think of what I should write next. At any time, day or night, often the words would just unexpectedly come to me and I would write them down and later arrange and co-ordinate them into the book. And, eventually, in such an unplanned way, it reached its present length.

A major reason so many of my people stay Amish is that, because of their sub-standard education and their limited contact with non-Amish people, few would assimilate well with the outside world. But, if they only knew of the many, interesting English people who they could become friends with and associate with, their own lives would then also become much more interesting. Those English people would be very willing to share with them and tell them of the many, many ways in which English life is so much better than Amish life. In fact, I think all Amish people should ask their best and most trusted English friends to clearly explain all that to them. They should also ask all their ex-Amish acquaintances if *they* ever regretted leaving. They would then, undoubtedly, be astonished and be more tempted than ever to embrace the English lifestyle. Still, most Amish will tend to keep to themselves and stay with the only lifestyle and religion they've ever known, despite often being very doubtful of its validity.

So, it is especially important that all religious people (*including the Amish*) consider all the pros and cons of their religious beliefs and take an impartial look at every controversial aspect of them. Otherwise, they probably will be "willingly" blinded and will just meekly follow and accept and *do whatever their leaders tell them!* That is what cult leaders prefer from their followers. In fact, a very devout and highly respected Christian pastor who was very familiar with Amish beliefs and doctrines, told me he believes the Amish *are* a cult. One similarity that they have with cults is that they think *more* is required to be saved than repenting and asking forgiveness and believing in and accepting Jesus Christ as their Savior, and that is to strictly obey the Amish Ordnung. I believe the Amish do meet most of the definitions of being a cult and that very many of them are more concerned about obeying the Ordnung and the teachings of Jakob Ammann than the teachings of Jesus Christ!

It's readily agreed that people are most vulnerable and gullible during their childhood and teenage years. So, of course, that's when parents in a cult try hardest to teach their children to accept their own beliefs, and it is also when the young ones are most likely to fall into a huge pit of deception. It must be realized that young children will believe almost *anything* that loving, highly respected parents teach them, no matter how unreasonable or absurd it might seem. The all-enveloping internal security that the Amish lifestyle offers to its members is much like that found in typical cults. And, their strange lifestyle and beliefs entice them to form a close-knit fellowship and comradery with each other, much like large groups of slaves did centuries ago.

A major reason I joined the Amish church is because many of my friends and acquaintances had already joined. I didn't realize that I, like them, had been successfully indoctrinated and that I should have *far* better reasons than that to join! But I'm sure the bishops were happy and content that we simply had such a superficial reason to join. Of course, they also were pleased that if others, in the future followed *our* reasoning, it would become a permanent and self-perpetuating process!

When I returned home and joined the Amish church after my two years at MMH, what really persuaded me and drew me back most strongly was, certainly not the Amish lifestyle, but my deep friendship with my family, siblings, cousins and all of my Rumspringa friends. I could hardly imagine *not* having a major and permanent friendship and affiliation with them throughout my lifetime. But, of course, all those desires and hopes and plans are little more than unfulfilled and vanished dreams and bygone memories now.

When I was growing up, I was warned not to read books written by Billy Graham or Dwight Moody, and that if Amish people read their books, they would almost surely be deceived. Now, much later in life, I believe those are exactly the type of books the Amish *should* be reading. However, many bishops and ministers would not trust themselves to read even a tiny portion of such books. *Or, of this book!* In fact, I suppose after the Amish bishops learn of the contents of this book, especially of *this chapter*, they will beg their people to not read it. They will consider this book to be a horrifying example of anti-Amish and anti-Ordnung propaganda. It might even cause some to wish my parents had stopped having children after their seventh child was born. As it turned out, though, I happened to be their eighth and final child!

It's extremely unlikely that any Amish ministers would participate in a serious discussion and debate about the validity of their own doctrines and the Ordnung, even with very well-informed people. In fact, each time I have ever seen anyone try that, the minister was very unwilling and would become agitated and quickly walk away and flee to a safer location. After all, why would any Amish person, especially a preacher, even consider leaving the church if it meant shunning in this life and hell in the next life?

Pertaining to the shunning issue, a very few bishops *might* be interested to know what "solution" I have. My most earnest request and plea is for all Amish people to *just stop the shunning!* And, if they did that, an added benefit would be a major reduction of the bishop's power. Certainly, no matter what the Bible says about shunning, it surely never meant for it to be done in the abusive and life-altering way in which the Amish practice it, especially the bishops and ministers!

What many Amish people fear most in their whole life is that they will be "deceived" (fahfiered) to the point where they'll leave the church. That's why they hardly ever dare to discuss or consider doing that. It does show the tremendous power of the brainwashing they've always been subjected to. And, by the time they realize that the "English" life is much better, and they're not automatically condemned to hell if they live that way, they're probably already married and obsessively urging their children to also always stay Amish! Those parents will faithfully and meticulously obey the Ordnung themselves, with the fervent and desperate hope that doing so will greatly impress the children and help to persuade *them* to stay Amish. That, along with achieving and earning outstanding respect from them, are two of their most effective "tools" of persuasion. But, at the same time, they know full well that some negative stigma will be attached to their own name if their children *do* decide to "go English."

Another strategy of the parents is to always appear respectful toward the bishops and never "bad-mouth" them, especially in their children's presence. Also, it seems two things in life that Amish parents (especially the bishops) always very strongly hope for, is that the children stay Amish and that the parents themselves never yield to the temptation of doubting or denying the validity of the Ordnung. They absolutely don't want to entertain the thought that it could possibly be silly and unnecessary.

It is a real dilemma and also blatantly hypocritical, when Amish people are very unhappy about being trapped in their lifestyle but are desperately begging their children to stay Amish. Many parents object strenuously to the cars and other "sinful" things the children have, even though they also had them during Rumspringa! Some parents *might* admit that to them, but would also include the fervent admonition, "Don't do as I did, do as I *say!*"

Also, parents who *did* have a car during Rumspringa, desperately hope their kids won't ask them if they had one, unless they are willing to lie and deny it. If they don't admit to it OR deny it, that is virtually a sure sign that they *did* have one. And, they would greatly dread if the kids knew that, or even just thought that!

To the Amish parents who are begging their children to stay Amish, I ask, "If *you* had been born and raised "English," do you *honestly* think you would have wanted to become Amish? If your answer is no, then *why* would you demand your children to be Amish? Would that not be the height of hypocrisy?" Really, just growing up Amish and obeying the Ordnung and all their "stone-age" type of rules is extremely demanding and exhausting, even if one never becomes a member.

A much more exciting and refreshing and logical idea would be if the parents, instead, encouraged the children to *not* stay Amish. But I have only heard of *one* Amish father and mother who did that. Most parents would consider such advice to be outrageous and disgraceful and completely "beyond the pale!" Still, it seems to me that all Amish parents who truly love their children and who want them to have happier and more fulfilling lives than *they* had, should also encourage them to not stay Amish. Having said that, I do want all Amish people to know that my goal is not to cause anger and grief for the parents, but to enable the young folks to have more pleasant and rewarding lives than they otherwise would have had.

When bishops and parents are begging rebellious teen-agers to stay Amish, the teens are only hearing *one side* of that very important argument! Ideally, they would also hear from English people who would be very willing and able to tell them from their own perspective, how much better English life is than Amish life. So, it's very easy to understand why Amish parents want their young folks to have as little contact with English society as possible.

A certain Amish preacher who is a cousin of mine, is considered by them to be the most "fiery," dedicated, and gifted preacher in all of Lancaster County. His oratory style is quite similar to what Rev. Billy Graham's was. I think it would be most interesting to debate him about the Amish religion, but I'm doubtful he would be willing to do that.

All Christian church denominations, except the Amish, at least to some degree try to evangelize non-Christians, and encourage and persuade them to join their church. Why do the Amish never even try that at all? Are they completely unaware of how strongly Jesus encouraged His followers to spread the gospel? Do the Amish refrain from that because they know how weak their message would be and how little hope of success they would have?

The Amish are correct when they say one can be a Godly Christian and still stay Amish. But should not all Christians, including the Amish, be constantly striving to grow in their spiritual life? Yes, because that is what the Bible teaches. Paul says in Galatians 5, verses 22-23, "The fruit of the Spirit is love, joy, peace, patience, kindness, goodness, faithfulness, gentleness and self-control." The Amish people should ask themselves if these attributes are becoming more and more evident in their lives because they have been faithfully listening to their Amish ministers. If not, maybe the ministers are not as well qualified as they should be. Amish people are taught from an early age, in a subtle but very persuasive and powerful way, that it is extremely important and absolutely necessary to strictly obey the Amish doctrine. That is, of not having cars or electricity, and of wearing their distinctive plain clothing and Amish hairstyles, along with many, many, other requirements that the church has had for hundreds of years.

But, will the Amish people ever learn that, in God's eyes, *it doesn't matter* what hair style is worn, or how wide the hat brim is, or what color socks or shoes are worn, or what type of suspenders one wears, or even if no suspenders are worn at all? Yet many Amish constantly monitor and judge each other on these and many, many other senseless and archaic rules and regulations of the Ordnung. But, if they ever realize and admit that most of the Ordnung is invalid and unnecessary, they will then feel a combination of astonishment and relief, but also chagrin and dismay that they were enslaved by it for so long!

One day, many years ago, I very sincerely questioned Dad why we had to wear plain clothing and a strange hairstyle and long untrimmed beards and do without so many modern things. With a worried look, and obviously concerned that I would ask such a loaded question, he told me that old Bishop D. Ira Stoltzfus often preached that there's a Bible verse which admonishes Christians to be "Ein Schpossiches Volk," meaning they should be *peculiar* people. Bishop Ira undoubtedly thought the most important message in that verse was that they should *look* peculiar.

In the late 1600s, Jakob Ammann apparently also believed, as do the present-day Amish bishops, that the verse Bishop Ira referred to, First Peter 2, verse 9, requires them to be a peculiar people. That verse specifically reads, "But ye are a chosen generation, a royal priesthood, a holy nation, a peculiar people, that ye should shew forth the praises of him who has called you out of darkness into his marvelous light." But, somehow and somewhere, apparently Mr. Ammann and the present-day Amish bishops, have decided that the word peculiar, in that verse, means that they should *look* peculiar, hence the centuries long tradition of Amish being required to wear plain clothing and strange and unchanging hairstyles. It's important to note that that Bible verse does not tell them to *look* peculiar, but instead, that they *are*, or should *be* peculiar. It obviously means that they should be peculiar, or different from the world, in the sense that they should be a holy nation and be faithful followers of Christ.

It was not until many years after I left the Amish church that I finally made that extremely important observation. And, because I've never seen it written or heard it explained in this way, I now feel strongly obligated to share it. I think many Amish would at least privately agree with my explanation if they just allowed themselves to consider it in an unbiased way. But there are also many who simply would not consider anything that sounds so radical to them, whether it seems to make sense or not. It's sad to know that, in any culture, such people usually continue to fully believe they are completely correct in their beliefs. And they would rarely change their beliefs even one iota, no matter how convincing an argument anyone might make.

Pertaining to the above-mentioned Bible verse, if Peter thought that he himself, along with other Christians, should *look* peculiar, *they* would have worn peculiar and plain clothing or hairstyles. And yet, nowhere in the Bible does it say or indicate that they did so. The Bible also never says or indicates that Jesus Himself ever wore peculiar, or plainer clothing or a different hairstyle than other people did. It would certainly seem that if that was necessary and important, He would surely have done so!

Hypothetically, if Jesus wanted to join the Amish church, would the bishops readily accept Him without question? Or would they think Him unfit because of His moustache and his non-Amish clothes? Would they demand that He also not have any "worldly" forbidden things? And would they greatly worry that He might condemn all their unbiblical legalism?

The Amish, of course, are required by the Ordnung to always practice humility in their daily lives. They know that Jesus Himself was an excellent example and a strong advocate of humility. But, starting with Jakob Ammann, the Amish seem to have equated humility with *not being allowed to have modern things!* It seems Mr. Ammann was the only leader of any sect to ever have *that* strange idea!

The Amish bishops even object to their people wearing sandals. But Jesus Himself and His disciples and practically all other people in biblical times, regularly wore sandals. So, one warm Sunday afternoon while visiting at a very self-righteous Amish man's house, I also wore sandals. He mildly objected to that. So, I told him of the Biblical account of Jesus wearing sandals and that that's good enough for me. He then reminded me that the Ordnung advises men to wear black high-topped leather shoes on Sundays, even in summertime (as he was!) I'm sure he knew, however, that I would not heed that advice!

Christians in biblical times, including almost surely, Jesus and his disciples, owned and played many different types of musical instruments. These included the harp, trumpet, tambourine, flute, lyre, cymbals, timbrel, and lute. In fact, there are some Scripture verses where the people are *commanded* to play such instruments, and even to *dance!* In Psalm 150 the Bible tells how God should be praised. Verses 3 through 6 reads, "Praise Him with a blast of the trumpet; praise Him with the lyre and the harp! Praise Him with the tambourine and dancing; praise Him with stringed instruments and flutes! Praise Him with a clash of cymbals; praise Him with loud clanging cymbals." So, why do the Amish object to these and other similar modern musical instruments? Also, the Bible does not indicate anywhere that Jesus and the disciples had a shorter or less "worldly" education than other people during that time. I suppose that even in Jakob Ammann's day, he preferred that his people, like the Amish today, have less education than non-Amish people. And that it was okay for them to read the Bible as long as they didn't seriously study and analyze it, very similar to what Amish bishops advise even today. I guess Jakob Ammann fully understood that the less educated his people were, especially about the Bible, the more willing they would be to obey him and to agree with his blatant legalism.

Could it be that eight thousand Amish bishops and ministers have an incorrect understanding of that Bible verse which exhorted those people that they are a peculiar people? Could it also be that Jakob Ammann perpetrated one of the biggest hoaxes in history, when he convinced his people that they must live such a regressive and primitive lifestyle, even though that is not commanded as being necessary in the Bible?

I'm sure many Amish people will want to strongly reprimand me and even condemn me for saying it's not necessary to live that way. Many will consider some of my statements to be blasphemy, or very nearly so. I'm sorry if they feel that way. I hope they will sincerely try to understand my perspective, and that it has never been my intent or desire to anger any of them or to lead them "astray." But, from my viewpoint, I have long felt a burden and even a distinct sense of duty to write these things. Especially since very few secular writers or other ex-Amish writers have provided substantive accurate and analytical critique of Amish religious beliefs and teachings. So, not only do I feel that what I'm writing here is very important and urgent, but I can't help but think, "If I don't write it, *who will?* And if not now, *when?*"

Because the brainwashing and indoctrination of the Amish people is all-encompassing and extremely effective, very few ever consider leaving the Amish church *unless* they become completely convinced that doing so won't jeopardize their salvation. I hope this chapter will be especially helpful in convincing them of that.

Maybe Jakob Ammann was completely sincere when he instituted all those extremely strict and legalistic rules and regulations. Maybe he fully believed that particular Bible verse requires people to *look* peculiar rather than to simply *be* peculiar, and to be Godlier in their Christian faith in comparison to other people. Nevertheless, even if people are completely sincere, they still may very well be completely wrong in their beliefs. Simply being sincere and *desperately hoping* that one's beliefs are correct does not ensure that they *are* correct. That's why it's very important for *any* religious group to not just blindly accept and follow their leader's teachings, but to carefully study and determine whether they are compatible and in accordance with Scripture.

The Amish may be more paranoid about false religions than any other sect. Some would take desperate measures toward those who seem to be "fahfierish" (promoting a false religion). One example was when I, as an innocent teenager, was reading one paragraph in an article about Charles Russell, the founder of the Jehovah's Witness church. I casually read it to my brother and he immediately tried to rip it out of my hands. Failing at that, he then tackled me, and we wrestled vigorously for some time until he gave up. He had remembered Mom once telling us of an Amish man who had joined that church, (Russell "gongah") as we called it, and that was considered so evil that his father only left him one dollar in his will. But I was astonished that my reading of that one paragraph had alarmed my brother so much! Still, I think many other Amish would have the same reaction.

Most Amish agree that there are many false religions that teach heathen beliefs. But how many Amish have ever *seriously studied whether their Ordnung is a false religion to them?* How many of them spend more time thinking about and obeying their *selfmade* Ordnung, than thinking about and obeying the *divine* teachings of Jesus Christ? So, of course, they should heed and obey *Biblical* advice rather than the legalistic advice of the Ordnung. Especially, since the Bible was here long before the Ordnung, and also had far more followers.

When I was growing up, we occasionally talked about various religious cults. And we also talked disparagingly about certain "sinful" Amish people who had left the church and began attending a "higher" church, perhaps even a worldly English church. We firmly believed that since we strictly obeyed the rules of the Ordnung, we surely were more righteous than they. But it never occurred to us that, in God's eyes, we really might not have been any better than those people at all! Or, that God might have looked *more* favorably upon them than us.

Now, more and more as I get older, I wonder with ever increasing amazement how I could have been so naive as to consider always staying Amish. Especially after having experienced "the good life" for two years at MMH. And, especially since modern society's standard of living has improved so much in recent years. How much will the Amish standard of living improve in the future? Will it even improve *at all?* These questions should be forefront in each young Amish persons mind who is considering joining the church. It seems they should be increasingly more reluctant to join, not knowing of all the amazing technology that surely is still to come and which the bishops will then also prohibit! So, for their own good, they need to sincerely and honestly evaluate all the pros and cons of Amish life versus English life. They should try to be fully aware of the *totality* of the huge and unnecessary burden of obeying the Ordnung throughout their lifetime. It would be especially burdensome if they entered into an Amish marriage and eventually were "required" to try to persuade all their children to stay Amish. And, how sad if someday they faced the horror and dread of being required or "forced" to shun their own children because they had left the church.

I think the three biggest reasons most teenagers decide to join the church and stay Amish for their entire life is, (not necessarily in this order) they do it because their friends did it, they think it's much more likely they'll get to Heaven if they do it, and joining the church enables them to avoid the intense scorn they'd otherwise receive from many friends and acquaintances. *That* scorn, however, is not nearly as difficult to endure as is the shunning that ex-communicated people have to live with.

Horace Greeley was a well-known author and statesman from the 1800s. He was famous for saying "Go West, young man!" as he encouraged those youth to seek freedom and opportunity. My advice to Amish teen-agers would differ by one word, "Go "English," young man!" And, pertaining to joining the Amish church, they should consider Nancy Reagan's famous words, "Just say no!"

It must seem obvious to many people that this books' overarching theme and message to the Amish people is, "YOU DON'T HAVE TO LIVE THAT WAY!" But most parents *do* strongly feel they have to live that way, while increasingly more of the young folks are becoming rebellious and now strongly disagree.

I expect that many people will accuse me of trying to tear Amish families apart with all of my "evil and deceptive rhetoric," as I try to convince them of how much better "English" life is than Amish life. But I am not at all trying to tear any families apart. Instead of shunning children who have left the church, Amish parents need to just *love and accept* them, and the children will love and accept *them* in return! And the parents should just calmly *ignore* the inevitable criticism that will come their way.

I also expect that most Amish parents will strongly criticize me because of many critical things I've written. I expect lots of former Amish people to do that too, because many still strongly empathize with the Amish. But I think most people who were never Amish, might be more in agreement with my viewpoints.

The Amish lifestyle is "comfortable" and non-threatening for those who choose to stay in it. So, it takes a lot of courage for them, especially church members, to become bold enough to "think outside the box" and break away from the only environment they've ever known and endure life-long shunning from their people. Most non-Amish people admire and applaud them, however, for showing so much courage and bravery when they do leave.

Still, because of the Amish peoples' extremely high birth rates and because of the amazing degree to which they accept the Ordnung and the Amish lifestyle, their overall church membership will undoubtedly continue to increase. But, more and more of them are now acquiring a new perspective and seeking a new freedom and are leaving the church at an ominously "accelerated" rate. Whereas in 1900, only about five percent left, now the figure is about ten percent.

Slowly, slowly, a new awareness is creeping into the "security" and solidarity of the Amish church membership. Slowly, ever so slowly, like a giant ship turning, more and more are acquiring a "strange belief" (fremmah glahva) because of various ex-Amish brethren teaching and sharing the Gospel with them from an evangelical and Biblical perspective. They now are willing and also understand that they need to stand up and oppose the oppressive and tyrannical decrees of the Ordnung, even though the bishops inevitably become very frustrated when any ex-Amish people try to educate and liberate their people this way. Indeed, there have been many times when both English and ex-Amish people have tried, with the noblest of motives, to "reach" Amish people and lead them to a better way of life. But, often, they are met with anger and rejection and an utter refusal to listen because they're afraid they will be "deceived."

Will the Amish bishops read any of my writings, even if only briefly? Will any of them try to read it with a completely open and unbiased mind? Will any of them dare to speak favorably about it to other bishops and ministers? I don't expect that any will. I have tried to explain as clearly as possible why I believe many of their doctrines and beliefs and the requirements of the Ordnung not only are completely unnecessary but are even in direct conflict with fundamental Scriptural teaching and readily accepted tenets of the Christian faith. But if the bishops ever become willing to compromise and allow their people to have the modern technology and the typical level of education that non-Amish people have, it would greatly enhance their lives in many, many different ways. All without jeopardizing their salvation at all! So, my passionate plea to the Amish bishops is, "Do not keep them in bondage and enslavement any longer, but "SET MY PEOPLE FREE!" And if that ever happens, many will shout exultantly, as Dr. Martin Luther King, Jr. did many years ago, "Free at last, free at last, thank God Almighty, we're free at last!"

Many Amish people will be truly angry at me when they read this. They will greatly fear that many of their young folks will be "deceived" and led astray. I will be accused of exaggerating and grossly distorting many facts, even though I have tried hard to be accurate. Some will think that I have vengeful motives and that I despise them because I have been ex-communicated and shunned. No, I am not seeking revenge and, in fact, many of them I still love dearly. And I don't despise them either, even though many of them will now despise me more than ever. Many will now also shun me more intensely than ever. Even so, I actually admire quite a few aspects of their lifestyle and beliefs. But I believe they are victims of the circumstances they were born into and I very much hope that I've shared many important truths that they will find helpful.

It saddens me when I think of how aggrieved my parents would be and how hurt my siblings will be when they learn of how critical I have been toward the

Ordnung and the Amish way of life. What would my mother say if she knew that her beloved "baby boy" would someday emphatically criticize and disparage the Ordnung that she and Dad always seemed to cherish and willingly obey? These thoughts do sometimes trouble me, but I strongly feel it is my duty to write what I have. And I very much hope it results in happier and more fulfilling lives for the Amish people.

I don't mean to be overly judgmental toward the Amish and I don't enjoy criticizing their religion and beliefs. I write these things, not to cause anger and dissension, but to illustrate that many helpful and logical changes could be made that would greatly enhance their standard of living without them losing their cultural identity. For instance, the bishops could allow them to have all the modern conveniences and at the same time simply require that they continue to have their traditional hair styles and beards and distinctive clothing that they've always had. If they did that, far more of the young folks would be willing to join the church and far fewer of the ones who are already members would be tempted to leave. And, because of their plain clothing, they would still be a "light to the world" as most of them hope and believe that it signifies.

I know there are thousands of Amish people who have many admirable and positive traits and characteristics. But, because so few are really aware of all the cultural and educational deficiencies of the Amish lifestyle, the vast majority of them, amazingly, will decide to stay Amish. Most of them *are* honest, hard-working people who try to live exemplary Christian lives and they deserve praise for that. Despite living the way they do, many really are resourceful and intelligent people. And, there actually are many appealing aspects of living the Amish lifestyle if it's embraced with enthusiasm and optimism. For some people, being Amish, despite all its deprivations, is thought to be better than the English lifestyle. Especially, since they might have always felt guilty had they chosen to be English instead.

Some people will complain that I have been far too harsh in my assessment of the Amish people and their lifestyle. But I would suggest to them and challenge them to live *exactly* like that for a long time themselves. I think they would then largely agree with me.

CHAPTER THIRTY-THREE

Permanently Leaving the Amish Church

THE AMISH STRONGLY EMPHASIZE the importance of keeping their Ordnung laws and faithfully obeying those rules. But Jonas Kauffman explained to me that none of that helps in gaining salvation and that only by repenting of our sins, trusting by faith and believing in Jesus, who died for our sins, and by His grace toward us, can anyone be saved. That certainly was a profound and wonderful revelation to me when I finally really understood it!

So, at that time, I became very interested in learning from the Bible, and from books written by Christian authors. I now realized more than ever how uninspiring and stagnant most Amish minister's sermons were. It seemed more obvious than ever that they didn't enjoy preaching and that it was actually a very unwanted chore for them. It certainly is understandable that they seem so sad and troubled and unwilling at the immediate moment in time when they are "elected" to become ministers.

I decided that I wanted to visit an English church, which I had never done before. I wanted to see how their services compared to Amish church services. I had listened many times on the radio to parts of English sermons, and always thought the preachers sounded enthusiastic and spoke with much knowledge and conviction. I was sure that visiting an English church would be a very interesting experience. But I didn't know which church I should go to. There were hardly any English friends who I knew that went to church regularly, and I did not want to go the first time by myself. Had I known how many fundamental evangelical Christian churches there were in Lancaster County, and had

I known how warmly I would be greeted, I certainly would have gone much sooner than I did.

At the same time, I was struggling greatly with the knowledge and the certainty that when I did leave the Amish church, I would surely be excommunicated and shunned and ostracized by the people who I was still very close to. Not only would that be painful for me, but I knew it would also be painful for my family, especially for my parents. So, I kept delaying my plan day after day and week after week, largely because I could hardly bring myself to hurt my parents that much. Of course, I had not told anyone about my plan to leave the church because I wanted to make sure no one suspected such a thing until I took that first step.

By mid-summer, 1976, I had formulated a two-step plan. I decided that some-time in late fall, I would go to Florida for a long visit to the Amish community at Pinecraft where Dave, John G. and I had visited a few years earlier. I had a few friends who lived there and I thought I'd hang out with them sometimes. The other part of my plan was that, instead of coming back within a reasonable time period as my folks would expect, I would just stay there until they strongly suspected that I no longer planned to be Amish. In fact, I considered possibly living there on a permanent basis.

While working at Stauffer's that summer, time passed slowly as I eagerly anticipated going to Florida in the fall. At least, now I had a definite plan and my life was no longer on a dead-end track. I could hardly wait to go back to the English lifestyle that I had known at MMH and I just *knew* that I would re-adapt really well to it!

Dave, John G, and I bought a nice motorboat, even though the Ordnung prohibits them. We frequently went to the Chesapeake Bay at Perryville, Maryland for boating and swimming on Sunday afternoons with Amish girls. Of course, we didn't tell our parents and I don't think they ever found out about it. We also played in a softball league at the Civics Grounds in Intercourse. The other players in the league were a mixture of English guys and a lot of Amish, half Amish and "used to be" Amish guys. My parents only mildly complained about that. I guess they knew I needed some recreation after all the freedoms I had at Morristown.

In late summer, three Amish buddies and I went to the shore for a few days at Rehoboth Beach, Delaware. We went in a van that one of them owned and at night we stayed at a campground. While on the beach we met two young English girls who we became friendly with. One of my buddies, Pidley Jake, and I asked them if they wanted to go to the movies with us and they agreed.

The movie we saw was *The Exorcist* and it was very interesting and we all had a fun time there. The girl who was with me was a pretty dark-haired girl named Anita. She asked me for my mailing address, which I provided. A few days after we got back from the shore, a letter from her came to our house. I felt fortunate that it happened to be me who brought the mail in that day. I think if Dad had seen it first, he would have confiscated and destroyed it. I had told Anita that I was Amish and that we had no phone, so she couldn't call me. I then sent her a reply letter and soon she sent me another letter, which Dad happened to confiscate before I saw it.

He demanded to know what it was all about. Dad was especially concerned because she had written, "I love you," under her name in the upper left-hand corner. I told Dad not to worry about it. He said he would only give me the letter if I promised not to have any more contact with her. I refused to make that promise and he refused to give me the letter! So, I never read her second letter and I'm sure Dad destroyed it. As it turned out, I did not have any further contact with her which, undoubtedly, was a big relief to Dad.

In August, 1976 I bought a car, a 1971 Ford Capri. It was the first car I'd had in more than three years. I kept it hidden behind Stoltzfus' Butcher Shop just east of Intercourse, about one mile away. Sometimes I parked it behind the old wooden schoolhouse in Hatville, where I had attended as a child. It was now no longer a schoolhouse but had been converted into an apartment building.

One Sunday afternoon as I was leaving from there, the gearshift broke off or became disconnected. I walked home and borrowed Dad's vice grip wrench out of the tool shed [without telling him, of course] and clamped it on to the broken section. For the rest of the day, I had a very odd looking but fully functional gear shift handle!

One Saturday night after being out with my buddies, I parked my car at the butcher shop and started walking home. As I came over the rise at Willis Futers' house, I was startled to see smoke coming from the south end of our house, about two hundred yards away. This was in the summertime, so I knew it would not be chimney smoke. Thinking the house was on fire, I immediately started running at top speed to get there. I ran around the north side of the house where Uncle Benny lived, and past the huge old walnut tree. As I raced around the far corner of the house, I almost ran straight into Dad. I may have startled him even more then the sight of the smoke had startled me a few moments earlier!

Thankfully, the house was not on fire. Dad was standing there, watching something burning on the sidewalk, right by his feet. It was a funny and bizarre looking straw hat that my brother had brought home from the beach. He had shown it to me earlier, and now Dad had found it and was burning it. It had on the front a caricature of a drunken sot, with bleary eyes, a bulbous red nose, and wildly unkempt hair along with a funny message on the front. Dad, however, was not amused by it, and had taken the liberty to burn and destroy it. He did, how-ever, offer to explain why but I really didn't need an explanation from him at all!

One Saturday afternoon in August of 1976, I was at Park City, which is a large shopping mall, one mile west of Lancaster. I saw a group of people standing outside and I recognized my cousin, Leroy, among them. He was one of Uncle Sammy and Aunt Mary's sons. Leroy was ex-Amish and I had not seen him in several years. He had been a church member but had now been excommunicated and shunned for a long time. He told me they were witnessing and preaching the Gospel to people that day. He said he had been attending evening classes at Lancaster Bible College and that he and his wife, Valerie, hosted a weekly Bible study group at their house in Lancaster. He invited me to come sometime and I was immediately interested.

He then introduced me to Elmer Kauffman, who I had not met before, but who happened to be my second cousin. Elmer told me he hosted Bible study classes at his parent's house and also attended classes at Lancaster Bible College. He invited me to his Bible study group, and I told him I would attend sometime soon. They told me that the people there were about the same age as I was.

I decided to go to the group at Leroy's house the following week, on a Tuesday evening. Elmer told me he would go right past our house and he offered to pick me up, to which I agreed. Of course, I didn't tell any of my family about it, since they strongly disapproved of attending English Bible study groups.

While we were eating supper, Elmer pulled into our driveway. Dad met him out on the front porch and Elmer told him why he was there. Dad told him to leave without me, and that he didn't want me to go with him. When he told me that, I told him I would go anyway. He didn't ask me how I was going. He probably already suspected that I had a car again.

Later, I walked to where my car was parked and went to the Bible study group at Leroy's house. There were about fifteen people there. What I remember vividly was how warmly they all greeted me and how friendly they were, even though I was a complete stranger to them. When the Bible study began, Leroy opened with prayer, praying out loud, and asking for wisdom and receptive hearts and minds. Then there were prayer requests and he prayed for all of them individually. After that, a specific part of Scripture was studied where everyone could participate in the discussion. Finally, at the end everyone had the opportunity to pray out loud if they wanted to, but I was far too self-conscious to do that.

Later, there was food and lots of social chatter and laughter. I was thrilled that God had chosen to bring me into this fellowship of true Christians. It certainly seemed to be exactly what I had been looking for. It struck me as being very odd and unreasonable that the Amish would object to something like this, where everybody was sincerely trying to study and interpret the Scripture verses correctly. Leroy and Elmer told me that the harsh legalism that the Amish people practice is completely unbiblical, and I quickly agreed with that. But, because of the intensive brainwashing I had experienced while growing up, I still thought for many years that the Amish Ordnung had some legitimacy!

Later in the week, on Thursday evening, I went to Elmer's Bible study meeting, and the format was similar but with fewer people. However, they also were very friendly to me. I continued to go regularly to both meetings each week, and certainly felt blessed each time. More importantly, I was learning valuable Scriptural understanding and Biblical insights on a regular basis.

Now that a completely new and wonderful chapter in my life had been opened, I had to totally rethink my plans of going to Florida. I realized that there was now no need for me to go there, because I had found exactly what I wanted and needed right here in Lancaster County. I have always felt that it surely was God's will that I happened to meet up with Leroy and Elmer that day at Park City.

Elmer invited me to go to church with him at Calvary Monument Bible Church, over at the mountain range, about five miles away. We met there that Sunday and, for the first time in my life, at the age of twenty-five, I attended an English church service. The pastor was Clarence Lefever, a friendly and very devout man, who was in his late seventies. Interestingly, in comparison to the Amish preachers that I'd always heard, he obviously enjoyed preaching, and certainly seemed a lot more enthusiastic and more qualified than any Amish preachers that I'd heard.

I was pleasantly surprised at how many people greeted me and chatted with me that day. I'm sure that strangers at Amish church services usually are not greeted that warmly. Even though many Amish undoubtedly feel that there's lots of appeal just in their quaint, comfortable and familiar old style of preaching, singing and worshipping.

I started attending church there regularly and, of course, I still had not told anyone in my family about it. I usually sat with Rick and his elderly friend, Lester McCrabb. I soon came to hold Lester in especially high esteem when I found out he had played major league baseball with the Philadelphia A's during the World War. Of course, the stories he provided about those experiences I found most interesting.

After I had missed attending two consecutive Amish church services, Dad, obviously alarmed, came up stairs to my room to talk to me that Sunday afternoon. When he asked where I had been, I told him I was attending another church, but didn't tell him it was an English church. I told him what Jonas had told me at work and that I fully agreed with him. Of course, Dad was very upset at Jonas because of that.

About that time, Mom came upstairs and joined us. She probably suspected what we had been talking about. When Dad sorrowfully told her that he thinks they have lost me, she sank down on the bed with an anguished moan and started crying as though her heart would break. I felt extremely sorry for her and tried my best to console her. I tried to comfort both of them but it seemed they were beyond that. Despite the sadness of the moment, I never wavered in that I was sure I was doing the right thing by going to the Bible studies and to the English church services.

Two weeks later, when the semiannual Ordnung church was held and I was not there, everybody knew that I must have gone "astray." Not just because that is a very important service in itself, but this was now the third consecutive Amish church service I had missed. Later that day, one of my brothers asked me where I had been and I told him I had been at an English church service. He scornfully asked me if I had now gone religious crazy. I told him no but didn't say any more, because I knew it would be useless to try to explain it to him.

All Amish church districts have services bi-weekly, and not weekly like other churches. I'm sure the bishops would not allow an Amish member to attend an English church service on the Sunday when there is no Amish service. In fact, I'm certain that if a baptized Amish church member attends or is baptized in an English church, even a very devout Christian church, the Amish bishop would excommunicate him even if he continued to attend the Amish church services.

The news that I had gone "astray," probably spread like wildfire. The next evening Deacon Davey and his wife came to visit me and Dad and Mom. Of course, he knew I had missed three consecutive Amish church services. When that happens, it is expected that the deacon then pays such an "errant" member a visit. Usually, his wife does not come along unless they think the situation is very serious, as I'm sure they now did. Davey tried for some time to convince me to confess my sins and come back to the church, but by now I was completely sure I would not go back, and I told him so. Shortly before they left, he made an amazingly rude and insensitive remark. He said to Dad and Mom, "I guess this is even harder on you then when your son Amy died." I angrily shook my head, but somehow managed to stay quiet, and I certainly was glad that they left soon afterward.

The next evening, Preacher Stevie Esh, came to visit me and my parents. Stevie was my favorite of the three ministers in our church. He had been a preacher in our church since I was about eight years old. He certainly was a good man and everybody liked him a lot. I had worked with him in the Amish carpenter gang.

Of course, he didn't say anything as rude as what Deacon Davey had said the night before, but he did try to coax me back to the Amish church, which is what I expected. Of course, my parents were sitting there too and they fully agreed with him. He pointed out the many reasons that he felt I should stay in the church but I had heard them all many times before and now I didn't agree at all anymore. I was very sad and frustrated, because I was sure I was doing the right thing, just as they were sure I was not doing the right thing.

Stevie was talking to me in a kind and gentle voice, and I hated to hurt him because he really was a very good friend of mine. Finally, I got so agitated that I jumped up and said, "I have to go outside now, before I say some things I might regret." I ran down past the garden, past the buggy shed and up the barn hill with my mind in turmoil. I put my arms and elbows up on the top board of the wooden fence, while trying to hold back the tears. I stared out over the western fields, and down over the hollow, where Henry's house and barn stood, and about one mile further west to where Stevie's house was. I remembered and thought about the many good times he and I had shared while thrashing wheat and harvesting corn together during my teen-age years, and later while working with each other in the carpenter gang. I felt a twinge of sadness and wistfully realized that those days were now gone forever. As I was trying to control my emotions, I knew that all this would be harder to deal with than I had anticipated.

After a while I went back inside the house and Stevie said he was sorry if he upset me, and I told him it was okay. Soon, we shook hands and he said he wishes me well. Then we said good-bye to each other and he left. Sadly, it was many years before I saw him again.

I suppose my parents were quite shocked about my leaving the church because I had never given them a hint of that, at least not verbally. I think they must have sensed my unhappiness, though, because of the sad demeanor I had much of the time. I guess they didn't dare ask me about it, though, being afraid their worst fear might become reality.

During the transition time of my leaving the Amish church. Dad briefly tried to persuade me to join a Mennonite church, rather than to go to a completely "worldly" one. And even though that plea failed, I suppose he and Mom and others appreciated that I had been a church member for three years and had at least given it "a good try." It does seem strange that neither my parents nor anyone else ever specifically asked me why I wanted to leave the Amish church. Of course, there are so many good reasons that someone would want to do so, that I think it would be obvious to everybody, even to the most devout Amish person. Still, there were frequent times when people made hurtful and insensitive remarks that I had to deal with. One Amish lady who was a good friend of our family said she wonders when I will come to my senses.

It was during this time that I wished more strongly than ever that some knowledgeable and well-meaning friend at MMH had given me sound counsel and advice and told me that joining the Amish church would be a huge mistake. But, of course, that never happened. Still, I'm glad I left when I did, before getting married and having children, which would have complicated things even far more.

Now that the news was out that I was leaving the church, I decided to rent an apartment and move out, as I saw no point in staying at home any longer. In November, I moved into a second-floor apartment in Lancaster, just two blocks west of the county jail. It had the smallest kitchen I had ever seen, but otherwise it was okay.

When I moved away from my childhood home that day, I knew I would never be moving back again. My family seemed to accept my moving out with an air of stoic resignation. Of course, the move to Lancaster was a bittersweet experience for me. On the one hand, I knew I had brought great sorrow into my parents lives by leaving the church. And, of course, it was very troubling to know I would surely be ex-communicated and shunned for the rest of my life. On the other hand, I now felt like a long-imprisoned bird suddenly freed from a cage. And it was a very welcome and liberating feeling to know that I would never be flying back into that cage again and that now I could again live a normal American lifestyle. And, unlike at MMH, I could do so on a permanent basis. How eager I was to see this unhappy saga of my Amish church membership now coming to an end! Indeed, that time period has been the most miserable three years in my whole life. What a relief it was to no longer be forced to obey the many, many senseless, stifling and archaic rules of the Amish Ordnung!

Still, in retrospect, would it not have been far less cruel to my parents if I had never come back from MMH and join the church, only to later leave and dash their hopes and dreams like I did? Yes, I'm sure that would have been far less painful for all of us than the circumstances I now find myself in. What is most painful for me about the ex-communication and shunning is that it has destroyed the close relationship I always had with all my siblings. And, of course, it's hurtful and very frustrating to know they will always consider me to be an evil and sinful person because I left the Amish church.

Meanwhile, for me it was back to full-fledged English life. Living in the city was certainly not as boring as at the farmhouse, even though I was now by myself again. My apartment was located along a busy street, East King Street, which was much noisier than where I had lived at the farmhouse. I had adjusted pretty well to it, however, until a car horn start blowing, loud and long, right outside the house at about 3:00 A.M., on two consecutive nights. The first night, I ignored it and it finally stopped. On the second night, I ran out to it and saw there was no one inside. I yanked up the hood and, with my vice grip wrench, quickly undid a battery cable from the terminal and the honking stopped immediately. I believe the car belonged to an Asian immigrant who lived nearby. As far as I know the car never went on another honking spree.

Another night I was wakened by a gang of rowdy people who were yelling very loudly below my bedroom window. I opened the window and screamed as loudly as I could for them to be quiet and, thankfully, the noise soon stopped.

There was a man who lived two doors up the street from me who liked to wear a dress and pretend he was a woman. I knew he was a man because I occasionally saw a five o'clock shadow on his face. Sometimes we'd see each other while shopping in the little grocery store across the street but we never spoke to each other.

My four Amish co-workers at Stauffer's still didn't know about my plan to leave the church. So, they were greatly surprised the first day I showed up wearing English work pants. I purposely wore black jeans the first day so as not to surprise them too much. Of course, the lack of my familiar broad-fall "barn-door" Amish pants and suspenders and my Amish straw hat were glaringly obvious, and within seconds they knew I was dressed English. All four of them fixed hostile stares on me, but only one of them tried to talk me out of being English. Mr. Beiler, an older man, undoubtedly thought it was his duty to do so, but he soon realized it was much too late for that. My English co-workers seemed to whole-heartedly agree with what I had done, and some of them even congratulated me for that.

When an Amish church member stops attending the Amish church and attends an "English" church instead, he is said to have gone "high." A long time ago it would also have been said that he had gone "gay," although that word now has a completely different meaning!

Often, when certain Amish reluctantly decide to stay Amish for the rest of their life, they try to console themselves by thinking that at least now they won't feel guilty like they're sure they would if they had "gone English." Would it not be so much better if they felt free to leave and enjoy the English lifestyle *and still not feel guilty?* After all, the Bible does not condemn anyone for simply living a *modern* lifestyle, but instead warns against living a *sinful* lifestyle.

How sad it is that a huge amount of anger, animosity and arguments occur between bishops, parents and teenagers because of disagreements about the Ordnung. Especially since there is *no Biblical advice* which demands any modern things to be prohibited *simply* because they are modern, which is so often done by the Amish bishops. And, yes, there were some "modern" things even back during Biblical times.

One of my Amish relatives, a man in his thirties, talked to me about some Amish who had left the church. He said in a scornful and disparaging tone that now they walk into an English "church house" with a Bible under their arm on Sundays. He was implying that it was conceited of them to carry it publicly like that. Of course, Amish people never take Bibles with them to their church services. There are not even any Bibles *at* the service, which many non-Amish people find astonishing. In fact, the only reading material that's there are the ancient Ausbund songbooks and the German prayer book.

A young Amish friend of mine was still living with his parents when he decided to start attending a non-Amish church. So, when he walked from the house to where his car was parked a half-mile away, he'd carry his Bible openly with him. His father did not want the neighbors to see him carrying the Bible, so he asked him to put it into a bag instead. What sad irony this picture provides, indeed!

One evening while I was alone in my apartment, someone knocked on the door. When I opened it, I was surprised to see Moses Esh, the Amish bishop from my home church district. As soon as he saw me, he said, "Hi, Yonie," and barged right inside before I could even respond or invite him inside. He started to survey my apartment with obvious disapproval. When he saw my tape player and a stack of eight track tapes, he asked me if they were all Christian tapes and I told him no. He shook his head, seemingly in despair. He told me of how wrong I was in leaving the church and, predictably, strongly urged me to come back. I very clearly and firmly told him I would not. He then did what he said was his duty to do and read me the statement which they do at that time. It was something about consigning my body to the devil so that my soul might be saved. I listened politely and when he was finished, we said goodbye to each other and he left. I don't believe there was a parting handshake.

If Bishop Moses was really concerned about my spiritual condition, why didn't he or any other preachers ever come and visit and counsel us during the two years we were at MMH? They must have known how vulnerable we were to all the "sinful" temptations that surrounded us every day. Even though he neglected that duty, he was quite willing to quickly excommunicate me *simply* because I stopped attending the Amish church. I had not been charged with any other violation of the Ordnung.

A few days later, I was notified in a letter from my parents that I had been excommunicated from the church. This was now the second time that had happened to me, but unlike the first time, I now knew that I would never rejoin and that I would be ex-communicated and shunned for the rest of my life. That certainly was a sad and sobering thought. Nevertheless, I was absolutely sure that I had made the right decision, and I have never regretted it at any time since. In fact, I feel certain it was the best decision I've made in my whole life.

A few weeks later during the Thanksgiving holiday, I was not invited back home for Thanksgiving dinner as I had always been before. So, I was very happy when Jim, Sr. and Jan Hicks, the parents of Jim, a friend from the Bible study group, invited me to their house for a wonderful Thanksgiving meal and a genuinely nice time visiting with their family.

The Amish men that I worked with at Stauffer's were slightly less friendly than before and, of course, they now would not eat at the same table in the lunchroom where I did. They also tried to avoid taking things from me, such as whenever I wanted to hand them something, even when it was a work related item. By the way, the Bible never states that shunning should be practiced to that extreme degree.

Aaron Glick was an ex-communicated ex-Amish farmer from Quarryville who frequently bought hay at the auction in Kirkwood. Whenever he tried to physically hand his payment check to the Amish clerk, he would be told to lay it on the counter instead. So, Aaron filed a complaint of discrimination with the Human Rights Commission in Harrisburg who, of course, eventually ruled in his favor, as they should have.

Some people feel that the shunning that is so prevalent among the Amish is largely unconstitutional because it violates people's religious freedom. They think that because the Constitution guarantees religious freedom, certain cases of extreme shunning could be and should be prosecuted in a court of law. If that ever happened, it certainly would be a most interesting case!

I continued to attend the two Bible study meetings each week and the Sunday services at Calvary Monument Church. I never once doubted that I had done the right thing by leaving the Amish church, and that I was now also doing the right thing by attending the Bible studies and going to Calvary Monument church.

At Christmas time, I was invited back home for the big annual Christmas dinner with my parents, siblings, nieces, and nephews. When we all sat down to eat, I sat by myself at the small table that had been put there for me. Nobody told me to sit there and I did not ask. I just knew that's where they wanted me to sit. It felt awkward, of course, but nobody was discourteous to me, and all in all, it went fairly well. At least I got a scrumptious Amish style Christmas dinner. Of course, I did not park my car at home, but parked it somewhere else in the neighborhood. I did still wear my Amish clothes that day.

Elmer had been attending Lancaster Bible College several evenings each week, and he asked me if I might be interested in doing that too. I decided that I would enroll there for one evening class. When I met him there for the first time, he showed me around and assisted me with registering for my class and helped me in any way he could. He was so happy for me and excited that I was taking a class there, that he shook my hand four different times during the course of the evening. The class I took was the Gospel of Matthew which lasted for a period of about three months. The teacher was Dr. Figart, an older gentleman who seemed to be the epitome of Godliness. I was struck by how earnest he was and that he seemed to be pouring his heart and soul into his teaching. There was certainly a profound difference between his style and the way the Amish preachers did it.

I was told by the Bible study group about a place called Y.F.C, or Youth for Christ, that was open for young folks, specifically high school alumni, each Friday evening. Jim Hicks and I regularly went their together. It was in a large auditorium with about one hundred people attending, with most of them playing volleyball. It would start at 7:00 P.M., and from 9:00 to 10:00 there was Bible reading and study led by Don Shenk. That was followed by more volleyball and it would close at 11:00 P.M.. I certainly enjoyed going there each Friday night and being with lots of Christian friends. I felt right at home there and didn't miss my Rumspringa activities at all, which I had done for so long.

In the fall, I took another evening class at Lancaster Bible College, [LBC]. I took First Corinthians, for a period of about three months. I was now attending church at Neffsville Mennonite Church, which was much closer to home then Calvary Monument was. There were also some of my friends from Y.F.C. who attended there. I had a few casual dates with girls from the Bible study group and from Y.F.C., but none of that became serious. However, the English girls generally were friendlier and not as shy as the Amish girls that I had pursued in the past.

The Ford Capri was now, more or less, on its last legs. So, after hitting a snowbank and crumpling a fender, I traded it in for a 1974 Pontiac Lemans, a much nicer and newer car. The salesman at the dealership where I bought it was John B. and he was more than a little friendly with me. I passed it off, thinking that it was just his nature. I was a little suspicious, however. My suspicions were confirmed when he showed up at my apartment, a day or so later, and started to make homosexual advances toward me. I told him very firmly and clearly that I was not at all interested. He apologized and quickly left my apartment and I never heard from him again. Later, I found out he was married and had a large family, including a loving wife and quite a few young children.

CHAPTER THIRTY-FOUR

Marriage, Children, and a Much Better Life

SOON AFTER I MOVED TO Lancaster, I took the necessary schooling to get my GED. So, I went to the Adult Enrichment Center, a decrepit old building on East Strawberry Street. That was not a good section of the city, but it didn't bother me. I'd either study the textbooks there or take them home. I did almost all my studying at my apartment, and after only about forty hours of study, I took the GED test at McCaskey High School and passed it successfully. I certainly was elated about that, since I hadn't had any high school education whatsoever, not for even one day. And, of course, I had no help from the Internet as that invention was still about two decades away.

I met an attractive young lady named Cindy Young while playing volleyball at Y.F.C. She and her family lived on a big dairy farm in Peach Bottom. A few days later I called Cindy and asked her for a date. So, we went to see a Corrie ten Boom movie at Strasburg that Saturday evening. Cindy's family lived about twenty miles south of Lancaster, and because it was in an unfamiliar area, I had trouble finding it. I had to ask for directions at two different farms and got there later than I had planned. Of course, there were no GPS devices back then. Soon after Cindy introduced me to her folks, she and I were on our way to see the movie. There were several sharp curves that we went around, with the tires screeching, but still arrived safely at the theater. We had a fun time there, but later Cindy said she almost ditched me because of my driving, but she decided to give me another chance. I made sure my tires didn't screech on our future dates!

Cindy's parents were quite old fashioned, but were good, hardworking people. The only TV in the house was in one of the boy's upstairs bedrooms.

Her dad was one of eleven children, having been raised in Virginia, then moved to Maryland, and finally to Peach Bottom, about four miles north of the Mason and Dixon line. Ray and Nancy had only one daughter, Cindy, and three sons Mark, Ralph and Morris. Ray was a partner with his brother Earl on the farm. Earl's farm was about a quarter of a mile to the north and together they owned about five hundred acres of land and one hundred thirty dairy cows. They were devout Christians and faithfully attended Faith Reformed Presbyterian Church in Quarryville each Sunday morning and evening. Cindy was attending nursing school in Lancaster and would graduate in a few months. We started dating regularly and she often went to Leroy's Bible study group with me. When she graduated from nursing school, she got a job at Masonic Homes in Elizabethtown and moved into a dorm room on site.

I would go back home every few weeks to visit my family about twelve miles away. Happily, they were no longer trying to persuade me to rejoin their church. At the time Cindy and I started dating, I also started attending the church in Quarryville where she and her parents were members, and where I also eventually became a member. The pastor was a devout young man named Jack DeBardeleben who I admired a great deal. He was only a few years older than me and I soon became good friends with him and his wife Debbie. Cindy and I continued to date over the winter months and into spring.

One Saturday evening I took her back home to visit my family and it went very well. They seemed to immediately like her and approve of her. Cindy had not only gone to the church in Quarryville with her parents all her life, but after graduating high school she had attended Covenant College, a Christian college in Chattanooga, Tennessee. I soon realized that she was a fine young Christian girl, as well as having an excellent sense of humor and being fun to be with. Also, she seemed to have many of the qualities I was looking for in a Christian wife and I often thanked God for bringing her into my life. As time went on, I felt more and more that she might be the one for me. By springtime, there was no doubt that we were very much in love with each other.

One Friday evening in May we went to the Ringling Brothers and Barnum and Bailey circus in Hershey, Pennsylvania. While one might not exactly expect a marriage proposal after an event like that, as it turned out, later that evening I asked her to marry me and she said yes. We decided the wedding would be at her church and it would be on October 7, 1978, the one-year anniversary of our first date. Pastor Jack would officiate and my new brother-in-law, Mark Young, would be the best man. I invited all of my immediate family but I really had no idea which of them might attend. When I told my parents of our wedding plans, they did not object and seemed quite matter of fact about it.

On the day of the wedding, a brisk, windy autumn day, my whole family including my parents, siblings, and in laws attended, along with Cindy's relatives and friends. Also, various friends of mine, including many from the Bible study groups. I had requested Pastor Jack to emphasize the importance of a strongly committed Christian lifestyle no matter what anyone's faith might be. At the end of the service, before Cindy and I started greeting people at the church entrance, I pulled the rope and rang the big old bell on top of the roof, as Pastor Jack had suggested. I was glad the photographer was able to get a picture of my mother as she was smiling and shaking hands with me. I'm certain that is the only picture I have ever seen of her.

My family all left soon after the service and, of course, did not attend the reception. I thanked them for coming. They were fairly friendly but had a rather solemn demeanor. I doubt that any of them had ever been at an English wedding before and I'm sure they had all been very curious about what the format would be like.

Shortly before they greeted us, I noticed that Dad was crying. I was sad to see that and wanted to console him but I didn't know what to say and so I said nothing. It's regrettable that at such an event, the parents of a non-Amish child would likely be crying rather than to be happy. Years later, I also saw my brother crying at the wedding of his son, who had left the Amish.

I soon became a member of the church where we had gotten married. Cindy and I were members there for a long time until we moved to the Leola area in 1999. After the wedding, we spent our honeymoon in the New England states and it was the perfect time for the fall colors. We visited quite a few tourist attractions and did a lot of sight-seeing. When we returned home eight days later, I only had eight dollars left in cash with me.

We had already bought a two and one-half story apartment building in Lancaster, a few blocks from where I had lived. The building we bought had three apartments and Cindy and I moved into the largest one, on the second floor. I soon got my first experience of being a landlord. Overall, it worked fairly well, although several times we had tenants who were quite undesirable. Cindy got a nursing job at the Mennonite home just a few miles away, much closer than where she had worked before in Elizabethtown.

Our next-door neighbor, Tom Carmitchell, was an older man who was reclusive and lived like a hermit in his large drab old brick house. It seemed he was angry most of the time, but when Cindy gave him some of her fresh homemade strawberry jelly, he became much friendlier toward us. Sometimes we would see him aimlessly wandering around downtown, and it didn't seem like he had any friends at all. He died a few years later and when his brother showed us through the house, it was incredibly cluttered and was a veritable firetrap.

The city had some land about one mile away that they rented to city residents as small garden plots. We rented a little plot there for eight dollars and planted vegetables the first two years we were there. Since we liked sports, we both played on softball teams. Cindy played on a girls' team at a park in Lancaster and I played at Strasburg. I also played basketball for my employer, Stauffer's, who sponsored a team in an industrial league and later I played on a city team at George Washington Elementary school, a few blocks away.

In 1980, Cindy and I were blessed with the arrival of our first child, Kevin, to our little family. My folks back home welcomed him and were happy to see him when we visited them. A black lady, Shelly, along with her granddaughter, Keisha, lived in our back apartment. Shelly would sometimes babysit Kevin. In 1981, when we moved to Peach Bottom we rented the upstairs apartment to Dane and his girlfriend, Cindy K. Dane was a smooth talker and an alcoholic. They had a three-year-old boy, Jared, who later, at the age of seventeen, was convicted of being an accomplice to the murder of a convenience store clerk in Lancaster. At that time his father, Dane, had already passed away at the V.A. Hospital in Lebanon, Pa.

In 1980, a few months before Kevin was born, I lost my job while the economy was already in recession. With jobs being scarce, I was fortunate that my father in law, Ray, offered me a job down at their farm, to fill a vacancy there. We moved into the farmhouse at the Yoder farm, which was the other farm that they owned, about one mile down the road. Even though I had grown up on a farm, it was again a big change moving from the city to the sparsely settled Peach Bottom area. Nevertheless, we were sure that moving from the city to the open country where Cindy's family lived, would be a good thing for us. The winter before we moved, in March 1981, I had been working at the Yoder farmhouse, remodeling it for our anticipated move there.

Precisely five days before our scheduled moving date, as I left there to go home to Lancaster for the night, I had a startling experience. While driving up the road toward the farm, I looked ahead and realized to my horror and consternation that the big old gray barn where Ray should have been milking was, literally, not there anymore. Instead there were lots of fire trucks there, and lots of smoke in the air. I quickly drove to the house and Nancy told me an electrical fire had been the cause of the barn fire and that she could not come down to the Yoder house to tell me, because of the fire hoses across the road. Also, she could not call me because there was no phone service to the Yoder house at that time, because an Amish couple had lived there previously. I hurried up to the devastation that had been the big dairy barn a few hours earlier. Fortunately, no one had been hurt and no livestock was lost.

I was afraid my new job might not materialize because of the fire, but Ray told me that they would rebuild the barn and they'd still need me to work for them. As it turned out, I helped them rebuild the barn soon afterwards. We moved to the Yoder farmhouse a few days after the barn fire and now I was working on a farm again. However, it was much different and much better than the Amish style of farming I had known, because now we had electricity, tractors and modern equipment. While I was never fond of milking cows, at least here it was much more modern than milking the Amish way. And living there was much quieter and more peaceful then living in the city had been.

In May, 1983, our second son, Jonathan, joined our little family. It was nice to be able to raise our boys there with their grandparents, Ray and Nancy, living only a fraction of a mile away. They were always as good to us as any grandparents could be. A few years later we bought a house in Wakefield, two miles away and moved there. In 1987 we were blessed again with our third and final child, another boy, named Matthew.

Later that year, John Fairfull, a friend from our church told me about his job as a union construction worker. He said there was lots of work available now that the economy was booming again. I became extremely interested when I was told of how much money I could earn in the carpenters union. John gave me all the information I needed and in July, I started working at a housing construction project and soon joined the carpenters union local in West Chester, Pennsylvania.

The following year I joined the massive road and bridge building project east of Philadelphia, which was the construction of Route 476, also known as the Blue Route. It was a major new highway, beginning at Chester at the south end and connecting with the Pennsylvania Turnpike at the north end. Bridge construction certainly was hard work and we worked in all kinds of weather, year-round. One memorable day, as the temperature reached 106°, Joe Bradley and I were swinging sledgehammers and busting concrete for much of the afternoon. While, of course, wearing the annoying and bothersome hard hats that we all had to wear. I might have sweated more that day than any other day in my life. However, I was now earning a lot more money and could support my family very nicely and I certainly was thankful for such a well-paying job.

One day in the summer of 1990, I was working on the Blue Route bridge construction project, near Route 30, in the Radnor area. I was with a group of other carpenters when something happened close by that seemed almost unbelievable. I was working with two other men on a scaffolding about twenty feet high that was attached to a bridge, and there were about ten other carpenters working nearby on the ground. Suddenly, one of them yelled, "Here comes a plane." We looked southward and saw a small three-seater airplane about one hundred fifty yards away, flying about fifty feet above the ground. It was moving more slowly than normal, and the wings were dipping up and down. My buddy, Joe McNaney, yelled, "That guy's in trouble". We didn't hear any engine noise and assumed the plane was gliding. It was about two hundred feet away and was heading directly toward our scaffolding as we watched in near disbelief. Suddenly, we realized we'd better get off the scaffold and down on the ground, because it seemed the plane might actually hit us. The pilot had thought of landing it a short distance away, but there was not enough room because other carpenters were working there. As we scrambled down to the ground, the pilot veered to his left over the parking lot of an office building. He saw that the parking lot was too full, so he flew to his right over the railroad tracks. He was now only about thirty feet above the ground and about a hundred feet away from us. A few seconds later, one plane wing clipped a utility pole and the plane spun partially around as it crashed to the ground. I immediately ran over along with Joe, Mickey Herron, and Tom Flynn. The pilot, who was injured and bleeding, was helping his sixteen-year-old niece out of the plane. It had already caught fire and was starting to burn rapidly. The pilot, Glenn Williams, yelled that his sister was trapped and unconscious in the plane and we have to quickly get her out. As Tom led the girl away to safety, Glenn, Joe, Mickey, and I desperately tried to free the trapped woman.

Suddenly, there was a frightful explosion, which I had been afraid might happen. Both Joe and I immediately dove away, headlong on the ground. When we realized we were not on fire, we jumped back up and again tried to rescue the woman. We yanked frantically on the crumpled door as the flames were now spreading rapidly, along with much more intense heat. With perhaps only seconds left, we finally got it open and quickly pulled her out and carried her to safety.

The other carpenters and a lot of people from the office building were now also there. Within a few minutes the plane was totally destroyed by fire, as emergency personnel in ambulances, police cars, and fire trucks rushed up. The lady we had rescued, Charlene Kenney, was hurt very badly and was quickly taken to a hospital in a Medevac helicopter.

Glenn, the pilot, from Allentown, later told us that for some unknown reason, both engines had quit, forcing him to crash land. He was, of course extremely grateful for our help. He and his niece, Beth, also went to the hospital for their injuries. which were not serious. Charlene also fully recovered after being in the hospital for quite some time.

Immediately after the accident, Joe, Mickey, and I were interviewed by the Philadelphia TV News team. I suspected there might be TV News footage of it on our local TV station later, back home. On my way home, I called Cindy and told her what had happened and told her to videotape that segment of TV coverage. So, she did that, which allowed us to view it later that evening.

The people at the accident scene were calling Joe, Mickey, and me heroes, but I told them I just did what I had to do. The next day there were numerous pictures and articles about the accident in all the local papers, including the Philadelphia Inquirer. Later, I was interviewed by a local reporter from our daily newspaper, the Lancaster Intelligencer Journal, which featured an article about the plane wreck and recognized me as the winner of the Lancaster Red Rose award. Eventually, Joe, Mickey, and I all received separate bronze medals and statements of recognition, along with grants of $5000 each from the Carnegie Hero Commission in Pittsburgh. They periodically give similar awards to people who risked their lives while trying to save others. We also received separate plaques from the state of Pennsylvania which Transportation Secretary, Howard Yerusalem, and several others brought to our construction site one day. In addition, we received plaques from the Radnor Township board of commissioners, and from the president of our local carpenters' union. Some of us received telephone calls from the Sally Jessie Raphael television show in New York, as they tried to make arrangements for us to be on their show. However, for whatever reason, that never materialized.

At that time, in 1990, it had now been fourteen years since I had left the Amish church. My life had long ago settled into a fairly predictable and more comfortable routine than when I was Amish. I can and will honestly say that I have never regretted my decision to leave the Amish church, and I'm sure that I never will regret it, despite my being permanently ex-communicated and shunned. One of my brothers told me once that he'd heard a rumor that I had regretted that I left. I then immediately told him that rumor was completely untrue. When I see or talk to my relatives or other Amish people, they usually are somewhat cordial to me, and I am likewise to them. However, because of the shunning procedures that are always lurking close by, I have not had much involvement with them over the years. My brothers were all married and were raising families of their own. In the forty- four years since I left the Amish church, there have only been three times that any of my parents or siblings came to visit us. And I doubt they will ever visit again after they have read this book. In fact, they might then not allow me to visit them anymore, which would sadden me greatly. But it is what it is, and I have to make the best of it. My brothers never ask or seem to have any interest in my day to day life, although I'm sure they're very curious. And, as I expected, none of my siblings ever invited Cindy and me to any of their children's weddings. But that didn't surprise us as that is part of the shunning process. I rarely allow myself to stop and grieve about all the "brotherly" good family times we could have had with each other, had it not been for the shunning. Never does a day pass, that I am not reminded of, or at least think about having been born and raised Amish. I have no expectation whatsoever that any of my brothers or sisters will ever leave the Amish church. I have never tried to persuade any of them to "see it my way" and leave as I did, knowing that would be utterly futile. All of them have always been "hard-core" Amish, which is not as sinister a term as it sounds, it simply means they are the least likely ones to ever leave. At this time, they are still all Old Order Amish, although several of my nephews and a niece have left, as I did. Dave Zook and John G., (Beatle) who were my best Amish friends for many years, are both married and have raised large families. John is still Amish, but Dave and his family attend a non-Amish church and he is also ex-communicated and shunned like me.

Brother John and his family were living in the old farmhouse back home, since he had bought the farm from my parents a few years earlier. My sisters, Suvilla and Lydia had a house built at the north end of the orchard and my parents lived there with them. Dad was still in fairly good health and often helped John on the farm.

Mother's health, however, had been increasingly declining for many years starting around 1976. At that time, she developed lameness in one leg and poor mobility in one arm. She had a brain scan and other tests done which showed one kidney was no longer functioning, so it was eventually removed. About six months later she suffered a serious stroke and could not walk by herself any longer. She had suffered from high blood pressure for many years. Eventually, the decision was made to take her to Dr. Ray Ever's clinic in Alabama for specialized treatment. That was much farther from home than she had ever been before in her life. Before that, the farthest she had been away was to the shore at Wildwood, N.J., in 1937, the summer after they had gotten married.

Dad and Mom and another Amish couple, Stephen and Arie Stoltzfus hired a van to take them to the clinic in Alabama. A few days after they arrived a sad and unexpected event occurred. During the third night they were there, Stephen, a diabetic, died of complications from not having taken enough insulin.

Chelation treatments had been started on Mom as soon as they had arrived, even though she really had not wanted to make the trip at all. After Stephen died, Mom became very discouraged and begged Dad to take her home. She said she would rather die at home. Dad reminded her that they had come an extremely long way and had already paid for thirty days of treatments. So, of course, they stayed. Mom got very tired during that long month when she was getting the chelation treatments every day. She was also very lonely because there were no other Amish people there in that area at all. So, they were both overjoyed when Jake, Benuel, and Suvilla came on a Greyhound bus to visit them for a few days.

Mom's chelation treatments involved getting vitamins and minerals intravenously in her arm every day for three hours. She was very glad when those treatments were finally over. Remarkably, at that time her blood pressure had returned to normal. I was surprised at that because I had been afraid that the clinic might only be a quasi-professional facility without the staff having proper accreditation and skills. Because Amish people usually don't have adequate health insurance, they often go to sub-standard places like that.

Even though the chelation treatments seemed to have been somewhat successful, Mom's quality of life was greatly diminished on a permanent basis. She suffered a major stroke in 1989. Sadly, she was then almost completely incapacitated and had to stay in a wheelchair. For the rest of her life she had many physical ailments, including sore eyes, bad nerves, bed sores and inability to swallow well anymore. She was remarkably patient, however and almost never complained. Eventually, she could not even feed herself anymore. Also, her speech had declined a great deal over the years, and by 1993, she could not communicate at all anymore. She was always glad to see us, though, whenever we came to visit, which we did frequently. Even though she could not even open her hand anymore, she would raise her arm a little and we would shake her hand.

During the last four years of her life, Mother had no use of her hands and no ability to communicate whatsoever, except to shake her head. Can anybody imagine what that would really be like? Her fingers were so crippled that she could not write at all anymore. If she was in pain or if she just had an itch, she could not convey that to anyone. If they had a typewriter or a laptop computer, she might have been able to slowly convey her wishes in that way. But, of course, they had no such things. And, because of being in an Amish household, there was no music, no radio, no television and no telephone that could have entertained her during the many long, dreary hours that she sat there. I think it would have been a real blessing to her if she had been allowed to listen to beautiful, soothing Gospel music from a radio. I think it is very unreasonable and cruel to not allow radios for people in such situations. Even when she could still talk, she said that she was ready to die. It certainly would have been understandable if she had become depressed and suicidal like her mother many years earlier but, thankfully, she apparently never was.

During her last few years, she couldn't attend church anymore, which she missed greatly. And since the Amish *never* record any church service events, she was never able to listen to any of the sermons or the singing. And, for those who do attend regularly, there is never any type of "artificial" music at all, such as a piano or organ or any musical instruments.

Mom's sister, Aunt Fannie, a widow, also lived a bleak and unhappy life at a very old age. She passed away in 2018 at the age of ninety-eight and her health was very poor, similar to Mom's. She sometimes said she doesn't understand why she doesn't die once. I'm sure Mom also felt that way.

Our neighbor, Abram B., also had lived a bleak and unhappy old age when he died at the age of ninety-three. In addition to the above-mentioned things which he didn't have, he couldn't even read since he was almost blind. He said it made for a lot of extremely long days.

As for Mom, at least she was blessed with plenty of visitors as she always had a lot of friends and relatives. I was glad that I had asked my parents, a long time ago, if they had forgiven me for having left the church, which I'm sure had almost broken their hearts. And I was thankful that they both readily admitted and told me that they had forgiven me.

In June of 1997, at the age of 82, Mom developed pneumonia and it appeared that she might not have much longer to live. Of course, we went to visit her that evening. She was in bed, apparently asleep. We sat in the living room nearby and sang her favorite gospel songs for her, hoping she would still be able to recognize our voices. Before we left, I held her hand and stroked her cheek. Something seemed to be telling me this would be the last time I'd be able to talk to her. Then, finally, I kissed her cheek and, with tear-filled eyes, I told her how much I loved her, and I thanked her for being such a wonderful, loving mother, before I said my final goodbye. I sensed that she still heard me even though she was completely quiet.

The next morning, on a Sunday morning, we received word that she had passed away. We were all glad that her earthly travails were finally over, and that she had gone to forever be with her Lord and Savior, Jesus Christ, in Glory. Later, at the viewing when Dad took me into the little room to see her, we both wept openly as we saw her in the coffin. I felt very sad because of all the sorrow I had caused her over the years. Dad privately told me later that he really appreciated that I had respectfully shaved off my moustache beforehand.

Mother's life had indeed been a very humble one in every aspect of the word. Still, she had throughout her entire life, always tried to do what was right. She was always patient, kind-hearted, gracious, and eminently fair with everyone. She had also been an extremely hard worker, often milking cows as needed or driving teams of horses in the fields. Her many farm duties included husking corn and spearing tobacco with the men, especially in her younger years. She had also spent an enormous amount of time in the gardens and kitchen, preparing countless delicious meals for her family, in addition to sewing almost all of our clothing. She never used language that could even be considered close to being obscene or profane. She had always been completely faithful to the tenets of the Amish Church and the Ordnung. She left a wonderful, inspiring, and Godly legacy that will always stay in the minds and memories of all who knew her, especially all of the ones in our family.

There was an exceptionally large funeral, with hundreds of relatives, friends, and neighbors attending. Later, at the Amish cemetery she was laid to rest next to her son, Amos, who had died at the young age of nineteen, many years earlier.

Dad was now eighty-three years old, but still often helped my brother, John, on the farm. He spent a lot of time sitting at the kitchen table, cracking walnuts from the big walnut tree behind the farmhouse. He also often visited with his old neighbors, Henry and Danny, who had also lived at their farms since the 1930s. Of course, he often visited his old English friend, Willis, who was also a widower now. Willis was now eighty-six years old and had lived his entire life in his old clapboard farmhouse, only about two hundred yards west of our house. Just six months after my mother's death, Willis also passed away.

When Dad was eighty-six years old, he started experiencing some very severe internal health problems. That resulted in a great deal of pain for him and he eventually required a colostomy which is always a very unpleasant and traumatic situation.

By that time Dad had also been suffering from two different forms of cancer, including bone cancer. It had been diagnosed as terminal and his treatments included frequent doses of morphine for pain. He was becoming increasingly confused and disoriented at times. During our last visit with him, he urged John and me and my boys to hurry out to the hayfield to bring the hay bales in before it rained. We gently told him there were no hay bales there to bring in. He also seemed confused about other things some times. We all suspected that he did not have much longer to live.

A few days later, we received word that he had peacefully passed away in his sleep. He died in June, the same month in which Mother had died five years earlier. Because of the weather being very warm, the funeral was held on the upper floor of the big old barn where Dad had spent many thousands of hours working, over a very long period of time. Despite such a mundane farming career, he had always seemed to enjoy his work and would often be happily singing, while faithfully milking his cows. He had been a typical Amish farmer, hardworking and honest, and devoted to his family and his church. He certainly had been a valiant old warrior of the Amish faith, having gallantly championed and defended it throughout his entire lifetime. He was well-liked by all who knew him, had a good sense of humor and a ready laugh, and was always willing to help others who were in need.

In a bittersweet way, it was good to know that his tired and worn old body, which had so often been battered and racked with pain from many broken bones and other injuries, would not have to endure any of that anymore. It certainly had been a long, harsh, and brutal road for him, struggling through all those sad and painful events. It seemed strange, and almost unfair, that his two brothers, Uncle Sammy and Uncle Benny, to the best of my knowledge, never had any broken bones at all during their lifetimes.

There was a very large funeral for Dad, and it was said then that he had been a post, or a pillar in the church. During the entire time of his and Mom's marriage of sixty years, they always attended church faithfully whenever their health permitted it. They had both lived lives of great simplicity and frugality but, seemingly, also of contentment. And I never, ever heard either of them complain that the bishops were too strict. Or, that they disagreed with any of the rules of the Ordnung. Certainly, their lives were fully committed and dedicated to obeying it.

My sisters, Suvilla and Lydia, who had never married, truly were the unsung heroes in the lives of my parents, especially during their old age. They lived with them throughout their lifetimes, lovingly and sacrificially caring and providing for them as best they could, despite the many burdensome and unreasonable demands of the Ordnung.

It saddens me that Mom and Dad never had many of the pleasures and advantages that a modern lifestyle could have provided them. And, sometimes it brings tears to my eyes when I think of how much pain and suffering they endured because of all the physical afflictions and misfortunes that came their way. It's also distressing to think of how hard they had to work throughout their lifetimes, with seemingly little reward. They, along with most other Amish families, experienced a tremendous amount of hardship and inconveniences because of the harsh and unrelenting demands of the Ordnung. But Mom and Dad did have many friends with whom they shared lots of enjoyment and happiness, for many years. And, because of their boundless courage and dedication, their lives may have been just as fulfilling and meaningful to them as typical non-Amish people's lives are.

During the final moments at the cemetery, everyone had a last opportunity to see Dad. It was then that I noticed for the first time that all the hair on his head and his beard was completely white, as he lay in his coffin in the bright afternoon sunlight. Of course, neither I nor any of my siblings had ever seen him without a beard, as that is an absolute requirement for all adult Amish men. Now he was being laid to rest alongside Mother and their son Amos, who had died at the young age of nineteen, forty years earlier.

I realized then, as someone who has seen the death and burial of both of my parents, that it gave me a profound sense of my own mortality. As I hope everyone would agree, by far the most important thing when we die is that we all are ready to meet our Maker. I fully believe that my parents were ready when they passed away, both at an old age. Like most Amish, they probably didn't feel sure they were saved, but I feel certain they were comfortably trusting that the God they believed in would call them home at the end. Despite the differences in our beliefs about Amish religious values and traditions, I have always fully believed that they faithfully tried to live their lives in ways that were pleasing to God. I will always appreciate that they were honest, hardworking, God fearing parents who were devoted to teaching us similar values.

Whereas all my sibling's lives have been far more predictable and mundane than mine, the choices I made have resulted in the long and winding road that I have experienced on my life's journey. God has faithfully brought me through all the highs and lows, and I feel that I understand Him, with all His marvelous attributes, much better now than I did in my younger years. At that time, I thought I should be fearful of Him rather than to love Him, but I have since found out that He truly is a God of love. I have met many fine Christians who have befriended me and taught me and shared with me many valuable insights along the way, for which I will always be grateful. I have learned that God is always in control, and that He is unchanging. He has given me a sense of serenity that I can feel each day, which I did not have in my younger years. I am grateful for all the blessings that He gives me every day and, may we remember at all times that He can always be found, even in our darkest hours. I have a profound understanding and respect for the people of my heritage, the Old Order Amish. I admire their simple faith and their amazing perseverance. Even though I will never again be a member of the Amish church, I will always feel a kinship and a bond with them. I will always be connected to them to some degree, even if now perhaps by only a thread. I wish all of them God's blessings and peace.

Acknowledgments

I WANT TO EXPRESS my deep thanks to many friends for their encouragement and support over the past seven years, as this book was evolving. At the top of the list is my very best friend, Linda Gail Hirsch, who has always inspired and motivated me. Also my sons, Kevin, Jonny, and Matt and my nephews, Wilmer, Amos, and Elmer. Other friends include Georgia Langford, Leon Stauffer, Wayne Kennedy and Mike Santaniello. I have also been inspired by ex-amish authors, Ira Wagler, Emma Gingrich, and Joe Keim. Last but not least is my friend, Marlene Brackbill who, many years ago, was the very first person to encourage me to write a memoir. So, here it is, with my sincere hope it will provide much entertainment for all who read it.

Author

Jonathan Fisher was born and raised Amish and is a former church member. In this multi-faceted, "one of a kind" memoir he explains in great detail many closely guarded facts, NOT REVEALED ANYWHERE ELSE, about the dreaded Ordnung of the Amish church, which demands strict submission to this dismal lifestyle and which may have been a factor in his grandmother's suicide. He resents that the Amish limited him to an eighth-grade education and, with poignancy and humor, tells of his childhood and Rumspringa years and of his defiance and rebelliousness which resulted in him being permanently shunned and ex-communicated by his people. He tells many quaint and amusing stories and facts about Amish life and he explains why their rapid population growth is sure to continue. He is saddened that his people are deprived of an enormous amount of modern conveniences and privileges which would make their lives vastly easier and more enjoyable. He yearns for their day of liberation when they are no longer enslaved to ' the harsh and bizarre demands of the Ordnung. With heartfelt sincerity, he implores the bishops to be more lenient, with the earnest hope they will someday have true peace with their people.